THE REVELATION OF ST. JOHN

An Inner Journey to Liberation

IRMA KORTE

THE REVELATION OF ST. JOHN

An Inner Journey to Liberation

Translated by Tarja Sagar and Patricia Taylor

Copyright © 2019 Irma Korte

Nemora Publishing / Nemora Kustannus
Espoo, Finland
nemora.kustannus@saunalahti.fi

On the cover: The Extinguished Sun and Moon and Fallen Stars, a 15th century miniature by Cristoforo de Predis. (Alamy)

Cover Design: BoD — Books on Demand. www.bod.fi

ISBN 978-952-69009-2-6
ISBN 978-952-69009-3-3 (EPUB)

Printing: BoD — Books on Demand, Norderstedt, Germany

Contents

INTRODUCTION

REVELATION AND ITS INTERPRETATION
Revelation as a myth — 14
Problems in interpreting a myth — 15
Conceptual and mythical language.
The cultural basis and universality in the interpretation.
Intuition and language.
Historical interpretations of Revelation — 20
Motives for the interpretation — 23
Revelation as a text — 26
The early text. The structure of Revelation.

I
THE NATURE OF REALITY
Chapters 4–7 of Revelation

4. HEAVEN
St. John's view of the reality — 29
The mythical heaven.
The enthroned, the elders, and the creatures.
St. John's heaven as a picture.
The throne and the enthroned.
Mineral–plant–animal.
The lion, the ox, the man, and the eagle. Lamps of fire.
The human image — 40
The vision of heaven as a personal experience of St. John — 41
The voices. Light. The praises.
The problems revealed by St. John's vision — 46
The sea. The location of the four creatures.
The torches and the eyes.
The symbolism of the numbers — 51

5. THE SCROLL AND THE LAMB
St. John's predicament — 52
The human image: general theory — 54
The ego and the Self. The universal Self. Man's cycle.
Consciousness and its content.
The human image in the vision of St. John — 63
The Lion. The Lamb.
Men, tribes, tongues, peoples, nations, kings, and priests.
The collective nature of the mythical images.
The direction of problem solving — 69
The spiritual experience and the necessity of change — 71
The playing and singing. The bowl.
The number of the angels. The angel.

6. **THE FOUR RIDERS, THE ALTAR, AND THE EARTHQUAKE**
   The human image: general theory   75
   The human image according to yoga theory.
   The mythical human image of the Bible and yoga theory.
   The chakras in Revelation.
   The human image in the vision of St. John   81
   Opening of the seals. The riders. The first rider.
   The second rider. The third rider. The fourth rider.
   The message of the four riders.
   The significance of the Self and the problem of evil   93
   The souls of the slain under the altar. The Self and evil.
   The demand for vengeance.
   The completion of the number of the slain.
   The blood. The white robe.
   St. John's shock   97
   The earthquake. The sun and the moon in St. John's vision.
   The sun and the moon in the life of modern man.
   The stars, the tree, and the wind. The receding sky.
   The mountains and the islands. The caves and God's wrath.

7. **THE CALMING OF THE WIND AND MARKING WITH SEALS**
   Quietude   107
   Strengthening of the Self   108
   The seal and the angels around the throne. The tribes.
   A multitude dressed in white. The palm. The numbers.
   Another angel.
   The significance of the inner quiet   113
   Anxiety and washing of the robes.
   Serving God and the presence of God.
   Thirst and hunger; the guidance of the Lamb.

II

THE INSUFFICIENCY OF THE OLD RELIGION

8. **THE SILENCE IN HEAVEN AND THE FIRST TRUMPET BLASTS**
   The silence   119
   The realization of the necessity of transformation   123
   The seven angels. Another angel.
   The beginning of the new transformation   125
   The first angel: the hail, the fire, and the burning.
   The second angel: a burning mountain and the transformation
   of the sea. The third angel: the falling star.
   The confusion   133
   The fourth angel: the darkening of the heavenly bodies.
   The angel–eagle.

9. NEW TRUMPET BLASTS: LOCUSTS AND CAVALRY
Opening of the unconscious 135
The fifth angel: the star. The bottomless pit.
Facing confusion and repressions 136
The smoke and the furnace.
The darkening of the sun and the air.
The locusts and the scorpions. The grass and the green things.
Seeking death. Locusts' breastplates, wings, and crowns.
Locusts' faces. Locusts' hair. Locusts' teeth.
The king of the locusts. The woe.
The release 146
The sixth angel: the release of the angels.
The altar and the horns.
The river Euphrates. The task of the angels.
The growing awareness 151
The horses. Those who sat on the horses.
The number of the horsemen.
The three plagues and the killing of mankind.
The incompleteness of the transformation 155
The idols and the demons.
Murder, sorcery, sexual immorality, and theft.

10. THE ANGEL AND THE BOOK
St. John's awareness continues to expand 158
The angel. Angel's book and his right and left foot.
The importance of the inner deepening 161
The cry of the angel and the thunder.
The prophesy about God's mystery.
Absorbing the teaching 163
Eating the book. The bitterness and the sweetness.
The prophesying.

11. THE MEASURING OF THE TEMPLE, THE TWO WITNESSES, AND THE ARC OF THE COVENANT
The advice to differentiate 166
Cognitive awareness and personal experience 168
The witnesses. The sackcloth.
The olive trees and the lampstands.
The life of the witnesses. The witnesses testify.
The witnesses are killed.
People see the witnesses' dead bodies.
The witnesses are resurrected and they ascend into heaven.
The problem of evil, Jesus' fate, and two systems of ethics 175
The witnesses and Jesus' fate. The courtyard and the temple.
The inner transformation 178
The earthquake and the death of the people.
The woe-cry and the sounding of the seventh trumpet.
The ark of the covenant.
Lightnings, voices, an earthquake, and hail.
The numbers 185

III
SPIRITUAL REBIRTH AND THE PROBLEM OF EVIL

12. THE BIRTH OF THE HEAVENLY CHILD AND THE DRAGON
    The spiritual renewal   189
    The birth of the mythical child.
    The rebirth in the vision of St. John.
    The woman in St. John's vision.
    "The womb of creation" and the universal Self.
    The problem of evil   199
    Mythical serpents. The mythical adversary.
    The problem of evil.
    The problem of evil in St. John's vision.
    The events of the vision: interpretations on the level of
    St. John's personal experience   213
    The dragon. The dragon's actions and designs.
    The birth of the child. The fate of the woman and the child.
    The war. The casting out of the dragon.
    The dragon persecutes the woman.
    The dragon persecutes the other children of the woman.

13. THE BEASTS
    The different forms of delusion in the human consciousness 221
    The beast rising out of the sea.
    The beast that came up out of the earth. The false prophet.
    The image of the beast. The making of the image of the beast.
    The image of the beast speaks.
    The image of the beast as a broader sense of self.
    Liberation from the delusion   235
    A further analysis of delusion in human consciousness   238
    The outer form of the beast.
    The deadly wound on the beast's head.
    The beast's blasphemies.
    The sign of the beast. The number of the beast.

IV
LIBERATION FROM THE OLD,

14. THE SINGING ON MOUNT ZION, THE THREE ANGELS, AND THE HARVEST
    Experiencing the sacred   247
    The Lamb and the 144,000 on Mount Zion. The song.
    The virgins. The first-fruits and their purity.
    The repetition   250
    The first angel. Another angel. The third angel.
    Inner transformation: agony and liberation   252
    Reaping the earth's harvest. Reaping the grapes.
    Trampling of the winepress.

15. THE VICTORY OVER THE BEAST AND THE DECLARATION OF THE FINAL PLAGUES
The liberation   263
The sea of glass and the victory over the beast.
The song of Moses and the Lamb.
The temple of the tabernacle of the testimony.
The new change begins   266

16. THE PLAGUES FROM THE BOWLS AND THE BATTLE OF ARMAGEDDON
The infused purification   268
The first angel. The second angel. The third angel.
The fourth angel. The fifth angle. The sixth angel.
The inner battle   275
The spirits of demons. The battle of Armageddon.
"I am coming as a thief". The seventh angel.
The results of the battle.

17. THE PROSTITUTE OF BABYLON
Introduction to the riddle of Babylon   284
Babylon as the wrong religion. Babylon as a sense of self.
The Babylon stage of development in literature.
The prostitute of the Bible and the women of Revelation.
The problem of the self.
Babylon in the vision of St. John   293
The wealth and femininity of the prostitute.
The prostitution and the clothing of the prostitute.
The intercourse between the prostitute and the kings.
The drunkenness of the inhabitants of the earth.
The drunkenness of the prostitute.
The prostitute on the mountains.
The reign over the kings of the earth.
The mother of abominations.
Those who bear the prostitute.
Liberation from one's own "I"   302
The seven kings. Destruction of the prostitute.

18. DESTRUCTION OF BABYLON
Desire-filled human nature and purification of the spirit   305
The characters in the vision. Interrelationships.
The merchandise. Other desirousness.
The problem of desirousness.
The events of the night of the spirit   313
The angel and the voice from heaven.
The destruction of the prostitute.
The torment of the kings, the merchants, and the seafarers.
The joy of the holy.
The incompleteness of the transformation   319
Babylon is thrown into the sea. The millstone.

V
THE HIGHEST LEVELS OF SPIRITUAL LIFE

19. THE ANNOUNCEMENT OF THE WEDDING OF THE LAMB, THE RIDER, AND LORD'S GREAT SUPPER
The new phase of evolution   325
Strengthening of the sense of oneness   326
The announcement of the wedding of the Lamb.
The wedding in myths and in religious literature.
The wedding of the Lamb and the bride of the Lamb.
The marriage supper. Worshiping God.
Infusion of the Holy Spirit or merging into the Om-vibration   332
The heavenly rider. The faithful and true Word of God.
The sword of the rider. The rider's robe, eyes, and the crowns.
The names of the rider. The warring nature of the rider.
Liberation from attachments and the delusion   340
The fate of the beast and the false prophet.
The fate of the beast's allies.

20. IMPRISONMENT OF THE DRAGON
The spiritual engagement or sabikalpa samadhi   345
Casting the dragon into the bottomless pit.
The power to judge. Thousand years. The resurrection.
The return of the dragon.
Liberation from the last attachments   350
The dragon deceives the nations.
The fire comes down out of the heaven. The fate of the dragon.
St. John's spiritual outlook   355
The enthroned. The judgment. The second death.

21. THE WEDDING OF THE LAMB AND THE NEW JERUSALEM
The spiritual marriage or nirbikalpa samadhi   359
The spiritual marriage in Revelation   363
Renewal. Returning home and the bride symbolism.
The wedding?
The holy city   367
The city of precious stones.
The form and the measurements of the city.
The foundation. The walls and the gates.
The nations and the kings of the earth.
The temple, the sun, and the moon are missing.

22. THE PARADISE OF THE NEW JERUSALEM
The paradise   380
Paradise in myths, in religious literature, and in dreams.
The paradise in Revelation.
The paradise of Revelation and yoga theory.
The highest enlightenment   386

ABOUT THE BOOK	391
NOTES	392
BIBLIOGRAPHY	443

The Bible quotations are taken from
the New King James Bible
unless otherwise mentioned.

INTRODUCTION: REVELATION AND ITS INTERPRETATION

"I, John... your brother... was on the island that is called Patmos for the word of God and for the testimony of Jesus Christ. I was in the Spirit on the Lord's day, and I heard behind me a loud voice, as of a trumpet, saying... 'What you see, write in a book.'" (Rev. 1:9–11.) These words in the beginning of Revelation are practically all we know about the author of the book and how it came about.[1]

Although the origin of Revelation by St. John the Divine is unknown, the text has continued to fascinate its readers for nearly two thousand years. As a text, Revelation lends itself to innumerable interpretations.

In this book, I assume that Revelation contemplates the central problems of man's spiritual life in a pictorial, so called mythical language. The word 'myth' is often used in colloquial language to refer to an untruth, but this is not the sense in which I apply the word. Myth, in the sense I use it, represents pictorial thinking which deviates from our normal thinking and language, and whose nature I will soon clarify. Whether the message we read into a myth is truthful or not, depends on the interpretation we give to it and our values.

Some of the problems, which I read from Revelation are philosophical by nature. They explore the very essence of reality and man, the riddle of evil and its existence, the significance of externally adopted religious beliefs, and of genuine spirituality. These eternal questions include ones about the spiritual lives of human beings with their different stages—not just in theory but as they personally experience them. I see the Book of Revelation as imparting an understanding of man's spiritual liberation beginning with the dissolving of the mental blocks and ending with the highest states of consciousness.

To support my interpretation, I will present many comparative examples from Christianity and other religions, mythology, philosophy, and from the dreams and experiences of modern man. The way I interpret these images is close to the explications of so called Jungian psychology, although I transcend the boundaries of psychology.

In my interpretation, I will emphasize the development of the problems I see as central, and so I hope the book can be read for the problems discussed in it.

Before offering a detailed interpretation, I will clarify the nature of Revelation as a myth, contemplate more closely the interpretation of myths, relate briefly different historical interpretations of Revelation, recount some personal experiences which have influenced my interpretation, and consider some textual problems. The interpretation of Revelation, however, stands well alone, and the reader interested mainly in this aspect of the book may bypass the introduction or refer to it later.

Revelation as a myth

Should Revelation truly be based on the visions by the prophet St. John the Divine, it represents a type of vision: the pictorial vision. A pictorial vision is sometimes seen as if it were a part of outward reality so that the visionary may not even realize at first that what he has seen is a vision and not a part of outward reality. More often, however, a pictorial vision rises in such a way that, for a moment, man's consciousness withdraws inward and he sees the vision with his 'inner eyes' as a sudden, bright picture. This kind of a vision is seen 'inside the head' in the same way as dream, mental or memory images, but unlike dreams, the visionary is awake and, unlike mental and memory images, the visions are spontaneous and include a strong sense of meaningfulness.[2]

The most commonly described subjects of visions in religious literature are saviours, saints, and different religious symbols, and the visions may include relatively few events. But the pictorial visions can also consist of long series of pictures, even as the visions by the Old Testament prophets often did. These kinds of visions can also be seen as a momentous flash, so that many things in them happen in one instance. Based on my interpretation, the essential point is that the rich pictorial language of these visions wells up, in large part, from the unconscious. For this reason, they are reminiscent of dream images, and dreams are part of mythical thinking. As I see it, should Revelation be a genuine vision, it is this kind of a serial-image vision and therefore mythical in nature.

Revelation's nature as a vision, however, has been sometimes questioned; instead it has been simply thought of as a literary work. For example, some researchers believe that one person has edited the book based on several sources, even fragments, whereas others suggest there have been several authors from different time periods.[3] These views find support in the fact that many of Revelation's images are derived, nearly as such, from the Old Testament or some other Judeo-Christian literature, and have, in places, connection even to the Babylonian and Greco-Roman sources.

Even if Revelation were a literary work, compiled or edited in some manner, and not a genuine vision, we can still interpret it as a myth. To begin with, it is based on the plentiful revelatory literature of the Middle Eastern and Mediterranean region, and presumably these writings have originally risen from the visions of the prophets. Secondly, mythical thinking and its intuitive understanding may be such strongly developed abilities in human beings that the editor or editors of Revelation have been able to compile the text so that it functions as a myth in a meaningful way.

It is also possible that Revelation was born as a result of a combination of processes mentioned above. Quite clearly, the original creator of Revelation has internalized the Judeo-Christian pictorial world. Perhaps he has additionally pondered the problems in Christianity so much that he has seen them, and solutions to them, in a deeply inward state as a series of mythical images. In writing down the visions, he may have even 'edited' his text according to his own intuition, knowledge, and literary sensibility. Nor can we exclude the possibility that there were—at least at times—more than one author; for example, the twelfth chapter of Revelation differs from the rest.[4]

Problems in interpreting a myth

Conceptual and mythical language

A myth follows a different logic and different laws than our conscious, so-called conceptual thinking. We express this thinking through ordinary language, which I will call conceptual language in the following.

Conceptual language is based on using conventional words that directly relate to reality; that is, in a particular linguistic association, a particular word is used to refer to a particular thing according to an established agreement. For example, the word 'fire,' in the English language, means the natural phenomena resulting from the burning of some substance: according to convention, fire is the name of that phenomenon.

Mythical thinking is the language of our subconscious. Along with other uses, it is the language of our dreams, and it is based on analogy. The creator of the myth intuitively finds analogies between different events and phenomena and uses mythical images to express what he sees. In my interpretation, a particularly important source of mythical images is formed by the analogies seen by different individuals between outward states and events and inner experiences and movements of the mind. For example, in the mythical world, fire can be both a phenomenon in outer reality and an inward state of consciousness that is experienced as hot and burning.

Mythical language has, presumably, been the earliest form of human conceptualizing, but over time, based on it, actual conceptual language was born, and at the same time the spontaneous understanding of the mythical language has faded. Mythical thinking, nevertheless, still lives in conceptual language as metaphors; generally, we do understand the meanings of metaphors without having to ponder them too deeply. For example, the mythical meaning of fire shows up in such expressions as fire of love, a fiery spirit, and burning desire. When I rely on different analogies in my interpretation, I try to present them so that they will be as easily understood as possible with the help of the metaphorical nature of language and common sense alone. Additionally, I support my interpretations by quoting literature where the particular pictorial language has been used in the sense I suggest.

An important difference between conceptual and mythical language is that the conceptual language, in its purest form, is extensively differentiated. Fire, indeed, is just that natural phenomena which the word 'fire' refers to, and many, even very theoretical, names have evolved for the 'inner fire,' such as, spiritual energy, fervour, desire, instinct, libido and so on. Typical to mythical thinking, on the other hand, is a holistic attitude; a mythical image is always experienced as broad and undifferentiated. Fire, for example, can be experienced within mythical thinking to include all those associations which, as a picture, it evokes.

Hence, one term of conceptual language can never call forth all the associations holistically experienced by the creator of the myth. Therefore, there is no one-to-one relationship between mythical language and conceptual language, nor can one mythical image be satisfactorily translated into one term of conceptual language. When, to support my interpretation, I present from literature quotations which use a specific image in the way I suggest, I don't intend to claim that this is the only possible interpretation. Rather, I recognize that the image has been used differently in other associations. Because I must use conceptual language in my interpretation, the whole interpretation is to be taken as an allusion or example of what is going on in the mythical world of Revelation.

Furthermore, conceptual language can be to a great extent separated from emotional experience. We may utter such words as burning love and, at the same time, feel nothing but coldness. Nevertheless, conceptual thinking is important because we can consciously differentiate and ponder matters with it. The mythical language, as the language of the subconscious, has a close relation to feelings, and the feelings provoked by the mythical images are generally spontaneous. Although we do not often understand the meaning of some dream—often we may not even remember the dream—it may still have had an impact on our feelings. It may have relieved us of tension, and, as a result, we may feel relieved even in our waking consciousness.

We can take advantage of the different natures of the conceptual and mythical thinking, because in concentrating on a mythical image and consciously pondering its meaning to us, we unite the levels of the subconscious and the conscious awareness. In this way, we bring into our lives a power of transformation which will enable us to walk the inner path into new worlds of experience. It is partly through this power of evoking feelings and experiences that the world's myths hold such a strong attraction to us even today.[5]

The cultural basis and universality in the interpretation

Revelation of St. John the Divine is characteristically part of Judeo-Christian religious tradition. Additionally, it belongs to the general Mediterranean culture. Its world of images, for example, reflects the plants, animals, climate, geography, and possibly also the historical and political events of the Mediterranean region.

At times, I interpret images with the help of other biblical texts. At other times, I compare Revelation's expressions with those of later Christian mystics, drawing on a common world of imagery. The philosophical and religious problems I see in Revelation are largely central problems of Christianity, and at times, in my interpretation, I will use words which specifically belong to the Christian tradition. Such words are, among others, 'killing' or 'mortification' of the desires and spiritual 'purification.' I use them, because I find them excellent 'translations' for the images in Revelation, although they tend to awaken problematic associations in modern man. In other words, I have strived to be faithful to St. John's own worldview as far as this is, for an outsider, possible.

The Mediterranean cultural tradition comes to play in my interpretation so that I present comparisons to St. John's visions from such mythologies and religions which may have influenced Revelation. These include the Babylonian and Egyptian mythologies as well as the Eleusinian mystery religion and Mithraic religion.

Another level of generalization I use to analyse Revelation transcends the boundaries of Christianity and the Mediterranean cultural tradition. It is possible to see Revelation as one of the world's myths, and it becomes part of human mythical thinking. For this reason, I offer comparisons to the images in Revelation from universal myths which have not influenced its creation. Additionally, I refer, at times, in a general sense, to the characteristic nature of the mythical thinking and the worldview it supports.

As strange as old and culturally distant myths may seem to us, they do not remain completely unintelligible to us; the reason is the common, universal material contained in human experiencing. Everyone has experiences, for example, about eating and drinking, and he knows, at least through others, about birth and death. Nearly everyone has also sensations about the basic elements of the outer world: earth, air, sky, fire, sea, sun, moon, stars and so on. When a mythical image is born from these kinds of experiences and sensuous observations—and there are many of them in Revelation—we can participate in them to transcend cultural boundaries.

The third and the most universal level of interpretation in my book rises beyond both Revelation's own cultural domain and the boundaries of mythical thinking. At this level, I refer to inward universal experiences and thus to more abstract ways of thinking and posing questions. Such basic experiences as feeling joy and sorrow, sensing right from wrong, striving toward goals and surrendering—these all belong to an inner yet universal realm of human experience. The pondering of existence and human fate, as well as of the meaning of life and death, are all universal experiences. Over time, human beings have lived those basic experiences extremely diversely, and they have given many different answers to certain questions about life and death. Yet, the core of the experiences and the existence of the questions form a thread which binds together the different time periods and cultures. This solid thread is expressed also in the concepts within different cultures: that is, we can find in widely different cultures words which mean, for example, good and bad, right and wrong, love and sorrow, existence and God.

As I, at times, move rather freely, crossing the boundaries of both Revelation's own cultural background and mythology, my interpretation is based on the idea that Revelation is a grand vision. It tells of archetypal human problems which are always contemporary, even though they appear in different ways to different people in different times.

Intuition and language

When the images of a myth touch men and women, they awaken their intuition. In its purest form, intuition transcends the images; it is as if it sees through, beyond and behind the images. But intuition must be captured through language if it is to communicate with others. And language, in an interpretation, is a limiting factor, because it inevitably carries in its wake the culture that it is a part of.

In my interpretations, I use different languages—biblical imagery, the language of the Christian mystics, images from the world's myths, the language of Oriental philosophy and religion, common theoretical language, and ordinary everyday language—to be able to free myself at least a little from language boundaries. To cross the boundaries to such freedom as intuition has is, however, impossible, and I wish that readers will use their own intuition to 'translate' the images into the language which is the most intimate to them.

If Revelation was a genuine vision, St. John has probably, through his intuition, realized immediately the inner meaning of his visions without even trying to analyse it on the level of conceptual thinking or language. When, during my interpretation, I use such expressions as St. John 'tells' or 'relates' to us something through his mythical image, this must be taken simply as a figure of speech.

Historical interpretations of Revelation

Revelation has been studied most often in Christian theological literature, which generally assumes that its historical background is the resistance to the Caesar-cult of the Roman Empire. The Babylon mentioned by St. John is, according to this interpretation, Rome, and the famous beast of Revelation is some Roman Caesar, possibly Nero. The destruction of Babylon reflects then the early Christians' belief in the rapid arrival of the final times which would include the destruction of the Caesar-cult as well. Some theological interpretations also see in Revelation general Christian teachings like the final judgment after death, the salvation of the Christians—this is illustrated by the holy city in Revelation—and the eternal damnation of the disbelievers which is, in Revelation, depicted by the fiery lake.[6]

All together the interpreters of Revelation form a motley group including scholars from different walks, individuals for whom it is a hobby, and many unusual people like clairvoyants and mediums. In reading classical literature alone, we notice quickly what a central place Revelation of St. John the Divine has in our own culture. We encounter brief references to it in the works of many writers, like Charlotte Brontë's *Jane Eyre*, Leo Tolstoy's *War and Peace*, Fjodor Dostoevsky's *Idiot*, and Thomas Mann's *Doctor Faustus*.[7] Broader views about Revelation have been presented—to mention a few different kinds of interpreters from different periods—by Emanuel Swedenborg in the 1700s, Friedrich Engels in the 1800s, and D.H. Lawrence in the 1900s. In the following, I will explain briefly their understandings as examples of the varied interpretations of the book.

Emanuel Swedenborg, a learned man who wrote about wide-ranging topics, was a clairvoyant and the father of the Swedenborgian religion. He saw in Revelation's prophesies some dogmatic differences between the Roman Catholic and the reformed church. In Swedenborg's interpretations Babylon represented the Roman Catholic religion which he saw as a degenerate form of the Christianity of his own time. The destruction of Babylon in Revelation was then, according to him, the description of the destruction of this church. Swedenborg's interpretations comprise altogether a few thousand pages.[8]

The socialist theorist, Friedrich Engels, assumed Revelation reflected the early Christians' desires for liberation. Engels emphasized that Christianity appealed particularly to the poor and the slaves who were the most oppressed individuals in the Ancient Roman Empire. Because certain failed slave rebellions had shown that earthly liberation from slavery was impossible, the oppressed hoped that God would avenge the Roman rulers and they themselves would find freedom in the life after death. Thus Babylon, which is destroyed in Revelation depicts, in Engels' interpretations, the Roman rule.[9]

The English author D.H. Lawrence saw Revelation as illustrating the repression of sensuality created by narrow Christian morals. The prostitute of Babylon, which is a grand mythical image in Revelation, was, according to him, the object of sensual desires unraveling from St. John's subconscious. But the prophet could not grant himself sensual enjoyment, and so he destroyed Babylon in his mental images in a frustrated fury.[10]

From my book's point of view, the more interesting interpretations are, however, those that emphasize the nature of Revelation as a myth and an illustration of man's inner life.

C.G. Jung, the best-known interpreter of myths in our own times, has also discussed Revelation, although he has not presented one continuous broad interpretation of it. He thought it quite possible that the author of Revelation was the same St. John who wrote the letters of John in the New Testament. Jung remarked that those letters exude love, and he assumed that in trying to acquire an absolute, all-forgiving love St. John must have repressed his negative feelings, such as bearing grudges and hatred. In the end these repressed feelings poured out of St. John's subconscious as vengeful visions, and these visions lived as part of Revelation. Another central idea in Jung's interpretation is that of God's dualistic nature as presented in Revelation's visions: God has a dark, terrible, and frightening side along with the good.[11]

Although the problems of repression and evil are in a central position also in my interpretation of this book, my work as a whole is different from that of Jung. I have, nevertheless, received insights from Jung's general theories and his interpretation of myths, and I refer, at times, to his writings.

In traditional Christian teachings, I know of no broad interpretation wherein Revelation would be consistently seen as an illustration of man's inner life. But I have found in the works of Christian mystics plenty of parables which contain images similar to those in Revelation. In their parables, the mystics have explained their own inner experiences. Sometimes, they have also directly referred to St. John's visions, and I have compared some of their references and parables to those in my interpretation. I want to emphasize though that I have picked the quotations from among many possibilities so that they support my interpretation. In fact, I found many of the quotations only during the final phases of my writing when my interpretation was already substantially completed. These quotations particularly come from the 16th century Spanish Carmelites, St. Teresa of Avila and St. John of the Cross.

Outside Western culture, Revelation has been interpreted by the Indian Sri Yukteswar Giri (1855–1936), and his disciple and successor, Paramahansa Yogananda. Although these interpretations discuss only a few verses, they are particularly interesting because they relate the mythical images in Revelation to Oriental philosophy and religion. These interpretations I found before beginning my final draft, and they have significantly influenced the general direction of my interpretation. As a result, Indian mythology, philosophy, and religion have provided an important comparison for my discussion of the images in Revelation.[12]

Among all my sources Revelation as an illustration for man's inner life is stressed most in an interpretation based on the information by the American Edgar Cayce. Cayce, who died 1945, was a famous medium who sank into trance-states, and during them, answered questions presented to him. The answers were written down, but while awake, Cayce did not recall them. When he was asked about Revelation, he stressed continuously, that every one of its images was a picture of man's inner state.

J.E. Irion has compiled Cayce's information and supplemented it with his own interpretations. Both Cayce's answers and Irion's text, however, are quite difficult to the point that the reader is advised on the back cover of the book, "Do not try to understand, simply read." Regardless of its difficulty, I find Cayce's answers to have connections to the interpretation I suggest. I found the book only toward the final stages of my work, but it has influenced my interpretation in one or two places by giving an impetus to alternative viewpoints. I refer to Cayce's information in places where his connections to my interpretation are the most essential.[13]

As widely as I have tried to search interpretations of Revelation, I have not been able to find them all. Even cautious estimates of the sources discussing Revelation, or at least mentioning it briefly, must be in the thousands if not millions. Therefore, I do not know whether there are other, even closer, comparisons to my interpretations than the ones mentioned above.

Motives for the interpretations

Obviously, no one can seriously believe that there is one and only one absolutely correct interpretation of Revelation. Why is it then that so many have wanted to present their own understanding about Revelation? One answer is the following: Revelation is the last text of the most profound book in our culture, the Bible. It is, as it were, the last word, and how we interpret this text crystallizes something about our own picture of reality. As a myth always does, Revelation functions as a mirror. It is the object of projection and activates the unconscious of the interpreter.

In the following paragraphs, I will relate briefly the background of my own interpretation and what influenced it; this will, perhaps, make it easier for the reader to approach my interpretation.

I first became acquainted with Revelation during the summer of 1980. The inspiration for my reading it came from this sudden realization: perhaps Revelation as the last book in the Bible would clarify essential problems in religion, and because I find the problems in religions to be connected to the problems in philosophy (even though the problems in religion and philosophy are discussed using different languages), would I not find in Revelation such problems as have engaged me in philosophy? Even at the first reading, the book opened as a meaningful and logical whole. Naturally, I knew that I had projected my own expectations to the text, but the experience was so enchanting that I returned to Revelation over and over.

When I now look back many years later, I cannot help but think that getting to know Revelation was one of the important turning points in my life. I see that the book began to function as my first true guide into the inner world. Later, many other doors have opened, like the door leading to the ancient Oriental yoga path. Yet, I have been able to find all other paths as well—or at least hints of them—in the visions of St. John the Divine. I see myself as having walked for many years through inner paths in the company of Revelation, watching my interpretations transform even as I have been transformed.

I see, also, that the influence of Revelation soon spread into my philosophical research, so that my interest in philosophy turned to mythical thinking and the issues in life imparted to us through the world's myths. Yet, for many years, I was unable to create for publication an interpretation about Revelation, because it kept transforming in my mind.

Soon after being introduced to Revelation, I noticed also that images similar to those in Revelation kept arising in my own dreams, although the feelings associated with my dreams were often different from those in St. John's visions. It is natural that, particularly during recent years while I have been writing the interpretation, images, and at times even series of events, from Revelation, have appeared in my dreams. Some of the images included lions, sheep, eagles, horses, frogs, great numbers of insects, hair, blood, white and red clothing, swords, bowls, palms, grass, mountains, islands, rivers, hail, earthquake, stars falling from the sky, fire falling from the sky, hiding in caves, burning, dying, waking from death, birth of miraculous children, multi-headed dragons, great signs in the sky, weddings, and brilliant jewels.

I could have written a book with interpretations based on my dreams and many other experiences associated with Revelation; it would have depicted one human being's long evolution through many stages. As a researcher, however, I have chosen another alternative. I have looked at Revelation as part of a broad mythical and metaphysical view of the reality which, in my thinking, it belongs to. And I have developed connections to those world myths, religions, and philosophies that can help to clarify Revelation's images and events.[14]

Although I have muted the purely personal aspect, my interpretation reflects partly also my own experiences and beliefs; otherwise I could not have written it. In the following, I summarize the motives behind my work.

First, I believe there are immense possibilities available for us in spiritual experience if only we step into our inner world. It is this world my interpretation describes as I see it imparted through the images and events in Revelation.

Secondly, I feel that the basic principles of the spiritual life have much in common. Our inner lives are individually colored and different cultures dress them in different beliefs and images. But the important point is this: understanding that all human beings are one in their deepest inner spiritual lives could destroy the walls separating peoples and nations and could level out the time barriers separating past and present events.

Thirdly, I suggest through my interpretation that it is not necessary to read into Revelation prophesies of a horrible destruction and end of the world, or of the terrible revenge awaiting the disbelievers, or fierce condemnations of immorality seen in black and white terms. These kinds of interpretations may be self-fulfilling prophecies and accordingly, Revelation can be, and has been, used to nullify the message of love otherwise imparted by the New Testament. Reading Revelation in negative ways would, for instance, justify the violent destruction of the enemy in the last battle of Armageddon. I want to ask through my interpretation whether these kinds of literal, externalized ways of reading are merely the dominating culture reflecting itself off the myth's mirror-surface.

I have encountered images comparable to the visions in Revelation in dreams of other people who have told me about them over the years, and I compare some of these to St. John's visions. I thank warmly the 'dreamers' who have allowed me to use their dreams and the associated experiences as my examples.

Revelation as a text

The early text

Theological research reveals that the birth of Revelation is often placed toward the end of the first century. The timing is based on the assumption that St. John was in exile on the island of Patmos during Caesar Domitius' reign (81–96 A.D.) when the Christians were persecuted. This dating is supported by Father Ireneus' (died c. 200 A.D.) mention of Revelation having been written during Domitius' times. The original copy of Revelation has, however, disappeared.[15]

Today, there are many known manuscripts of Revelation by St. John the Divine. The earliest complete text which is included in the so called Sinaiticus-manuscript found in the Sinai monastery, dates back to the beginning of 4th century. But an earlier, so called Chester Beatty p^{47}-papyrus from the 3rd century, already includes a large portion of Revelation. The early manuscripts known today and written in Greek, differ from each other in many places, although the differences are minor.[16]

The structure of Revelation

The first chapter of Revelation forms an introduction wherein St. John discusses the task given to him. The next two chapters consist of the letters to the seven churches in Asia Minor. I will not give a detailed analysis of these beginning chapters although I will refer to their imagery at times. I assume that St. John approaches in the first three visions the problems which are significant to him, but it is only after the letters that he needs to confront his problems consistently, step by step.

I interpret the happenings of the visions as if St. John himself really lived through all of them, at the same time experiencing and learning new things. This is, however, just a way to present my interpretation. It is said in the first verse of Revelation: "The Revelation of Jesus Christ, which God gave him to show his servants—things which must shortly take place" (Rev. 1:1).

I

THE NATURE OF REALITY

Chapters 4–7 of Revelation

In the chapters four, five, and six St. John the Divine presents a vast picture of reality as the basis for further visions. He begins with a macrocosmic vision and moves gradually toward the microcosm, the human being. In these chapters St. John also wakes to the fact that his understanding of the reality and his inner life contain unsolved riddles. He is shocked to admit this, but at the same time, it is liberating. The seventh chapter illustrates the healing and the sense of wholeness following the liberation.

4. HEAVEN

St. John's view of the reality

The mythical heaven

"I looked, and behold, a door standing open in heaven. And... a voice ... said, 'Come up here.'" (Rev. 4:1.) In the vision following this account, St. John tells us what he sees in heaven.

Heaven as a mythical image can refer both to the macrocosm and the microcosm. As a part of the macrocosm, the mythical heaven refers to the most essential sphere of reality, regardless of how 'essential' is specifically defined. Applied to the microcosm, or the human being, heaven represents high states of spiritual consciousness. Within Christianity this symbolism was used by St. Teresa of Avila who spoke of "another heaven" when she referred to certain spiritual realms of the soul.[1] Because we experience superior good and stronger intuitions in these high states, it is appropriate to refer to our inner heaven as the superconscious. In the following interpretation of the heaven of St. John, I emphasize the macrocosm, as I assume St. John in this first actual vision in Revelation is describing the nature of the universe.

The enthroned, the elders, and the creatures

"And behold, a throne set in heaven, and one sat on the throne" (Rev. 4:2). "Around the throne were twenty-four... elders sitting" (Rev. 4:4). "And around the throne, were four creatures" (Rev. 4:6). The essential parts of St. John's heaven consist of the enthroned surrounded by the elders and the creatures. I will begin an analysis of St. John's heaven by comparing it with a universally accepted understanding of the macrocosm derived from philosophy, religion, and mythology. In this tradition, reality is perceived as an original oneness or unity from which either two or four primary principles detach—which then, in turn, become the source of further principles. In other words, reality is essentially a oneness or a whole, but this oneness breaks into different forms. I will call these separate forms 'the level of duality' or simply 'duality' and 'diversity' in contrast to the original oneness.

In ancient Chinese philosophy, the original oneness is called Tao. It was not manifest, yet, from it, sprang forth everything that exists. "Tao begets one. One begets two. Two begets three. Three begets myriad creatures." In Indian tradition, the original oneness in its non-manifested form is Brahma. As a manifested creation, reality, however, is divided into basic principles, and according to the Indian Samkhya philosophy these principles are comprised of *prakriti*, or the original matter, *buddhi*, or universal wisdom, and the basic elements: ether, air, fire, water, and earth.[2]

In Spinoza's philosophy, the original reality was the Substance which Spinoza also called God. This Substance revealed itself through different attributes and modes, and therefore, these manifested forms can be thought of as corresponding to the concept of duality. Hegel referred to the oneness as the Absolute, but he explained that one must study reality also as a changing and evolving form, and so it is to be examined through different opposites and concepts.[3]

A worldview wherein duality and diversity are born from the original oneness is universally common in different mythologies and in the creation myths of different religions. The original oneness—be it the cosmic egg, the all-embracing sea, the original man or God—divides into parts. The cosmic egg, for instance, is native to Orphism and Finno-Ugric beliefs. A kind of original sea appears in the creation story in the Hebrew Scriptures where God "made the firmament, and divided the waters which were under the firmament from the waters which were above the firmament." In our times, an Indian saint, Anandamayi Ma, taught, "The Great Mother, Mahamaya, is the origin of the Creation. When the desire for divine play was aroused in her, She became two, Ma and maya, the cosmic illusion, and hiding behind the veil of maya She stepped onto the earthly stage."[4]

Similarly, the enthroned in the heaven of Revelation is the original oneness, the Substance, the ultimate existence or divinity. The elders and the creatures surrounding the throne represent duality as manifestations of ultimate existence, manifestations which take the form of mythical images.

The numbers of the elders and the creatures, twenty-four and four, are numbers commonly associated with the universe in a mythical worldview. For example, in Babylon, a pair of stars was associated with each of the twelve signs of the zodiac, and these twenty-four stars were also deities, and they were called the judges. The Babylonians divided each of the twelve months in two, so that the year was comprised of twenty-four minor months. I mention this only as a comparison as I do not know whether the Babylonian worldview has influenced the symbolism in Revelation.[5]

The number twenty-four is central also in the Indian tradition as the previously mentioned Samkhya philosophy recognizes twenty-four basic principles in the universe. Actually, in the Samkhya, there are twenty-five basic principles, but the first one is *Purusha* as the basis of reality comparable to the enthroned in Revelation. In Indian literature, Swami Sri Yukteswar draws a parallel between these twenty-four principles of the Samkhya philosophy and the twenty-four elders of Revelation. Also, according to Indian understanding, one of the great time-periods is twenty-four thousand years. During this time the world will first rise to a great flowering only to deteriorate again before its next ascent.[6]

Perhaps because of Indian and Babylonian influences the ancient Persian creation myth also presents twenty-four deities. Because of the greater duality of the Persian mythology there are, however, two sets of deities, one, good and the other, evil.[7]

The number four, as well, is in many ways associated with the cosmic relationships and the keeping of time. The twelve signs of the zodiac have been often depicted in a circle, because they constitute one full year. Every third sign establishes one of the four main directions of the universe—corresponding to the terrestrial North, South, East, and West. Likewise, the belief that the creation has four original elements is common. In his *Timaeus*, Plato named these as earth, air, water, and fire. Sri Yukteswar Giri presents the Indian notion of four ideas of the universe: time, space, Om—the basic vibratory force of the universe—and *anu*, the atom.[8]

In ancient Greek and Rome, the belief was that humankind evolves through four major cycles; the highest was the golden age, followed by the silver and bronze ages, and finally by the iron age, during which men's and women's evolutionary state was at its lowest. We can find the same basic concept about the four major cycles in India and Persia. In India, these cycles are called *Satya, Treta, Dwapara* and *Kali yugas*, with Kali yuga being the cycle when the mental condition of human beings is at its lowest level.[9]

St. John's heaven as a picture

The above outlined conception where two and the multitude are born out of one, is visually depicted in what are called mandalas. A mandala is usually a circular figure which has been divided into segments, but it often contains other forms like squares and triangles.

Especially in the Oriental cultures, such as Tibet, the mandala is a sacred figure used in rituals and meditation practices. The detailed illustration and the messages carried by the imagery vary depending on the rituals and the nature of the practice; generally, however, the center of the mandala is the most sacred position. In the mandalas belonging to the more demanding practices, the center represents the undivided oneness, and the segments and other figures along the periphery of the mandala, symbolize the different manifestations of reality. In concentrating on the mandala, the meditator endeavors to approach its center: he strives to transcend the diverse manifestations of reality represented by the segments of the mandala, to experience the oneness symbolized by the center. We could say that in the mandala the macrocosmic and the microcosmic levels merge, for the purpose of concentrating on the mandala is to lead the meditators into their inner centers or into their deepest, or highest, states of consciousness. According to the Oriental understanding, it is then that they experience also the ultimate level of reality.[10]

Although the use of the mandala is not as evident in the Western cultures, here, too, we can find similar geometric realizations. Plato, in his *Timaeus,* presents the universe as circular at the same time as he explained that it consists of four basic elements. This view was later carried over to neoplatonism, and, for example, influenced the design of the rose windows common during the Middle Ages. The designers of the Chartres cathedral were directly inspired by neoplatonic sources. Also, in the works of the Christian mystics, there are circular figures which they have used to illustrate their understanding of reality. In these figures, generally, the center is God, and the layers closest to the center are the hierarchies of the angels; 'cruder' levels of reality may be depicted along the edges. We can find these kinds of circles, for example, in the works of Hildegard of Bingen and Jacob Boehme.[11]

The dreams and imagination of the modern person also offer interesting material. C.G. Jung noticed figures similar to mandalas appearing in his patients' dreams, imaginations, and art therapy. These mandala likenesses appeared especially when his client was sincerely seeking inner wholeness after, say, having been harassed by fragmentation and confusion. Jung found in himself a similar tendency. He believed that men and women, spontaneously, guided by unconscious and archetypal experiences, trace reality and their own essential selves with the help of mandalas.[12]

The mandala principle can be applied, also, to the heaven described by St. John. The enthroned in his vision would be the center of the mandala. The creatures and the elders would form the imagery along the periphery. St. John does tell us that the creatures and the elders are assembled around the throne, even if he does not explicitly explain that they create a circle. He does, however, use expressions derived closely from the Greek word *kuklos*, a circle, a sphere, and an orbit. Some contemporary English translations of Revelation, in fact, define the placement of the elders as a circle by saying directly, "in the circle around the throne."[13]

The interrelationships of the creatures and the elders around the throne are also open to interpretation. The elders are mentioned first, and their title might lead us to believe them to be the more primary principles; thus they could be closer to the throne. On the other hand, it is said about the four creatures that they are not only around the throne but also in the middle of it—a peculiarity I will return to later. These details, however, are not very important to the mandala as a visual image. The four creatures could be seen, as it were, a summary of the twenty-four elders. In his vision St. John explains each of the four creatures to have six wings (Rev. 4:8), thus, each creature could be seen to represent six basic principles, adding up to twenty-four basic principles.

St. John's vision of heaven, viewed as a mandala, is represented in certain medieval Christian church windows, which may have four small roses or other ornaments surrounding a great central rose. Such a window can be seen, for instance, in the Saint-Denis church near Paris—a church from the 12th century.[14]

The throne and the enthroned

In this vision St. John presents the center of heaven both as the throne and the enthroned. The throne appears later on in several visions in Revelation. In this chapter St. John describes the elders sitting on the thrones, "Around the throne were twenty-four thrones, and on the thrones I saw twenty-four elders sitting" (Rev. 4:4). In the second chapter of Revelation the angel of Pergamon is told, "I know your works, and where you dwell, where Satan's throne is. And you hold fast to my name." (Rev. 2:12–13.)

In general, a throne is a fit symbol for power and authority. When St. John in the beginning of his fourth vision speaks of the throne and the enthroned, apparently referring to God, he is perhaps regarding God as the ruler of all there is. The elders, as their names would lead us to believe, could be interpreted to have thrones because they are the more important and dominant principles of reality. Satan's throne would tell us that within the domain of the Pergamon church evil, or the mythical devil, is the ruling principle.

I suggest yet another interpretation for the throne, one which complements the meaning of dominion, power, and importance. The "throne" may refer to the idea of God generally and the "enthroned" may refer to various specific meanings and connotations which St. John attributes to God. This reading would account for St. John's personal experiences with God later on and his consequent changing understanding of divinity.

Mineral–plant–animal

The way St. John the Divine describes the central elements of his heaven—the enthroned, the elders, and the creatures—follows partially the ancient mythical delineation, mineral–plant–animal. St. John relates the enthroned to precious stones, "And he who sat there was like a jasper and a sardius stone" (Rev. 4:3). The creatures—or more accurately, three of them—St. John relates to animals: "The first living creature was like a lion, and the second living creature like a calf, and the third living creature had a face like a man, and the fourth living creature was like a flying eagle" (Rev. 4:7). Furthermore, the creature with a human face is an animal in a sense that the Greek word *zōon* used for a creature in this connection, refers to an animal as well.

The mineral–plant–animal pattern is not fully expressed in the vision. St. John does not define the elders through plant-like images. But the connection to plants is hinted at in the earlier mentioned window design of Saint-Denis church if it were interpreted to be a visual depiction of the heaven in Revelation. In it, three of the four ornaments surrounding the great central rose depict animals, and the petals of the central rose are comparable to the elders.

In mythology, the mineral–plant–animal pattern is used to express deviation from the normal. A phenomenon removed from the ordinary human experiences is described through minerals; a phenomenon expressed through animals is close to us. This sense of deviation can be applied both to the macrocosm and the microcosm. It can express favorable, disadvantageous or neutral differences. The context and the particular characteristics of the images tell us what kind of difference and distance is in question. I will refer to this in more detail later on. For now, I will mention only a few examples of mineral, plant and animal symbols used in a macrocosmic environment.

In a religious worldview, divinity, or God, is both the most primal and the highest sphere of reality. A stone is strong and endures, and so it lends itself well to symbolizing God as the most lasting constituent in the universe. Stone symbolism appears in various religions as sacred stone, like the round stone altar of Tarakeswar in India and the black stone of Kaaba in Mecca.[15] A good example of plant symbolism on the macrocosmic level is the cosmic tree. A mythical image is typically multi-layered and complex, but we might see the cosmic tree basically to represent the constant change in the universe: birth, growth, withering, and destruction. Animals have been used in different mythologies to identify the constellations and the stars, which in mythical worldviews often represent the lower deities, or cosmic forces and principles.

If we superimpose John's vision on the mineral–plant–animal configuration, the elders would again be placed close to the center, or the enthroned. Even the elders' clothing reflects this sacredness when St. John writes, "Twenty-four elders sitting, clothed in white robes" (Rev. 4:4). White, in general, is associated with purity and lack of color, alluding to higher, original and sacred realms of existence.

The lion, the ox, the man, and the eagle

Perhaps the nearest parallel to the four creatures of Revelation—a lion, a calf, a man, and an eagle—can be found in the Old Testament in the Book of Ezekiel, where the prophet sees in a vision four beings, with four faces, namely those of a lion, an ox, a man and an eagle.[16] Despite the difference between the use of the word calf and ox, the parallel is close because the Greek word *moschos*, which St. John uses, can be translated with the word 'ox,' as several translations do, and I will use this word. Later, in Christian symbolism, these four creatures have been utilized to represent Jesus' four most important disciples: the lion symbolizes St. Mark; the ox, St. Luke; St. Matthew is associated with an angel; and St. John, with an eagle. The lion, the ox, the angel, and the eagle are also the images surrounding Saint-Denis' rose window.

The symbolism of the four creatures of Revelation may also relate to the signs of the zodiac which apparently were used already during the time that Revelation originates from. Should we visualize the zodiac as a circle, Leo the lion and Taurus the ox can be placed in two of the main directions, whereas Aquarius and Scorpio will occupy the other two. Perhaps Aquarius could be seen to parallel the creature with a human face in Revelation, but a scorpion and an eagle have little in common.[17] At any rate, the creatures arranged according to the four main directions well fit the symmetrical mandala pattern I have assumed to lie behind St. John's vision.

The lion, the ox and the eagle—and naturally the human being as well—were popular figures in the ancient Babylonian mythology. There they were often depicted with wings, perhaps to illustrate their significance as cosmic or spiritual forces. Along with the usual zodiacal signs including the lion, the ox and the human-like figures, the Babylonian astronomy recognized a star referred to as an eagle. Records of this star have survived on tablets containing astronomical observations.[18] I do not know, however, whether the lion, the ox, the man, and the eagle ever were presented as a group of four in Babylon; I have not found a source citing such an assemblage.

An integral unit of four beings—a wild beast, a domestic animal, a man, and a bird of prey—is found in the Egyptian mythology where Horus had four sons: one with a head of a jackal, another with a head of a dog, the third with a human face and the fourth with a head of a hawk. Their duties were, among others, to guard the four main directions.[19]

The text does not give any guidelines as to what the lion, the ox, the man, and the eagle might symbolize. St. John does mention these creatures again in the sixth chapter, but only sparingly. Nevertheless, I suggest for the creatures an interpretation which is based not only on the allusions of the sixth chapter, but also on a wider metaphysical-mythical foundation. The central features of this viewpoint can be found universally within different religions and mythologies as well as in philosophies where reality is seen to transcend empirical observations. For these reasons, I call it metaphysical-mythical.

I see this thinking running thread-like through St. John's work and I would need to explain it even if I did not explicitly associate it with the four creatures.

Characteristic of this metaphysical-mythical view of reality is an assumption of a basic level of the universe, a kind of original form of energy, out of which the whole creation develops. In the Bible, this foundation is the Word, Logos, which, as stated in the Gospel of John, was in the beginning "with God." In Revelation, the Word is Amen, and it is called "the beginning of the creation of God" (Rev. 3:14). In Indian religions and philosophies, the basic level of the universe is often perceived as a vibration or energy, and it is called Om. Om is sometimes written *Aum* as it is compared to or even taken to be, the Amen of the Bible.[20]

Of the four creatures in Revelation I interpret the lion to represent such basic energy in the universe. Usually the animals as myth and dream images illustrate the type of energy the person is involved with, such as instinctive, innate drives. In a cosmic context, an animal provides a natural symbol for universal energy. In mythology, the lion is often the king of the animals. The other animals, or energy forms, are subservient to him. Thus, the lion represents a kind of basic energy.

A second characteristic feature of a metaphysical-mythical approach can be described as the cosmic force which initiates change. In the Bible, this change is the creating done by God as described in the beginning of the Old Testament, but the early Christian Gnostics speculated much about the different ways the creation was done, and about the deities, or demiurges, who performed it. Indian literature assumes a propelling force, which produced the visible manifestation. The force is directed outward from the unmanifested reality, from the original oneness, materializing the manifest universe.[21] In a metaphysical-mythical view, when the creation comes about, it is the basic, original energy crystallizing gradually to a grosser form, so that eventually different forms of matter are born.

The ox serves well as a mythical image for such a propelling force. His horns reflect the forward thrust, and the land is plowed with his help, making it easy to associate him with the material. Even his massive form is a ready symbol for sheer physicality.

A third basic assumption in the metaphysical-mythical approach is that spirit is omnipresent. The universe in the mythical worldview is never just mechanical, lifeless machinery. Regardless of the form of any particular worldview—be it animism or one of the more evolved religions—it recognizes the presence of spirit. We could say the human being is the most evolved manifestation of the spirit because only human persons are aware of their own existence in a deeply conscious way. Yet, even men and women, in their normal everyday consciousness, do not fully manifest their spiritual potential. They do not, in their usual everyday state, live conscious of the divine omniscient, omnipresent Spirit, which transcends the creation, and is characterized by absolute oneness. A human being as a mythical image, nevertheless, represents well the spirit and intelligence manifested in the creation.

A fourth characteristic of the metaphysical-mythical approach is the assumption of the cyclical unfolding of creation. This aspect appears, particularly, as a myth of returning to an original state. For example, in the Bible, God created human beings and exiled them from His presence. Yet, it is their duty to find their way back to union with God, back to paradise. This return happens in the last few chapters of Revelation. As St. John states, God is the beginning and the end (Rev. 1:8 and 21:6). Christianity, however, does not adopt the belief in the cyclical recurrence of creation as does, for instance, Indian mythology. In Indian mythology, periodically, from an unmanifest reality, a manifest one is born. After a certain vast period in existence, this creation returns back to an unmanifest state; after a time of rest, a new manifest universe begins again.[22]

We can interpret the eagle as representing this kind of cyclical development. The eagle is born from an egg, which is a symbol of original oneness. Having matured, it preys from the air upon the animals down on the ground, thus departing from its original oneness and subjecting itself to material bondage. After consuming its kill, the eagle is free from constraints again, and soaring through the skies, it defies gravity and the material world. In the same way, the metaphysical-mythical view of reality maintains the need for the spirit to free itself victoriously from the power of the material in order to return to ultimate oneness. The spirit of victory is often emphasized through eagle symbolism; for instance, in the Old Testament the powerful kings were compared to the eagles.[23]

All four creatures mentioned by St. John can also be seen as different stages in a vast, evolving cycle. The lion represents the beginning of creation. The ox is the powerful creative force revealed in the lower forms of life. The figure with the human face symbolizes humankind who find that the meaning of their existence may lie in their return to their Source. The eagle mythically represents the final stage of the cycle—the end, which means also a returning to the beginning. The similarity of the beginning and the end is illustrated in this worldview through the predatory nature of both the eagle and the lion. The eagle in mythology appears also as the king of birds, just as the lion is the king of the animals.[24]

The metaphysical-mythical characteristics explicated above can be found also within various Western philosophies. For example, in ancient Greece, Heraclitus took fire to be the basic principle in the universe. He also saw that the changes that fire goes through are cyclical; he said fire ignites and burns out according to its own measure. In his philosophy, mythical fire was closely associated with the Logos, and so, it was a fire of Reason or the Spirit. Hegel might be mentioned as another philosopher who uses as his central theme the self-alienation of the Spirit followed by its return to itself.[25]

Lamps of fire

"And there were seven lamps of fire burning before the throne, which are the seven spirits of God" (Rev. 4:5). The number seven—like the number four and twenty-four—is used often in mythical views of reality, as well as in early astronomy. Babylonian astronomy devised several groups of seven. The most important one was the seven known planets, which included the sun and the moon. All these planets were believed to have an association with different deities. In India, the macrocosm is divided into spheres according to how prominent each is and in what way various basic universal principles are manifested in them. Sometimes these spheres are classified as the seven higher and the seven lower ones; sometimes all of reality is divided into seven spheres or *swargas*. Swami Sri Yukteswar, in fact, identifies Revelation's seven lamps of fire as the seven swargas of the Indian worldview; the highest, *Satyaloka*, is completely spiritual, and the lowest, *Bhuloka*, material.[26]

The seven lamps of fire, or the seven spirits of God, can be interpreted as different subtler and grosser forms of cosmic energy; fire is both a form of and a fitting symbol for energy. I assume the lamps of fire illustrate for St. John also the depth of reality as swargas do for Indian holy men. Portrayed as a mandala, heaven may represent a cross-section of the macrocosm.

The human image

In a metaphysical-mythical view of reality, the macrocosm and the microcosm correspond to each other: the microcosm portrays the macrocosm and vice versa. In Christianity, this is expressed in words, "God created man in his own image". In ancient Greece, Plato in his *Timaeus* perceived the macrocosm and the microcosm to mirror each other. Likewise, various Indian philosophies assume that the macrocosm and the human being are made up of the same elements.[27]

The parallel nature of the macrocosm and the microcosm can also be understood by examining the idea of a human being or man's archetype. According to Platonic Christianity, the prerequisite for all creation is its eternal idea in the mind of God: St. Augustine and Meister Eckhart believed this.[28] Human archetype need not be envisioned as separate from the rest of reality, but it can be seen in the ideal nature of the macrocosm. In this way, we can interpret St. John's heaven to reflect also man's archetype.

Particularly interesting in this respect is the Oriental viewpoint, which specifies seven different energy spheres both in man and in the macrocosm. In man, these different spheres, or levels, are manifested as seven main energy centers, called *chakras*, lotuses and *patalas*.[29] I suggest that in St. John's vision of heaven the seven spirits of God refer to the macrocosmic spheres of reality. The seven spirits of God will be transformed in the following visions, however, in such a way that the human being is indeed more readily recognized in them.

I see evolving from the mandala of the original heaven, which can be seen also as man's archetype, a tangible human being. At the end of Revelation, a new mandala, the holy city of Jerusalem, will be described. In my interpretation, this concluding mandala symbolizes men and women as spiritually fully evolved. Having reached this stage, their evolution is completed; they have progressed from the beginning till the end, and the beginning and the end are both mandalas.

The vision of heaven as a personal experience of St. John

"And behold, a door standing open in heaven. And... a voice... said, 'Come up here'... Immediately I was in the Spirit." (Rev. 4:1–2.) These words of St. John tell us about his altered state of consciousness. They reveal the heaven of Revelation to be also that "other heaven," the superconscious, which is within St. John himself. When consciousness transcends its usual everyday state of mind, a heightened state of awareness flows in, sometimes in a sudden floodlike outpouring. A door has opened in heaven. In this deeply withdrawn state the bodily sensations will cease, and St. John experiences himself, literally, to be "in the Spirit."

The voices

"And the first voice which I heard was like a trumpet speaking with me, saying, 'Come up here'" (Rev. 4:1). "And from the throne proceeded... thunderings, and voices" (Rev. 4:5). A voice like a trumpet has already spoken to St. John in the first chapter of Revelation. There he compares the voice also to the "sound of many waters" (Rev. 1:10 and 1:15).

The voices and sounds mentioned by St. John can be identified as sounds one actually hears in a deep, inward state. In Indian texts these sounds are generally referred to as *nada*, or often simply as Om. Om is the sound that we can hear in a deep state of meditation. When we are able to withdraw our life force from our senses and reach a deeper, more primal, state of consciousness, we will hear the Om. The Indian

Paramahansa Yogananda, in fact, interprets the sounds in Revelation, like those of the trumpet, the sound of many waters, and the thundering, to be the sound of Om.[30]

In India, the concentration on the Om-sound is an acknowledged yoga practice, believed to noticeably deepen and transform the consciousness. Yoga teachings associate the Om-sound with the energy centers, the chakras, explaining that the different sounds emanate through different chakras. The lowest chakra delivers a humming, buzzing sound, like the sound of bumblebees. The actual Om-sound flows forth through the fifth chakra, located in the vicinity of the neck and the throat. This rumbling sound is rhythmically fast-paced, with a tone color of a roar or a boom. Thunder, waterfall, or ocean roar are fitting illustrations for this sound as is a trumpet blast. Finally, the combination of all different manifestations of the Om-sound is heard from the sixth, so called *ajna* chakra, on the forehead, or rather, from its polar point at the base of the scull in medulla oblongata.[31]

In Christian literature, St. John of the Cross, or Juan de la Cruz, a Spanish mystic from the sixteenth century, describes this sound in his work *The Spiritual Canticle*, quite possibly based on his own experience. He explains that this sound heard by the soul is like thunder or like the roar of many currents. Yet, he claims it to be an immense, spiritual, inner sound, not a material one: it fills the soul with a spiritual strength. St. John of the Cross relates also that the author of Revelation, St. John the Divine, heard this sound, when he said he heard thunder and the sound of many waters.[32]

Another example within Christianity comes from St. Teresa of Avila. In her book *The Interior Castle* she tells of the "great noises" describing them in the following way:

> There seem to be many rushing rivers and waterfalls in my head, and I hear the singing of birds, as it were; not in the ears but in the upper part of the head where the higher part of the soul is said to reside.

St. Teresa points out that, "all this turmoil in my head does not ...hinder praying or what I am saying, but rather, my soul is very strong in her rest, love, longing, and clear understanding."[33] The sounds mentioned by St. Teresa compare well to the actual Om-sound (the rushing rivers and waterfall) and to the more easily heard twittering form (the singing of birds), both of which can be heard at the same time.

It is possible to hear the Om-sound with no knowledge of the above explained theory. I believe many people have had this experience. Modern man, unaware of the descriptive history behind the sound, may compare this rhythmic roar, for example, to the powerful sound of an approaching train.[34]

The empirical evidence from people having survived a clinical death suggests that the Om-sound is apparently heard sometimes at the time of this transition from life to near-death. Some accounts include descriptions of roaring, booming sounds, of the howling of the wind, of drumming, or the sound of rushing water. Other sounds, too, such as buzzing, easily recognized as a form of Om-sound, have been recorded from these near-death experiences. That these sounds are heard during the death process can probably be ascribed to the withdrawal of life force from the sense organs.[35]

Forms of the Om-sound heard in a deeply withdrawn state may have been familiar also to some folk traditions. The old Finnish-Karelian folk poetry, for example, speaks of the rapids of Tuonela, a land associated with death, but a realm which one may reach without having to die physically. I suggest that this latter way of reaching Tuonela refers to one's entering a deep state of trance. The universal custom of employing drumming in a variety of rites to assist in reaching a trance state may also be connected to experiencing the Om-vibration.[36]

When Revelation characterizes the Om-sound in different ways—sometimes it is thundering, sometimes the voice of the trumpet or the sound of many waters—these images reflect also appropriate symbolism. For example, the thundering functions in the Bible as the voice of God and the symbol for His power.[37] In St. John's vision, the thundering originates from the throne, the image I have associated with God's reign and the God-concept. I will return to the symbolical meaning of the sound of the trumpet later when the trumpet blows appear more decisively.

Light

"And from the throne proceeded lightnings" (Rev. 4:5). In other words, the throne in St. John's vision is radiant, emanating bright light. Light is one of the more common features in visions. In the following, I will explain a way of seeing light, which will clarify St. John's vision of heaven, as well as some of the other visions in Revelation.

In a deeply withdrawn state, the meditator can see within his forehead a sphere of light. Like the Om-sound, this is an actual experience. This light has been called the spiritual eye, the third eye, and the eye of intuition. This light can be seen as either extremely bright or as a soft, circular luminosity, a ring of light. Or it will appear as an illuminated central light surrounded by a bluish sphere with a golden halo. If the concentration is very deep, the central light is seen as a clearly defined star. The following is a description of one experience: "Masses of whirling light appeared [within my forehead]; the radiance gradually formed itself into an opal-blue spiritual eye, ringed in gold and centered with a white pentagonal star."[38]

Concentration on the light in this way is a meditation practice in the Oriental yoga tradition. The Indian Paramahansa Yogananda, for example, often speaks of this light in his books.[39]

In Christian literature, Ignatius Loyola tells of having often seen Christ as a sun. It could well be that he has seen the spherical light of the spiritual eye and with it intuited the presence of Christ. We can also find in the Bible a passage which easily lends itself to an interpretation of the light of the spiritual eye as explained by Paramahansa Yogananda, who reads Matthew 6:22 in this way. One of the meanings for the Greek word *haplous* is a reference to health, and so within some languages the passage is translated, "If your eye is healthy your whole body is illuminated," but *haplous* also carries the meaning of 'single,' and so the passage can be equally well translated as the English King James version does, "If therefore thine eye be single, the whole body shall be full of light."[40]

Apparently this light can be sometimes seen at the time of death, according to some who have survived a clinical death. Different folk traditions, as well, may have references to this kind of light, as perhaps is the case in the Finnish-Karelian lore. The poems of the earlier mentioned Tuonela rapids speak of a burning whirl, and a burning whirl is, indeed, a good description of the round spiritual eye, which may emerge with a whirling motion. Furthermore, it was a required feat for ancient Karelian heroes to shoot a star from the sky—which may be a reference to the star seen in the center of the spiritual eye.[41]

I find it quite possible that during his vision, St. John is seeing the light of the spiritual eye. He describes heaven in further detail, "And there was a rainbow around the throne, in appearance like an emerald. Around the throne were... twenty-four elders sitting... and they had crowns of gold on their heads." (Rev. 4:3–4.) The center of the heaven, or the throne with lightnings emanating from it, together with the enthroned, would form the central light of the spiritual eye. The rainbow, with a reference to a green emerald, would correspond to the blue sphere. In the biblical times, emerald was a valuable, highly esteemed precious stone, and the definition of color was, in general, more vague; the difference between green and blue for instance, was not all that exact. The elders, with their golden crowns, would form the golden halo, although crystallized to a mythical image as elders.[42]

Of course, St. John's heaven is not merely an analog to the spiritual eye. Rather, there are several elements involved. More likely, he is seeing a more complicated, more pictorial vision, superimposed, as it were, on the spiritual eye.

The praises

In the vision, the four creatures and the twenty-four elders praise God. These praises do not add new material to the vision, but they may be emotionally an important experience. Perhaps while hearing these praises, St. John realizes and feels more deeply issues which he has already experienced in his vision, and this internalizing propels him further on his inner path.

Similar incidents occur throughout Revelation. Time and again, different entities raise their voices in a choir. The biblical translations usually present these praises as poems, and mostly they only reiterate the previous events. In general, I will interpret them only when there are mythical images involved, ones which I find essential in understanding the whole. In this chapter, there is no new mythical imagery in the verses delivered in a poetic form. The eighth verse simply praises God. The last verse praises God as the creator of everything there is, which is logical, as in this vision St. John in a way reconstructs the creation of the entire world as he traces the basic elements of reality.

The problems revealed by St. John's vision

The sea

"Before the throne there was a sea of glass, like crystal" (Rev. 4:6). The sea, the earth, the underground, and the air form the structure of the mythical worldview along with heaven; they appear again and again. Therefore, I will explain some of the mythical meanings that the earth, the air, the sea, and the underground convey.

Normally we live on the earth's surface and breath air. The earth and the air, even if they are used as mythical images, are thus connected to our usual daily environment and ordinary consciousness. We can envision the structure of our everyday experiences as consisting of earth and air in both a normal and in a mythical sense. In fact, this is how the world is defined in Finnish where *maailma*, the world, literally means 'earth-air.' On an individual level, earth most commonly refers to physical being and ordinary awareness, whereas the air denotes such value experiences as do not, however, belong to the higher spiritual states of consciousness symbolized by the mythical heaven. In its broader meaning, the earth symbolizes the entire level of physical existence and creation, and then the earth is the earthly realm with heaven as its opposite.

The sea is a foreign element for human beings, because we are not readily capable of living under water. On an individual level then, the sea symbolizes both in dreams and in myths the unconscious and that which is potential, that which has not become actual, or something which we have not 'made our own.' The sea, however, is abundant with fish for the fisherman to catch and to receive nourishment from, even as we can draw new experiences and inspirations from the ocean of our unconscious. On the macrocosmic level the sea represents that which is potential and even chaotic—that which has not yet been organized to a comprehensive pattern. This kind of symbolism can be found, for example, in the creation myths with a primordial sea, which reflect the human understanding about the beginnings of the cosmos and perhaps even about the origins of the human consciousness. When, in the creation myths, the primordial sea divides into parts, or an island is formed in it, the original chaos, or in more neutral terms, that which is potential, begins to be defined and become actual.[43] From a psychological point of view, these myths reveal the emergence of structure, the first isles of awareness, from the unconscious.

The underground realm appears in Revelation sometimes in the form of caves or as a bottomless pit. In modern psychological terminology, the underground can well represent the subconscious, although the term 'subconscious' is often used interchangeably with 'the unconscious.' I have not given either a strict definition, although the mythical sea and the underground do differ from each other. The most important difference between them, as mythical images, is that the sea is by far vaster. In myths part of the sea may be also in heaven. The sea as the unconscious includes that which is potential in the superconscious as well as in normal everyday consciousness. The sea and the underground differ from each other in this respect also: that we can much more readily live in caves underground than we can under water in the depths of the sea. Thus the caves may symbolize the unconscious especially at those times when we are already in a process of realizing certain levels of it. The sea in myths often represents yet a deeper realm of the unconscious, a realm more strange and unfamiliar.

When St. John perceives the sea in heaven, he thereby recognizes that both in his understanding of reality and in his personal experience there is something more to be realized.

Why does St. John compare the sea with glass and crystal? To understand his meaning, it is helpful to return to the mandala symbolism of his heaven. St. John follows here probably the mythical mineral–plant–animal pattern to locate the sea in his heavenly mandala. Glass and crystals are both minerals. The sea of glass and crystal belongs to the center of the mandala as does the enthroned who is also defined in terms of minerals or precious stones. The sea of glass then reveals that there is something lacking in St. John's understanding of divinity and that there are problems to solve in his highest, or deepest, experiences of it.

Glass and crystal are hard and translucent materials. They cannot be cut with an ordinary knife, but light will pass through them. Perhaps St. John finds his problems to be so deep and difficult that he cannot penetrate them with ordinary thinking. He can grasp them only through the ray of intuition. There may be some significance in his mentioning glass first—as if to say that his recognition of a problem (this sea of glass) is one step forward. The next step will be further enlightenment, symbolized by crystal, for crystal refracts light better than glass. This sea of glass presents an essential moment of his vision; from there on follows a veritable avalanche of events.

Our modern conscious perception of reality is not the same as that which is imparted by Revelation, but the problems St. John encounters in his vision are familiar to us. A spiritual person continually ponders the nature of God and the possibility that human beings can get to know Him. A philosophically inclined person thinks about the meaning of existence and the riddle of life. Even a person with a worldview based on the natural sciences may find himself wondering, "What if human evolution does not stop at the level we have reached so far? What if we develop yet different forms and kinds of senses and abilities? How would I then experience myself and what might then be the reality which I would experience to be as natural as I now perceive the world to be?" The more deeply we examine this kind of question, the clearer it becomes that we have yet to realize and experience much that is essential. Like St. John the Divine, we find ourselves facing the sea of glass both in the center of our perception and in our experience of reality.

The location of the four creatures

"And in the midst of the throne, and around the throne, were four living creatures" (Rev. 4:6). The heaven of St. John is not a logical mandala. The beings which are supposed to be only around the center turn out to be also in the middle, in the most sacred space. In any case, the enthroned is the most holy being for St. John. The creatures "give glory and honor and thanks to him who sits on the throne," and even the elders fall down before the enthroned (Rev. 4:9–10).

To our ordinary way of thinking, it does not seem realistic to have the creatures simultaneously occupy both the middle and the surrounding area of the throne. In mythical reality, however, it is quite possible to think of an entity as being in two places at the same time. Such double spatial existences suggest a break or division in one's consciousness or perhaps it warns of the approach of change. [44] In any event, we need to explain further the double location of the creatures in St. John's vision.

The Greek expression *en mesō*, which in the phrase *en mesō tou thronou* has been translated "in the midst," is broad enough to convey several ideas. Some English translations use the meaning "on each side of the throne," or they refer to the location in a more general way by saying "in the center, round the throne itself." In other languages, one can also find a translation "in front of the throne."[45] These differences in choice of words possibly derive from the strangeness of the subject matter, for in the next chapter of Revelation the exact same phrase in all cases has been translated to mean "in the middle of the throne" (Rev. 5:6). The many available choices in translating this particular passage aside, I suggest an interpretation which untangles some of the strangeness apparently included in the original biblical text—the creatures appearing both in the midst and around the throne.

Of the creatures, the lion is in a unique position to represent the foundation of the universe, the Amen of Christianity, the Word of God. On the one hand, Amen refers to God, as it says in the Gospel of John, "And the word was God."[46] On the other hand, Amen is closely connected to the creation for it is written in Revelation, "Amen... the beginning of the creation of God" (Rev. 3:14). Amen, representing God, belongs to the center of the mandala, but Amen as the foundation of the creation may be farther away from the center, and closer to the periphery of the mandala.

The three other creatures, in my interpretation, clearly represent the realm of duality. The fact that they also occupy the middle of the throne and do not just sit around the throne, suggests that St. John envisions the sacred center of the mandala in terms of duality. Absolute oneness is not yet found in his heaven because he has not yet realized nor experienced it himself. By portraying the creatures in the middle of the throne, he admits he has discovered a problem. A central issue in Revelation is this problem of defining the most sacred erroneously in terms of duality whereas he should be seeing it and experiencing it as a oneness.

The torches and the eyes

So far I have interpreted the seven torches in heaven to represent the different cosmic energy levels, and the seven energy centers of the human archetype. A mythical image, however, is always multi-dimensional. The torch is likely to convey more than one message. Here the torches may also emphasize the need to study and understand matters ever more deeply, as if we need to be further illumined by torches.

The heavenly symbols allude in another way to the need to study: the creatures in heaven have an unusual number of eyes. "And around the throne, were four living creatures full of eyes in front and behind" (Rev. 4:6). "And the four living creatures, each having six wings, were full of eyes around and within" (Rev. 4:8).

In my interpretation, these creatures are mediators between ultimate reality and the more tangible creation. With eyes both in front and behind, that is, mediating between the divine and the material worlds, the creatures seem to tell St. John to look ever more closely both worlds as though with multiple eyes. Usually we don't see what is behind us, and so eyes in back point out a strong need for seeing and understanding what is about to be revealed.

Since the creatures are described as having eyes within, they probably have eyes under their wings. St. John probably wants to see what there is under the wings. There are, as it were, secrets about to be revealed from underneath the wings, even as there were secrets emerging from the sea of glass. The creatures will, indeed, have a significant role in the sixth chapter when they begin to reveal to St. John new aspects of man's nature. According to my interpretation, creation, even the tangible human person, is still hidden from St. John's gaze. He must re-visit the world's creation, proceeding gradually from the spiritual to the more material beings. The creation process, for him, has not yet reached the concrete human person.

The numbers of the torches and the wings—seven and six—also carry a reference to change. The numbers play an important part in Revelation. In the following, I explain the basic symbolism associated with them.

The symbolism of the numbers

I use the following interpretations for the most important numbers in Revelation, which apply here well, although they are not to be taken as universal guidelines.

Number one symbolizes oneness.

Number two expresses conflict, the tension between the thesis and antithesis.

Number three illustrates change. The three components are like the thesis, the antithesis and the synthesis—the different phases of change.

Number four symbolizes a harmonic whole, consisting of parts. If the number four is used to refer to a human being, it suggests a wholeness that has been reached through a process of differentiation.

Number five, in Revelation, connects with something undesirable and evil like anxiety or other such feelings. One might say the wholeness of four is disturbed when the fifth element comes along—dissonance has been created. (In myths, however, the symbolical value of the number five varies widely. The ambiguous quality is, in a way, built into the structure of the number five. For instance, geometrically, five can read as an irregular pentagon, the center point of the square or the peak of a pyramid).

Number six is associated with change and action. Six being the outcome of two times three, it speaks of change brought about by a conflict.

Number seven is a symbol for the completion of the process of change. In Revelation, this symbolism is clarified by looking at the seven as the sum of six and one. Six will then represent change, and one, a feeling of liberation and oneness which results from the change being brought to completion. The seventh step is the final stage and apex of transformation, as it were.

Number ten in Revelation is associated, like the number five, with anxiety. Should we think of ten as two times five, it would symbolize anxiety rising from conflict.

Number twelve in Revelation, as in the Bible in general, is the number of perfection. If the number twelve is used to refer to human persons, we might say they have become perfect, for instance after going through three transformations, each time reaching a new wholeness (symbolized by four).

5. THE SCROLL AND THE LAMB

St. John's predicament

"And I saw in the right hand of him who sat on the throne a scroll written inside and on the back, sealed with seven seals" (Rev. 5:1).

In his previous vision, St. John awakened to the sea of glass in the middle of heaven. In my interpretation, this means that he had come to understand that his spirituality is deficient in theory and in practice, and now he begins to examine his situation more closely.

In the vision, the scroll illustrates the whole of reality, the macrocosm. The exterior of the scroll is that part of reality which is visible and easily understood, or, as it were, 'read.' The interior of the scroll is the more spiritual and inward realm, perhaps even the divinity, which St. John has been all too unaware of. That he has not yet 'read' that part of the scroll means he has not yet experienced God. Within Christianity, a similar-type interpretation of the scroll in St. John's vision is given by St. Bonaventure, a Franciscan monk and scholar from the 13th century. According to him, the inside of the scroll is the Creator himself and the outside, the creation.[1]

This macrocosmic interpretation is complemented by the microcosmic view wherein the scroll is St. John's own consciousness. Written on the scroll is his present level of awareness. It includes his beliefs about God—possibly an assumption of His omnipotence, goodness, and righteousness—as well as his present spiritual experiences. But all this has proved to be insufficient. Therefore, the interior of the scroll is filled with script, and because it cannot be read (the scroll is sealed), the inside of the scroll represents the unconscious. Here, I interpret the seals preventing St. John from reading the content of the scroll to be mental blocks in his consciousness. There are seven seals or problems to solve and so he will have to transform spiritually. (The number seven, as explained earlier, symbolizes the process of change and the succeeding liberation.) The scroll is held by the enthroned because St. John's present problem deals with his inadequate understanding of the nature of divinity and of whatever is most sacred.

The scroll in the vision was probably inspired by the will used in the ancient Rome. This document was secured by the witnesses' seals, usually seven in number. General information was written on the exterior of the will, but only that which was on the inside was legislative.[2] It is the same in St. John's vision: that which has been written on the inside is essential.

Anyone who has admitted his incompleteness can easily see himself in St. John's position. When we begin to examine ourselves, we may notice that we have avoided problems and opportunities to further develop ourselves. It is vital to break those obstructions in order to open to new possibilities.

"Then I saw a strong angel proclaiming with a loud voice, 'Who is worthy to open the scroll and to loose its seals?'" (Rev. 5:2.) In this verse St. John wonders, how he could open his consciousness and break the mental blocks. When he asks, *who* could break the seals, he is really pondering which faculties in his own nature he ought to develop to initiate the inner change.

"And no one in heaven or on earth or under the earth was able to open the scroll, or to look at it" (Rev. 5:3). St. John's mental blocks are so strong that he is unable to get started. His present experiences of the superconscious state symbolized by heaven are not enough to help him. Nothing "on earth," in other words, nothing in his conscious beliefs, serves to aid him. Nor is the deadlock opened by anything from underground or the subconscious.

"So I wept much because no one was found worthy to open and read the scroll, or to look at it. But one of the elders said to me, 'Do not weep. Behold, the Lion... has prevailed to open the scroll and to loose its seven seals.'" (Rev. 5:4–5.) Probably the weeping releases St. John's tension enough so that he is able to experience new inspiration. When one of the elders speaks to him, perhaps he intuitively feels connected to higher levels of reality. Now he knows what it is in him he needs to develop to make spiritual progress. But, I need to precede the interpretation of this realization with a broader introduction.

The human image: general theory

In describing the image of human beings that I believe to be in the background of Revelation, I begin from the empirical level and proceed gradually to those more spiritual and deeper. This will reverse the order of the events of Revelation, but the presentation will be clearer.

The ego and the Self

First, let us consider man's external behaviour, his sense perceptions, thoughts and feelings, and his different faculties—such as the ability to act, to observe, to think, and to feel—through which he functions in the world. This is the most concrete level of the human image I refer to in my interpretation.

But the human being does not experience himself simply as the sum of his actions and ideas. Rather, he feels himself to be the one who acts, observes, thinks and feels. We say: I act, I see, I think, I feel. As a *preliminary* definition, when man is the controller in charge of his body and conscious of himself as himself, I call him the ego. This is the second level of the human image in my interpretation.

In the literature, the term 'ego' is used in a variety of meanings. There are also many other terms used approximately in the same sense as I am using 'the ego' here. Christianity, for instance, has the expressions "the center of the senses," "the sensory part of the soul," "the lower part of the soul," and "the old man." In Oriental literature, as in the *Bhagavadgita*, the concept I am speaking of as the ego, is expressed through words "I am the doer," or speaking more theoretically, the ego, in Indian philosophy, is referred to as *ahamkara*.[3]

The ego is a broad and variously used concept. Human beings can, for instance, at times experience themselves as the entities performing a skill like that of thinking, although they usually feel themselves to be authorities also in a more lasting, broader sense. In its deeper meaning the ego, indeed, refers to one's sense of self as a separate entity. However, even this kind of understanding of one's self varies. It may be narrow if our conscious experience is comprised only of limited awareness and a few clear feelings. When our experiences expand to include the altered states of consciousness, our sense of self will broaden accordingly. I will examine these issues more closely in chapters thirteen and seventeen.

Thirdly, I recognize in the human image a level more spiritual than the ego. I call this level the Self. Christianity expresses this deeper state of consciousness by speaking of the center of the soul, its deepest center, the soul's interior, its ground, its most spiritual or higher part. In Western philosophy and psychology, the deeper level of the human being is referred to as the real self, the deeper self, and the Self, but depending on the theory, the meanings associated with these terms vary. In Indian philosophy, the deeper level of man is called *Abhasa Chaitanya* or *Purusha*, and within the Indian religion it is called *Atman*.[4]

We can view theoretically the deeper level meant by the Self as the foundation of man's specific abilities and the ego. Meister Eckhart referred to the deeper level of the soul as the ground of the soul, and he explained that all man's abilities spring forth from there.[5] In the following passages, I will describe the ego and the Self in ways that are essential to my interpretation. In other words, I have adapted these concepts to the human image that I find emerging in Revelation. Because persons experience their bodies through their senses and thought processes, I will discuss the concepts outlined above only on the level of human consciousness, an approach sufficient for the theoretical account intended in this book.

The ego-consciousness is characterized, first of all, by duality. When the person acts as the ego, his consciousness has an object he is acting upon. This object can originate from the outer world as a thing, a person, or a happening, but one's consciousness perceives it, in any case, as a sensation or a visual memory created by something external. The object can also be an idea created purely by the person himself. In either situation, the person in question and the object of his attention are separate from each other. The human consciousness can thus be said to be divided in two: the doer and the object. We can observe this separation even in everyday speech as we say: I think of something, I have memories, and so on.

The second characteristic of the ego-consciousness is desirousness: in ego-consciousness persons are attached to the objects of their desires, and the attachment expresses itself through the suffering they feel when unable to fulfill their desires. A desire can be a positive wish, or it can be negatively charged as in wanting to avoid something. Also, the desires may differ ethically—they may be more or less valuable—but as long as there is an attachment, they are part of the ego-consciousness. I use the word 'desire' referring to the wish that is part of ego-consciousness, and when I want to emphasize this aspect, I will use the expression 'ego-desire.'

The third important characteristic of the ego-consciousness, its goal orientation, is a result of attachment: persons as egos try to satisfy their desires. They see various objects as good or not depending on whether they fulfill or frustrate their desires, thereby causing them pleasure or sadness. Such judgments further enhance the dualistic aspect of the ego-consciousness.

I will sometimes refer to this ego-consciousness simply as "ordinary consciousness."

On another level of consciousness which we refer to when we speak of the Self, we experience high, spiritual values and deep intuitions. Such values include bliss and love, when love is devotional or brings a sense of fulfillment experienced as joy and happiness. In Christianity, the interior of the soul or the ground of the soul—or whichever name the Self is given—is thought as the organ through which one knows God.[6] The ground of the soul is the organ of spiritual love, bliss, and intuition. These higher spiritual experiences and intuitions are marked by opposite characteristics to those of the ego-consciousness: oneness instead of duality, surrender instead of goal-strivings, and freedom from attachments instead of desirousness.

Human beings may awaken to a high spiritual experience through some mental image of an object in the external world, but in an actual spiritual experience—if it is deep enough—the persons undergoing that experience do not feel a separation between themselves and the object which has caused it. During extreme spiritual experiences, they do not even feel themselves to be separate entities; they will merge into oneness. For this reason, both literature and the religious texts speak of the intense spiritual experience as a state of oneness. For example, in his book *Siddhartha*, the writer Herman Hesse describes the moment of Siddhartha's illumination with words, "All is one." The dissolving of a separate I-ness accompanied with a new spiritual experience can eventually become a permanent state. Within Christianity, St. Paul's well known words "I live; yet not I but Christ lives in me" can be easily seen to describe such a state.[7] Also, it is typical in a deep, intuitive state to experience oneness differently from ordinary thinking. In such an experience a person identifies with that which is being intuited.

To experience oneness, the person has to be able to give in to it completely. In literature, high value experiences are, in general, described with words denoting surrender; for example, Hesse speaks of Siddhartha's illumination with words such as "to have surrendered, belonging to oneness."[8] As long as men and women have ego-desires, they will strive to attain their objectives. This effort will distract them from absolute devotion and prevent them from experiencing oneness; that is why freedom from attachments is essential for experiencing oneness and devotion.

It is true that the Self also has one goal, wish or aspiration, but it is different from that of the ego marked by desire-driven striving and longing. The aspiration of the Self is not directed toward the external world, but its only desire is to fully express itself. This desire can be called spiritual love when love refers to the aspiration to become perfect.[9]

In the following, I will refer to human consciousness as that of oneness when it relates to high spiritual experiences and intuitions. Oneness often implies altered states of consciousness: the experience of bliss, the fulfillment of love and high spiritual intuitions.

In addition, the Self has another function besides that of experiencing high spirituality. The more we are freed from attachments, the more we are able to use our skills in a new, detached, and unselfish way. Eventually, we will not experience ourselves to be separate doers even while performing actions. Nor do we feel any longer "I am the doer." St. Paul apparently had come to realize this as he writes, "I labored... yet not I, but the grace of God which was with me."[10]

Naturally, also unselfish, detached persons will strive to reach some goals. They love everyone universally and want to do good. While acting, they also are observant of and discriminating toward the material world. In this way, there is some duality in their consciousness, but they are not attached to their goals. Should they not be able to reach their goals, they will neither feel frustrated nor suffer for it—they may simply try again.

This state of consciousness, wherein one acts without attachments and ego-desires, is the third one to define. It is the one through which a saint thinks and acts. Its accurate name would be detached consciousness of duality, but in general, I speak of it simply as detached or unselfish action and similar expressions. Together, the consciousness of oneness and the ability to act without attachments could be called the consciousness of the Self, because both of them are innate to the Self.

In the human image described in this book, the ego is a shell, as it were, covering the Self, and essentially that shell is formed by the attachments created by the ego-desires. When the attachments fall away, the Self is liberated.[11]

The ego and the Self, like the states of consciousness I have used to describe them, are abstractions. In reality, they are intertwined in many ways. For example, the Self striving for expression manifests itself first through an ethically valuable action, even if this was tainted by the ego's suffering in failing to reach the goal. Also, one person alone can, at the same time, have strains of all the previously differentiated states of consciousness. Clearly, for instance, the difference between attachment and detachment is not sharp. Love and joy often have desires that belong to ego-consciousness mixed in them. But they can also belong to the state of consciousness characterized by oneness. During one's spiritual evolution, a person thus gradually moves from the ego to the Self, from attachments to freedom, and from selfishness to desirelessness.

These concepts of the ego and the Self are fairly easily understood within the modern scientific worldview, at least if the relatively common spiritual experiences and unselfish actions are included in the concept of the Self. The Western theoretical literature does use the concepts of the ego and the Self, although their contents are somewhat different from the ones presented here. For example, in Jung's theory the ego means the center of a woman's or man's conscious mind, and the Self, or *Selbst*, refers to the person as a whole or to the center of one's total being.[12]

The universal Self

There is yet a deeper level of the human image than that of the Self, one which belongs to a metaphysical-mythical worldview. This level is the common spiritual foundation both of all human beings and the rest of the creation. I will refer to this level as the universal Self. This concept may appear foreign to the scientifically oriented modern man, but in order not to violate the concept of reality presented in Revelation, we need to make certain assumptions. During St. John's spiritual quest and visions, his definition of the universal Self will gradually emerge. For now, I will explain the universal Self more generally by comparing it with ideas presented in the Bible and in Indian philosophy.

The universal Self is to be seen as a high state of spiritual reality existing in an objective sense, but also available for man's personal experience. As a state of consciousness, which can be experienced by man, the universal Self can be seen as an extreme form of the individual Self; when the attachments have completely fallen away, the human being moves from the boundaries of the individual Self to the universal Self. In the early stages of Revelation where we are at present, the universal Self is easiest seen as the space or borderline between the ultimate divinity and the individual Self.

In Christianity Christ bears connotations of the universal Self. He is the metaphysical, spiritual foundation of all things as expressed in Paul's letter to the Colossians: "he is the image of the invisible God, the first-born over all creation: For by him all things were created ... All things were created through him and for him. And he is before all things." The meaning of Christ as a basic universal principle becomes evident in the Bible especially when the existence of the Son before the earthly life of Jesus is emphasized. For instance, Jesus himself says in the Gospel of John, "Before Abraham was, I am."[13]

In the Indian philosophy *Kutastha Chaitanya*, also called *Purushottama*, can be compared to the universal Self. Swami Sri Yukteswar explains that Kutastha Chaitanya is the omniscient love aspect of the ultimate divinity, *Parambrahma*. The individual expressions of the Self, called in India *Abhasa Chaitanya* or *Purusha*, are reflections of the spiritual radiation from Kutastha Chaitanya and Purushottama respectively. Swami Sri Yukteswar explains further how the ego is built up over the Kutastha Chaitanya and Abhasa Chaitanya. The Oriental texts do not always differentiate clearly between the individual and the universal Self. Atman, Purusha, the Self, and so on, can refer to either the individual or the universal Self, and sometimes even to the ultimate spiritual reality. In any event, the Oriental texts commonly present that deeper spiritual level as the foundation for creation, and also for the more specific human being. The Indian Ramana Maharsi expressed this by saying, "The Self is the pure reality in whose light the body, the ego and all else shine."[14]

Man's cycle

According to the metaphysical-mythical worldview, human evolution unfolds in a cycle, and it is possible to see the above-mentioned levels of human consciousness differentiated in such a way as to also form a cycle. The beginning is oneness or God, and gradually from this foundation the ordinary human being, the ego, emerges through the universal Self and the Self. This cycle manifests our human alienation from God, and it can be referred to as a descent. Alienation occurs with the creation and Fall of man. In religious language, this descent refers also to spiritual death, whereby the layers of ego cover the Self.

When human beings have fallen to the lowest level, to the level of the ego, they will have to begin the ascent to the Self, the universal Self and in the end to the oneness that is God, who is both the beginning and the end. This journey is a returning back into oneness with God, and it can be depicted as traveling up an ascending arch. The journey is that of the continuous death of the ego. The more the ego dies, the more freely and universally the Self manifests itself, and the more substantively it is born and resurrected.

In the Bible, the descending arch is presented in Genesis, wherein man's alienation from God, his falling from the paradise, is described through the mythical first human being, Adam. The life of Jesus, on the other hand, can be seen as mythical depictions wherein the essential stages of the ascent are crystallized. (Naturally, to interpret the life of Jesus as a myth does not exclude the historical reality of it, nor is it possible to exhaust a myth through one interpretation.) Every human being must surrender to ego's death, not unlike Jesus did when he surrendered to death. When the ego dies, the Self experiences resurrection, even as Jesus was resurrected. Finally, man's spiritual evolution culminates in experiencing the universal Self, which transcends the ordinary boundaries of human consciousness; this is like the ascent to heaven which followed Jesus' resurrection. The thought of the death of the ego and the liberation of the Self has, of course, been discussed openly in Christian literature. In the Bible it is expressed with words, "He who loses his life... will find it."[15]

The mythical cycle of descent and ascent can also be expressed with the words of St. Paul in the first Epistle to the Corinthians, "For as in Adam all die, even so in Christ all shall be made alive."[16]

Similar thought is found in Oriental culture, where the process of creation is generally thought of as the descent from the higher to the lower, from the infinite to the finite, and from the real to the unreal. The origin of all things is from the highest level and human beings are to return to it.[17] The death of the ego and the resurrection of the Self is in the Oriental literature often expressed with conceptual terms instead of through mythical images. For example, in the words of Ramana Maharshi, "The 'I' thought is the ego and that is lost. The real 'I' is 'I am that I am'... Where the 'I' vanished, there appears an 'I-I' of itself."[18]

The transition from the individual Self to the universal Self is also presented clearly. Paramahansa Yogananda explains that man must make his ability to love universal, because it is love that breaks the narrow boundaries of the I, and when man eventually is able to experience universal love, his consciousness is transformed to the Kutastha Chaitanya consciousness. Paramahansa Yogananda calls this consciousness both Christ Consciousness and Krishna Consciousness to stress the similarity between the Indian and the Western religions.[19]

In myths, a human cycle—or some part of it—is perhaps seen best in the universal theme of a journey. In these myths, the hero leaves home for a foreign country, and doing so becomes alienated from the original spiritual home. Eventually the hero, however, begins to long for home, and after many difficulties is able to return there. Such mythical travelers include the Greek hero Odysseus and the prodigal son of the Bible.

This kind of cyclical development can be found also in Western philosophy and even in scientific literature, although with partial similarities only. In philosophy, humanity's cycle is perhaps best presented by Plato, who believed that human souls have been created from one totality. At first, all souls are equal, but they change according to the life they live, and material from fire, water, earth, and air is transmitted to them. According to Plato, man must then become free from the "affliction of change" by living right, and he must return to "the state which was his first and the best state."[20]

Hegel, also, in his philosophy describes a type of man's returning to the Spirit. In the evolution of the Spirit, men rise up over the narrow boundaries of their isolated states by joining into larger units and finally they can realize Spirit in "absolute knowing."[21]

One of the cornerstones of Jung's psychology was the assumption of the human being's internal change which he called individuation. During the process of individuation a person first became an individual, but in the final stages individuation meant essentially a strengthened sense of one's Self. Jungian psychoanalysis explains the process of individuation as the development of human beings from the undefined state of childhood to the attainment of a personal ego and then to the Self, when in the latter part of the life one begins to see the relative nature of his ego. To what extent the individuation of the Jungian psychology resembles the spiritual journey in my interpretation of Revelation must in such a brief account as this be left unresolved. Jung did, however, call the Self "the God in us," and he explained that a detachment from emotional ties occurs at the completion of full individuation. Additionally, Jung and the analysts influenced by him, have often interpreted religious symbolism using the ideas derived from the theory of individuation.[22]

Consciousness and its content

To understand the symbolism of Revelation, it is essential to make a philosophical distinction between consciousness per se and its content. This distinction can be made also in regard to the consciousness of oneness that a person experiences as the Self and as the universal Self but this differentiation must theoretically be made by an outside observer. When I want to emphasize human consciousness, I will use expressions like 'subjective side' and 'the level of consciousness,' and when I wish to stress the content of consciousness, I will use expressions like 'the objective side' and 'the level of spiritual reality.' These latter expressions come from the fact that the subject matter in Revelation deals with experiencing deep levels of spiritual reality. In religious worldviews, these levels are assumed to exist objectively. Human beings do not create those spiritual levels of reality, but they participate in them through their personal experiences.

The human image in the vision of St. John

Before I return to the events of St. John's vision, I will describe the mythical images in this vision as well as some in further visions of Revelation.

The Lion

St. John describes the lion in his vision with the words, "The Lion of the tribe of Judah, the Root of David" (Rev. 5:5). These definitions refer to Christ, because according to the Bible Jesus was from the family of Judah and David, and he was called the son of David. (The expression "the root of David" actually means the descendant of David.) I interpret the Lion to be the symbol for the universal Self, because Christ can be seen as the Christian symbol for the universal Self. In Oriental culture, the lion as the universal Self could be identified as Krishna. In the *Bhagavadgita* Krishna, who represents God or Atman, says, "Among the wild animals I am the lion." In general, in India the lion is a common symbol for Atman.[23]

Because one of the four creatures in heaven is like a lion, there are two lions in Revelation. Yet, there is no contradiction since the universal Self, symbolized by the Lion of the tribe of Judah, and the basic vibration of the universe, symbolized by the lion as one of the creatures in heaven, are similar, even though not equal. They both serve as a foundation for the more tangible creation.[24]

The Lamb

"And I looked, and behold, in the midst of the throne and of the four living creatures, and in the midst of the elders, stood a Lamb as though it had been slain" (Rev. 5:6). The Lamb, like the Lion, refers in the biblical symbolism to Christ. For example, John the Baptist says of Jesus, "Behold! The Lamb of God," and St. Paul writes, "Christ our Passover was sacrificed for us."[25] For this reason I interpret the Lamb to symbolize the universal Self. In the visions of St. John the Divine the Lamb, however, encapsulates the meaning of the universal Self in a human cycle with more definition than the Lion does, since St. John tells of the Lamb, "A Lamb... having seven horns and seven eyes, which are seven spirits of God sent out into all the earth" (Rev. 5:6).

According to the theoretical guidelines I have presented, the universal Self has two meanings in the human cycle. On the one hand, it functions as "the first born," through which everything is created, or in words of the Bible, "All things were created through him." On the other hand, the universal Self represents a high state of the return phase of a person to original oneness. In the early visions of Revelation St. John is interested in the creation of the world and of human beings, but the symbolism of the sacrificed Lamb derives so essentially from the philosophy associated with the return, that I need to speak of this aspect also while interpreting the Lamb.

In the process of creation, the Lamb can easily be associated with the mythical ox referred to earlier since the Lamb has horns like the ox has. The horns then connect the Lamb to the creative power of God.[26] St. John is saying that all of creation occurs by means of the universal Self. The Lamb has also seven eyes, which are "the seven spirits of God." These spirits appeared in the previous chapter where they were compared to torches. In my interpretation, the torches symbolize different forms of spiritual energy, manifesting in persons as seven energy centers or chakras. Because everyone has these chakras, these spirits have indeed been "sent out into all the earth" as St. John says. That the spirits of God show themselves in this vision as the eyes of the Lamb reveals that the Lamb functions like a medium through which the spirits are being sent into human beings, that is, to creation.

The fact that the Lamb in St. John's vision has been slain explains the way by which a human person can return to God: through sacrificial death of the ego. The return of the human being to God can thus be crystallized in one archetypal mythical image: that of the slain, sacrified Lamb. (In referring to the sacrificed lamb the English translation capitalizes the word Lamb.) Thus I interpret the live lamb to be the symbol for the ego, and when it has surrendered to die, it becomes the Self.

In myths, man's different evolutionary stages are often depicted through animals, which symbolize the characteristics of the stage in question. The live lamb represents such an ethically high evolutionary state that attachments have nearly all disappeared, but not yet so fully that the ego has completely died nor the universal Self been entirely lived. Through his whiteness the lamb is associated with innocence, and lamb follows the shepherd in a sheep-like way. Similarly, those who have advanced on their journeys, have already freed themselves from their undesirable tendencies and able to follow their deeper intuitions, and they need not any longer strive to control their unruly wanton desires. Furthermore, the lamb surrenders to be slaughtered. Likewise, those who want to become perfect must eventually allow their "old I" to die. Only then can they reach the level symbolized by the sacrificed Lamb. These characteristics associated with the lamb—innocence, mildness, and submission in the face of death—appear in the Bible in several places. For example, it is written in Isaiah, "He was led as a lamb to the slaughter, and as a sheep before its shearers is silent, so he openeth not his mouth."[27]

The similarity of the sacrificed Lamb and the Lion in Revelation can be explained through the understanding that when man completely dies as an ego, he is transformed from a lamb to a majestic lion. This kind of symbolism appears often in Oriental literature, where according to a popular parable persons are in fact fearless lions or lionesses though they had imagined themselves to be weak sheep.[28]

From the perspective of the ascent or return phase of the human cycle the horns of the Lamb symbolize the universal Self striving to express itself as fully as possible in the lives of human persons. The universal Self functions as if a deep spiritual power from within pulling or pushing men and women forward on their spiritual journey. In a more mythical sense, the universal Self functions as a guide for humanity, and in Christianity, Jesus even used the shepherd-parable in referring to himself; the universal Self thus guides and tends the ego-lamb. In the Oriental tradition, this function of the Lamb would be like that of the Guru influencing man from within.[29]

The eyes of the Lamb symbolize the deeply spiritual, intuitive ability 'to see' needed on a person's return journey and this sight or guidance is given by the universal Self. Additionally, the chakras, like eyes that are sent into all the world, have an important function during the human beings' return to the Source. (This will be further dealt with in the following chapter.) As there were seven horns, so there are seven eyes all of which symbolize the need for deep change and liberation.

The idea of the universal Self as man's guiding force is not altogether strange to the scientific literature either, if we allow some margin of freedom in claiming parallels. Jung assumed the existence of a profound collective unconscious beneath the personal unconscious of the individual human being. He also defined archetypes as innate tendencies to experience and to cognate in certain ways as functioning on this unconscious level. Jung assumed further that the collective unconscious and its archetypes guide man's inner evolution in a deep, although often inconspicuous way. The individuation process is, according to Jung, a collectively innate tendency; a tendency produced by nature itself. Individual persons can, however, hinder the unfolding of their own individuation, and this may lead to psychic problems, anxiety and feelings of frustration in their lives.[30]

Men, tribes, tongues, peoples, nations, kings, and priests

"You [the Lamb]... have redeemed us to God by your blood out of every tribe and tongue and people and nation, and have made us kings and priests to our God; and we shall reign on the earth" (Rev. 5:9–10). The new mythical images mentioned by St. John—tribes, tongues, peoples, nations, kings, and priests—describe human beings on a more concrete level than do the Lion and the Lamb. We are still engaged with the basic ideas of the human image but not yet with physical personal man, as St. John is still involved in creating the foundation for him.

The tribes, the tongues, the peoples and the nations are composed of individual men and women who, in Revelation, symbolize the most concrete level of the human image. One individual person as a mythical image represents some particular characteristic, ability, desire, or mental state. Within Christianity, St. John of the Cross, for example, uses similar symbolism in speaking of "people of the lower part of the soul" and "the inhabitants of the house of the senses" when he refers to different abilities, mental states, likes and dislikes of the soul.[31] The tribes, peoples, and nations depict different classes of abilities and characteristics. Naturally, we can differentiate between an ability and a class of abilities, or a characteristic and a class of characteristics, only by agreement. For example, the mythical image of "the tongues" mentioned by St. John could symbolize the different forms of the ability to communicate. "The tongues" would then consist of such skills as the ability to speak and write, hear, gesture and so on.

At times, however, it is appropriate to interpret literally the individuals, peoples, tribes, and nations recounted by St. John in his visions. A myth has always many levels.

Most translations and manuscripts of Revelation do not use the word 'king,' *basileus*, in these verses.[32] However, for clarity, I interpret the king briefly here because kings are important components of St. John's human image. First the king, *basileus*, functions in Revelation as a ruler in general, when the Lamb is called the king of kings (Rev. 17:14 and 19:16). Secondly, kings in Revelation mean different kings of the earth. And man is the king of the earth when he acts as the performer of one of his abilities, for example, as a thinker or one who wills. In general, the kings of the earth in Revelation refer to man as one who acts, and that can be—as we have seen—either a desirous individual or one who is free of attachments. To say that the Lamb is the king of these kings emphasizes once again the importance of the universal Self in the metaphysical-mythical human image.

The priest belongs to the realm of sacred life, and therefore, as a mythical image, he represents the Self in one way or another; and I assume that the priest, as opposed to the Lamb, belongs to the level of the individual Self.

I interpret the more exact meaning of St. John's words in these verses only in the notes because the interpretations repeat what has already been said and also anticipate future events.[33] However, the words, "we shall reign on the earth" are interesting at this point. When these words are applied to the creation sequence, they tell us that St. John will soon progress in his reconstruction of the creation story. He will describe the emergence of the concrete human being: the birth of the men and women who live on earth, human beings endowed with ordinary consciousness and physical bodies.

The collective nature of the mythical images

Several of the mythical images St. John presents in this vision as well as at other times in Revelation are collective in a sense that they consist of many individual units. He speaks about people and nations and tongues. These collective images are important for the symbolism to function, because St. John uses them as a way to express the gradual changes taking place in him. For example, the more people are dying, the more St. John's ego is undergoing gradual death. Similar use of mythical imagery appears in the *Odyssey*, when Odysseus during his journey back home transforms inwardly: he is freed from his ego and matures spiritually. At the same time, the large crew of Odysseus' ship, which I see as a mythical image for Odysseus' ego, is killed one by one.

Collective, majestic mythical images fit well the nature of Revelation also because it is a grand, archetypal vision. It deals with matters that are essential to all people, that is, literally to all nations and tongues.

'Large' images are common also in dream symbolism. I stress this, because I believe it points out the possibility of interpreting Revelation as a picture of a man's or a woman's inner life regardless of its grand symbolism. In dreams, an 'immense' symbol can represent, for instance, the vastness of the personally observed inner experience; no doubt a spiritual transformation is always impressive for the individual undergoing it. But a magnificent dream image can also reflect the nature of the archetypal change; one who is going through a change may feel himself to live—using Jung's terminology—on the level of the collective unconscious. Yet, at other times, having many people appear in one's dreams can reflect fragmentation and a confused state of consciousness, which also often is part of the inner change.

In the following dream, which reflects the inner change of a person, there are large images of several individuals. The dreamer, who did not know anything about the above described symbolism, had been living through a period of transformation. Previously an intellectual extrovert, the woman's awareness of her inner experiences strengthened during the time of the dream. The inwardly lived experiences in myths are often represented by a woman, because the inner state of a woman's body likens to an image of inwardness. Man's sexual anatomy in myths, on the other hand, is associated with outward directiveness and with goal oriented, analytical thinking.

I see a battlefield. Large armies of men are engaged in combat. One by one the warriors are killed. When finally all of them lay dead, a group of women rise up from underground.

The direction of problem solving

Now I will return to the events in St. John's vision where we left off at the verse, "Do not weep. Behold the Lion of the tribe of Judah, the root of David, has prevailed to open the scroll and to loose its seven seals" (Rev. 5:5). After this, the Lamb becomes the center of attention, "And I looked, and behold, in the midst of the throne and of the four living creatures, and in the midst of the elders, stood a Lamb... and he came and took the scroll out of the right hand of him who sat on the throne" (Rev. 5:6–7). In the following visions the Lamb then opens the seals. Thus the Lion and the Lamb essentially depict the same idea as I mentioned earlier.

That the Lamb is the one to open the seals tells us about St. John's realization: the problem he became aware of at the sight of the sea of glass is so deep that to solve it he must transform spiritually. He must learn to love in a new universal way, and he must see matters through bright, high intuition. These are the qualities the Lamb represents when interpreted from the subjective point of view, that is, on the level of human consciousness. This kind of bright, deep intuition is born when the consciousness becomes quiet. It can then tune in to a level of higher spiritual reality which is symbolized by the Lamb when seen from a more objective point of view. When such intuitive understanding has been awakened in aspirants, it leads them onward in their spiritual journey by removing hindrances from their consciousness. Thus the Lamb in Revelation functions as a guide, as it were, and breaks the seals of the scroll.

In St. John's vision, the function of the Lamb is important, in the first place, in regard to the most central problems in Revelation: St. John's need for a correct God-concept and for a deeper spiritual life. When the Lamb enters the vision, St. John's concept of God and his personal experience of spiritual life are beginning to change. He understands that the universal love symbolized by the Lamb is central in religion, and he begins also to live this love. But he needs the Lamb at this time in his visions also because he wants to understand the world's creation and the place of the Lamb as the one through whom all things are created.

The realization of the importance of the Lamb becomes obvious in the vision because the Lamb steps into the center of the heaven. St. John sees the Lamb in the midst of the throne, the four creatures and the elders (Rev. 5:6). The meaning of the Lamb is emphasized also in the following way, "Now when he had taken the scroll, the four living creatures and the twenty-four elders fell down before the Lamb" (Rev. 5:8). Because the four creatures, including one like a lion, bow to the Lamb, St. John is portraying the Lion–Lamb as representing a higher and more important principle than the creatures. And it should be like this. In Christianity, the Son or Lamb–Christ is closest to the Father. The poetic verses of the vision also emphasize the significance of the Lamb, "Worthy is the Lamb... to receive power and riches and wisdom, and strength and honour and glory and blessing!" (Rev. 5:12.)

The central events of this vision of St. John, the appearance of the Lion–Lamb and the Lamb becoming the focal point, can be understood in a more general way than in light of the religious problems alone. When we have admitted to ourselves that our understanding of reality and ourselves is incomplete, we begin to seek direction for our transformation. The first important realization is then, "My transformation must mean a deepening of my inner life. For such a change to be genuine, it is not enough simply to absorb new outer concepts about the nature of the reality."

The spiritual experience and the necessity of change

Having found the direction for the inner change, St. John feels relief; his life seems light and happy. There is some worry mixed with his sense of relief, though, because St. John realizes he is facing a long process of change. These matters can be seen in the symbolism of the final verses of the chapter: the playing, singing, bowls of incense, and the number of angels.

The playing and singing

"The four living creatures and the twenty-four elders fell down before the Lamb, each having a harp... and they sang a new song" (Rev. 5:8–9). The instrument mentioned by St. John the Divine is called *kithara* in Greek. Different translations refer to it as a variety of stringed instruments like the harp, and sitar, but all of them carry the same symbolism. The song that the creatures and the elders are singing, is fittingly a new song, for St. John has realized something new.

Music in myths and dreams is a common symbol for an experience of high value; for example, in the Indian mythology, Krishna by his flute lures the listener into spiritual ecstasy. In Finnish folk poetry the singing, along with the playing of the *kantele* by Väinämöinen, functions in a beautiful way as mythical images for the love of nature and the joy of life.[34] I have found uplifting singing and playing in dreams to reflect personal spiritual experiences, happiness and feelings of integrity.

Describing personal spiritual experience as music is proper: although produced with instruments, music itself is, as it were, in the air, in the mythical world of values. Furthermore, human beings can give in to the spell of music with abandon without first having to analyze it or understand it intellectually. It may be, also, that the playing as a mythical image in St. John's vision, comes from the nada-sound heard in a deeply withdrawn, inward state. The instrument in St. John's vision brings forth a bright, plucked sound, which is one of the forms of the Om-sound.[35]

The bowl

"The four living creatures and the twenty-four elders fell down before the Lamb, each having... golden bowls full of incense, which are the prayers of the saints" (Rev. 5:8).

A bowl and its content in myths commonly symbolize value experiences. Our consciousness is like a bowl, and the value experienced is the content of the bowl. The bowl fittingly symbolizes a spiritual experience because we are to be receptive and yielding, like open vessels, for the spiritual experience to occur. Should the content of the bowl be liquid, the bowl symbolism reflects well the nature of the ultimate spiritual experience. We feel the content of the experience fully inside our consciousness, if you will, without longing or striving for anything outside the experience, not unlike the liquid at rest remaining completely inside the bowl. Our value experiences are various in qualities and in grades of intensity, and so there are also different kinds of receptacles in myths. One of the most famous is the Medieval Arthurian Holy Grail, which is commonly associated with the search for spirituality.[36]

In Revelation, the bowl seen by St. John symbolizes the experiencing of spiritual holiness in the stillness of prayer. Also, in the bowl, there is incense which is "the prayers of the saints," and usually there is smoke rising from incense. I interpret this to mean that St. John's devoted quietude includes a wish, which he sends off like smoke rising from the bowl. Different from purely spiritual experience, this wish is goal-oriented, and probably has to do with St. John's success in the spiritual change which he intuits is approaching. This wish reveals that St. John does not yet, at this stage of the journey, experience absolute stillness. He is not ready for it.

The number of the angels

"Then I looked, and I heard the voice of many angels around the throne, the living creatures, and the elders; and the number of them was ten thousand times ten thousand, and thousands of thousands" (Rev. 5:11). According to the interpretation I have suggested, thousand expresses oneness, because its first number is one. Should there be only the number thousand in the vision of St. John, it would symbolize experiencing absolute oneness. But when St. John writes "thousand times ten thousand," this adds dispersion to the experience. Number ten, in Revelation, connects to anxiety, which is clearly evident in the second chapter which reads, "You will have tribulation ten days" (Rev. 2:10). The anxiety is natural in this vision, as well, when St. John realizes, regardless of his spiritual experience, that he has a long and difficult journey ahead.

The angel

Angels appear often in Revelation. Already in the beginning of this vision, St. John says, "Then I saw a strong angel proclaiming with a loud voice, 'Who is worthy to open the scroll and to loose its seals?'" (Rev. 5:2.) Toward the end of the chapter, St. John writes, "Then I looked, and heard the voice of many angels" (Rev. 5:11).

Good angels in myths and folk beliefs are light-emitting beings, who play the flute, the harp, some other stringed instrument, or perhaps the horn. In Revelation, the angels also play the trumpet. It is easy to understand these general abilities of angels when we recall the light that is seen and the sound that is heard in the state of meditation.

While seeing the light of the spiritual eye, one experiences exaltation, love, and sometimes one begins to perceive the light as a living personage. Earlier I used as an example the remark by Ignatius Loyola that he often saw Christ as a sun, which perhaps tells of his having felt a personal presence in association with the spherical light. Some people who have undergone a clinical death have explained that the light they saw during the experience, emanated love, and they have called the light a light-being.[37] I myself also felt this sense of something personal when I, unexpectedly, saw that extremely bright light the first time. I did not associate it with angels, but when the light suddenly appeared in my forehead, the feeling that it caused was so beautiful and special, that I personified it spontaneously and sighed, "Please, do not go away!"

The sound of Om may be heard while seeing the light. As I have explained before, this is heard in a variety of ways. According to yoga teachings, different chakras emanate different sounds. From some of the lower energy centers flow the flute and harp-like sounds, and the actual Om-sound is then such a roar, thundering or drumming, that it can be described as the sound of trumpet blows.[38]

In myths, the angels also deliver messages. This errand of the angel is already evident in the Greek word for an angel, *aggelos* (pronounced *angelos)*, as it means more generally a messenger or harbinger. The angel's capacity as a messenger is natural, because we are intuitive in a deep state of meditation, and so we receive new realizations or 'messages.' Thus I interpret the angel, as an experience, to be a person's intuition.[39]

The intuition associated with the Om-sound can be such a modest incidence that a person may only afterward realize that she understands some matter in a new way and with an intuitive certainty. But intuition can also be a bright, sudden state of consciousness, during which one realizes many new things in a flash. A person meditating may also hear mentally in his head definite words—along with the Om sound—whose content seems quite surprising [40] Such an experience could be aptly described by saying that while the thunder is roaring, the angel delivers secrets in a loud voice. This kind of description does appear later on in St. John's visions (Rev. 10:3).

When St. John tells us about angels in Revelation, undoubtedly he sees them as pictorial visions. But it need not be wrong to assume that such experiences, associated with deeply withdrawn states as I have outlined above, have also influenced his angel vision.

6. THE FOUR RIDERS, THE ALTAR, AND THE EARTHQUAKE

The human image: general theory

St. John continues to explore the creation of men and women. A material human being of flesh and blood is already born in this vision, but to interpret the vision, I need to speak further of the metaphysical-mythical human image.

The human image according to yoga theory

According to Oriental teachings, the core of human energy system consists of seven important energy centers, or chakras. Yoga theory states that cosmic energy enters this system through the medulla oblongata located at the base of the skull opposite to the sixth highest center called *ajna* chakra. From there the energy, or *prana*, is dispersed into the head and the body, flowing to the lower chakras along the energy channels called *nadis*, located in the vicinity of the spine, and further along the lesser nadis onward to the different body parts. There are finer and grosser forms of prana corresponding to the different forms of cosmic energy, and this prana circulates in the body making its various functions possible; in this way prana forms the basic energy foundation for the physical and psychic functions.

The greater energy channels, where prana circulates, are located in the spinal region, and in India they are called *ida* and *pingala*. These are understood to be polar to each other: ida is cool and pingala warm. Additionally, in the spine in between ida and pingala, there is a third, innermost energy channel called *sushumna*. Sushumna reaches from the lowest center, the so-named *muladhara* chakra in the vicinity of the genitals, to the top of the head, where its destination is the highest chakra, *sahasrara*. Sahasrara is also called the thousand-petalled lotus, but it is not always thought of as an actual chakra. When energy reaches sahasrara, a person experiences bliss and oneness.

The sushumna nadi of average human beings is said to be closed, so that energy does not flow in it. Should we then wish to experience bliss, we must open the sushumna and send energy up through it all the way to the sahasrara. (This happens by withdrawing consciousness and the life energy.) While the energy ascends upward through the sushumna it passes through all the chakras strengthening their functioning. This is called by yoga teachings the opening of the chakras. The more the energy is passed through the sushumna, the more the chakras open. And the more that energy is drawn up to the sahasrara, the more we are liberated inwardly until finally we experience bliss.[1]

Yoga theory also points out that the nadis are not nerves, although sometimes they are talked of as such for the sake of simplicity. Rather, they are channels for life energy, or astral energy, and accordingly this level of being is also referred to as the astral body. There is also a deeper level than the astral body called the causal body. Often when yoga theory discusses a person's subtler levels than the physical body, it speaks of the subtle body, or the body formed by the subtler substances. All these different bodies are thought of as layers over a person's deepest core, Atman.[2]

Oriental literature mentions frequently that the advanced yogi sees with his 'inner eye' the network of prana I have described.[3] Its main features are generally accepted in that cultural tradition. As a matter of fact, some of this yogic concept has been adopted by Western schools of medicine, as far as acupuncture points are believed to be parts of this subtle body.

The mythical human image of the Bible and yoga theory

The Old Testament describes the creation of the human being in the following way, "Then God said, 'Let us make man in our image, according to our likeness'... So God created man in his own image, in the image of God he created him." In the following chapter the Bible recounts this creation, this time describing it thus: "And the Lord God formed man of the dust of the ground, and breathed into his nostrils the breath of life; and man became a living soul."[4]

Analyzing these two accounts in terms of yoga theory, the first man, the one whom God created in his own image, is man's Self, whereas the man created from the dust of the ground symbolizes the more tangible levels of human being. However, even the man created from the dust of the ground does not yet depict the physical body, but rather the subtler levels of human being, because the dust of the ground as a mythical image would probably be more likely to represent the subtle body. Within Christianity, this kind of interpretation about the creation myth of man, was presented by Origen c. 200 A.D., when he explained that the man which was created as the image of God refers to the inner aspect of man, and the one created from the dust of the ground, the outer.[5]

The above quoted Bible verse can be understood to trace also the descent of the cosmic energy into man's subtle body as God breaths the life force into man's nostrils; the nose is located approximately at the level of the medulla oblongata through which, according to yoga theory, the cosmic energy enters the subtle body.

The biblical creation myth continues next with a description of paradise, "And the Lord God planted a garden eastward in Eden; and there he put the man whom he had formed. And out of the ground the Lord God made every tree grow that is pleasant to the sight and good for food; the tree of life was also in the midst of the garden, and the tree of the knowledge of good and evil." If we see the man created from the dust of the ground as the subtle body, then the description of paradise would symbolically describe the properties and functions of this subtle body. In Christianity, the paradise of Eden, indeed, has the connotation of the soul in a state of mercy. This idea can be developed further by applying yoga theory.[6]

In the light of this theory, the biblical paradise is a mythical image of man's energy structure. The beautiful and nourishing trees of paradise are the different energy channels of the astral body and the different types of energy flowing through them, 'nourishing' that body. The two most important trees of the paradise describe the two most important parts of this energy structure.

The trunk of the tree of life is formed by the sushumna nadi and the foliage in top of it, by the thousand-petalled lotus which is the sahasrara. Thus this tree resembles a palm tree. This part of the prana structure is the tree of life, because man experiences bliss when the energy flows in it. Ida and pingala nadis and their tributaries, the lesser energy channels, can be included in the tree of life as its branches, but the sushumna and the sahasrara are the most important parts of the tree.[7]

The trunk of the tree of the knowledge of good and evil is formed by the ida and pingala nadis only, and its branches are those lesser energy channels which flow in the astral body and to which the energy flow of ida and pingala is connected directly. This tree looks like a fig tree, where the lower branches are near the ground. When man's energy structure is limited to this tree, he cannot experience bliss, but is confined to the outward consciousness maintained by the prana flowing in this part of the energy system. In the biblical myths, this limitation takes place when man eats from the tree of the knowledge of good and evil; in a more general Christian language, he then loses his state of mercy. In the biblical creation myth, God indeed warns man not to eat from this tree.

The myth of the Fall—following the creation myth in the Bible—represents yet a little more tangible stage of the human image. When Adam and his wife eat from the tree of the knowledge of good and evil, the human energy distribution becomes limited to that tree: man's life energy begins to circulate only in the ida and pingala nadis and in the lesser energy channels. In the biblical myth about the Fall, the fig tree plays a part in the events, as right after the Fall Adam and Eve protect themselves with the large leaves of the fig tree. The material human being, which we now are, is born from this Fall. When God gives Adam and Eve clothes of leather, man, having been an astral being, now takes on a more material physical form, and when Adam and Eve are sent away from paradise after the Fall, man moves completely away from the pure and harmonious energy system, which had made it possible to experience bliss. After man's Fall God places cherubs to guard the way to the tree of life; this way to the tree of life is a fitting mythical image for the sushumna nadi.[8] While the cherubs guard the way to the tree of life, man is no longer able to enter the state of bliss through sushumna. Yoga theory expresses the same idea by explaining that the sushumna nadi is closed at its lower end.

In Indian symbolism, the human energy system on the astral level is generally described as a tree, but there the tree usually is presented upside down to emphasize that human life energy is part of cosmic energy; human beings draw energy from heaven with the upside-down roots reaching out to it. In Indian literature, the human prana system is also associated directly with the tree of the knowledge of good and evil of the Bible.[9]

I find it natural that there are similarities between the Oriental human image and the biblical myths. The original creators of the myths were prophets and other exceptional individuals, who have personally experienced the vast dimensions of human existence. They have often disguised their knowledge in mythical robes and these have become legendary tales. Bible scholars believe that the sections concerning paradise derive from the ancient oral traditions of the Middle-East.[10]

Using the terminology I have presented earlier, the energy of the tree of life, or sushumna and sahasrara, compares on the level of human consciousness with the consciousness of oneness. Should we include ida and pingala nadis along with the lesser energy channels in the tree of life, the energy flowing in them compares with the detached consciousness of duality. (Here ida and pingala nadis and the lesser energy channels have been purified, meaning that man is free from attachments. These matters will be defined more clearly in the last few chapters.) The energy of the tree of the knowledge of good and evil can be compared to ego-consciousness. The implication of this interpretation is that the Fall means that man has limited himself to ego-consciousness.

According to the interpretation I am suggesting, the biblical creation myth and the myth about the Fall present, in a sense, a cross-section of the different levels of the human being. They begin the description from man's innermost level and advance to the outermost and the most gross level, that of the physical body and the desire-filled ego-consciousness.

The chakras in Revelation

In his previous vision, St. John described the scroll that was sealed with the seven seals. From here on his visions unfold to the beginning of the eighth chapter in the way that the Lamb opens those seven seals. Later the visions are paced by the blasts from the seven trumpets and the pourings out from the seven bowls (till the end of the sixteenth chapter). Thus St. John's inner change takes place in seven steps.

I associate the seven-step symbolism of Revelation with the seven chakras. I assume that St. John travels back to paradise along the pathway of the tree of life. On this pathway, he opens the seven chakras proceeding from the base upward. In Revelation symbolism, the seventh step does always form the climax—the liberation, experiencing oneness or bliss—in the same way as according to the yoga teachings the seventh chakra, sahasrara, is the center for experiencing bliss. That the seven-step series of events is repeated tells us that St. John opens the chakras gradually; he walks the pathway of the tree of life in a spiral, as it were, so that the opening of the chakras is ever deeper at each new cycle.

It is especially fitting to interpret the opening of the seals by relating them to the chakras because yoga teachings specifically speak of the opening of the chakras. The seals and the chakras are similar also in their circular appearance; chakra means a wheel, referring thus to a spherical form.[11] This approach does not, however, exclude other interpretations; for example, to open the seals that have closed up a book can be well related to opening of the human consciousness, and the seven-step serial event describes generally a completed cognition and transformation process.

The symbolism of the seven steps appears also in the three first chapters of Revelation which I did not interpret. In the first chapter St. John sees seven lampstands (Rev. 1:12), and the second and the third chapters are comprised of letters, which he addresses to the seven churches of the Asia Minor. In the light of yoga theory, the lampstands would be energy centers, or rather, more accurately, their locations in the human body, as St. John sees only the lampstands, not the fire, or the energy itself. The seven churches can also be seen to symbolize the chakras, because they are said to be "the seven lampstands" (Rev. 1:20). In his epistles, St. John mentions of each church something good and something which needs improvement. He also presents cautions and encouragements for a deeper spiritual life. The epistles addressed to the churches can be seen as St. John's introspection. During them, he understands that in the realm of each chakra, his experiences are deficient, like lampstands, which have not been ignited to light the way. And so he needs to set out to travel the inner road of the tree of life.

To my knowledge, the similarity between Revelation of St. John the Divine and the chakra teachings was first presented in 1894 by the Indian Swami Sri Yukteswar. His disciple, Paramahansa Yogananda, has further supported this view. The American Edgar Cayce also presented in his trance states an interpretation of Revelation based on the energy centers. Today references to the chakra symbolism of Revelation are quite common.[12]

The human image in the vision of St. John

Opening of the seals

The sixth chapter is especially interesting in the light of the chakra teachings, because in this vision the chakras appear in two different ways which partly overlap, and partly diverge. On the one hand, St. John advances along the pathway of the tree of life, as though climbing upwards along its trunk at the same time as the seals are being opened, and he understands reality in an ever-deeper way. On the other hand, the chakra teachings are present as subject matter to be realized in such a way that St. John's concept of the human being becomes step by step more real and substantial as he follows in his vision the descent of the cosmic energy into the human being from the higher chakras downward.

Because the sixth chapter of Revelation obviously connects with the chakra teachings, the vision could be approached by examining these connections more closely. For example, every energy center has its own function within the human body and consciousness, and these functions vary depending on the individual's particular evolutionary stage. But instead of following the chakra teachings in more detail, I will assume that St. John sees what he needs to see in order to solve his spiritual problem. He thus begins to see the structure of human consciousness in such a way as will clarify human development and the cycle wherein human beings become alienated from God. He will then seek out possibilities for their return.

The riders

While the Lamb opens the four first seals, the four creatures each send off a rider. Just as the creatures symbolize the basic principles of the macrocosm, so now St. John examines how the macrocosmic principles appear in man, the microcosm. In this way he follows the metaphysical-mythical assumption that the macrocosm and the microcosm are comparative in their nature. The four riders then represent in St. John's vision the basic principles of human life. According to yoga teaching, human beings receive an important part of their energy from cosmic energy, and the four riders tell us that indeed this cosmic energy gets transferred into human energy.[13] The horse in this vision would represent the energy itself, and the rider on its back, the human consciousness corresponding to that energy.

The horse as an image of men's and women's energy foundation is also common in dreams. In average dreams, the horse most often symbolizes their animal drives. The relationship between the horses and their riders tells about the dreamers' relationship to their own basic drives. For instance, someone who wears her horse out by whipping it on relentlessly may be reflecting a tendency to urge herself to such demanding accomplishments that the strain depletes her natural energy flow.

In the following interpretation of the four riders, I assume St. John is interested in the function which these basic principles have in the creation of the human being. For this reason I link my interpretation to the biblical creation myth and the myth about the Fall.

The first rider

"Now I saw that the Lamb opened one of the seals; and I heard one of the four creatures saying with a voice like thunder, 'Come and see.' And I looked, and behold, a white horse. And he who sat on it had a bow; and a crown was given to him, and he went out conquering and to conquer." (Rev. 6:1–2.)

St. John does not tell us what the creatures that send the riders look like; speaking of the creatures he merely says: one, the second, the third and the fourth. I assume, however, that the creatures appear in the same order as in the fourth chapter, so that the first rider is sent off by the creature looking like a lion. Because the lion in my interpretation symbolizes the basic level of the universe, a kind of original energy, the white horse represents the same basic energy in man. Applied to the creation myth of the Old Testament, the sending off of the first rider is like the breathing of the life force into the man created from the dust of the ground. In this way, St. John begins to see the human being as the subtle body, or the body of energy.

Applying yoga theory, we might say that the white horse is the finest and most original form of prana. In India this kind of identification would be explained by reference to basic human elements. These range from the subtler to the grosser ones in this order: ether, fire, air, water, and earth, the ether forming the background to which the other grosser energy forms are attached. When only four elements are distinguished, fire is usually the most subtle one. The white horse of Revelation might then represent in man the function of the mythical ether—or alternately that of the fire—as the white horse is the first one to be sent off. Instead of prana, different cultures have their own names for the human life force, such as *chi* in China.[14] It is not necessary, however, to interpret the white horse according to any one specific theory; a general assumption of man's basic energy foundation is enough.

Man's cyclical evolution requires that human energy returns to the highest and most subtle form at the end of the ascent. So it is that toward the end of Revelation, when St. John is approaching the state which is both the beginning and the end, the rider of the white horse indeed appears again.[15]

White with its seeming lack of color fittingly describes the beginning and end of life—the stages without the variety and color of everyday events. Perhaps this is the reason many cultures associate white with birth and death, the beginning and the end of human life. The color white appeared earlier as a symbol in Revelation: in the fourth chapter the elders were dressed in white clothing. I explained that white, denoting purity, symbolized the original as well as the highest and holiest states of consciousness. The whiteness of the first horse corresponds to this relationship within yoga theory too, because ajna chakra—the polar point for the medulla oblongata where the cosmic energy is said to enter the human being—is white according to this theory.[16]

The rider on the white horse, according to my interpretation, is the form of human consciousness corresponding to a human being's basic energy. This is a kind of pure consciousness, a state of mythical paradisiacal innocence or mercy, similar to the original state in the paradise before the Fall. During the return journey, it refers to a pure and high state of consciousness revealed in a person who has become a saint.

The rider has a bow because from the pure, paradisiacal, original state, the more material characteristics of human beings are, as it were, shot off with a bow. The original state of paradise is the starting point for the birth, or creation, of the more material human being as described in the early chapters of the Old Testament.

St. John uses the Greek word *stephanos* of the rider's crown. This actually means a wreath made of palm leaves, and it is a symbol of victory, as in antiquity the winner of a race was crowned with a wreath. The wreath-crown has the same meaning of victory in St. John's visions. The victory that St. John talks about in Revelation, means, of course, man's return to the paradise of oneness with God. Before this triumph man must, however, walk victoriously through his whole evolutionary road from the beginning till the end, and it is perhaps for this reason that St. John says the rider goes out as "conquering and to conquer." The circular shape of the wreath is also appropriate to illustrate human alienation and return, for the aspirant has, as it were, traversed a full circle by the time of returning to that state which is both the beginning and the end.

The second rider

"When he opened the second seal, I heard the second living creature saying, 'Come and see.' And another horse, fiery red, went out. And it was granted to the one who sat on it to take peace from the earth and that people should kill one another; and there was given to him a great sword." (Rev. 6:3–4.)

In his envisioning the second rider, St. John comes a step closer to an awareness of the more material side of a human being. In the light of biblical myths, he begins to trace the Fall of man whereas according to yoga theory, the second horse would represent a grosser form of prana descending to the lower chakras.

The second creature, who sends out this rider, was in the fourth chapter said to look like a calf or a young ox, and in my interpretation it represented the power of change, which is now activated and begins to transform man to a more tangible being. In a 'finished' human being, the red horse represents the active energy, and the rider on the horse symbolizes the corresponding quality in the human consciousness. Thus the rider could be said to represent willpower, which is essential also during the return journey, because man needs to change himself inwardly to be able to ascend back to pure consciousness.

Red is an appropriate color for this horse because it relates, in many ways, to action and activity. Red is commonly experienced as an active and even provoking color; it may derive these associations from the nearly aggravating clarity with which red shows off against the green background of nature. In the Bible, a purplish red reflects royalty, and in Revelation the king symbolizes the one who acts. We will also see throughout Revelation that red represents a more superficial and unholy—even evil—level than does white. Thus red clearly is associated with a more material human being than white. In yoga theory, two of the chakras lower than ajna chakra, the second and the fourth from the bottom, are said to be red.[17]

The sword of the rider on the red horse, I interpret generally to symbolize a goal-oriented attitude, as the warrior strives towards his goals with the help of his sword. When Adam and Eve in the biblical myth receive, after the Fall, leather clothing—a physical body—they become aware of their physical needs and the necessity of attending to them. In fact, the Lord says to Adam after the Fall, "In toil you shall eat from it all the days of your life."[18] The consciousness of the material man tied to his physical body is thus generally marked by a goal-oriented attitude or a drive to satisfy his needs.

The errand given to the second rider, to take the peace from the earth, means that the human consciousness will come to a state of transformation. The original state of oneness and peace is broken when the human being with a physical body and an ordinary consciousness is formed after the Fall. The expression used by St. John "that people should kill one another," symbolizes well the inner conflicts rising from continuous change.

When applied to the return journey, the characteristics of the second rider tell us how women and men must use their willpower to make progress on their inner road. They must kill in themselves new attachments, or such qualities as inhibit their spirituality; that the "people should kill one another" also refers to this effort.

The third rider

"When he opened the third seal, I heard the third living creature say, 'Come and see.' And I looked, and behold, a black horse, and he who sat on it had a pair of scales in his hand. And I heard a voice in the midst of the four living creatures saying, 'A quart of wheat for a denarius, and three quarts of barley for a denarius; and do not harm the oil and the wine.'" (Rev. 6:5–6.)

Should the senders follow—as I assume they do—the order mentioned in the fourth chapter, the new rider is sent off by the creature looking like a human being. St. John examines how the spirit appears in a more material human being. I believe he sees the spirit expressed basically in two different ways: one symbolized by the scale and the words "a quart of wheat for a denarius, and three quarts of barley for a denarius", and the other by the oil and the wine and the caution not to ruin the oil and the wine.

The scale held by the rider symbolizes all evaluation, weighing and pondering. The symbol for the goddess of justice, for example, is the scale, because she weighs right and wrong. In its broadest sense the scale symbolizes duality, which I defined in the previous chapter to be a basic quality of ordinary human consciousness; therefore, the third rider seen by St. John tells us more about the emergence of the material human being. The same duality of consciousness can be seen also in the myth about the Fall. After eating from the tree of the knowledge of good and evil, Adam and Eve discover themselves to be naked: man began to see himself as an object and to weigh his own state. At the same time, he became obliged to evaluate himself as he became aware of the differences between good and evil.

The words "a quart of wheat for a denarius, and three quarts of barley for a denarius" also include evaluation in expressing the wheat to be three times the value of the barley. I associate these words with the meaning the duality has on the return journey. The traveler must use his critical thinking to decide what in life is valuable and what less so to know which direction to go. But even good judgments help the traveler only if he makes them his own, or 'eats' them, and perhaps it is for this reason St. John suggests the parable of grain or food.

In myths, the grain, however, has a fairly superficial meaning. It is associated with analytical thinking and evaluation. Farmers grow the grain, zealously till the ground and harvest the crops. Similarly, man cultivates his own consciousness and receives from it the fruits of new thoughts and evaluations. He ponders them in his mind as if he were chewing grain. In the words of Christ when he says that the ear of wheat must die, the ear of wheat is actually the same as the ego.

The symbolical meaning of oil and wine is deeper than that of the grain because they are the internal core-essence which is extracted from the fruit by crushing it. The peel and the flesh of the fruit represent the more superficial consciousness or even the ego, but the extract is like that sense of Self and love we experience when the ego dies. The Old Testament prophet Zechariah says, "Grain shall make the young men thrive, and new wine the young women." Here the male symbolizes the conscious and striving side of the consciousness and the female, the deeper level whereby one can experience spiritual values.[19]

Thus, I interpret the words "do not harm the oil and the wine" to refer to the experiencing of the spiritual values, and the words emphasize the necessity of surrendering love during the return journey. Though analytical evaluations are important for the traveler, they retain their duality and may hinder a person's sense of surrender to oneness, and so the warning not to harm the oil and the wine is appropriate.

The caution is timely also because in the mythical Fall human consciousness of oneness is shadowed by the ego with its desires and duality. The ability to experience oneness or high spiritual values decreases when one begins to experience lesser values like pleasure and ordinary joy. With these positive feelings come also their negative opposites, namely sadness and pain, expecially when one is frustrated in their pursuits. I feel the words "do not harm the oil and the wine" to point out that human beings should not be content with a low and negative emotional life. They must feel positive values on as high a level as they are able to, and try to cultivate them even further.

The third horse of Revelation is black—a deep darkness for St. John perhaps, because it represents a whole field of problems, especially those having to do with confronting self-evaluation and his own inferior value experiences. A dream of a black image usually means that the dreamer is not being consciously aware of or has not personally experienced the matter represented by that image. Yoga theory states the third lowest chakra is the color of the dark clouds and the fourth from the bottom has black coloration along with the red.[20]

These interpretations of the second and the third rider and their symbols are in harmony with both Western and Eastern philosophy. Western philosophy separates three basic ethical concepts: power, justice, and love. Three different ethical systems have been built around these concepts. The basis of the ethics of power is the willpower, which I associate with the rider on the red horse and his sword. An essential part of the ethics of justice is critical evaluation, and in St. John's vision this is symbolized by the scale. The core of the third form of ethics, the ethics of love, is the experience of love, which in Revelation is symbolized by the oil and the wine. In Oriental culture, these matters are presented by explaining that a human being's most important avenues to liberation are action, wisdom, and love. (The fourth main avenue to freedom is the yoga path.)[21] Perhaps the vision of St. John tells us that the most essential of all these paths is that of love: one should not harm the oil and the wine.

The fourth rider

"When he opened the fourth seal, I heard the voice of the fourth living creature saying, 'Come and see.' And I looked, and behold, a pale horse. And the name of him who sat on it was Death, and Hades followed with him. And power was given to them over a fourth of the earth, to kill with sword, with hunger, with death, and by the beasts of the earth." (Rev. 6:7–8.)

The fourth rider is sent out by the creature looking like an eagle. This rider then depicts the cyclical development of man: his alienation from God and his return to God.

As far as alienation is concerned, the fourth rider represents the 'finishing touches' of human separation from oneness with God. Separated from God, men and women are tied to physical bodies, and therefore, to physical death. The horse ridden by Death in St. John's vision represents thus the characteristics belonging to the physical body: aging, deterioration, and dying. The rider Death on the horse represents human awareness of the necessity of death. Similarly, the biblical myth about the Fall stresses man's mortality when the Lord, while dressing Adam and Eve in leather clothing, says to Adam, "For dust you are, and to dust you shall return."[22]

In relation to alienation, the rider Death can also be interpreted in a more abstract way. The issue may be spiritual death when the soul loses its innocence during the Fall. Tied to the physical body and a slave to its needs, men and women become filled with desires, and these desires separate them from God. For example, St. John of the Cross expresses this idea appropriately by saying, "The appetites kill a man in his relationship with God."[23]

On the journey whereby men and women return to God, Death refers to the death of the ego. That is, human beings have to mortify their attachments and ego-desires in order to return to God. St. John of the Cross, for instance, says that "The soul cannot fully live new life unless the old man dies completely," and he specifically stresses the mortification of desires.[24] When human beings in the end are fully free from attachments, they overcome the power of matter and return as free souls, or eagles, back to their original state.

Most people do not, however, become fully liberated from their ego-desires in one lifetime; thus they will not be able to return to oneness with God. For the return to become possible, the metaphysical-mythical worldviews assume either that the road continues after death, or that people live more than one life on earth. The former case suggests a purgatory where people are gradually purified from their desires in the after-death state and, once pure, united with God.[25] The latter case is explained by the idea of reincarnation. As long as persons have not reached full liberation, they will exist, for a time, in the after-death state apart from their physical bodies and then incarnate again on earth. During earthly life they then continue to mortify their desires till they gain final liberation. After that they are not forced to incarnate again.

Keeping the above images in mind, we can see that the horse ridden by Death symbolizes the urge for detachment from those desires which keep us tied to lives on the physical plane; and the rider Death on the horse represents the awareness of the necessity of the death. But now that awareness can embrace both the physical death and the death of the ego because a deep realization of the necessity of the physical death may also lead to the death of the ego. The Hades following the Death refers to the state after physical death.

According to my understanding, one cannot deduce from Revelation what specific form St. John believes the return will take, but it is possible to see references to reincarnation in Revelation. In the third chapter of the book we read, "He who overcomes, I will make him a pillar in the temple of my God and he shall go out no more" (Rev.3:12). In Indian literature, this verse has been interpreted to explain that as long as man has not "overcome," or found the ultimate oneness with God, he is to "go out" or to return back to the cycle of birth and death.[26]

The idea of reincarnation has not, in general, belonged as clearly to Christianity as it has to Oriental religions. There are, however, moments in the Bible which seem to imply that reincarnation was considered a possibility in exceptional cases like that of a prophet. For example, the Old Testament ends with a prophecy about the new coming of Elijah, "Behold, I will send you Elijah the prophet before the coming of the great and dreadful day of the Lord." Later on Jesus says of John the Baptist, "And if you are willing to receive it, he is Elijah, who is to come." During the first centuries of Christianity, when Revelation originated, some Gnostics supported a general belief in reincarnation, and in ancient philosophy, ideas of reincarnation were clearly visible in Plato's works.[27]

But now I will return to the fourth rider, Death, who was given the power "to kill with sword, with hunger, with death, and by the beasts of the earth." In this list of death-causes, death, *thanatos*, has been interpreted in most translations to be an illness leading to death, a pestilence. I interpret these details of the fourth rider, also, from the viewpoints of both alienation and return, or from the viewpoints of spiritual death and the death of the ego.

When man dies spiritually, he begins to use his own will in a selfish way, filled with desires, so that he feels himself to be separate from others, and even in opposition to them. His selfish will, or sword, kills him in this way. When the question is that of the death of the ego, killing with the sword means self-discipline and discrimination; the aspirant uses his willpower to cut off those desires which he understands to enslave him.

In dreams, fairy tales, and old legends, the sword may also be a magical weapon like a sword of light. A sword like this symbolizes intuition rather than willpower or discrimination; with a sword of light the warrior, as it were, creates light in the midst of darkness. The sword of intuition is indeed a valuable weapon in slaying the ego, as we will see later on in St. John's other visions.[28]

Hunger as a mythical image refers both to mental and spiritual hunger. The meaning befits spiritual death especially, because individuals continuously create new needs for themselves and seek to satisfy them. Yet they are never satisfied; they do not gain lasting happiness even when all their outward needs and desires have been fulfilled. They feel a constant compulsion to seek that 'something else,' and overcome by this feeling they are, as it were, starving. St. John of the Cross points out that those who are slaves of their desires are always unsatisfied and bitter, like someone always hungry.[29] In the end seekers may come to understand that they can find lasting happiness only by learning to feel love and joy within themselves. It is then that their desires for external, material things begin to fall away.

Pestilence, in the Bible, refers to a variety of epidemics like smallpox and cholera. The abscesses and boils belonging to pestilence make the person swell abnormally. This kind of bulging and bloating denotes metaphorically all kinds of ego-inflation or egoism. Egoism causes arguments in human relationships, and so an unpleasant atmosphere develops wherein anxiety and bitterness and different forms of spiritual death spread like epidemics. These disturbances can, however, eventually lead to an inner change, so that the person suffering from them will begin to seek liberation. Then the old person finally dies, as during the biblical times people often died of a pestilence.

The beasts of the earth, finally, as mythical images are our own animalistic, egoistic desires and instincts, a common meaning often given to the beasts both in religious texts and in secular literature.[30] If we are not able to direct our lives in reasonable ways, our desires will tear us into fragments and increase the chance that we will experience a most difficult spiritual death. Finally, we perhaps reach such a state of futility and anxiety that we cannot continue in our former behaviours, but instead we begin to seek liberation. Thus can our fear of approaching spiritual death make room for the death of the ego.

The fourth horse in St. John's vision is said to be pale. Speaking of plants, the original Greek word *chlōros* means yellowish green, and speaking of people, a sickly color. An English scholar of Revelation,

John M. Court, apparently has strived to combine the different meanings of the original Greek word by suggesting the horse to be yellow or bilious looking.[31] For the purposes of my interpretation, these are excellent descriptions; the word 'bilious' is particularly fitting with bile symbolizing bitterness. Having been driven away from the paradisiacal, pure, original state of consciousness, having fallen into the physical body and become spiritually dead, a human being is painfully aware of the troubles and suffering in his body and life; he is also well aware of death. He is suffering like a bilious patient. In yoga theory, the lowest, or muladhara chakra, is yellow.[32]

The message of the four riders

I feel that the vision of the riders in Revelation—as well as the biblical envisioning of the Fall—presents, in a succinct, mythical form, those basic human conditions which we are tied to as physical and psychic beings. I will reiterate briefly.

The necessity of satisfying our needs is a basic human condition. This requires goal orientation and duality, or the separation into the subject and the object, and in general, the ability to discriminate, which all make it possible to satisfy our needs.

Also, part of the human condition is the ability to experience values both in a positive way as pleasure and joy, and in a negative way as sadness and sorrow. Physical death and the awareness of it are, of course, part of the human existence. These basic conditions lead to suffering: it is not always possible to satisfy our needs, and illness and death bring sorrow. But suffering also leads one to seek liberation, and it is possible to become free, if we find that deep spiritual level which is the foundation for our material being. Expressed more mythically, it is the Fall that eventually leads to our desire to return back to paradise, wherefrom we once were driven away. The words in the second chapter of Revelation, "Remember therefore from where you have fallen; repent and do the first works" (Rev. 2:5), already suggest the idea of the falling and the return.[33]

The significance of the Self and the problem of evil

The souls of the slain under the altar

"When he opened the fifth seal, I saw under the altar the souls of those who had been slain for the word of God and for the testimony which they held" (Rev. 6:9).

From this verse on, I begin to interpret the visions of St. John based on the idea that he has moved on to the theme of the return to oneness, or God. I feel he has satisfactorily analyzed the creation of the human being, and at the same time, has revealed man's Fall and his spiritual death. St. John does later on speak briefly a few times of the problems of the creation process, but according to my interpretation, the latter part of Revelation describes mostly the different stages of the return journey.

The new phase of the visions begins when St. John sees the altar, and I assume the altar to continue the function of the sea of glass which appeared in front of the throne in the fourth chapter (Rev. 4:6). I associate the altar with the sea of glass, because both of them are located in front of the throne, although this is not directly said to be the case with the altar. Generally, the altar, however, is the place where humankind is in front of God, or the enthroned, and a few chapters later Revelation explicitly speaks of "the golden altar which was before the throne" (Rev. 8:3).

The altar suggests to me the idea of universal love, or expressed more theoretically, the universal Self. More accurately, the altar is the subjective side of the universal Self, whereas the Lamb symbolizes its objective side. (The basis of this interpretation will become apparent as the altar evolves and changes during the visions.) When the altar now appears in St. John's vision, he realizes that there has not been enough of universal love in his life. Earlier he had experienced the vision of the sea of glass, or the unconscious and an awareness of potentiality. But now that which is potential is beginning to become actual.

The souls of the slain, which St. John sees under the altar, are, however, more apparent in the vision than is the altar. I suggest a multi-layered interpretation for these souls.

The Self and evil

The souls of the slain mainly refer to the death of the ego. While still alive, the slain people were components of the ego, and once they had been killed, the ego died. Then the soul was set free from the slain people so that these souls are now 'parts' of the Self. These souls, too, symbolize the Self, but unlike the altar, which denotes the universal Self, the souls of the slain represent the level of the individual Self. I feel these souls to be under the altar because they are, as it were, the first seedlings of the universal Self or the altar. As a reminder, the universal Self is the extreme form of the individual Self; only after the ego has died completely will a woman or man live fully on the level of the universal Self. But at this stage, St. John experiences personally only that small part of the universal Self which is symbolized by the souls of the slain. Thus, St. John uses the image of several souls to illustrate the gradual death of the ego and the strengthening of the Self. (Naturally, the deepest level of the human consciousness is already whole and complete, but to express the transformation, one needs to rely on speaking of the parts.)

Possibly, the souls of the slain are under the altar also to give us the impression that they are found in a secret place. When St. John finds these souls in a secret hiding place, he realizes that in every spiritually dead human being—as in himself—the deeper level of being has been pushed aside. (Revealing a secret hiding place is a natural continuation of St. John's earlier images as he is beginning to see what is hidden in the sea of glass, and he is already able to peek into the scroll a little, and even read some of it.)

Secondly, I associate the souls of the slain with the problem of evil. St. John must have wondered how it is possible that God has allowed His true prophets and apostles to be killed. I believe this to be so because the souls St. John sees are the souls of those people "who had been slain for the word of God and the testimony which they held." In general, the issue then is the problem of evil: how can an omnipotent, good, and righteous God allow evil and wrong? I assume additionally that St. John has, till now, repressed the problem of evil as something too painful to confront, and therefore the souls of the slain are now revealed, as it were, from a hiding place.

The problem of evil has caused anxiety for several Old Testament prophets; for example, Habakkuk pondered, "You are of purer eyes than to behold evil, and cannot look on wickedness. Why do you look on those who deal treacherously? And hold your tongue when the wicked devours one more righteous than he?"[34]

The relationship between the omnipotent God and evil has bothered philosophers, theologians, and other people for centuries. For example, in *The Confessions* of St. Augustine of Hippo, who died in 430 A.D., we can find heart-breaking descriptions of the deadlock this problem created:

So, where then the evil comes from, when God has created everything and God is good... Where is the evil from? Or was the substance He used for creating everything something bad, and as He shaped and organized it, He left in it something which He did not transform into good? But why? Or was He, regardless of his omnipotence, unable to transform all of the substance into good, so that no evil would have been left in it? Such thoughts did I harbor in my sick heart, weighed down and anxious for the fear of death and hopeless search for truth.[35]

I assume that the meaning of the Self and the problem of evil are 'layered' in St. John's visions, so that at times I see them both in the same mythical image. This is natural, because those two matters are connected. When St. John has repressed the problem of evil, this repression has kept his spiritual life in paralysis, and his Self has not been able to get free. But only by progressing spiritually could he understand the problem of evil in a deeper, more satisfying way.

The demand for vengeance

"And they [the souls of the slain] cried with a loud voice, saying, 'how long, O Lord, holy and true, until you judge and avenge our blood on those who dwell on the earth?'" (Rev. 6:10.) I interpret this crying of the souls now in two complementary ways: on the one hand, it has to do with the dying of the ego and the strengthening of the Self, and on the other, with the problem of evil.

In the first reading, the souls or actually the Self is crying out in a loud voice, proclaiming its existence. The vengeance on those dwelling on earth means that the ego must die more completely. Vengeance is a good expression here, as St. John must feel that his ego-bound conscious mind which embraces all those who dwell on earth, has, until now, taken up too much of his spiritual life. Even his God-concept has been too narrow and so his personal experience of love has been ignored both in his life and in his concept of God.

In the second reading the cry from the souls, "How long, O Lord, holy and true, until you judge and avenge our blood", is an anxious question like those asked by the prophet Habakkuk and St. Augustine about the problem of evil. Perhaps St. John's sense of justice demands judgment and vengeance, because he has seen how his fellow Christians have been persecuted, even as he himself was sent to exile.

The completion of the number of the slain

"It was said to them that they should rest a little while longer, until both the number of their fellow servants and their brethren, who would be killed as they had been, was completed" (Rev. 6:11). The words reveal that St. John realizes that his ego must die more fully. More people need to be killed, because St. John cannot solve the deepest riddles of life, to which the problem of evil belongs, without inner transformation.

The blood

The slain express their demand for vengeance by a reference to their own blood, "How long, O Lord, holy and true, until you judge and avenge our blood on those who dwell on the earth?" (Rev. 6:10.) Blood is the essence of the human being in the same way as oil and wine are that of the oil-bearing fruit and grapes. Therefore, the blood symbolizes the essence of the human being, the Self. More generally, the blood symbolizes love, because to experience the Self means to live love itself. In Christianity, this blood symbolism is expressed especially in the Holy Communion, because in drinking the blood of Christ the person receives the spiritual love of Christ in order to experience it in a personal way. In St. John's vision the reference to avenging blood emphasizes that the blood ought to be drawn from new people —that is, from the different components of consciousness—so that they would transform into 'parts' of the Self.

The white robe

"And a white robe was given to each of them" (Rev. 6:11). A cloth is a symbol like that of a vessel in the sense that it can enclose something, and vessel-like symbols in mythical associations express the subjective side, or man's own consciousness, in contrast to the objective content of consciousness. We may have several layers of clothing which may conveniently illustrate different levels of the consciousness. That we can change clothing, dress and undress makes it easy to express through clothing changes in states of consciousness.

In ordinary dreams, a person's outfit may depict a superficial state of consciousness, perhaps a role which the dreamer has adopted. In spiritual associations, however, clothing generally symbolizes deeper states of consciousness. For example, the apostle Paul speaks about "the new man" as if it were clothing to be put on, "You put on the new man, which was created according to God in righteousness and true holiness."[36]

Here white as a mythical image in Revelation represents the level of holy and original existence. When the souls of the slain are given the white robes, St. John, as it were, locates those souls: they belong already to the level of the Self. They are the ones who have reached the original and holy spiritual home. Because those who have returned home are those who are also victorious, it is said in the third chapter of Revelation, "He who overcomes shall be clothed in white garments" (Rev. 3:5). In Christian literature, the white cloth as a symbol can be found in St. John of the Cross, who speaks of "the pure white inner tunic" and says, "The soul cannot be clothed in a better inner tunic or robe than this white cloth of faith, for it is the foundation and the beginning of the robes of all other good qualities."[37]

St. John's shock

The earthquake

"I looked when he opened the sixth seal, and behold, there was a great earthquake" (Rev. 6:12). An earthquake is a common dream image which appears in connection with strong psychic changes.[38] An earthquake expresses powerfully the depth of a change: both the surface of the earth, being the conscious, and the inside, being the unconscious, are shaken. In St. John's case, the quake results from the process of cognition and transformation which he has experienced. He has realized that his spirituality is immature: his Self has not been liberated and his religious worldview has problems which he has so far repressed.

The sun and the moon in St. John's vision

"And the sun became black as sackcloth made of hair, and the moon became like blood" (Rev. 6:12).

In the first place, the sun is a metaphor for brightness. For example, the light associated with visions and deeply withdrawn inward states can be well compared with the sun as St. John does in the first chapter of Revelation. There he sees "one like the Son of Man," whom he describes with words, "His countenance was like the sun shining in its strength" (Rev. 1:16).

In Revelation, the sun, however, has another meaning along with brightness, when the sun refers to a celestial body, and I feel this is associated with an ancient mythical function of the sun. In the old patriarchal cultures the sun has for millenniums been the symbol for God, and sometimes it has been the divinity itself. For instance, the ancient Egyptian *Pyramid Texts* from 2400–2200 B.C. have been interpreted to mean that Atum was the unmanifested, ultimate divinity, and Re, or the sun, was its manifest form.[39] Therefore, I assume the sun in St. John's visions to symbolize such a God-concept as can be derived from the characteristics of the sun as a celestial body.

The sun is up in the sky, far from men and women, so that the 'sun-god' is marked by separation and alienation. The sun affects the alterations of day and night, light and dark, so that the definitions characterizing this God-concept have clear opposites. The sun is up during the day, so it represents the consciousness or awareness of the daytime: this God-concept is based on conscious thinking and conceived with the intellect. In its most narrow sense, the sun in Revelation represents in my interpretation man's outward, more or less anthropomorphic concept of God as a good and righteous judge. But in St. John's visions, the sun has also a broader meaning which is connected to justice in a more general way. Yet, in the broadest sense, the sun apparently symbolizes a superficial, externalized God-concept, one built by the conscious mind. In the Bible, we can find this kind of emphasis in the God-concept in the Old Testament if we interpret the religiousness of the Old Testament simplistically; for instance, if we think that in the tablets of law the Lord is only ordering human beings to do the right and commanding them to stay away from the wrong.

St. John's God-concept has not, of course, been entirely based on the Old Testament; Jesus had emphatically taught the message of God's love. But I assume that this kind of sun-god, as an externalized God-concept, has been one of the threads in his religion, and now he is analyzing his relationship to it. For the sake of simplicity, I will, later on, speak of the sun as St. John's old concept of God, but it is important to keep in mind the above reservations.

At the same time that St. John finds the Self to be ever more central in a spiritual life, he finds his old concept of God to be wrong. God must no longer be associated simply with the sun shining in the sky, and so in St. John's vision the sun turns black. Because sackcloth during the biblical times was the dress for sorrow, repentance, and misfortune, St. John's simile, "the sun became black as sackcloth made of hair," means that he lays his old God-concept down to grieve and to repent its own incompleteness.

In the mythologies of the patriarchal cultures, the moon has had a lesser meaning than that of the sun. For example, while Atum-Re was the highest god in Egypt, the god of the moon, Thoth, even while respected, was clearly secondary.[40] As a general mythical image and as part of a patriarchal culture, the moon expresses something which is thought of as secondary to something valuable, or as something complementary to a valuable entity. Additionally, the moon can symbolize something which has remained in the shadow of the night: we are at least partly unaware of it and so have not fully experienced it.

I assume that for St. John the moon stands for that of which too much has been left out in his old God-concept, and this part left out is love. Thus the moon symbolizes God as love, and when it now in St. John's vision becomes like blood, a new concept of God—God is love—becomes emphasized in his spirituality. (Here, too, the blood symbolizes love.) The sun turning black and the moon becoming blood, could be also interpreted to mean that St. John is ever more clearly moving from the Old Testament God-concept over to the New

Testament one. But even St. John's new concept of God is still one of alienation; it finds its symbolical form in a celestial body, the moon. Of course, this is natural, as St. John has not yet been able to fully experience love, or realize his Self.

The sun and the moon in the life of modern man

To move from the world of the sun into that of the moon, or in general, to see the sun growing dim and being embraced by the darkness, is a disquieting event. Often it is like a gateway or the first step into an inner world. Because the problem is important, I will now interpret the sun and the moon in more detail in the life of a modern person. This interpretation will also clarify further the role of the sun and the moon in St. John's vision and his inner transformation.

Because the sun is up in the sky during the daytime, it is associated with daytime consciousness, or awareness. This level of consciousness has its own characteristic principles and laws. On the level of conscious awareness, we use, for instance, conceptual language and organize the world with the help of cause and effect relationships, linear time, and three dimensional spatial coordinates. Although we do not always recognize these basic principles, they form a general frame of reference, which is well symbolized by the sun. We perceive the world on the level of conscious awareness in the light of these principles, even as we see the world during the daytime in the light of the sun. Additionally, this frame of reference is common to all of us and our conscious minds are tied to its inner laws whether we like it or not. Similarly, the sun as a celestial body represents for us a common experience, and its function is outside our power.

Because the moon is in the night sky, it is related, as a mythical image, to the night's consciousness. This consciousness is the world of dreams, and more generally, the unconscious, because the unconscious in the human mind remains, as it were, in the darkness of the night. This level of consciousness is characterized by different principles and laws than those of the conscious mind. To begin with, the language of the unconscious is that of the myths, a topic which I examined in the introduction. Also, experiencing feelings is closely linked to the unconscious: in order to really feel something the source of the experience must touch us on a deeper level than that of the conscious awareness. It must reach into the unconscious. Human beings shape their lives following the directives of feeling and of the unconscious both of which form a sort of super-individual frame of reference. In a broad sense, the moon symbolizes this frame of reference that reaches beyond the mere individual.[41] But because the moon is far from our own field of experience, it can refer only to an early stage in finding a new attitude and outlook on life.

Modern women and men live largely in the world of the sun, because we live as if dependent on our conscious mind. But if we want to advance to the spiritually deeper levels, we need to find the world of the moon as well: we must open to that potentiality of our consciousness which is in the unconscious. This is so, because to be able to go within, we need to let go of our ingrained old beliefs and to release any resistance in the unconscious. Today, it is fashionable to say that in undergoing this kind of transformation we activate the right hemisphere of the brain, which has remained unused while we have mostly relied on the left hemisphere.

In modern life, this kind of a change need not have anything to do with the deeply spiritual or, especially in a traditional sense, religious experience. The change may happen simply because we come aware of possibilities of any sort that formerly remained hidden from us. The transformation itself can take different forms depending on the particular phase a person is living through. A strong experience like an overwhelming love, a deeply aesthethic experience, or a parapsychological experience, may initiate the change. If the experience is gripping enough, the individual in the midst of it feels his previous ability to experience life (when it was limited by his normal awareness) darkens or even disappears for a while; the old cognition appears meager next to the newly opened possibilities. The transformation can also come as a result of an emotional crises. The joy and the meaningfulness of life are dulled, for example, by over-intellectualizing. The depressed person may feel himself to be in the middle of a crisis as if he were in complete darkness, till a new way of experiencing opens for him. These kinds of emotional disturbances are like inner earthquakes, which open whatever is blocked in the consciousness. Eventually the turmoil leads to a renewed understanding of life, because after such experiences, it is easy to admit the sun is not enough and the moon is indeed important.

The following dream describes this change. The dream is by the same woman who had the dream of the fighting armies used as an example in the fifth chapter:

I walk along a road and meet people. The whole landscape and the people bathe in sunlight, as if in an impressionistic painting. But now I come to a wall and I am engulfed by darkness. I hear a voice say, "It is here that the journey begins." Next, I am on the other side of the wall and I see the moon on the night sky. It is beginning to transform strangely. Its outline becomes alive and flaming, sparks fly from it. I am afraid; I sense danger and fear this to be the end of the world. But the dream continues and I find the way onward.

The stars, the tree, and the wind

"And the stars of heaven fell to the earth, as a fig tree drops its late figs when it is shaken by a mighty wind" (Rev. 6:13). In this verse St. John describes the results of his inner disturbance.

The mythical worldviews often present the stars and the planets as lesser gods; in ancient mythology, two examples are Venus and Mars. Expressed in modern language, the star-gods were different abstract qualities, like love and warfare, which were used to organize reality. These mythical star-gods functioned thus as the guiding stars for the human life.

Because the stars as celestial bodies are up in the sky, I interpret the stars in Revelation to be those beliefs which St. John has adopted more or less outwardly; he has not experienced their content intimately. When the stars fall to the ground St. John's present spirituality begins to disintegrate. He realizes that his religion has largely consisted of mere beliefs. Getting rid of all sense of alienation is not, however, possible at this stage, as indicated by the fact that the blood-colored moon remains in the sky. Nor does the darkening of the sun mean that St. John would be fully liberated from the alienation symbolized by the sun.

The tree can symbolize also a more general concept than that of the human energy system which I examined earlier. In a general sense, the tree expresses inner experience and its fruits the nourishment which the inner life brings to that human beings and pass on to others. The trees and their fruits reveal symbolically different states of consciousness depending on their more exact characteristics.

In Revelation, St. John uses the word *olunthos* for the fruits of the fig tree which fall down to the ground. There is no unanimous agreement as to the exact meaning of the word, and the different Bible translations use expressions like "unripe," "untimely," and "late." Usually, in the New Testament, the word *sukon*, which means a ripe fig, is used for the fruits from the fig tree. Then *olunthos* could be thought of as the unripe fruit, and this would be appropriate in St. John's vision. St. John realizes his earlier inner life has been unripe. He must let go of the old, and so the unripe fruits fall from the tree.

Earlier I associated the fig tree with the tree of good and evil knowledge because of its geometric form and because it has been mentioned in the biblical myth about the Fall. A similar interpretation is partly supported by other biblical fig tree symbolism, which is strongly two-fold. On the one hand, the fig tree fruits are nourishing and sweet food; this does become evident in the biblical symbolism. On the other hand, there are surprisingly many places in the Bible where the fig tree and its fruits have been used in a cautionary way. For example, Jesus curses the fig tree which does not bear fruit. At other times, the figs are "rotten," or figs "could not be eaten, they were so bad." The Bible also stresses the necessity of caring for the fig trees.[42] These kinds of comparisons relate the fig tree well with the tree of knowledge of good and evil, because human beings can use the abilities symbolized by this tree, like their willpower and ability to think, either well or poorly, either to draw closer to or to become more alienated from God. Thus all persons are to cultivate these abilities carefully to bring forth good rather than poor harvest.

With the above in mind, the stars falling to the earth like the unripe fruit from the fig tree can be interpreted in following words: St. John realizes his previous spirituality has been merely like the unripe fruit from the tree of good and evil knowledge. True spirituality would be the fruit from the tree of life, such as the personal experience of love and joy.

The wind, if interpreted on the psychological level, is the mental process. It is said, for instance, in the *Bhagavadgita*:

> When the mind follows the senses
> which continuously roam this way and that
> the understanding flies away
> like the boat tossed about by a strong wind.[43]

In Revelation, the unripe fruit of the fig tree falls as a result of a strong wind, signifying that St. John is inwardly shaken; a powerful storm has tossed his consciousness about.

That the stars should fall in a storm like the unripe fruit of a fig tree represents another common event, one which can touch a modern person as well. Certainly, many of us have at one time awakened to find that our beliefs and outlook in life are immature. Our discovery comes as a shock, like an inner storm, and we realize that we must give up our old views.

The receding sky

"Then the sky receded as a scroll when it is rolled up" (Rev. 6:14). The sky which recedes is St. John's old superconscious, or the way he has until now experienced spirituality. When that turns out to be unripe, too shallow, he gives it up.

The simile of the scroll used to describe the receding of the sky, is familiar from the previous visions. The scroll, however, need not refer to the scroll of the previous chapter, although wrapping up the scroll at this point is a logical symbol. Six of the seven seals of the scroll have been opened by now, and at every opening St. John has become aware of new issues, or he has, as it were, read the scroll. (In a mythical reality, to be able to read the scroll, it is not necessary to wait till all the seals have been opened, but rather at the opening of each seal one is able to read more of the scroll.) The seventh seal is the only one remaining closed, and the opening of it indicates the highpoint of the transformation, a spiritual exaltation. Such an experience in itself is something more than ordinary cognition, and so St. John need not actually read the scroll any longer—at least for now. Therefore, the scroll is well put aside.

The mountains and the islands

"And every mountain and island was moved out of its place" (Rev. 6:14). The moving of the mountains and the islands out of their places describes, as well, St. John's inner turmoil.

In different mythologies, a mountain often expresses the upward dimension of human consciousness toward higher values and a more exalted spiritual life. That is why, as a place, the mountain is associated with gods. For example, the Bible narrates how the Lord and Moses met on Mt. Sinai, and in ancient Greece, the gods lived on the Mt. Olympus.[44] In St. John's vision, the mountain fittingly symbolizes his God-concept. It also symbolizes, more broadly, his most worthwhile spiritual experiences and the beliefs and outlooks he associates with these experiences. All these have become the focus of change, and the transformation has reached the very foundation of his spiritual life. Therefore, the mountains in St. John's vision move out of their places, or from their foundation.

An island, in myths, symbolizes often the conscious level of the psyche at the times when it is experienced as being surrounded by the unconscious. This kind of experience is associated especially with times of deep inner changes, when we experience ourselves to be, as it were, surrounded on all sides by the sea of the unconscious, or by new potentials. During such a phase we live withdrawn in our own world, as one lives on an island removed from the rest of the world. The heroes of myths are often on an island when they are involved in a deep inner change; for example, Odysseus roams in an archipelago while he is maturing inwardly. St. John has realized that so far his spiritual experiences and his understanding of a spiritual life have been merely islands in the vast sea of the unconscious, and thus, incomplete. Therefore, they are to move out of their places: the change must be profound.

The caves and God's wrath

"And the kings of the earth, the great men, the rich men, the commanders, the mighty men, every slave and every free man, hid themselves in the caves and in the rocks of the mountains, and said to the mountains and rocks, 'Fall on us and hide us from the face of him who sits on the throne and from the wrath of the Lamb! For the great day of his wrath has come, and who is able to stand?'" (Rev. 6:15–17.)

A cave is part of the underground, which on the psychological level represents the subconscious. As a mythical image a cave reveals that a connection has been made to the subconscious, because a cave usually has an opening leading outside. The cave is appropriate in this part of Revelation, because St. John has been able to create a new contact to the subconscious levels of his psyche; his consciousness has already opened while the seals have been opened. In myths underground places, in general, are stages for a deep inner change. One of the feats the mythical heroes are universally expected to accomplish is that of descending underground, or into the underworld; for example, one of Heracles' heroic achievements in the Greek mythology was a visit to the underground Hades.[45]

The reference to the wrath of the Lamb and the enthroned is a typical projected expression often found in myths: it is not that the Lamb and the enthroned are angry, but that St. John himself feels anxious. The reason for his anxiety is his realization that he has not recognized the true meaning of the Lamb and the enthroned. While writing his vision, he converts his dismay into their anger. In Christian literature, the impact of God's wrath on one's anxiety is expressed by St. John of the Cross:

> I cannot... explain, how severe this anxiety is, nor can I describe, how painful grows the trouble the soul feels and experiences. I can only refer to the words of Jeremiah speaking of it, "I am a man, who see my own poverty under the whip of His wrath."[46]

The kings of the earth, the great men, the rich, the commanders, the mighty men, every slave, and every free man—all these represent St. John the Divine's thought patterns and ways of experiencing up until this time. But now as a result of his inner turmoil and overwhelmed by great anxiety he must live through everything again. When the kings, the great men and others ask the mountains and hills to fall on them, St. John is really wishing he could surrender to searching and finding what is new from the deep levels of the unconscious.

7. THE CALMING OF THE WIND AND MARKING WITH SEALS

Quietude

"After these things I saw four angels standing at the four corners of the earth, holding the four winds of the earth, that the wind should not blow on the earth, on the sea, or on any tree" (Rev. 7:1). The wind symbolizes, here as elsewhere, mental activity. Therefore, the wind dying out means internal quieting. This analogy is used also in the *Bhagavadgita*:
> Like a lamp burning steadily,
> sheltered from the wind:
> such is the yogi
> who controls his thoughts
> and practices yoga.[1]

The fact that the angels are holding winds that cover all main directions suggests that St. John's inward stillness reaches throughout the whole earth, that is, throughout all of his conscious mind. The stillness is so deep that the ocean, or St. John's unconscious, has calmed down as has the earth. And as represented by the tree, even his life energy is in a state of rest.[2]

We experience inner tranquillity with the intensity possible according to our spiritual maturity. When our superficial states of consciousness which are tied to desires and duality become quiet, room is created for experiencing the deeper state of oneness, and so we feel joy, happiness, and love during the quietude. If an experience like this is strong enough, it will release a change: in its light, we will see ourselves and perhaps the whole of reality in a new way. Although the change essentially means healing—it is generated by the experience of joy and happiness—there may also be anxiety. As a result of the quietude, for example, we may realize ever more clearly our many attachments and wasteful strivings, and this realization may create anxiety. If we do not indulge in self-deceit and rationalization, but will face our mistakes, we will become at least partly free from old entanglements. This liberation will be a preparation for a still deeper quietude because it is attachments which have kept our consciousness 'on the go,' as we have been pursuing the objects of our desires. In this way, the transformation continues.

The previous chapter ended with St. John turning inward as represented by the kings, the great men and others being drawn into caves. Now this turning inward leads into inner stillness. The stillness does not, however, reach its culmination until the first verse of the next chapter, when the last, the seventh, seal is opened.

St. John's vision in this chapter continues, "Then I saw another angel ascending... and he cried... to the four angels to whom it was granted to harm the earth and the sea, saying, 'Do not harm the earth, the sea, or the trees till we have sealed the servants of our God on their foreheads.'" (Rev. 7:2–3.) St. John foresees in these verses the anxiety caused by the process of transformation following the quietude. During the transformation, his conscious awareness and the unconscious as well as life energy are, as it were, injured, because of the painfulness of the change. It is then that the angels harm the earth, the sea and the trees. But the apprehensive phase St. John is referring to does not begin right away; it will not begin till the second verse of the eighth chapter. This is why the angels are not yet allowed to harm the earth, the sea, and the trees. First St. John savors the healing caused by the quietude—a happy event in itself.

Strengthening of the Self

The seal and the angels around the throne

St. John's vision reveals that a seal, indeed, is pressed on the foreheads of the God's servants, as St. John says right after the angel has announced the task, "And I heard the number of those who were sealed" (Rev. 7:4).

The seal can be interpreted to be the round light which I spoke about in the fourth chapter, and which the meditator may see in his forehead during a state of deep withdrawal. According to the chakra teaching, the seal on the forehead would be the ajna chakra, which is located at the point between the eyebrows. The Oriental yoga tradition counsels the meditator to concentrate on this spot. The seal could also be viewed as a round mandala. Then it would symbolize the experiencing of healing and oneness.[3]

But a seal carries also the idea of ownership, and this probably has an important meaning in St. John's vision. Certainly, he feels that during the inner stillness he becomes God's own. In Christian literature, St. Teresa, as well as others, speaks of a seal in a similar sense alluding to ownership. Her description about the pressing of the seal reveals other characteristics typical of the inner stillness which help us to understand St. John's vision. St. Teresa describes the experience of utter surrender and spiritual union in the following way:

> God wants the soul to emerge from a state of quietude marked with His seal... Truly, the soul does not do anything more than wax would when someone proceeds to press his seal on it. The wax does not press it on itself... but remains still and agreeable.[4]

We can prepare ourselves for a spiritual experience by quieting the mind as much as we can, but the experience itself, the joy and happiness we feel during quietude, is characteristically spontaneous in the sense that we do not feel we have caused it or created it ourselves. Theoretically this is logical: when the ego-cover is removed, the Self flows forth of itself. In religious language, this spontaneous emerging of the Self is expressed by the concept of mercy.

The expression "the seal of the *living* God" used in Revelation, tells us something more about St. John's feelings (Rev. 7:2). During the withdrawal, a personal way to experience divinity as joy and spiritual love opens up to him. This personal experience is different from experiences caused by his old, externalized, and thus *dead*, God-concept.

We might see the light of the spiritual eye and the mandala figure in the vision in another way, too, because St. John says that the angels stand around the throne and praise God, "And all the angels stood around the throne and the elders and the four living creatures... saying, 'Amen! Blessing and glory... to our God.'" (Rev. 7:11–12.) The angels assembled around the throne praising the glory of the God do create an image of a spherical illumination with a brighter central light.

The tribes

According to St. John, those marked by a seal are "of all the tribes of the children of Israel" (Rev. 7:4). Interpreted as mythical images, the tribes of Israel symbolize the different aspects of one individual; the people of Israel is like an archetypal man. The various events and wanderings by these people, as related in the Bible, represent the human evolutionary stages and changes in a person's internal life. (I want to stress again the fact that a mythical interpretation does not exclude the historical reality of the events.)

For instance, the exile of the Israelites and the slavery in a foreign land can be seen as mythical images for ego-consciousness. Being in a foreign land describes well human alienation from God, or a state of ego-consciousness. Christian literature uses the expression of exile commonly in this kind of symbolic meaning; the analog is found, for instance, in writings by St. Teresa of Avila. The wish of the people of Israel to return to the promised land reflects women's and men's desire to return to their spiritual home, or to oneness with God. St. John of the Cross speaks, for example, of the promised land of divine union.[5]

St. John the Divine experiences a deep spiritual transformation as a result of his inner stillness. This occurrence corresponds to the vision of part of the people of Israel becoming God's own; that is, the transformation is from ego to the Self. In St. John's vision this transformation is symbolized by pressing a seal on the foreheads of the children of Israel. Others have used, instead, more ordinary mythical images, such as returning home.

A multitude dressed in white

"After these things I looked, and behold, a great multitude which no one could number, of all nations, tribes, peoples, and tongues, standing before the throne and before the Lamb, clothed in white robes" (Rev. 7:9).

The multitude seen by St. John reiterates, on a higher level, the transformation from the ego to the Self, described by the pressing of the seal on the foreheads of the children of Israel. In the case of the children of Israel, St. John was careful to count out all the numbers: there were twelve tribes and within each of them a certain number of people were marked by the seal (Rev. 7:4–8). Now he stresses the fact that the multitude he sees is so vast no one can count it. I suggest this change derives from something he has experienced. When the deeper level of consciousness, the Self, is strengthened, it is experienced as an inner sense of wholeness; we become more whole, if you will. Thus a change from separate parts to a united whole, where one cannot distinguish the separate parts, is a natural expression for the strengthening of the Self.

The idea of the multitude symbolizing the strengthening of the Self is expressed also through the white clothing, as in the case of the souls of the slain mentioned in the previous chapter.

The souls envisioned in the previous chapter were under the altar, for one thing, because St. John had not understood their meaning well enough. The multitude, which St. John sees in this new vision, is "before the throne and before the Lamb", and St. John sees this vast group clearly, "I looked, and behold, a great multitude" (Rev. 7:9). The symbols of the Self thus, as it were, emerge from their hiding place under the altar out into the open space before the throne and the Lamb. At the same time, the meaning of the Self in a spiritual life becomes ever more obvious for St. John. The change is initiated by St. John's inner quiet which has made the nature of true spirituality clearer to him.

The palm

"A great multitude... clothed with white robes, with palm branches in their hands" (Rev. 7:9). The palm is associated in many ways with the Self, reinforcing the fact that the multitude dressed in white, indeed, is 'a part' of the Self.

In the previous chapter, I assigned the palm the meaning of the tree of life; the tree of life, in turn, symbolizes the experience of oneness and bliss. (As explained before, the straight trunk and the top foliage describe well the sushumna nadi and the thousand-petaled lotus, sahasrara, crowning it.) When the energy symbolized by the palm tree becomes ever more real for St. John, he feels joy and happiness.

In the region where the Bible originates, the date palm thrives in the desert oasis and is a valuable source for nourishment. In the Bible itself, the palm appears especially as temple decoration; for example, in the temple vision by the prophet Ezekiel, the palms are the most important decorations. The palm has also been used generally as a symbol for victory and peace.[6] All these associations with the palm tree are very fitting here because the strengthening of the Self means that at least part of St. John has, as it were, already found its way to the oasis and to its delicious nourishment as well as into the inner temple; that part of him has been victorious and reached peace.

The numbers

"And I heard the number of those who were sealed. One hundred and forty-four thousand of all the tribes of the children of Israel were sealed." (Rev. 7:4.) After this, St. John counts out the tribes, calling them by their names. There are twelve of them, and he says there are twelve thousand sealed in each tribe (Rev. 7:5–8). Not all, but only those one hundred and forty-four thousand Israelites became God's own so far, because St. John's transformation from the ego to the Self is not yet complete.

The numbers St. John mentions form a multiplication of twelve times twelve thousand. This figure can be compared with that of the holy city appearing in the end of Revelation, which measures twelve thousand times twelve thousand (Rev. 21:16). Those sealed by God's seal form an embryo, as it were, for the holy city, which illustrates spiritual perfection, or the fully manifesting Self. Thus it is natural to have the number twelve appear in both mythical images. In this seventh chapter, the numbers interpreted geometrically form a rectangle, whereas the holy city, as a geometric form, is a square. St. John has yet a long journey ahead of him on the pathway of the tree of life before he finds the harmonious wholeness symbolized by the square.

Similar transformations of geometrical forms appear also in dreams. I followed such changes in my own dream imagery long before I noticed the same symbolism embedded in Revelation. For instance, in one series of dreams a dining table gradually changed from a long, rectangular table to a square one, while the inner nourishment I was receiving was becoming more wholesome.[7]

Another angel

The angel who asks the four angels not to harm the earth, the sea, or the trees, and who apparently seals the servants of God, is described by St. John in the following way, "Then I saw another angel ascending from the East" (Rev. 7:2).

In the Greek of the New Testament, East is expressed with the words "the rising of the sun", and in different languages some older translations use this expression.[8] East, however, is a better translation, because the rising of the sun creates an image of the sun as a celestial body, which, in Revelation, symbolizes St. John's old concept of God. Therefore, the rising of the sun would not bring good tidings. On the contrary, St. John is trying to rid himself of the sun during the course of Revelation. East, on the other hand, is the direction of the awakening light. The angel from East symbolizes such light as provides the intuitive experience which is transforming St. John.

The significance of the inner quiet

In the last few verses of the chapter, St. John ponders the meaning of his experience. The content of the verses mostly reiterates events, but considering Revelation as a whole, there are interesting mythical images in them.

Anxiety and washing of the robes

"These are the ones who come out of the great tribulation" (Rev. 7:14). St. John experienced deep anxiety in the end of the previous chapter when he felt himself to be the target for the anger of the enthroned and the Lamb and sighed, "The great day of his wrath has come, and who is able to stand?" In his anxiety, St. John turned inward, he grew quiet, and this inner quiet became a moment of joy and love. Anxiety, and perhaps even the shame he felt as he realized the incompleteness of his old spirituality, was swept away while joy overtook him. At the same time he was freed from his attachment to his old alienating beliefs. They were displaced by new, sweeter feelings: joy and love.

St. John refers to this change again and clarifies it with the following words, "They washed their robes and made them white in the blood of the Lamb" (Rev. 7:4). Because St. John's consciousness is purified from attachments and anxiety, the transformation he experiences is manifested as washing of clothes, that is, the cleansing of consciousness. Apparently he feels he has actually washed himself in universal love for the robes have been washed in the blood of the Lamb. (This blood, as usual, reflects spiritual love.)

To wash a cloth in blood does not, of course, in everyday reality produce a white cloth, but it must be so in the mythical reality of Revelation. White, in Revelation, is the color of higher spiritual levels of reality, and washing in the blood of the Lamb means experiencing those levels.

Serving God and the presence of God

"Therefore they are before the throne of God, and serve him day and night in his temple. And he who sits on the throne will dwell among them." (Rev. 7:15.) When a deeper state of consciousness has opened in aspirants, it can manifest itself continuously if they concentrate on it. It stays, as it were, at the back of their minds, even when they are otherwise involved in activity and even when they encounter outer as well as inner difficulties. Religious literature often calls this state "practicing the presence of God."[9] Human beings are in this way, by some portion of their being, constantly, night and day, in the temple of God, in His presence.

The latter part of the verse lends itself to a few possible translations. St. John uses the verb *skēnoō* and the preposition *epi*. Most commonly this verb means to live, to dwell, but the corresponding noun, *skēnē* along with a dwelling has the meaning of a tent and a booth, and particularly the tent of the Testimony, or tabernacle. The most common meaning for the preposition *epi* is 'on' and 'upon,' although there are also other ways of interpreting it, depending on the context. Therefore, different translations use, for example, such expressions as "he…will protect them with his presence," "he…will shelter them with his presence," and "he…shall spread his tabernacle over them." I use the last translation, because it is the most concrete, and as such it is appropriate in mythical language.

The tabernacle continues the symbolism of the white robes; both a tabernacle, or a tent, and a robe are vessel-like symbols. The tabernacle is spread—or more accurately, will soon be spread—over those dressed in white, making them one whole unit. Thus the tabernacle expresses a new degree of wholeness in St. John's spiritual transformation: the deeper level of his consciousness, the Self, increases from representation by a robe to the symbolism of a tabernacle. It is then capable of embracing ever greater degrees of spirituality and is nearing the universal Self. The Christian literature does speak of the spiritualized soul, at times, as a tent where God dwells.[10]

The tabernacle, however, expresses also St. John's present incompleteness, if we compare his state to the one at the end of Revelation. In biblical times, the tent was the shelter for the nomadic people within the Middle-Eastern cultures. The well-known tent of the Bible, the tabernacle of the Testimony, functioned as the temple for the Israelites during their migrations. St. John, also, is still a wanderer on his way to his spiritual home, making it appropriate to depict his consciousness as a tabernacle when he does experience holiness. The Palestinian Bedouin tent was a rectangle like the biblical tabernacle; perhaps we can infer from this that the shelter mentioned by St. John had the geometric form of a rectangle, which would reflect an early form for the square holy city.[11]

When spiritual consciousness has opened in men and women, it protects them, because with its help it is easier to cope with the difficulties in life. I suggest that the tent, the tabernacle, functions also as a general symbol for this protection.

Thirst and hunger; the guidance of the Lamb

"They shall neither hunger any more nor thirst any more; the sun shall not strike them, nor any heat" (Rev. 7:16). When we are open to experiencing love and to living a life of holiness, we receive mythical living water to drink and manna to eat, and we feel spiritually nourished. An alienating, too externalized religion will suffocate the personal spiritual experience in life, just as the merciless Mediterranean sun will scorch nature's greenery. Here, too, the sun has the connotation of a negative, too external religiosity.

"The Lamb who is in the midst of the throne will shepherd them and lead them to living fountains of waters. And God will wipe away every tear from their eyes" (Rev. 7:17). The verse reiterates the essential message of the early chapters: the Lamb, or the universal Self, is central in true spirituality. As a theoretical realization, this centrality is expressed in the vision by the concept of God having received a new content: the Lamb has moved over to the midst of the throne. Theory, however, is not enough. St. John himself must be open to experiencing the level of high spiritual reality symbolized by the Lamb. The Lamb must guide St. John onward to ultimate perfection. The living fountains of waters and the wiping away of tears, are general symbols of happiness, and they are repeated somewhat transformed at the end of Revelation when the state of the paradisiacal happiness promised here will come to pass.

II

THE INSUFFICIENCY OF THE OLD RELIGION

Chapters 8–11 of Revelation

The sense of freedom St. John the Divine described in the previous chapter, will climax in the first verse of the Part II. After that, he becomes aware of the insufficiency of his earlier spirituality. The images in the visions transform in a logical progression as St. John's awareness deepens. They describe also in a more general sense the nature of man's spiritual transformation.

8. THE SILENCE IN HEAVEN AND THE FIRST TRUMPET BLASTS

The Silence

"When [the Lamb] opened the seventh seal, there was silence in heaven for about half an hour" (Rev. 8:1). Whereas in the beginning of the previous chapter only the sea and the surface of the earth with its trees had calmed down, now St. John's inner peace deepens so that it reaches heaven, or the superconscious. I assume that the deep inner silence experienced by St. John is an experience in oneness. When the movement in ego-consciousness comes to a standstill, a deeper state of consciousness, or the consciousness of oneness, overtakes him.

A half, as a mythical number, reflects generally something small. Therefore, half an hour, in a mythical sense, describes a short period of time. Analyzed further, a half is one divided by two—one expressing oneness and two, duality. A silence which lasts for only half an hour is an experience in oneness wherefrom St. John returns quickly to his normal everyday awareness, characterized by duality. It is also possible that, momentarily, his consciousness is divided, as it were. His normal awareness may be present, but, at the same time, a new dimension of deep silence and experience in oneness opens up for him.

An experience in a new state of consciousness is called by Western psychology an altered, or heightened state of consciousness or a peak experience. Western religion, and sometimes philosophy, thinks of these experiences as supernatural and mystical. Thus the level of ego-consciousness, marked by duality, is thought of as the normal state of consciousness, and that which extends beyond the level of ego-consciousness is considered supernatural and mystical. In these terms, all experiences in deep silence and oneness are thought of as supernatural, although they are natural in the sense that a diverse group of individuals, at different times, within various cultures, actually have experienced them and talked about them.

The descriptions of these experiences have several common basic features. To begin with, the person feels that ordinary life begins to appear like a dream or darkness when compared to life during peak experiences. Secondly, the experiences are marked by a deep sense of reality: although the experience itself may have lasted only a moment, the person having lived it cannot doubt its truthfulness. Even if he should try to deny it, he will, nevertheless, notice having changed due to the power of the experience. This may manifest as a sudden spiritual awakening, but the change can also be more gradual. Also, describing these experiences is difficult, because their nature extends beyond the normal consciousness characterized by duality; thus descriptions often contain paradoxical remarks like "lofty deeps" and "a superessential nothingness."[1]

The individual quality of these mystical states, however, varies. What is emphasized in them may be, for example, oneness, the holistic nature of the existence, timelessness, freedom, reality, simplicity of life and its meaningfulness, or universal love. Revelation speaks here simply of the "silence in heaven," which refers to superconscious stillness. I suggest, however, parallels to St. John's experience which explain more deeply the nature of the experience and its impact on the sequence of events in Revelation. My parallels vary in their quality, intensity, and time span, as I assume that St. John describes here a long period in human life in a crystallized form, during which the new dimensions of consciousness begin to open.

My first example is from Bernard of Clairvaux, a Christian mystic from the twelfth century, because he refers to this particular section in Revelation while describing a mystical experience. Also Gregory the Great and William of Saint-Thierry, a contemporary of Bernard, offer similar interpretations regarding the silence in heaven mentioned in Revelation.[2] Bernard combines the imagery from Revelation with that from the Old Testament's Song of Songs, and he also draws from Paul's Second Epistle to the Corinthians:

> When, for a moment, the heaven has become silent, perhaps for half an hour, she rests calmly in that dear embrace. She herself sleeps, but her heart is awake, for a moment, allowed to see into the hidden secrets of the truth, which she will rejoice in once she has returned to herself. During that moment she sees the invisible and hears matters which she cannot, nor is allowed to, speak of.[3]

St. Teresa describes the momentary opening of a new state of consciousness, which she calls "an intellectual vision" in the following way:
> When the Lord should feel it best, it happens, that the soul in prayer and fully conscious is suddenly uplifted to a state where the Lord allows it to understand great secrets... [Although the experience] transpires quickly, it leaves its imprint deep into the soul... It reveals to the soul how everything is seen in God and how He already has everything in Himself... God suddenly and indescribably reveals in Himself some truth, which makes all other truths seem like darkness.[4]

St. Teresa emphasizes—and this is interesting in understanding St. John's visions—that during those moments, the soul realizes that also evil deeds take place in God. God is like "a grand and beautiful mansion or a palace," and St. Teresa asks:
> Could the sinner leave this palace to perform evil deeds? No, certainly not, but those awful, shameful, and evil deeds, committed by us, the sinners, happen inside this very palace which is God himself.[5]

Perhaps it is because of this kind of an experience, wherein the person irrefutably realizes that everything—including evil—happens within one totality, that St. John must examine his idea of God in a new way. God cannot be any longer simply a contrasting good force opposite to evil.

Within Western philosophy, an experience in oneness which transcends the boundaries of the ordinary consciousness, can be found, for example, at the end of the *Tractatus Logico-Philosophicus*, an early work by Ludwig Wittgenstein. He writes, "To experience the world as a limited whole is a mystical experience."[6] Thus Wittgenstein describes the experience through a paradox; in our normal thinking, total reality cannot have limits or boundaries, because there is something yet beyond any boundaries. I understand that Wittgenstein also felt truly awake during these experiences, since he explained in his letters, "Our life is like a dream. But in our best moments we wake up just enough to realize we are dreaming. Most of the time we are fast asleep."[7]

Perhaps St. John, as well, after experiencing a deep inner quiet, finds his old state of consciousness to be like dreaming. He wants to wake up permanently, and so the silence in heaven initiates a new transformation process on his inner journey.

As a parallel in Oriental culture to St. John's inner quiet, I present an experience in *satori* from the Zen Buddhist tradition. Satori means the opening of a new state of consciousness. It is said that this new state of consciousness is first experienced as brief moments, becoming more lasting only in time.[8] The Zen teacher generally guides his student to satori by leading him into a dead end on the level of normal thinking; the many well-known *koans* of Zen literature to be solved by the student aim for this. When the student cannot find his way out of a dead end, he gives up and momentarily, out of necessity, lets go of dualistic thinking. He will then experience satori: he will experience existence in a new way, free from dualistic differentiations and decisions. Zen philosophy expresses this phenomenon in the following way:

There is nothing difficult about the great way,
but avoid choosing!
If the mind is at peace
the wrong ideas disappear of themselves.[9]

I assume that St. John's experience of inner silence or of deep peace destroys his old religious beliefs which were based on dualistic thinking.

I will present also one more personal experience in oneness, which I know, to emphasize the reality of the message of Revelation in modern life:

I sit quietly, withdrawn inward. Suddenly, a new dimension opens in my consciousness. I see, or experience, the *whole of reality* in a way difficult to describe. I experience it through identifying with it, if you will. I realize, at the same time, that this totality cannot be superseded, because it is a complete whole. Everything that exists is in it as oneness. Regardless of what my form of existence would be, I could never end up outside it as it does not have an outside. Measured with our normal perception of time, the experience lasts only a brief moment, yet it is indisputable, like truth itself.

Because in Revelation, the silence in heaven happens after the Lamb opens the seventh seal, St. John experiences the inner quiet as the peak of the transformation process described by the opening of the seals. According to chakra symbolism, he has reached the seventh chakra or sahasrara. The intensity and duration of the transformed state of consciousness varies depending on how fully the life force has moved up to sahasrara. Because St. John's inner journey has not yet come to its conclusion, this silence in heaven is not yet complete lasting bliss, but only an ephemeral peak experience.

The realization of the necessity of transformation

The seven angels

"And I saw the seven angels who stand before God, and to them were given seven trumpets" (Rev. 8:2). The seven angels seen by St. John symbolize a new intuitive process of transformation and realization. When he sees the angels, he realizes that his inner changes must continue. Later the angels take turns sounding the trumpets, symbolizing the different stages of transformation.

In the Bible, the sound of the trumpet is one of the symbols for the voice of God. Interpreted in the Oriental tradition, the trumpet sound reflects the Om-sound. However, the trumpet here is also for other reasons an appropriate symbol. During his previous transformation process, St. John opened up many obstructions in his consciousness. Now he needs to become more clearly aware of that which was left hidden behind those blocks, or seals, and is presently being revealed and proclaimed by the angels through their trumpet blows. The Greek Artemidorus, who in antiquity explained the meanings of dreams, interpreted the meaning of the trumpet by saying that it reveals hidden things because of its penetrating sound.[10]

Another angel

"Then another angel... came and stood at the altar... which was before the throne...Then the angel took the censer, filled it with fire from the altar, and threw it to the earth. And there were noises, thunderings, lightnings, and an earthquake." (Rev. 8:3,5.) The vision continues to take place in heaven. Thus St. John remains in a heightened state of consciousness, although now, as the angels are prominent, it is a state of intuitive realization.

Because the actions by this other angel happen after the silence in heaven and before the trumpet blows, I assume them to depict St. John's intuitive vision about the meaning of his superconscious peace. According to my interpretation, the altar of this vision is the altar in the sixth chapter, which symbolizes universal love, or more theoretically expressed, the subjective side of the universal Self. The censer is St. John's individual consciousness as it experiences holiness and spiritual love. And when the angel puts fire from the altar into the censer, I believe St. John understands intuitively that he experienced the universal Self during a moment of deep peace and its accompanying sense of oneness. He felt that all boundaries disappeared within everything that exists, and this vanishing of boundaries allowed the experiencing of universal love.

Fire emphasizes the nature of certain experiences and of love, in particular, as powers which transform and purify human beings. (St. John describes this transforming power of fire more clearly as the vision progresses.) Throwing the fire from heaven to the earth symbolizes thus the effect St. John's 'heavenly,' superconscious experience has on his earthly being. The experience in deep peace and universal love symbolized by the silence in heaven, changes him irrefutably.

The thundering, noises, lightnings, and the earthquake I interpret to express St. John's return from his transformed superconscious state back to an ordinary state of consciousness. I assume St. John hears these sounds as his life force descends. This is one possible way to read the progress of St. John's vision, because only the chakras lower than sahasrara emit the Om-sound.[11] The direction of action from heaven to earth probably reflects also the strongly altered state of consciousness returning back to a more normal earthly one. The earthquake symbolizes once more St. John's inner turmoil initiating the transformation which will soon begin.

St. John explains yet more clearly the angel's actions: "[The angel] having a golden censer, came and stood at the altar. And he was given much incense, that he should offer it with the prayers of all the saints upon the golden altar which was before the throne. And the smoke of the incense, with the prayers of the saints, ascended before God from the angel's hand." (Rev. 8:3–4.) The smoke from the incense symbolizes, in my interpretations, prayerful request.[12] St. John realizes that he has a transformation ahead of him. He wants to be successful in it and success is what he is praying for. But the smoke also darkens the surroundings, and as it rises toward God, it obscures Him. Certainly St. John then realizes that his old image of God has dimmed along with the new experience, and so he must search for new answers and change himself.

The beginning of the new transformation

"So the seven angels who had the seven trumpets prepared themselves to sound" (Rev. 8:6). After this, the angels blow the trumpets, and the latter part of the vision occurs during the first four trumpet blows.

It turns out that during the trumpet blows from the first three angels, something is thrown from heaven onto the earth. Interpreted in a general sense, the movement from heaven toward the earth symbolizes here, as well as in the fifth verse, the impact of St. John's experience of the 'heavenly' stillness. It impacted his more 'earthly' being, or everyday awareness, his ordinary experiences of what is worthwhile, and his unconscious mind.

The movement from heaven to earth can also express the experience which in Christian literature is called infusion. Infused experiences are characterized by such spontaneity that the person undergoing the experience does not feel himself to be the source of the events, but rather, is overtaken by it. The experience, as it were, pours into him, transforming him. Christian literature includes both blissful and afflictive infusions; the former are called grace, the latter are associated with purification. Infused experiences appear especially on the higher levels of inner life. In St. John's visions the symbolism of infusion becomes clear toward the end.

The transition from heaven to earth fittingly symbolizes giving up alienating religious attitudes; this interpretation is especially appropriate when something is thrown from heaven onto the earth or the sea. This meaning applies well to St. John's vision, because due to his experience in superconscious peace, it is ever clearer to him that what he himself experiences is the most essential aspect of religion, rather than what he believes to exist in heaven; thus he is ready to give up some of his old externalized beliefs.

The different meanings I have presented for the throwing of something from heaven to the earth are interlinked, but in my interpretation, the resolving of alienation has the most important place.

This resolution of alienation, like many other problems I see Revelation engaged in, is also a human event transcending any religious concerns. Our concept of reality is most often formed in our youth through learning from external sources and later in life through absorbing the surrounding culture. Should we, as modern persons, step into the visionary process of St. John, we would at this stage awaken to an ever more profound spiritual experience. As a result of this experience, we would begin to give up our flawed, narrow beliefs, till now considered definite truths.

The first angel: the hail, the fire, and the burning

"The first angel sounded: And hail and fire followed, mingled with blood, and they were thrown to the earth" (Rev. 8:7). From this verse on, St. John begins to describe the effects of his experience in heavenly peace.

Hail is mentioned as a plague in the Bible already in Exodus and there are devastating hailstorms in the Mediterranean countries even in our times.[13] This plague-like nature of the hail symbolizes the anguish felt during infused purification. The anguish is often connected with strong inner transformations, which is what St. John now is living through; surely he suffers while he realizes in the light of his experience in superconscious peace how shallow his previous religion has been. And because St. John's anguish follows immediately after the superconscious state he experienced during the silence in heaven, it is fittingly described as hail falling from heaven.

However, the hail of the vision is mixed with blood—and blood, in Revelation, symbolizes love. Therefore, regardless of anxiety, St. John feels also love awakened by the experience in inner peace. The integration of love and anguish is also more generally characteristic of intensive, inner transformations. We may, for example, experience the change brought about by love so strongly that we are frightened and feel distress; yet we feel the life filled with love to be deeply worthwhile. One might explain it to be the ego which during such changes feels anguish, as the transformation means its partial disappearance, but at the same time the Self is liberated, and this is experienced as the joy of love.

The fire mingled with blood that is thrown upon the earth in this vision reiterates the earlier events of the vision, as in the fifth verse "another angel" took fire from the altar and threw it on the earth. I assume that in both cases the fire flowing from heaven tells of the superconscious experience of love and its results; and St. John describes this change caused by love more clearly by explaining what effect the fire has on the earth.

"And a third of the trees were burned up, and all green grass was burned up" (Rev. 8:7). Some manuscripts say here that also a third of the earth burned up, and I follow this version, because it fits Revelation well. Because of love, part of St. John's old ways of experiencing and perceiving are burnt up, and now he is freed from them. Other Christian sources also use the concept of purification in a similar manner where it is often compared to burning in fire. For example, according to St. John of the Cross the souls "are purified and liberated from impurities... through loving and dark spiritual fire," and by this loving and dark fire St. John of the Cross means the integration of love and anguish. In Oriental cultures, the burning off of *karma*, or the effects of one's actions, is a common concept; for instance, in the *Bhagavadgita*, karma is said to be burnt off by the fire of wisdom.[14] Burning in fire illustrates well an intensive transformation, because the mental tension in this kind of change is like spiritual fire.

When a third of the earth burns, it means that part of St. John's religious beliefs formed through his conscious awareness, or the earth, burns away. And when a third of the trees as well burns away, St. John experiences the transformation also on a deeper level than conscious awareness; he experiences it on the level of the life force. The fact that St. John mentions the earth and the trees separately, and that the change in both of them is the same, can be interpreted with the help of the yoga theory, because according to it, every thought corresponds to a certain energy flow, and a change in either one means a change in the other.[15]

Grass in St. John's visions is a new mythical image. Because grass, like trees, belongs to the plant world, it expresses a deeper level of the life force than that of animal instincts. Unlike the trees, grass is an annual plant. Therefore, it is an appropriate symbol for a more superficial level of energy which is susceptible to changes; men and women can, for example, have basically healthy and energetic constitutions, although during daily activities they are superficially drained until they recover again overnight. When in the vision all green grass is burnt up, St. John undergoes a forceful change in his more superficial, fluctuating energy level. On a deeper and more lasting level symbolized by the trees, the change is only partial, as only a third of them is burnt. In a general sense, it is easier for human beings to change superficially rather than deeply.

The second angel: a burning mountain and the transformation of the sea

"Then the second angel sounded: And something like a great mountain burning with fire was thrown into the sea" (Rev. 8:8). The mountain represents again, as in the sixth chapter, St. John's beliefs about God. I associate the mountain in this vision with some aspects of St. John's externalized God-concept. He is not yet fully able to give up this concept of God. Therefore, the sun and the moon do not fall down from the sky. But he is ready to give up some of the aspects of his old God-concept, and so a burning mountain is being cast into the sea.

In Revelation, the mountain ends up specifically in the sea, because the resolution of the alienation affects St. John deeply, descending even into his unconscious. The burning of the mountain tells us that St. John's old beliefs are burning away: he is becoming free from them. The mountain does not, however, burn off completely in the vision—otherwise it could not fall into the sea—and this is probably so to depict St. John becoming only partially free from old ideas. But the matter can be examined further. In a strongly felt transformation we often come to notice that there are both right and wrong aspects to our beliefs and values, and now St. John is beginning to give up what he realizes to be untrue. Untruths burn off, at least partly, but that which has some truth to it, he wants to absorb in a new way, and this is the part that falls into the sea.

"And a third of the sea became blood" (Rev. 8:8). When St. John is becoming even partly freed from his former beliefs, he is able to experience deep love that penetrates even the unconscious, and so the sea becomes blood. I believe that the true part of St. John's perception of God, which did not burn off, was St. John's belief that God is love. However, he needed to be able to experience love ever more deeply and personally, and it is this kind of change St. John is going through when the sea becomes blood. The change is not yet complete, though, as only a third of the sea becomes blood. Perhaps his old, false beliefs burning away as the mountain was burning were his perception of God existing separately from human beings as an anthropomorphic good and righteous judge.

"And a third of the living creatures in the sea died, and a third of the ships were destroyed" (Rev. 8:9).

In myths and dreams, the creatures in the sea symbolize fairly universally the contents of the unconscious. Some of the well-known sea creatures in myths are sea-monsters, which reflect a person's unconscious fears, or repressed desires, which one has experienced to be like monsters. Thus the dying of the sea creatures in St. John's vision tells of a deep, inner transformation. Even some of the content of his consciousness, which he has not yet experienced clearly or become aware of, dies. St. John is liberated from such contents, and at the same time, his ego dies more at the level of the unconscious.

A ship is used to travel the sea, and generally the sea in myths describes the unconscious. The journey across the sea is particularly important on a spiritual path, because a genuinely spiritual life must be so deep that even the unconscious becomes familiar for the traveler: ever new potentials must become actual. Therefore, it is natural that the heroes in myths sail the oceans with the ship depicting all that which helps them in their inner journeys. Above all, the ship helps the heroes to stay up on the water. Although, at times, they may be swallowed by the sea-creatures or they may dive for treasures, they may not drown fully in the mythical sea, as this would mean a permanent regression or serious psychic disorder.

Because a ship is made by human hands, as a mythical image, it is thought to hold those spiritual teachings that are created by human beings. Thus a ship can symbolize, for example, the superficial or the deeper wisdom of women and men, general spiritual teachings, or those transmitted by a particular culture. This kind of ship symbolism is common in the Oriental cultures, where, for instance, in the *Bhagavadgita* we find an expression "with the boat of wisdom you may cross the sea of miseries."[16]

When, in Revelation, a third of the ships are destroyed, St. John realizes that part of those beliefs on which he has relied during his spiritual journey up until now, are useless, and he gives them up.

It is possible to interpret the events of the vision in this part of Revelation in a way which is appropriate for the modern person. The mountain would mean any belief or value that we have absorbed outwardly and which we feel to be central to our worldview. The burning of the mountain would reflect the emotional relinquishment of that belief, or more precisely the part of that belief which we are beginning to find untrue. Casting the mountain into the sea would mean ever deeper absorption of that which we find to be correct in our belief, and the sea becoming blood would symbolize the deepening intensity of personal experiences followed by a transformation. In our situation, the destroyed ships would be those less important beliefs, which we now feel to be useless and free ourselves from.

The third angel: the falling star

"Then the third angel sounded: And a great star fell from heaven, burning like a torch... and the name of the star is Wormwood" (Rev. 8:10–11). The stars were interpreted earlier as representing St. John's beliefs concerning the nature of spiritual reality. These stars or beliefs are subservient to those represented by the sun and the moon.[17] When one of the stars in the vision falls burning from heaven, St. John defines one of his previous beliefs more closely. The quality of this belief symbolized by the star is revealed by the name given to it: Wormwood.

Wormwood, *apsinthos* in Greek, is actually a plant with a characteristically bitter taste. In the Bible, it is used to refer to poison, and in a more abstract sense, misfortune and injustice. It is said in Jeremiah, "Behold, I will feed them with wormwood and make them drink the water of gall." In Lamentations, a long sequence of misfortunes is described with words, "He has filled me with bitterness, he has made me drink wormwood," and the prophet Amos cries out a judgment, "You who turn justice to wormwood, and lay righteousness to rest in the earth."[18] As the wormwood represents generally something evil, and because St. John sees the Wormwood-star during his vision, I believe that he continues to struggle with the problem of evil.

That the mountain burned, means St. John has abandoned part of his externalized God-concept, whose good and righteous aspects were symbolized by the sun. This good 'sun-god' has been a convenient concept, because in St. John's mind it had an opposite—evil. But where, in the final analysis, did evil as an opposite to the good sun-god come from? St. John has not examined this completely; he may have in fact repressed the problem, as I suggested in the sixth chapter, and so the existence of evil in his worldview has been an important but mystifying principle. Evil has been like a mysterious lodestar left in darkness, a poisonous star on the night sky, and its opposite, the good and the righteous God of judgment, has been like the sun in the daytime sky.

Now that the Wormwood-star burns in the vision, St. John is able to partially let go of the mystifying principle of evil. In the same way, he has already partly discarded his beliefs in a God, who is merely a good and righteous judge existing outside men and women. These rejections are a natural result of his experience in oneness presented at the beginning of the vision; having experienced the whole of reality as oneness, as a single whole, St. John realizes the superficial, dualistic nature of his previous spirituality and tries to give it up.

St. John expresses the burning of the star through a simile, "burning like a torch." Perhaps the comparison tells us that St. John from now on strives to examine the problem of evil, as it were, in the light of a torch, rather than to repress it in the darkness of the night.

"And it fell on the third of the rivers and on the springs of water ... and the third of the waters became wormwood" (Rev. 8:11). Because the sea gets its water from the streams which originate in springs, the streams and the springs symbolize generally the deepest levels of the human consciousness. But it is possible to analyze St. John's symbolism from the basis of yoga theory, where the streams would be—like trees and other plants—streams of life force. The springs would be the chakras, from which, according to yoga theory, the streams of life energy flow. Compared to the trees and other plants, the streams of water would be deeper streams of energy, because the water, like the minerals, belongs to lifeless nature.

If St. John's vision is interpreted in this way, it has progressed logically from more superficial levels to deeper ones. His ordinary awareness, or the earth, and the respective energy channels, the plants, were the first to be transformed. After that, the transformation continued in the sea, that is, his unconscious mind, and now the change occurs in the deep energy channels and chakras.

When the streams and the springs in the vision partially become wormwood, St. John realizes that his spirituality has until now been partly wrong, like toxic water. Perhaps he feels that instead of true life energy, poisonous water has flowed through him. More precisely, the life energy in St. John has flowed in inappropriate ways, responding to inappropriate states of consciousness; as explained earlier, according to yoga teaching, the different states of consciousness correspond to the flow of certain energies.

Perhaps St. John at this stage of his visions awakens to the realization that his old spirituality has essentially been a fear of evil. He has believed in the good and righteous God of judgment so that God would protect him from all that is evil and wrong. But now, as a result of his experience in heavenly silence, he understands that his fear is like a poisonous drink, wormwood. Its opposite is inner silence, the mythical living water of peace, oneness, and joy.

"And many men died from the water, because it was made bitter" (Rev. 8:11). It is not easy for St. John to admit that there have been wrong, even harmful aspects in his previous spirituality. All this is for him something bitter to drink. However, when he drinks the bitter water, his ego further dies as is represented by the many people who die in the vision.

The general interpretation of the Wormwood-star as an unsound belief concerning evil can be appropriately applied to our life as ordinary modern individuals. We might be thinking along these lines: "All those who do not believe in the same 'good' things as we do, are wrong; they are evil people." Deflecting evil to others, however, will hinder our inner deepening, as we will thus avoid examining and correcting our own faults. Such an attitude as one's lodestar in life is then like a poisonous Wormwood-star. But if we are able to admit the harmfulness of this attitude, we take a new step toward freedom regardless of the bitterness of the change.

The confusion

The fourth angel: the darkening of the heavenly bodies

"Then the fourth angel sounded: And a third of the sun was struck, a third of the moon, and a third of the stars, so that a third of them was darkened; and a third of the day did not shine, and likewise the night." (Rev. 8:12.)

St. John's liberation from the alienating spirituality expressed by this vision, is not complete. That is why the sun, the moon, and the stars symbolizing the various aspects of this unsound spirituality, lose only a third of their brilliance in St. John's mind. Also otherwise in this vision, St. John has used the amount of a third to describe the partial nature of his transformation; for example, only a third of the sea became blood.

In the midst of his inner transformation, St. John feels confused. His day consciousness, as well as his night consciousness, are partly in a state of inner darkness, and so a third of the day and the night darken in the vision.

The angel–eagle

"And I looked, and I heard an angel flying through the midst of heaven, saying with a loud voice, 'Woe, woe, woe to the inhabitants of the earth, because of the remaining blasts of the trumpet of the three angels who are about to sound'" (Rev. 8:13). The original manuscripts present here, most often, the eagle, instead of the angel, and nearly all translations mention the eagle. Therefore, I interpret the verse with reference to the eagle. However, the symbolic meanings of the angel and the eagle applied to this verse, are roughly the same.

The eagle has already appeared in the fourth chapter, where the fourth creature was like an eagle, and it was also embedded in the sixth chapter, where a creature, which looked like an eagle, said, "Come!" to a horse and its rider, the Death. At that time, I interpreted the eagle to express cyclical evolution and human beings' return to oneness with God, which happens when they are finally free from ego-desires and attachments. It is this kind of return that St. John is now involved in.

Birds in mythical connections symbolize experiences. We feel ourselves separated from this everyday 'earthbound' life; our spirits fly high up in the sky, if you will. We speak of high thoughts, high values, and of heightened states of awareness. Depending on the quality of the birds, they symbolize different experiences transcending the everyday consciousness. Here the eagle clearly represents a prophetic intuition. That it flies in the middle of the sky emphasizes, perhaps, the loftiness of St. John's problem and the importance of his intuition. Birds carry the same meaning of high intuition in myths, particularly at the times when they function as messengers for the gods. The eagle has this connotation, for example, in the Greek mythology.[19]

If we assume that the eagle in Revelation is like an ordinary eagle, it would be a dark bird. Black is appropriate in this part of St. John's vision, as dark birds can, in myths, carry threatening or anxiety-laden meanings.[20] St. John would feel anxiety in realizing the difficulty of the problems ahead of him and in anticipating what he must bear in solving them. Thus, there will be more trumpet blows and those on earth will suffer.

9. NEW TRUMPET BLASTS: LOCUSTS AND CAVALRY

Opening of the unconscious

The fifth angel: the star

"Then the fifth angel sounded: And I saw a star that had fallen from heaven to the earth" (Rev. 9:1). The star St. John is talking about may be the Wormwood-star of the previous chapter, which fell from the sky down to the earth into streams and springs. Although the Wormwood-star burnt out as it fell, perhaps something of it was left. This could mean that St. John in this vision continues to deal with the problem of evil symbolized by the Wormwood-star. However, I interpret this new star seen by St. John differently. I assume that it crystallizes all those incidents from the previous chapter when something—hail, fire, mountain and Wormwood—fell from the sky onto the earth. At the same time St. John began to resolve his alienation. I assume the new star symbolizes St. John's new understanding about religion derived from the events from the previous chapter: an individual's personal experience, rather than externally adopted beliefs, is essential in religion.

The bottomless pit

"And he opened the bottomless pit" (Rev. 9:1–2). With his new insight, St. John understands that his own consciousness must become the focus of his spiritual life. He himself must change deeply. Psychologically speaking, he must open his unconscious and approach its content in a new way. As an underground environment, the bottomless pit indeed represents the unconscious.

The new step in the inner transformation is possible for St. John because he has removed the mental blocks in his consciousness, that is, he has broken the seals. He has also given up some of his old beliefs during the first trumpet blasts. Therefore, his unconscious mind can further open up so that its 'inhabitants,' or those contents he has been unaware of and has not experienced clearly, can surface.

Facing the unconscious is a stage of inner transformation. Often it is initiated by an incident which has touched one's feelings deeply, a moment comparable to the quietude in heaven described by St. John in the beginning of the eighth chapter. In our lives such an incident can be external like a serious illness or the death of a loved one, but it can also be purely inward, an intensely lived experience. It may be that, taken by surprise, we quickly realize that the attitudes about life and death and existence we have harbored until now are insufficient. We are shaken, and it is then that the repressed contents of the consciousness—the fears, the traumas, the problems, the lies, and the conflicts—begin to emerge.

Facing confusion and repression

The smoke and the furnace

"And he opened the bottomless pit, and smoke arose out of the pit like the smoke of a great furnace" (Rev. 9:2). In this stage of intensive transformation, St. John is first engulfed by confusion; he finds himself in the midst of concealing smoke. The verse tells us additionally that St. John's unconscious is at present like a furnace. Psychologically the appearance of a furnace like this at the depth of the human consciousness can be understood based on our knowledge of repression. When we repress something, we metaphorically, as it were, press it downward psychically; we refuse to be aware of it. But what is repressed works its way upward to be acknowledged and experienced, and the conflict creates such friction and heat that an underground furnace is formed.

The darkening of the sun and the air

"And the sun and the air were darkened because of the smoke of the pit" (Rev. 9:2). The confusion of St. John has to do with the sun, or his old God-concept, and the air, or his value experiences.[1]

According to my interpretation, St. John has already admitted that his concept of God symbolized by the sun is partially wrong. This change essentially resulted from the superconscious experience in quietude that befell him in the beginning of the previous vision. Because of that experience he had to admit that God is not just a judge existing outside of the human being. However, St. John has not yet been fully able to give up his old God-concept. He would now like to continue his introspection, but he finds himself at a loss.

Perhaps St. John wonders about the nature of his superconscious experience during quietude. Undeniably, he has experienced it himself, but how should the boundaries of human value experiences (symbolized by the ubiquitous air) be determined? Does the air, perhaps, reach all the way to heaven? This is something St. John does not know, and so the air is concealed in the smoke. The greatest reason for St. John's confusion, however, may be the following problem: if man's own experiences are the most important factors in religion, what significance is left for God? Perhaps St. John thinks to himself, "There must exist divine righteousness and certainly God exists irrespective of human beings. How could I completely abandon that God which is like the sun on the sky?" St. John will find answers to these kinds of questions only after a long inner transformation. For now, the sun is covered by smoke because of these confusing questions.

The sun and the air being concealed by smoke is an appropriate image also for modern women and men because it is perplexing for anyone to have an experience of such deep quietude that it seems to open up a new dimension in reality. We ask, "How does this fit in with our normal thinking (which is symbolized by the sun in the broader meaning given to it in my interpretation)?" And furthermore, "If I acknowledge those experiences and begin to adapt to them, will my value system (represented by the air) darken so completely that I will be misled by mysticism?"

The locusts and the scorpions

"Then out of the smoke came locusts" (Rev. 9:3). These locusts symbolize well such contents of St. John's consciousness as begin to emerge from his unconscious—the bottomless pit.

Describing the contents of the consciousness as flying insects is appropriate as even in modern language, we may refer to the thoughts buzzing or racing around in our heads. Both Occidental and Oriental literature are rich in these kinds of metaphors. For example, St. Bonaventure, in describing St. Francis of Assisi as having been bothered by disturbing thoughts, compares them to flies. The Indian Paramahansa Yogananda writes that he, even as a young child, noticed how man's troubles are like "a cloud of mosquitoes" and "the buzz of insects."[2]

The more distant from human beings an animal is biologically, the more distant from the ordinary is the level of consciousness it symbolizes in dreams and myths. Thus the levels of consciousness represented by insects are generally closer to the unconscious than those represented by mammals.[3] However, all animals, unlike minerals and plants, have the ability to move from one place to another, and thus, in mythical thinking, they are found closer to the everyday consciousness than the minerals and the plants. Therefore, the locusts in St. John's vision are likely to be such contents of the consciousness which he is largely not yet aware of, although they are beginning to surface.

In the southern parts of the Mediterranean, flocks of locusts can destroy all vegetation in the area they descend upon, leaving behind a desert and famine. That is why the locusts are mentioned in the Bible as one of the great plagues in Egypt.[4] As a mythical image, this plague-like nature of the locusts fittingly reflects the anguish brought about by one's inner change: the devastation caused by the locusts is like the painful diminishing of the previous I, or the ego, as the transformation progresses.

"And to [the locusts] was given power, as the scorpions of the earth have power... And their torment was like the torment of a scorpion when it strikes a man." (Rev. 9:3,5.) "[The locusts] had tails like scorpions, and there were stings in their tail. And their power was to hurt men." (Rev. 9:10.)

In myths and dreams, stinging animals like bees, scorpions, and snakes, may convey certain realizations to the person who envisions them. These realizations can be painful when they reveal to individuals their self-deceits and shortcomings. Perhaps it is for this reason that Dante described the agony of hell by saying, "they were much stung by the bees and the gadflies."[5]

In mythology, a snake bite, on the foot in particular, is a common subject. In Greek mythology, Philoctetes is bit by a snake on his foot. In the Egyptian myths, the god Ra meets with the same fate, and in the Bible, the subject appears during the Fall, where the snake is given the power to strike human beings at their heels. In these cases, the encounter probably illustrates an impulse rising from some deep level of a person's being and its emotionally painful effect, which in the end may turn out to be either harmful or potentially good.[6]

The scorpion sting as a mythical image is much the same as the snake bite because a scorpion normally crawls about the ground and stings with its tail which it flings over its back. Scorpion stings are also painful, and the stings of the larger species can be fatal. Additionally, in biblical times, a type of whip with spikes was called a scorpion.[7] For these reasons I assume St. John uses the locust–scorpion stings to describe the anxiety he experiences during the early stages of his dawning awareness.

The anxieties caused by St. John's locust experience may also derive from the fact that apparently there are vast numbers of them, as in the Bible the locusts function as a symbol not only for a plague but also for a great number. The prophet Jeremiah uses the image by saying, "they are innumerable, and more numerous than grasshoppers."[8] Thus St. John feels that innumerable repressed problems, anxieties, and conflicts are emerging out of his unconscious.

Any modern person who dares to introspect deeply, might feel similarly. This kind of an experience is typical especially during the early stages of a strong transformation process, but it is particularly painful when the consciousness has already been partly purified. In St. John's case, some purification happened during the previous vision, when part of the earth and the trees and all the grass burned off, and when some of the people and creatures of the sea died. Even a partial purification of the consciousness brings calmness and inner peace. When someone used to a state like this is engulfed by the countless problems pouring out of the unconscious, he experiences the ensuing confusion as an acute, psychic pain.

The grass and the green things

"They were commanded not to harm the grass of the earth, or any green thing, or any tree, but only those men who do not have the seal of God on their foreheads" (Rev. 9:4). Those men who do not have the seal of God on their foreheads symbolize St. John's spiritually immature level, or the level of his ego. He feels anxious because he is becoming aware that his ego may endure torment.

The fact that no green thing—the grass or the trees—may be harmed defines a difference from the previous chapter where all the green grass and the third of the trees were burnt. We may assume that new grass has grown where the old burnt off; St. John feels that the life force symbolized by the grass has been replenished. Now he needs this life force, along with that symbolized by the trees, to be able to bear the difficult transformation he will be facing. That is why the grass and the trees may not be harmed. In accordance with this change, St. John is more aware of his inner transformation in this chapter. In the previous vision, the events were presented mostly with symbols from plants and the lifeless part of the nature. In this chapter, the images are provided by animals and men.

Seeking death

"In those days men will seek death and will not find it; they will desire to die and death will flee from them" (Rev. 9:6). The same idea appears partly already in the fifth verse, "And they [the locusts] were not given authority to kill them, but to torment them for five months" (Rev. 9:5).

St. John's ego ought to die in order for his deeper I, the Self, to be liberated ever more fully. But the ego's death is difficult. On the one hand, St. John wants to change; yet on the other, he is not able to let go of his attachments, his sense of self-importance and his rationalizations. He cannot admit having been decisively wrong. He suffers when struggling with his attachments, and in the vision his suffering is depicted by people being tormented. Since he will not surrender, his ego cannot die off; hence his vision shows death escaping whoever seeks it.

St. John's anguish lasts for five months. Evil and the mythical number five are connected in this context in many ways. The torment itself is a distressful, 'evil' experience. The problem of evil—why it exists at all—returns to disturb his inner harmony. A further connection with the number five refers to the fifth angel sounding a trumpet to initiate his torment. In the tenth verse, St. John once more reiterates the length of the agony, "And their power was to hurt men for five months" (Rev. 9:10).

Locusts' breastplates, wings, and crowns

"And they had breastplates like breastplates of iron" (Rev. 9:9). A breastplate is used to cover something up. Hidden under it is that which St. John needs to become aware of. However, he cannot see it because of the covering. The breastplates also protect the locusts. Apparently St. John feels that he cannot push his problems—which the locusts represent—back into the bottomless pit. He cannot stop their progress, as they are shielding themselves to withstand any such turning back. St. John is not able to solve his problems, and yet he cannot repress them either. The impasse is greatly distressful.

"And the sound of their wings was like the sound of chariots with many horses running into battle" (Rev. 9:9). Perhaps something which St. John cannot see is hidden also under the locusts' wings. At the same time, he feels that those invisible problems are attacking him violently. The battle is paraphrased also in the seventh verse, "And the shapes of the locusts were like horses prepared for battle" (Rev. 9:7). It is an inner battle that is waging in St. John.

"And on their heads were crowns of something like gold" (Rev. 9:7). Here St. John uses the word *stephanos*, which means both a crown and a wreath. In the sixth chapter the wreath has already been associated with victory and other symbolic meanings referring to the return to oneness with God. The wreath-crowns of the locusts thus emphasize the fact that St. John cannot repress the problems symbolized by the locusts. The locusts move onward victoriously, although, as they win, the actual winner, of course, is St. John. When he has solved the riddle of the locusts, he will be able to return closer to God on his spiral pathway.

In the second chapter of Revelation it is said, "Be faithful until death, and I will give you the crown of life" (Rev. 2:10). The golden crowns seen by St. John are the precursors of this crown of life. According to chakra theory, the life energy moves up to the top of the head to the sahasrara when the spiritual victory is finally won.

Locusts' faces

"And their faces were like the faces of men" (Rev. 9:7). The locusts are monsters composed of parts from different kinds of creatures.

In myths, some parts of a monster may consist of animals, reflecting an animalistic quality. (Mythically, some animals are experienced as sacred; other animals, or at times the same animal, would be considered shameful.) The human part, on the other hand, represents a certain degree of human culture, and belongs to the more controlled, conscious realms of life. Perhaps the locusts in St. John's vision have received human faces because St. John no longer wishes to repress the problems represented by the locusts; he does not squash them into facelessness, but tries to meet them face to face, if you will.

Locusts' hair

"They had hair like women's hair" (Rev. 9:8). As a mythical image, the hair generally represents the thoughts 'growing out' of the head, as well as mental images. For example, St. John of the Cross explains, while interpreting the symbolism of the Bible, that hair depicts man's thoughts and affections.[9] During biblical times, it was common for women to have long hair, and long hair can carry either a positive or negative value.

Personally, I have met several people who, during a creative stage in their lives, have dreamt of masses of hair and beautiful flowers growing out of their heads. The dreamers themselves perceived these dreams as expressions of happy creativity. Long hair has a connotation of vitality also in the biblical story of Samson, as when he says, "No razor has ever come upon my head... If I am shaven, then my strength will leave me, and I shall become weak."[10] Long hair is, however, negatively charged in a situation where a correct spiritual solution to a problem in life calls for an absolute surrender to an experience of profound value. Surrender requires giving up the thoughts and mental images symbolized by hair. It is this kind of mythical import hair has when Buddhist nuns and monks retire from the world. At that time, although there are also practical considerations, their hair is shaven as a sign of relinquishing and surrendering.

In a positive sense, the locusts' hair in St. John's vision depicts that creative force with which he wants to solve the problem symbolized by the locusts. The vision may include some negative purport associated with hair as well, because the locusts' long hair may indicate that St. John is not yet able to solve his problems in a profound way: by surrendering to deep spiritual experiences.

Also the fact that St. John refers to the hair as women's hair, may be significant. Its meaning can be fully understood only after St. John presents three important female images of Revelation: the celestial woman, who gives birth, the prostitute of Babylon, and the wife of the Lamb. Briefly, the celestial woman and the wife of the Lamb represent a sound, deeply spiritual life, and the Babylonian prostitute the wrong kind of spirituality, one which is too superficial. It is this kind of problem that we deal with in the case of the locusts. Now many thoughts about both genuine and superficial spirituality spring forth from St. John—like the countless hairs which symbolize them. Because he has not yet been able to organize his problems properly, there seems to be an incredible number of ideas. In the Bible hair often appears as a metaphor for a great number. For example, "Innumerable evils have surrounded me; my iniquities have overtaken me... They are more than the hairs of my head."[11]

Locusts' teeth

"And their teeth were like lions' teeth" (Rev. 9:8). In myths, the mouth and teeth of beasts generally depict the threatening quality of those mental states which are symbolized by these animals. Thus St. John feels that his problems are difficult enough to be threatening. Perhaps he ponders to himself, "What will be left of my old religion if I examine it thoroughly, and how will I be able to bear the scrutiny and not be crushed by confusion and devoured by anxiety?"

In Revelation, the lion itself, however, is defined more clearly than simply as a beast: in earlier chapters it has represented, according to my interpretation, high spiritual levels of both the universe and of human consciousness. It was during the quietude in heaven that St. John must have felt he contacted the deep levels of spiritual reality. But no matter how beautiful they are, dramatically altered states of consciousness can later be experienced also as threatening. They call for reassessment of everything old, and require a person's total renewal. Thus they actually are a threat to one's ego. Possibly, a new realization begins to form in St. John's consciousness: he must, in his inner life, give ever greater significance to the levels of existence and consciousness symbolized by the lion. Indeed, it may seem to him that the locusts—with their mouths resembling those of the lions—are about to roar out the importance of these deep levels.

The king of the locusts

"And they had as king over them the angel of the bottomless pit, whose name in Hebrew is *Abaddon*, but in Greek he has the name *Apollyon*" (Rev. 9:11). The king of the locusts is not mentioned before the end of the locust section. Therefore, I assume that the king represents a new stage in St. John's transformation. The difficulty with problematic situations often lies in the fact that there are too many separate conflicting components involved, and so the whole problem is like a buzzing swarm of locusts. But eventually St. John can distinguish a king in the swarm. Then the problem symbolized by the locusts begins to take on more definition, and St. John, for the time being, begins to feel a sense of wholeness.

Since the king of the locusts is also the angel of the bottomless pit, he is associated with the different rulers of the Underworld, as well as with other mythical underground beings whose best-known features include some kind of frightfulness and evil. But in myths, these beings can also be beneficial, because the journey through the Underworld, even if it is frightening, will often bring the hero wisdom and teach him to know himself. The ruler of the Underworld, Lucifer, has a function of imparting wisdom in this way, as revealed in the literal meaning of his name, 'one who delivers light.' Because the angel of the bottomless pit acting as the king of the locusts leads the locust army, he brings the locusts into St. John's view and shows him what is emerging from his unconscious, or from the bottomless pit. Thus we can interpret the angel of the bottomless pit also as intuition, or that which brings light, although at present, the anxiety derived from destroying the ego is emphasized. In St. John's vision, the angel of the bottomless pit is appropriately called the Destroyer, which is the meaning of both Abaddon and Apollyon.

The name of the king of the locusts, Apollyon, is nearly the same as the name of the Greek god Apollo, who was a multifaceted god belonging to the ancient mythology. He is characterized by many features similar to those of the angel Apollyon of Revelation. For example, in the *Iliad*, Apollo appears as the destroyer who brings death. He kills animals and men with his arrows, and Homer describes his progress saying, "He strode on in fury, like the night he moved on." Some researchers suggest Apollo's name derives from the ancient Greek word meaning 'to destroy.'[12] Apollo's role as an archer also connects him with St. John's vision, because the arrows shot off by the archer can sting painfully like the locust–scorpions.

Apollo uncovered the guilt of men and cleansed them of it. Similarly, the angel Apollyon discloses to St. John his faults, that is, his repressions. In Greece, Apollo was also the god of fortune-telling, as the oracles of Delphi were under his surveillance, and it was through the oracles that he revealed to people their future and the will of the gods. According to a tradition which is younger than the *Iliad* and was possibly created by the poet Aeschylus, Apollo was associated with light.[13] All this connects Apollo with intuition, which in my interpretation of Revelation is also symbolized by Apollyon.

Additionally, the Greek Apollo protected nature from threatening destruction. Perhaps it is a coincidence brought about by the fragile Mediterranean ecology that Apollo, in protecting the plant growths, is called the destroyer of locusts.[14] Be that as it may, when the angel Apollyon appears in St. John's vision, the locusts disappear from Revelation. When St. John through his intuition (that is, under the guidance of the angel Apollyon), has acknowledged the existence of his repressions, the transformation can continue, and the locusts must make room for new mythical images.

To acknowledge one's repressions is a long process in a human life. If we strive for inner honesty, we need to go through this process many times as we pass through the different stages of our lives.

The woe

"One woe is past. Behold, still two more woes are coming after these things" (Rev. 9:12). St. John uses the woe-cry to emphasize the anxiety caused by the transformation. As a symbol, the woe-cry has evolved from the end of the previous chapter, where the angel–eagle said, "Woe, woe, woe to the inhabitants of the earth, because of the remaining blasts of the trumpet of the three angels who are about to sound!" (Rev. 8:13.) At that time, there were three trumpet blares left: the fifth, the sixth, and the seventh. St. John has described the effects of the fifth trumpet blast, and thus it is the time for the sixth angel to sound the trumpet.

The release

The sixth angel: the release of the angels

"Then the sixth angel sounded: And I heard a voice from the four horns of the golden altar which is before God saying to the sixth angel who had the trumpet, 'Release the four angels who are bound at the great river Euphrates'" (Rev. 9:13–14).

Releasing of the bound angels symbolizes well the freeing of St. John's intuition. When the locusts, or the repressions, have been let out of the bottomless pit, St. John need no longer spend energy in repressing the problems in question. His inner life becomes more balanced and his intuition begins to flow more freely.

The altar and the horns

St. John hears the voice from the four horns of the altar, one that demands release of the angels. The altar, in my interpretations, has represented universal love, or more theoretically, the subjective side of the universal Self. More accurately, the altar symbolizes universal love at that stage when St. John does not yet experience it in full measure. Only after he makes progress on his inner path as the visions of Revelation evolve and he learns to love ever more fully will he finally experience the universal Self completely. Then the holy city, the bride of the Lamb, appears in Revelation; the bride of the Lamb symbolizes the fully manifested universal Self from its subjective side. The Lamb, on the other hand, symbolizes throughout Revelation the objective side of the universal Self.

In this vision, there are four horns on the altar. Therefore, we might assume that the altar is square or rectangular. This shape supports the interpretation I have earlier given to the altar because it visually depicts the form of the holy city, which at the end of Revelation is described as a square.

Horns have appeared earlier on the Lamb (Rev. 5:6), making it natural for the altar to have horns also. The horns of the altar and the horns of the Lamb carry the same meaning of the desire of the Self to express itself freely without the limitations imposed on it by the ego. When the horns in St. John's vision speak out, it is because of this impetus. The Self 'wants' to strengthen itself, and this can happen only if the spiritual intuitions—the angels—are set free from the bonds created by attachments.

The horns of the altar and their speaking add a new stage to the evolution of the altar as a mythical image. To summarize: the fourth chapter presented a sea of glass symbolizing that which is potential or that side of spirituality which had remained hidden. After that, in the sixth chapter, St. John saw the altar from under which the souls of the slain were revealed. Then that which was potential began to actualize and what was hidden began to emerge. In the eighth chapter, we saw in front of the throne the altar and an angel casting some of its fire onto the earth. Thus the altar began to function through the angel, that is, through intuition, to transform St. John. Now the altar has received horns and a voice comes forth from them, making the altar an ever more dominant mythical image in the inner dynamics of the visions. Because the altar is in heaven, we can probably assume that St. John's spiritual evolution is directed even more clearly than before from the superconscious: the divine infusion in his inner transformation is emphasized.

The river Euphrates

The angels to be released in the vision by St. John, are bound along the Euphrates River, which is one of the grand mythical images in Revelation. Although mentioned there only twice, it extends geographically for almost two thousand miles and hence creates a vast mythical image. In fact, Revelation calls it "the great river Euphrates." It is such an interesting mythical image that I will discuss it in greater depth.

In the Bible, the Euphrates River is mentioned the first time in Genesis before the Fall. "Now a river went out of Eden to water the garden, and from there it parted and became four riverheads. The name of the first is Pishon; it is the one which encompasses the whole land of Havilah, where there is gold. And the gold of that land is good... The name of the second river is Gihon; it is the one which encompasses the whole land of Cush. The name of the third river is Hiddekel; it is the one which goes towards the east of Assyria. The fourth river is the Euphrates."[16]

If we compare the biblical images to those of yoga teachings, we find that the human energy system is represented by a river's tributaries as well as by the trees of paradise in the Bible. We are then examining the streams of astral life force. In the beginning of man's creation—when a more tangible man is just beginning to emerge—this energy system is in the 'paradisiacal' or harmonious state, both inwardly and outwardly. The most inward and spiritual energy flow is probably described by the river Pishon mentioned in the myth first for it is said that the gold of the land of Havilah which it encompasses is good. Assyria with the Hiddekel, that is the Tigris, and the Euphrates associated with it, would describe the outer energy systems.

After the paradise sections, the meaning of the Euphrates River in the Bible changes dramatically. For example, in Jeremiah, the Lord complains about the people of Israel, "They have forsaken me, the foundation of living waters... And now, why take the road to Egypt, to drink the waters of Sihor? Or why take the road to Assyria, to drink the waters of the River [Euphrates]?" The Euphrates has thus acquired a meaning opposite to that of living water, and Assyria, which in the creation myth appeared as a part of paradise, has become a mythical strange land. The Euphrates and Assyria then represent man's alienated state, or ego-consciousness, as does Egypt. Analyzing this further, the Euphrates River and the Sihor, that is, the Nile, which make Assyria and Egypt fertile with their waters, are those energy streams which sustain ego-consciousness.[17]

The interpretations I suggest for the Euphrates, the Nile, Assyria, and Egypt derive from geographical and historical associations. The Euphrates River flows through the ancient kingdom of Assyria, and, similarly, the Nile, through Egypt. The Jews were in slavery in Egypt and later emigrated to Assyria against their will. The most important reason for the change in the meaning of the river Euphrates in the Bible, is its connection to the mythical Fall, which also changed the nature of the human energy system. Earlier, in the sixth chapter, while interpreting the symbolism of the trees in the paradise, I analyzed the impact of the Fall on the human energy system. I will now reiterate some of that analysis focusing the interpretation on the mythical image of the great river.

Applying the yoga theory, the great mythical river is the energy stream flowing through man's spine, which in the tree symbolism is depicted by the trunk of the tree. I feel that it is this great energy-stream which the river Euphrates of Revelation symbolizes. But the great mythical river changes when the quality of the energy stream flowing through the spine changes. In the inner great stream of an ordinary, ego-bound person, the energy flows in the ida and pingala nadis, whereas the sushumna is yet empty of energy, or nearly so. The sushumna of a saint living in a state of bliss, on the other hand, is fully open. Therefore, his inner stream has been transformed into the river of paradise. Because St. John is still on his way to paradise, the symbolism of the strange land is emphasized in his inner stream: it is called Euphrates.

There are places, however, in the Bible, where the river Euphrates has a narrower meaning than I suggest above. For example, in the previous quote from Jeremiah, the spring of the living water abandoned by the people of Israel is like the sahasrara on the top of the sushumna, that is, the center of experiencing bliss, and the Nile and the Euphrates are like the ida and the pingala nadis. (As explained before, ida and pingala are, according to yoga teachings, located on opposite sides of sushumna.) Similar narrower meaning for the river Euphrates can be seen in Genesis, when God says to Abraham, "To your descendants I have given this land, from the river of Egypt to the great river, the River Euphrates." The promised land is thus in between two great rivers of two strange lands, even as sushumna is between ida and pingala. The River Jordan of the promised land would, in the Bible, be a fitting symbol for the sushumna-nadi. (The mythical viewpoint, of course, is only one of many dimensions in an interpretation.) Furthermore, in India, the three major energy streams, ida, pingala, and sushumna, are symbolized by the three great rivers: the Jamuna, the Ganges, and the mythical Saraswati.[18]

One universal, grand mythical river is the river of the Underworld. It, too, in its own way, will shed light on the meaning of the Euphrates River. Analyzed on the level of experience, the river of the Underworld, naturally, has to do with human sensations at the time of death. In an ordinary death, man gradually loses his bodily feeling and the functioning of the senses. Energy withdraws from the surface more deeply inward and finally along the major channels from the base upwards. The dying person may experience this final stage, as if he were moving through a dark tunnel hearing sounds at the same time, possibly even the roaring of the river. These sensations have been recounted by many who have experienced clinical death.[19] That dark tunnel could well be the dark river of the Underworld along which people (according to a universal myth) travel to the kingdom of death.

Many central practices taught by yoga theory, the so-called *pranayama* practices, have to do with drawing the life force along this great channel located in the spine and the head.[20] The existence of a vast inner energy stream is well known to anyone who has practiced pranayama with concentration.

In Revelation, the River Euphrates forms a logical step in the evolution of the mythical images in St. John's visions. In the previous chapter, he had progressed in his symbolism to the streams and springs, or to the energy streams and chakras, and now he continues the symbolism adding the major stream of energy along which, or inside which, the most important chakras are located.

Because St. John has by now dismantled many mental blocks, the stream of his life force can travel more freely. (According to yoga theory, changes in one's state of consciousness affect the flow of life force, and vice versa—a phenomenon which has become evident already in Revelation.) The angels being released along the river Euphrates are the states of consciousness associated with the freed life force: they represent new intuitive realizations and experiences.

The task of the angels

"So the four angels, who had been prepared for the hour and day and month and year, were released to kill a third of mankind" (Rev. 9:15). When his intuition is freed, St. John's feeling for life broadens and brightens. Now it is possible for him to let go of his self-importance and to admit his mistakes. He is freed from his attachments and so his ego begins to die. At this stage, the dying, however, is only anticipated. I interpret the expression "a third of mankind" to refer to the second stage of the three-part transformation process which began in the previous vision; at that time, St. John said, "many men died" and in several places he related to the change as "a third."

The number four—there are four angels to be released—possibly emphasizes a healing. St. John is beginning to become a more 'whole' person. He is progressing on an inner path during which he will gradually be transformed into the mythical square holy city. Additionally, the number of the angels associates them with the four horns of the altar.

The growing awareness

Since St. John's intuition was freed up during the angels' release, his problems begin to organize. Therefore, a new mythical image appears in the vision: the army of the horsemen (Rev. 9:16). This image of an army extends in a logical and easily recognizable way the image of the locust army, thereby expressing a new stage in John's growing awareness and organizing of his problems. Similarity is evident already in the fact that St. John previously compared the locusts with "the horses prepared for battle" and the buzzing of their wings with "the sounds of chariots with many horses running into battle" (Rev. 9:7,9).

The horses

"And thus I saw the horses in the vision... and the heads of the horses were like the heads of lions" (Rev. 9:17). "For their power is in their mouth and in their tails; for their tails are like serpents, having heads; and with them they do harm" (Rev. 9:19). While the locusts' teeth were "like lion's teeth," the heads of the horses are now "like the heads of lions". And while the locusts had tails like scorpions to harm with, the horses have tails like serpents to harm with.

The shift from the lions' teeth to the heads like those of lions indicates that the frightening aspect of the problems which previously bothered St. John has decreased. The problems no longer threaten to crush him. However, the horses' serpent-like tails, capable of harming people, tell us that the growth of St. John's awareness is still painful. The fact that the horses' power "is in their mouth," alludes to the possibility that the horses will soon be able to speak. Perhaps they will use their mouths to share information, and St. John will receive new realizations. This is probably reflected also in the fact that biologically a horse is closer to a human being than is a locust. The shift from locusts to horses thus points out that St. John's problem has moved closer to his awareness and therefore will be easier for him to recognize.

Those who sat on the horses

"And thus I saw the horses in the vision: those who sat on them had breastplates" (Rev. 9:17). The verse speaks of an important change, which came about when St. John shifted from locusts to horses: unlike the locusts, the horses have someone sitting on them. A human being who controls the animal form has thus entered the mythical image of the problem. This means that St. John feels he has gained more control over his problem.

The way I see the change evolving in St. John's vision is that the human component of the locusts, the face, has separated and become personified by its own mythical image, the horseman. Also, the locusts' breastplates have been transferred to those who sat on the horses. The breastplates themselves have apparently changed as well, because St. John said about the locusts' breastplates that they were "like breastplates of iron" (Rev. 9:9). The horsemen, however, simply have "breastplates." I interpret these differences, too, to mean that St. John feels he is approaching the solution to his problem. The mythical image under the breastplate is no longer as far from human experience as is the insect body of a locust.

The number of the horsemen

"Now the number of the army of the horsemen was two hundred million and I heard the number of them" (Rev. 9:16). In the usual translation, the number of the horsemen is said to be two hundred million, but St. John presents this number with the help of two numbers which translate more literally to 'twice a myriad' and 'myriad.' As myriad means not only a large number in general, but also ten thousand, some translations express the number used by St. John with the words, "Twice ten thousand times ten thousand." St. John's words are, on the one hand, marked by the number two, and on the other, by number ten. Using the symbolism of the numbers I have presented earlier, number two represents conflict, and it is the conflicts in his own spirituality St. John is resolving. The number ten symbolizes anxiety, which in this connection is that of his growing awareness and transformation. The great number of the horsemen probably expresses St. John's feelings that there still are a vast number of problems to solve. He also feels again rather fragmented, although the buzzing flock of locusts has already become somewhat organized.

The three plagues and the killing of mankind

"And out of the mouths [of the horses] came fire, smoke, and brimstone" (Rev. 9:17). "By these three plagues a third of the mankind was killed—by the fire and the smoke and the brimstone which came out of their mouths" (Rev. 9:18).

When the fire, the smoke, and the brimstone come out of the mouths of the horses, it is as though the horses were speaking. But they speak a mythical language, and the messages are embedded in the mythical images of fire, smoke, and brimstone. Because the fire, the smoke, and the brimstone come out of the mouths of the horses, or animals, I assume St. John is still only beginning to grow aware of his problems.

I interpret the fire, again, as a symbol of spiritual energy. When he sees the fire, St. John realizes, that the right kind of spirit and love already burn in his spiritual life. This has already been expressed in earlier visions, especially by the quietude in heaven (in the beginning of the previous chapter which led to throwing fire from the altar onto the earth). Yet, regardless of its positive meaning, the fire appears in this vision as a plague, because, in the light of his new spiritual experiences, St. John sees the insufficiency of his previous spirituality and thus he suffers.

The smoke emanating out of the horses' mouth indicates that St. John realizes his spirituality includes also sides that are obscure, as if they were covered by smoke. It is not easy for anyone to admit his spirituality to be insufficient and obscure, and therefore St. John sees the smoke, too, as a plague.

Brimstone is sulphur, and in the Bible, it is a symbol for God's anger and punishment. An example: "For it is the day of the Lord's vengeance...Its streams shall be turned into pitch, and its dust into brimstone." Burning stone and similar images, like glowing embers, are also associated with anxiety. Engulfed by deep anxiety, we feel as if we are scorched in a slowly burning fire or on hot stones; for example, St. John of the Cross compares his spiritual trial to his heart being scorched with glowing embers.[21]

The burning of stones and other minerals tells us that a furnace is forming in those deep recesses of human consciousness which are represented by these minerals. In the beginning of this chapter I interpreted the furnace from the viewpoint of repression, and now I will continue this interpretation adding that the brimstone symbolizes the repressed contents of consciousness. When there is brimstone coming forth from the horses' mouth, St. John realizes that there still is something repressed in his consciousness which he has not yet resolved. It is not easy to admit it, and thus also the brimstone becomes a plague.

Admitting one's own imperfection, which St. John has now been able to do, brings a feeling of release. When a person yields in this way, he lets go of his rationalizations, which he had previously used in order to prove himself right regardless of everything. He is liberated. Thus, in Revelation, St. John's ego can be said to further die symbolized by the vision of a third of the people being killed because of the fire, the smoke and the brimstone.

Describing the horsemen, St. John mentions also the colors of their breastplates, "[The horsemen] had breastplates of fiery red, hyacinth blue, and sulfur yellow" (Rev. 9–17), which is to say the colors of the breastplates resemble those of the fire, the smoke, and the brimstone. According to yoga theory, red, dark bluish, and yellow are colors of the chakras lower than the ajna chakra; thus, the transformation in question probably has to do with the changes in the lower chakras only.

St. John speaks of the horses' harmful, serpent-like tails only after he has told us about the killing of the people. Apparently he feels that the opening up of his sense of awareness must continue to be painful even after the present dying of the ego. The final verses, as well, emphasize the incompleteness of his transformation.

The incompleteness of the transformation

"But the rest of the mankind, who were not killed by these plagues, did not repent of the works of their hands" (Rev. 9:20). If the keys of interpretation I have given are used here, too, people who have not been killed would be those sides of St. John's ego which have not yet died. Because women and men as egos feel themselves to be the performers of their actions, "the works of their hands" is an appropriate expression.

The idols and the demons

"They... did not repent... that they should not worship demons, and idols of gold, silver, brass, stone and wood, which can neither see nor hear nor walk" (Rev. 9:20).

In the most general sense, an idol is any ego-desire that controls the human mind. When we strive to fulfill this desire, our actions must comply with the requirements for success. Then we, as it were, worship the desire, and the preoccupation of satisfying it directs our life. The desire is like an idol we bow to. A similar interpretation can be found in St. John of the Cross, who says the idols are "our alien attachments."[22] Because the ego-desires differ in their ethical value, St.

John, in Revelation, refers to them with attributes of different value: gold, silver, brass, stone, and wood.

The reference to idols by St. John the Divine can, of course, also be interpreted as a general emphasis on the fallacy of an unsound religion. In the final account, an unsound religion is simply a human being's belief in his own religious ideas. Those ideas are like idols, and this kind of religion is dead compared to a genuine spirituality or to vibrant, high states of consciousness.

For the demons mentioned by St. John, I suggest only one interpretation, supplementary to the previous explanation. When our ego-desires are extremely strong, we strive to accomplish them, as if we were possessed by demons, and thus we worship those demons while submitting to being driven by them.

Murder, sorcery, sexual immorality, and theft

"They did not repent of their murders or their sorceries or their sexual immorality or their thefts" (Rev. 9:21).

I interpret murder in this reference as I did the people killing each other in the sixth chapter. Murdering of people thus means inner battles in general, and killing of the ego in particular. Interpreted in this way, these mythical images convey the idea that St. John's inner transformation must continue, and that the ethically more profound aspects of his ego must 'kill' those of lesser value.

Sorcery, expressed in modern language, refers to a variety of parapsychological powers and phenomena, and their uses. The Bible relates to these phenomena in different ways. For example, St. Paul is strictly against sorcery, but the miracles performed by Jesus are presented openly and approvingly. Another accepted incident is found in Exodus, where the Lord counsels Moses and Aaron to perform miracles in order to gain victory over "the wise men and the sorcerers of Egypt."[23] Perhaps St. John has till now regarded the parapsychological powers as important, and now he understands that he is not yet fully free from that attitude. Possibly he wants to stress, additionally, that the parapsychological experiences and abilities can lead many astray from genuine spirituality.

In the Bible, sexual immorality, prostitution or fornication, as a metaphor, means erroneous spirituality. For example, in Hosea, we read. "The land has committed great prostitution by departing from the Lord."[24] The metaphorical fornication means the union of the human consciousness with the wrong values, that is, one enjoys satisfying the ego-desires. This meaning is found in St. Teresa, who writes, "Are there other unions [than those with God]? Of course! Should we linger in trivialities and love them too dearly, the devil may charm us, but not like God, not so that the soul would be flooded with delight and contentment, with peace and joy."[25]

Finally, theft leads us to think of how a flawed religion and our many attachments rob from us of a great treasure—spiritual peace and bliss. Jesus speaks of this kind of theft in his parable about the sheep, "The thief does not come except to steal, and to kill, and to destroy. I have come that they may have life, and that they may have it more abundantly."[26]

10. THE ANGEL AND THE BOOK

St. John's awareness continues to expand

The angel

"And I saw still another mighty angel coming down from heaven, clothed with a cloud. And a rainbow was on his head, his face was like the sun and his feet like pillars of fire... and [he] cried with a loud voice, as when a lion roars." (Rev. 10:1,3.)

Because an angel symbolizes intuition, the above verse tells us that a new intuitive vision, which will help St. John to examine his problems, is about to appear. In the end of the previous chapter, St. John has admitted that along with admirable qualities, there are repressions and unresolved issues affecting his spirituality, and it is these that he is now trying to recognize intuitively. Because the angel steps down from heaven, it suggests an element of divine grace and the effect of the superconscious in the inner transformation process.

Keeping in mind the evolution of St. John's visions, the angel advances the image of the locusts and the armies of horsemen. I assume that this step forward is a result of John's growing awareness.

Whereas the locusts were covered by iron breastplates and the horsemen with ordinary breastplates, the angel is clothed with a cloud. I infer from this that St. John feels that he is drawing nearer to the solution to his problems. He is beginning to gain intuitive understanding of them, although his intuition does not yet flow completely freely. The angel's head and feet are portrayed vividly, not unlike the descriptions of the locusts and horsemen, where on the one hand, the head was emphasized, and on the other, the lower end, the tail.

A further analysis shows the lion to be a common denominator in the recounts of the locusts, horsemen and the angel. Earlier, St. John compared the teeth of the locusts to those of the lions, and the heads of the horses to the heads of the lions, and now the mighty angel cries out "as when a lion roars." The change involving the lion in these mythical images reflects clearly the shift from threat to realization.

Because in this vision the lion-principle simply proclaims something, it no longer threatens to crush St. John with his teeth.

The rainbow over the angel's head can be compared to the golden wreath-crowns the locusts wore. The rainbow appeared already in the fourth chapter, where it was surrounding the enthroned. At the time, I interpreted it as a geometric ideogram. But the rainbow as a mythical image illustrates appropriately also the connectedness of heaven and earth. Apparently it is for this reason that the rainbow in the Old Testament symbolizes the covenant between God and man. In Genesis, this covenant means God's promise never again to destroy the mankind through flood.[1]

In the New Testament, the rainbow no longer appears as a symbol for covenant, but the covenant between God and humanity is still talked about, "For this is the covenant that I will make... None of them shall teach his neighbour, and none his brother saying, 'Know the Lord,' for all shall know me, from the least of them to the greatest of them."[2] I assume that in Revelation St. John strives for this kind of new relationship between God and himself: he strives to establish an intimate union with God. That St. John uses a symbol derived from the Old Testament shows that he feels his final union with God to be far from realized. But he believes his new intuition, the angel descending from heaven, will lead him closer to the attainment of union, and this is indicated by the rainbow on the angel's head. Because the final union with God, in the vocabulary of Revelation, means also the final victory, the rainbow on the angel's head and the locusts' wreath-crowns expressing victory, are fittingly analogous.

Whereas the locusts' faces were like those of men, the angel's face is like the sun. The angel's face like the sun is a symbol for the brightness of intuition. Thus the change from a human face to a face that is like the sun, reflects the transition from ordinary human understanding to intuitive understanding. But the angel's face appearing like the sun may also tell us that St. John must wait for a further intuitive realization to solve the problems which are tied to his old religion; as explained before, in my interpretation the sun symbolizes also his old God-concept.

St. John describes the feet of the angel saying that they were like "pillars of fire." Fire appeared at the end of the previous chapter, where it came out of the horses' mouth, and at that time, St. John realized there were already some authentic elements in his spirituality, namely, love and spiritual fervor. The angel's feet of fire suggest that, for St. John, spiritual fervor includes such intuitive clarity as will support his inner journey.

Because the angel is a singular grand mythical image, unlike the locusts and the horsemen who were numerous, St. John feels himself more whole now that he has reached an intuitive stage in the expansion of his awareness.

The angel's book and his right and left foot

"And he had a little book open in his hand" (Rev. 10:2). In the fifth chapter, St. John saw a sealed scroll held by the enthroned. At that time I interpreted the scroll both on the macrocosmic and microcosmic levels. It represented reality itself as well as St. John's consciousness. I assume that this little book is St. John's consciousness only, and because the book is open, St. John feels now that his consciousness is open. Therefore, he is ready to learn new things.

"And he [the angel] set his right foot on the sea and his left foot on the land" (Rev. 10:2). In interpreting this verse, I apply the more common mythical meanings whereby the sea symbolizes the unconscious and the land, conscious awareness.

A deep personal experience, which includes an emotional element, is usually connected to the unconscious, or the mythical sea. Cognition, on the other hand, is part of the conscious mind, or the mythical land. Emotional experience and cognition, however, are intertwined in many ways, and they both have a part in a deep transformation. Perhaps this is why an angel stands both on the sea and on the land connecting them with his body.

In his vision, St. John possibly regards personal experience and the unconscious to be more important than conscious awareness, because the angel places his right foot on the sea. The most common mythical meaning for the right-hand side is the depiction of the more correct, or important, alternative. These meanings are carried also in many languages as homonyms, so that in addition to the right-hand side, right means 'morally correct.'

The importance of the inner deepening

The cry of the angel and the thunder

"And [the angel] cried with a loud voice, as when a lion roars. And when he cried out, seven thunders uttered their voices." (Rev. 10:3.) The mythical images of the previous vision, the lion's teeth and the lion's head, have created an impression that St. John has expected 'the lion principle' eventually to say something. And now St. John indeed hears the lion speak—apparently along with the Om-sound. But then the vision takes a surprising turn.

"Now when the seven thunders uttered their voices, I was about to write; but I heard a voice from heaven saying to me, 'Seal up the things which the seven thunders uttered, and do not write them'" (Rev. 10:4). Why is St. John not allowed to write down what he hears?

Probably the reason is that the angel symbolizes insufficient intuition, as he is shrouded in a cloud. Therefore, regardless of the angel's intuitive quality, the message St. John hears, represents an all too ordinary level of realization. The message is such that St. John could write it down, and so it probably describes relatively conscious thinking. But cognition, although already partly intuitive, is not enough to understand genuine, deeply spiritual life. This requires a personal experience in the highest states of consciousness, that is, in oneness.[3]

The angel, as a symbol for a somewhat lower state of consciousness, can be interpreted also from the basis of the chakra theory. Then it is possible to associate the angel with the ajna chakra, the sixth highest chakra. The angel's face—like the sun—creates an impression of the spherical light of the spiritual eye and thus of ajna chakra. While St. John is climbing the path of the tree of life, again and again, from the base upward, he must at every turn further open each chakra. In this vision his task is to open wider the ajna chakra so that his intuition would be further enlightened. St. John would then have at this time two more steps to climb up the tree of life. First, his life energy would move ever more fully into the ajna chakra, and after that, up to the sahasrara.

When something is sealed up, it cannot be read before the seal has been broken. This means that St. John may think he cannot solve his problems before his present ability to intuit has deepened. Analyzing the seal further, it is an appropriate symbol for ajna chakra which is located in between the eyebrows and seen by the meditator in a deeply withdrawn inward state as the spherical light of the spiritual eye. In our everyday life, while engaged in solving a problem, we often feel that we are concentrating on the spot between the eyebrows. Also, in body-language, concentration is commonly reflected in wrinkling the forehead or the eyebrows. Therefore, to seal up symbolizes, in this connection, concentrating the life force into the ajna chakra, and more generally, deep concentration.

St. John hears the advice to seal something from heaven. This voice is likely to symbolize a higher, more purely superconscious intuition than the angel. St. John follows this intuition and already the latter part of the chapter expresses deep concentration. The clarity following the concentration is then described in the next chapter.

The turn St. John's visions have taken is quite normal in inner transformations, since our ability to intuit is tied to our present state of consciousness. When we move forward on the inner path, new vistas open. Then we realize also our own incompleteness in a new way, and we must often recognize it to be greater than we had imagined.

The prophesy about God's mystery

"And the angel whom I saw standing on the sea and on the land lifted up his hand to heaven and swore by him who lives for ever and ever, who created heaven and the things that are in it, and the earth and the things that are in it, and the sea and the things that are in it, that there should be delay no longer, but in the days of the sounding of the seventh angel, when he is about to sound, the mystery of God would be finished, as he declared to his servants the prophets" (Rev. 10:5–7).

These verses anticipate the culmination of St. John's present transformation process symbolized by the sounding of the trumpets. After St. John has first followed the given advice, deepened his intuition and gained clarity, he will feel relief. When the intuition deepens, the life force will be in the sixth, or ajna chakra. But liberation requires an even deeper state of consciousness than this. According to yoga theory, the life force must move into the highest center, the sahasrara, during the seventh step of the transformation process, and that is when a person experiences the bliss of oneness.

In Revelation, the seventh angel will sound the trumpet at the end of the next, the eleventh, chapter. It is then that St. John lives in a state of oneness more fully, and in that experience he finds a satisfying solution to God's mystery, that is, God's mystery is finished or fulfilled.

The prophesy about the fulfillment of God's mystery is declared by the angel standing on the sea and on the earth, but he motions with his hand toward heaven, and swears by God's name. Perhaps this is to stress the deeper superconscious origin of this anticipating intuition. The angel's words, that there should be no delay, emphasize the fact that God's good tidings will soon be fulfilled and St. John need not wait for this much longer.

Absorbing the teaching

Eating the book

"Then the voice which I heard from heaven spoke to me again and said, 'Go, take the little book which is open in the hand of the angel who stands on the sea and on the earth.' And I went to the angel and said to him, 'Give me the little book.' And he said to me, 'Take and eat it.'" (Rev.10:8–9.)

The most common mythical meaning for eating is the absorption of something. In everyday language, when we do not want to accept or cannot understand a matter without some thought, we say we need to chew on it. As a mythical image, eating can be often interpreted also as internalizing, because while taking in nourishment, the one who eats absorbs the matter more fully, or he internalizes it, becoming at the same time a more inwardly directed person.

Because at the core of a genuine spiritual life there is a personal inner experience, eating is one of the more universally common religious rites. For example, eating is a part of the Christian ritual called Holy Communion, wherein one eats a wafer and drinks wine. A sacred repast was central also in the Mithraic religion which preceded Christianity in the ancient world. In the Mithraic religion, sacred foods were milk, wine, and honey.[4]

That which is eaten expresses what is being absorbed. In St. John's vision, the consumed item, unlike any in the more common religious rites, is a book, which I have interpreted to be St. John's consciousness.[5] Thus eating the book may seem a strange image, but in mythical reality there is nothing strange about eating our own consciousness. In fact, we must do it, should we wish to absorb its contents in an ever-deeper way.

If we identify the open book of this vision with the earlier microcosmic scroll that had its seals opened, it clarifies the events at the end of the chapter, but the identification is not necessary. When the last seal was opened in the beginning of the eighth chapter, the scroll became an open book. After that, St. John, accompanied by the sounding of the trumpets, read the same book over. At every trumpet call, he has had to understand more of the matters left in the unconscious, or hidden in the book. The open book expresses all that process of expanding awareness and transformation that St. John has been through since the beginning of the eighth chapter. When St. John is counseled to eat the book, he is being asked to internalize what he has learned in an ever-deeper way.

While assimilating anything thoroughly, one must concentrate on it in a deeply withdrawn state. We can understand the symbolism of Revelation in such a way that both sealing something up and eating a book actually signify the same thing—deep assimilation. While eating the book, St. John thus follows the advice to seal up what he has heard earlier.

The bitterness and the sweetness

"And he [the angel] said to me... 'It will make your stomach bitter, but it will be as sweet as honey in your mouth.' And I took the little book out of the angel's hand and ate it, and it was as sweet as honey in my mouth. But when I had eaten it, my stomach became bitter." (Rev. 10:9–10.) Based on what I have said of the book above, I suggest only one interpretation to the sweetness and the bitterness of it, although it is possible to see this in other ways, as well.

The sweetness of honey which St. John tastes in his mouth, is the after-effect of the experience in quietude that he lived through in the beginning of the eighth chapter (Rev. 8:1). Probably St. John feels great happiness that he has experienced a new, higher state of consciousness—quietude and oneness—and that such a state would even be possible for a human being. The sweetness of that state lingers, when he remembers it, like honey, and when he does taste it again, he assimilates the experience in quietude more deeply.

Because of its sweetness and because it is collected by the bee, which is a flying insect, honey is in different mythologies associated with high spiritual experiences. Earlier I mentioned the Mithraic religion, where honey along with wine and milk was a sacred food, but honey as a symbol for spiritual values appears also in Indian literature. There, according to a popular metaphor, the human consciousness is like the bee, which quietly drinks the sweetness of honey from the flower.[6]

The bitterness in St. John's stomach reflects his memory of the anxiety caused by his broadening awareness and by the transformation he endured after his experience of quietude. In his visions this stressful stage was depicted variously as hail, as the falling of a mountain and a star, and as locusts and horsemen. That anxiety still comes through as bitter while St. John continues to digest his book or consciousness.

While St. John eats the book, that is, while he assimilates what he has learned, he is building a foundation for the climax of the processes of transformation and consciousness expansion. Only a personal inner experience can bring about a deep transformation. Thus Revelation crystallizes yet another universal and essential stage of the human transformation process—internalization—in a fitting mythical image of eating a book.

The prophesying

"And he said to me, 'You must prophesy again about many peoples, nations, tongues, and kings'" (Rev. 10:11). Having eaten the book, St. John is ready to continue his introspection.

11. THE MEASURING OF THE TEMPLE, THE TWO WITNESSES, AND THE ARK OF THE COVENANT

The advice to differentiate

"Then I was given a reed like a measuring rod. And the angel stood saying, 'Rise and measure the temple of God, the altar and those who worship there. But leave out the court which is outside the temple, and do not measure it, for it has been given to the Gentiles.'" (Rev. 11:1–2.) Measuring symbolizes differentiation and examination. Thus St. John must continue to analyze his religion, because he has not solved all the problems in it.

The different parts of the temple mentioned in the verse symbolize the different sides of St. John's spirituality. The courtyard depicts the external aspect of a religion and the temple and the altar the inward aspect. The temples of the Jews—for example, the tabernacle and the temple of Solomon—had one or more courtyards, which the visitor had to pass through in order to enter the temple.

Interpreting the verse in this way, we can see that the courtyard is associated with an earlier mythical image that appeared in Revelation, the sun, which has represented St. John's old God-concept. The courtyard and the sun relate to each other also in the sense that the courtyard of the Jewish temple actually was an open-air space. A courtyard, however, expresses a milder estrangement than did the sun because it is located next to the temple rather than far away in the sky. Therefore, the courtyard has the capacity to symbolize the way St. John has in his life manifested the spirituality represented by the sun; for example, he must have sincerely tried to follow all the rules regarding right and wrong taught by his religion.

But the vision specifically says that the courtyard has been given to the Gentiles. In this way, St. John is being cautioned about spirituality that is too externalized. And because St. John need not measure the courtyard, he need no longer focus on the problems of his old religion. Instead, he is to understand better the new spirituality, which is more inward and is depicted in the vision by the temple, the altar, and those worshiping there. It is these, therefore, that St. John must measure.

The temple, as an expression of the new spirituality, symbolizes the way in which St. John has strived to establish in his life the religion of love, although he has not been able to do so in full, personal measure. This interpretation is based on the observation that compared to the altar and the holy of the holies, the temple itself is an outer structure. It is the altar and the holy of the holies as parts of the temple that symbolize the personal experience of love. The symbolism of the temple is similar to that of the moon, although the alienation reflected by the temple is not as pronounced as that of the moon. The temple and the moon are akin also in the sense that the temple of the Jews actually was dimly lit.

The altar, which is central in the temple, symbolizes universal love. Theoretically, the altar is thus the subjective side of the universal Self, whereas those who worship by it represent the level of individual Self.

So far, St. John has experienced only a glimpse of universal love, and therefore, he has not yet realized the universal Self in himself. But he must strive for this, and the first step toward the change is to understand in what way love is the central content of religion. That is why St. John is advised to measure the temple, the altar, and those worshiping there. The analysis and understanding of these matters will then lead him to an inner transformation. By the end of this chapter, St. John will see the temple open so that the holy of the holies is revealed. (More accurately, he sees the arc of the covenant, which was kept in the holy of holies.) According to my interpretation, St. John then personally experiences love and bliss ever more deeply.

The opening verses of the chapter can be interpreted also in a general way. Change is often initiated by some realization, "What I have understood so far is superficial, as if I had merely entered the courtyard. I must move onward through it to examine my own consciousness and the deeper levels of existence. To understand them is the foundation for experiencing them in a personal way."

Cognitive awareness and personal experience

The witnesses

"And I will give power to my two witnesses, and they will prophesy" (Rev. 11:3). The witnesses can be seen as a new link in the chain of mythical images St. John has created as the visions have evolved, although their connection to the earlier images is not obvious.

The mouth is emphasized in the witnesses' forms as was those of the locusts, horses, and the mighty angel. The witnesses speak, and later St. John notes that fire proceeds from their mouths (Rev. 11:5). When the witnesses witness or preach and speak, they finally disclose what St. John has in his previous visions tried to become aware of. The fire proceeding out of the mouths of the witnesses is like spiritual fervor: it reveals secrets and inspires change. In contrast, the cry of the angel in the previous vision represented a realization which was still too superficial.

The two witnesses are like the two feet of the angel, which St. John talked about in the previous vision. At that time, one of the angel's feet was on the earth and the other on the sea, emphasizing that the transformation must involve both cognition and personal experience. I believe that the witnesses symbolize both the cognitive awareness and the personal spiritual experience and that there are two of them to stress this twofold nature of the inner transformation.

That there are two witnesses also symbolizes the conflict associated with the number two. Thus, St. John's inner life is at the present time in a state of conflict. More than that, he has reached an impasse. As long as he is not consciously able to solve his spiritual problems, he cannot continue his spiritual transformation on the level of personal experience. But as long as he does not *live* his spirituality, in other words, experience the deepest states of consciousness, he is unable to perceive authentic solutions to his problems.

We could say the vision about the witnesses tells us what St. John discovers while measuring the temple, the altar, and those who worship, and that the measuring leads him to a growing awareness and spiritual transformation.

The sackcloth

"And I will give power to my two witnesses, and they will prophesy... clothed in sackcloth" (Rev. 11:3). The sackcloth-metaphor appeared already in the sixth chapter, where "the sun became black as sackcloth made of hair" (Rev. 6:12). Since in the era during which Revelation was written, it was customary to wear sackcloth when one was grieving, repenting or seeking healing, so the witnesses wearing sackcloth suggests that St. John grieves over his own insufficiencies.[1] He realizes that he needs improvement.

The olive trees and the lampstands

"These [witnesses] are the two olive trees and the two lampstands standing before the God of the earth" (Rev. 11:4). The oil from the fruits of the olive tree symbolizes in these interpretations human being's core-essence, love.[2] But in the tree itself the oil is only latent, and therefore, the olive tree represents only a person's potential ability to open up to spiritual love. The lampstands are still unlit. As explained earlier, the lampstands are like chakras which have not yet fully opened, or 'lit up.'[3] The lampstands illustrate insufficient awareness, because we cannot see with the help of the lampstands alone. As mythical images, the olive tree and the lampstand thus emphasize St. John's present inadequacy both on the level of spiritual experience and cognition, yet they acknowledge the potential for growth.

The life of the witnesses

The different stages of the witnesses' life, which form the central content of this vision, tell us how St. John continues to grow. In the mythical images of the vision, St. John's cognitive and spiritual changes are interlinked, as it were, and that is why I interpret the same images to depict both cognition and spiritual transformation. Cognition supports spiritual transformation and vice versa. This mutual support enables St. John gradually to open the deadbolt of insufficient awareness and inadequate spiritual experience that have restrained him.

The life of the witnesses can be organized in a following way: First, *the witnesses testify.* Then, *they are killed* and *people will see their dead bodies.* Finally, the witnesses *are resurrected and ascend to heaven.* I interpret these different stages first as general mythical images and then consider theoretically what exactly St. John will realize and come to experience through them.

The witnesses testify

"And if anyone wants to harm them, fire proceeds from their mouth and devours their enemies. And if anyone wants to harm them, he must be killed in this manner." (Rev. 11:5.) Because the witnesses symbolize St. John's potential for growth, their enemies are such qualities as would hinder his inner growth. These qualities are, for example, self-importance, fear, hesitancy, and complacency. But St. John has already been through so much inner preparation that his transformation cannot be prevented. The enemies are killed, and as they die, St. John's ego further dies. Because the enemies are killed specifically with fire, it is his spiritual fervor, wisdom, and love which destroy the threatening qualities or faults.

"These have power to shut heaven, so that no rain falls in the days of their prophesy" (Rev. 11:6). As a mythical image, a drought is an emotional and spiritual dry spell; even in colloquial language, we commonly relate to something dull and lacking in feeling as 'dry.' Because St. John speaks expressly of the ceasing of the rain, he apparently feels that divine grace has come to an end in his life. This is a natural reaction, because the witnesses' testifying symbolizes a discriminating attitude. Often analytical thinking leads to one's consciousness feeling barren since it interrupts the simple devotion requisite for personal spiritual experience. But inner dryness may also be a result of some subconscious problem which inhibits us from yielding to a sense of wholeness; this, too, applies to St. John's situation, because he has not been able to solve all his subconscious problems.

"And they have power over waters to turn them to blood" (Rev. 11:6). The time spent in prophesying by the witnesses is, in real life, a long period of transformation. Along with dry spells, this period includes feelings of liberation and joy. Expressed theoretically the transformation St. John is undergoing means that his sense of Self is strengthening. When the ego dies, the Self is liberated, and it is this strengthening of the Self, or the core-being, that 'the waters turning to blood' symbolizes. Water becoming blood is a miracle similar to the changing water to wine performed by Jesus at the wedding in Cana; both blood and wine are a core-extract.[4]

"And they [the witnesses] have power... to strike the earth with all plagues, as often as they desire" (Rev. 11:6). The words tell us St. John finds the transformation so difficult that it is like a plague.

The witnesses are killed

"Now when they finished their testimony, the beast that ascends out of the bottomless pit will make war against them, overcome them, and kill them" (Rev. 11:7).

A beast is any content of his consciousness that St. John had earlier repressed. When he repressed it, he figuratively pushed it out of his immediate reach and into his subconscious. That repressed material continues to bother St. John to the point that it takes on the image of a beast. Now, however, regardless of everything, it ascends from the depths, that is, St. John becomes aware of it and experiences it openly. Because it is not easy to grow aware of that which has been repressed and to administer to it, the change is recounted as warfare. St. John feels that a war is being waged in him. He would rather not know about his difficulty nor deal with it, but he is not able to ignore it either, and so the beast wins, and St. John's transformation goes on.

A more obvious interpretation for the beast is to associate him with the problem of evil that has engaged St. John. He has been wondering, "How is it possible that an omnipotent, good and just God allows evil and wrong?" He has admitted already in the sixth chapter that the problem exists, but has not found a satisfactory answer for it. Interpreting the verse in this way, the ascent of the beast from the bottomless pit denotes a new step in solving the problem of evil.

To understand St. John's new realization, I want to remind the reader of the quietude in heaven, which was described in the beginning of the eighth chapter. The silence in heaven was interpreted to be an experience in oneness, wherein St. John experienced everything that exists as one whole. To continue this interpretation, I assume that St. John thinks of that oneness or wholeness as God. Then evil is undeniably part of God *in some way*: God has his 'beastly' side. I suggest that this realization is the beast ascending from the depths and killing the witnesses. As the witnesses die by the force of his realization, St. John changes.

In addition to the cognitive realization, the beast can be interpreted on the level of personal experience. Then it symbolizes the feelings connected to the problem of evil in St. John's mind. The conflict between a good God and evil must have created much anguish in him, as an unresolved conflict would. He has, perhaps, felt an outright rage and a desire to retaliate for all the deplorable unfairness in the world. But he has repressed all these feelings as too negative and difficult, and so they have grown to become a beast shackled in the bottomless pit. When that beast now comes up, St. John experiences openly his own difficult 'beastly' feelings, and then his old way of experiencing feelings, symbolized by the witnesses, disappears, or dies.

This idea in Revelation can be seen as an example of the universal mythical subject, where the beast, or more generally, some evil being, kills what is good. For example, in the Egyptian mythology, the evil Set kills the good Osiris, and in the Bible, Cain kills Abel.[5] These myths can be interpreted on the individual level so that the good and the evil express the different sides of the same person. We identify easily with our 'good' aspects and repress that which we regard as bad in ourselves. If the repressed material, however, is brought to awareness and dealt with, we change, and the overtly one-sided, conceited sense of I disappears, or dies.

There are excellent parallels for the beast of this vision in the more theoretical literature. For instance, Rudolf Steiner crystallized this kind of teaching into a figure of "a guardian of a threshold," which referred to that part of our being which we are not aware of. According to Steiner, facing the guardian is an important and necessary step on the spiritual path. He explained also, that we can perceive the guardian intuitively and that it is "a frightening, nearly terrifying being." C.G. Jung called the dream image summarizing all that which we are not aware of in ourselves, "the shadow." The shadow is a good expression, as the unrecognized parts of our consciousness follow us as persistently and are often as overlooked as our shadow.[6]

In our lives as modern men and women, these mythical images—the beast that ascends from the depths, the guardian of a threshold, and the shadow—can be any repressions which are difficult for us to become aware of and to experience openly.

People see the witnesses' dead bodies

"And their dead bodies will lie in the street of the great city which spiritually is called Sodom and Egypt... Then those from the peoples, tribes, tongues and nations will see their dead bodies... and not allow their dead bodies to be put into graves." (Rev. 11:8–9.)

That people see the dead bodies of the witnesses means St. John is seeing or becoming aware of the immaturity symbolized by the witnesses. That people do not allow the bodies to be put into graves means St. John is no longer willing to deny his deficiencies or to repress them underground into the subconscious.

The city as a mythical image symbolizes human consciousness, and that which exists in the city represents the contents of consciousness. Often a city depicts our general state of consciousness, not unlike the realistic cities where we perceive a general characteristic atmosphere. The cities of Sodom and Egypt mentioned in the vision thus reveal to us something of St. John's feelings after the witnesses have been killed.

In the Bible, the city of Sodom is known for its sins, implying that St. John feels he has previously lived practically in sin.[7] But even as Sodom as a city was destroyed, so, too, St. John's 'sinfulness,' or immaturity, has now been killed. However, Sodom was perhaps chosen for the mythical image in St. John's vision for the reason that, while a transformation culminates the process and the person involved in it is finally able to admit his mistakes, he tends to judge himself too harshly.

Egypt symbolizes alienation and bondage, because there the Israelites were in slavery under alien rulers. Therefore, using Egypt as a mythical image, St. John feels that his old spirituality alienated him from God; genuine spirituality had been under slavery, as it were. Perhaps St. John here, too, exaggerates his own inadequacy, because Israelite's slavery in Egypt takes place in the early pages of the Bible. Another possibility is that St. John makes use of Egypt in a more general sense to describe an early stage of spiritual exile. When the witnesses are said to die in the city of Egypt, St. John is beginning to be freed from his old views and so is ready to move to a place higher than Egypt.

"And those who dwell on the earth will rejoice over them, make merry, and send gifts to one another, because these two prophets tormented those who dwell on the earth" (Rev. 11:10). During their lives the witnesses tormented those living on earth meaning St. John suffered in trying to admit his deficiencies and conflicts. When he finally succeeded, that is, when the beast killed the witnesses, he feels relief and so people rejoice. St. John begins to see things differently. That is why people living on earth give gifts to each other symbolizing those new realizations brought by a new sense of freedom.

The witnesses are resurrected and they ascend into heaven

"Now... the breath of life from God entered them, and they stood on their feet... and they heard a loud voice from heaven saying to them, 'Come up here.' And they ascended to heaven in a cloud." (Rev. 11:11–12.)

Although the death of the witnesses as an experience has been difficult for St. John, it means liberation. When his repressions are admitted to and lived through, as it were, energy is not spent restraining them but instead can be directed toward growth. The resurrection of the witnesses and their ascent to heaven depicts this kind of inner growth. The process by which St. John comes to realize his problems is an intuitive one that is increasingly controlled by his superconsciousness. The witnesses now symbolize his spiritual experiences wherein the heavenly levels or superconsciousness is prominent. But St. John's transformation is not complete: the witnesses ascend to heaven in a cloud, and a cloud is like a veil. (The mighty angel of the previous chapter was, similarly, shrouded in a cloud.) In effect, St. John does not yet see clearly nor live completely openly.

Death and resurrection present central subjects for different mythologies. For example, in an ancient Egyptian myth, Osiris, who had been killed by Set, was resurrected by Isis. In ancient Greece as part of the Eleusinian mysteries, there is a myth about Kore, who descends into Hades, but is allowed every spring to rise as high as the Olympus, the abode of the gods. On a more immediate and popular level, both myths reflect the seasonal cycles, the dying of the plants and their renewal, but they were also part of religious mysteries and thus illustrate spiritual transformation.[8]

"Now... they [the witnesses] stood on their feet, and great fear fell on those who saw them... and they ascended to heaven... and their enemies saw them" (Rev. 11:11–12). When people see the resurrection of the witnesses, it means that St. John is observing (through introspection) what is happening to him. Being overcome by fear is a likely result of a strong inner transformation although it is also deeply gratifying to anyone who experiences it. St. John perhaps mentions the witnesses' enemies because a deep transformation easily activates our stagnant sides. During the transformation, we are sensitive to the stress created by the conflict between the old and the new, and thus we resist the change.

The problem of evil, Jesus' fate, and two systems of ethics

The witnesses and Jesus' fate

The vision of the two witnesses by St. John follows closely the events of Jesus' life. Jesus was killed, he was dead for three days, was resurrected and ascended to heaven. The witnesses are killed, they are dead for three and a half days, are resurrected and ascend to heaven. Revelation explains also that the great city, Sodom, and Egypt, where the witnesses' bodies lay about in the street, was the city, "where also our Lord was crucified" (Rev. 11:8).

I understand the analogy to mean that for the author of Revelation the problem of evil was particularly burning in the case of Jesus' death. God's goodness, omnipotence and righteousness, on the one hand, and the cruelty and injustice of Jesus' death, on the other, seem to conflict most incongruously. Why was Jesus, who was so completely good, killed? Why did not a good, all powerful and just God prevent it? If Jesus, by his death, can be said to have saved people from eternal damnation, could not an almighty and good God save people in some other way than by demanding Jesus' death?

Biblical research has pointed out the fact that there were different notions about the meaning of Jesus' death during the time the New Testament was written down.[9] Therefore, it would be natural to assume that St. John also pondered these problems in the mythical language of his vision. C.G. Jung of our own times spoke of Jesus' enigmatic death poignantly:

Who is this father who would rather slaughter his son than forgive his imperfect... creations? What does this cruel and primitive sacrifice of the son attempt to reveal? God's love?

It is an unexpected shock, when this highest Goodness will deliver his mercy only after having received his own son as a sacrifice... What blindness not to notice the garish light this leaves God in! And how conceited seems the talk about him as love and the highest good.[10]

I feel St. John finds the answer to this kind of problem in the events of his vision, and I will relate it by interpreting Jesus' death with the help of two different theoretical ideas, the ethics of justice and the ethics of love.

Central to the ethics of justice is the logic of the act being followed by a reward or punishment: an act must have just consequences. Should this logic be applied to religion without further consideration, God appears as a righteous God of judgment. Once people sin, the God of judgment will demand punishment, or in other words, he exacts settlements for sins. In this thinking Jesus' death is experienced as a redemption for sins with the idea of suffering as the means of atonement. The problem in Jesus' case regarding a strict demand for righteousness is that he has done no wrong but is merely a substitute—he suffers in atonement for others. Yet, despite this fact, a God of judgment stands behind Jesus' death for He demands punishment for sins.

When the beast kills the witnesses, St. John seems to be thinking: "If God demands punishment for people, he is nothing more than a righteous God of judgment, and if he asks for the sacrificial death of Jesus, who is fully innocent, before he would consider human sins redeemed, he is a beast after all." If we think of such a realization as the beast ascending from the bottomless pit, it should be easy to understand why St. John had repressed it into the subconscious, and that now having ascended, it transforms him dramatically. In the final account, this realization requires that we question the reality of this righteous God of judgment and reconsider our idea of God.

The essence of the ethics of love is simply the call to love. And to be able to live out an ever deeper and more universal love we must change inwardly. Within the ethics of love Jesus' death and resurrection can be seen as general mythical images of an inner transformation. We must voluntarily surrender to the death of the ego in order to be resurrected as the Self. It is possible to see Jesus' death as a mythical image for atonement and redemption also within the ethics of love, but in this case the terms refer to the inner transformation and liberation we experience when the "old I" in us dies. Love will overtake us, and love will wipe away all that is flawed. When the death of the ego and the resurrection of the Self continues, we will finally experience love as immeasurable bliss. In this ecstasy, we will know God, for God is bliss. (I emphasize again that examining the subject matter through mythical images does not exclude other dimensions.)

This kind of explanation for Jesus' death based on the ethics of love can be seen in the mythical images of Revelation, as St. John experiences a deep inner transformation during the death and resurrection of the witnesses. At the same time he, perhaps, comes to see Jesus' death in a new way, and is relieved from the anguish brought about by the seeming unfairness of that death and by his consequent repression of the whole problem. Possibly he feels now that Jesus surrendered to death in order to guide men to a new, deeply spiritual path—away from the bondage to the ego and toward resurrection of the Self—and that everyone ought to follow this path. Later in Christian history, Meister Eckhart expressed this thought in saying that Jesus died so that I would die to the world, and similarly Mother Teresa of Calcutta taught us that it is only by dying with Jesus that we can rise with him.[11] Perhaps St. John feels also that Jesus' death and resurrection, considered as mysteries of religion, emphasize the metaphysical and universal truth of the ego's death and the resurrection of the Self.

The courtyard and the temple

The two different systems of ethics outlined above will also help to define as mythical images the courtyard and the temple seen in the opening verses of the vision. The courtyard can be interpreted as a phase of the ethics of justice in one's spiritual evolution. When individuals come to understand the requirements of righteousness, they will follow human moral laws and will be considerate of others in their actions. They will go beyond the boundaries of narrow egoism, and perhaps, will act with the good of the community in mind. If they are religiously inclined, their God-concept is based on the ethics of justice and defined in terms of the moral laws. The stereotypically interpreted

Old Testament religion, where the commandments and laws were central, is one such religion. From a more general perspective, the ethics of justice belongs to that frame of reference which we use in our ordinary conscious thinking; the idea of sin and redeeming punishment compares well to the principle of cause and effect.

Conforming to righteousness is a necessary and valuable stage in ethical development, but in a deeper spiritual sense, righteousness alone is not enough. Devoid of a living, personal experience of love, the aspirant has not reached a genuine, deeply spiritual life, but has, as it were, stayed in the courtyard without entering the temple itself. Especially in religion, remaining in the courtyard reflects immaturity, because at its extreme it means nothing but a belief in a righteous God of judgment external to human beings. Therefore, the courtyard in St. John's vision has been given to the Gentiles and need not be measured.

The temple symbolizes the ethics of love considered abstractly, whereas the altar and those who worship by it symbolize personal experiences in varying degrees. And when St. John in the beginning of the vision is urged to measure these parts of the temple symbolizing love, it carries an important message. St. John is counseled to understand the meaning of love in spiritual life so deeply that he would no longer feel obligated to see Jesus' death in the light of his old religion —as a matter of sin and redeeming punishment—but would realize it from the basis of ethics of love, and would, in the end, experience spiritual love in himself.

These realizations already liberate St. John regardless of his not having been able to solve the problem of evil completely, and this sense of freedom releases an ever-deeper change in him.

The inner transformation

The earthquake and the death of the people

"In the same hour [as the witnesses were ascending to heaven] there was a great earthquake, and a tenth of the city fell. In the earthquake seven thousand men were killed." (Rev. 11:13.) The transformation St. John has experienced has been so agitating he is inwardly shaken. His previous state of consciousness symbolized by the city is partly destroyed; the number "a tenth" in the verse expresses agony.[12]

The dying of people means, once more, the dying or diminishing of St. John's ego, which happens as he experiences the inner earthquake. This is the third time people die while the trumpets are sounding. I interpret this to bring to conclusion the three-part transformation process, where twice earlier a third of the different creatures were killed (Rev. 8:9,11 and 9:18). Now the number of the people being killed, "seven thousand," tells us that the transformation process symbolized by the sounding of the trumpets from the seven angels is coming to a close, and soon the last, or the seventh angel, indeed will sound his trumpet.

"And the rest were afraid and gave glory to the God of heaven" (Rev. 11:13). Although St. John's ego has not completely died, he is beginning to understand how deep and immense the spiritual life is. He knows that on the spiritual path men and women must transform themselves entirely; they must abandon their ego-desires and give glory to God.

The woe-cry and the sounding of the seventh trumpet

"The second woe is past. Behold, the third woe is coming quickly. Then the seventh angel sounded." (Rev. 11:14–15.) The first woe-cry was presented just before the sounding of the trumpet by the sixth angel (Rev. 9:12), and this second woe is similarly presented just before a trumpet blow, the seventh one. After the seventh sounding of the trumpet, poetic praise follows, reflecting St. John's sense of relief. The last verse describes the climax of St. John's present transformation.

The ark of the covenant

The last verse begins with the words, "Then the temple of God was opened in heaven, and the ark of his covenant was seen in his temple" (Rev.11:19). We have come to the seventh step on St. John's spiral pathway. Thus we might expect the verse to describe St. John experiencing an ever higher, more completely transformed state of consciousness. Such an interpretation is indeed appropriate. Heaven denotes here as before the superconscious, and the temple in heaven is the internalized, holy level of the superconscious. By including the ark

—the sacred chest—in the temple, the verse pictures an even holier, deeper level of the superconscious than that symbolized by the temple. The inner structure of the soul is described in a similar way in Christian literature. For example, St. John of the Cross explains that the soul has several centers, one inside the other, as it were, the innermost one being the most holy.[13] The ark of the covenant as a mythical image will tell us more precisely what St. John's state of consciousness is now like.

The actual historical ark was a chest where the tablets of the Law were stored. The ark was gilded both inside and outside. God promised Moses that He would appear to Moses when he would sit on the cover of the ark, "the mercy seat." Later, according to the Bible, God was actually heard speaking to Moses from the mercy seat.[14] During the Exodus of the Jews, the ark of the covenant was the most important object in the tabernacle, and it was kept in the holy of the holies. After the Exodus, the ark was finally placed in the most sacred, innermost room of the temple built by Solomon on Mount Zion in Jerusalem. However, the temple was destroyed long before the time of the New Testament, and it is not known what became of the ark.[15]

The ark of the covenant symbolizes the union between God and humankind. This union was discussed briefly in the tenth chapter in connection with the rainbow, because the rainbow was the first symbol for the covenant between God and humankind. I assume that Revelation speaks—as is found in other sections of the New Testament—of the covenant as the promise that men and women will eventually learn to know God personally.

When St. John uses the ark of the covenant rather than the rainbow as the symbol for the union, he feels he is approaching the fulfillment of the promise, as if he were already visiting the holy city on Mount Zion. However, because the ark of the covenant is an image carried over from the Old Testament, and because it was lost during the destruction of Solomon's temple, the union has not been fully accomplished nor is it yet permanent. For these reasons, I suggest that the ark of the covenant symbolizes a transient state of consciousness, wherein a woman or a man personally experiences divinity.[16]

A similar interpretation of the ark of the covenant can be reached by analyzing it as an object. A chest is like the human consciousness, and the contents of the chest are like the contents of the consciousness, or that which is experienced. Because the ark of the covenant was a sacred golden object, it symbolizes the most valuable, holy level of consciousness. On this level we experience spiritual bliss, love, oneness and divinity. Christianity often refers to these high states as union, because the soul and God are said to unite when the soul experiences spiritual bliss. In this symbolism, the soul is seen as feminine and like a bride. In the union she receives God who is like the bridegroom, and as such is seen as the masculine principle. This can be understood as a kind of a sexual analogy and a similar analogy can be derived from the ark of the covenant as well. The chest is a container and thus the feminine aspect, and the content of the chest is the masculine aspect. It was the Law given by God that was kept in the ark, and therefore these commandments can probably be taken to symbolize Him in a general sense.

In this light, the union between God and us is fulfilled in the state of consciousness symbolized by the ark of the covenant. When we experience ecstasy, we get to know God personally as the God described by the ethics of love and the New Testament. The soul and God unite in the state of bliss, and this, according to the Christian mystics, eventually leads to a marriage, a permanent bliss. Thus the union between God and the human soul culminates in a spiritual marriage.

Along with union, we can find in the literature many other expressions for the states of spiritual bliss. Within Western philosophy Spinoza spoke about "the intellectual love for God," and such expressions as *samadhi* and "an experience in cosmic consciousness" are common in the Eastern texts.[17]

In Christian literature, St. Bonaventure, in his book *The Soul's Journey into God,* speaks of the ark of the covenant in terms of symbolism similar to that described above. Bonaventure describes six different steps in meditation or prayer which lead to a mystical ecstasy of the soul, and he compares these steps to a journey into the holy of the holies. According to Bonaventure, in the early stages of the meditation practice, the aspirant stays in the temple courtyard, as it were. Then he moves into the temple itself, and eventually enters the holy of the holies, where he sees the ark of the covenant with its mercy seat. At this stage the prayer already means inner illumination of the soul, but after that there is yet to come the full, mystical ecstasy. For Bonaventure, ecstasy means final union with God, and is the last, or the seventh step on the journey of the soul.[18]

St. John of the Cross, also, speaks metaphorically much in the same vein as Revelation while quoting the prophet Jonah, "You have cast me out of Your sight, but I will see Your holy temple yet," and he interprets the words to mean that seeing God's temple is a blissful experience, one of "enjoying sweet contemplation." At another time, St. John of the Cross interprets the ark of the covenant itself to mean that the soul is striving for spiritual perfection.[19]

Although St. John the Divine describes his experience simply as one of having seen the ark, I will now suggest a few parallels from literature that are similar to my interpretation. I have chosen such examples as will help clarify St. John's progress as revealed in my interpretation and the consequences that the seeing of the ark has for him. St. John describes these consequences in the following chapter, and I will return at that time to the examples presented here.

The first example comes from St. Teresa of Avila. She compares the stage when the soul first begins to experience spiritual bliss to wedding preparations. According to St. Teresa, in the first union between the soul and God, the soul-bride and the God-bridegroom meet each other "face to face." After this comes the engagement and finally the marriage. Applying St. Teresa's symbolism to Revelation, seeing the ark depicts those first meetings between God and the soul which are only brief face-to-face moments. In Revelation, also, the mythical wedding comes later. In the words of St. Teresa:

> For the brief moment [the union] lasts, the soul, indeed, is without her senses, as it were, so that she cannot think if she wanted to... In a word, she is completely dead to the world to live more fully in God... I know not whether there is even enough life left in the body to breath... God itself so overwhelms the soul that when she returns to her senses she cannot doubt she has been in God and God in her.[20]

> His majesty is pleased with the soul and it is His gracious wish to have her know Him ever more closely, and He will arrange for them to meet face to face...We can say it happens in this way as it lasts only a moment. Then... the soul sees secretly who this Bridegroom, whom she will accept, is. She could not in a thousand years comprehend with her senses and abilities

what she now grasps in a single moment... After this one moment alone, the soul is more worthy to be given [to God].[21]

The next example comes from the Indian Paramahansa Yogananda. In it, he gives an account of his first experience in cosmic consciousness:

The soul and mind instantly lost their physical bondage... The flesh was as though dead; yet on my intense awareness I knew that never before had I been fully alive. My sense of identity was no longer narrowly confined to a body but embraced the circumambient atoms... My ordinary frontal vision was now changed to a vast spherical sight... An oceanic joy broke upon endless shores of my soul. The spirit of God, I realized, is exhaustless Bliss; His body is countless tissues of light... The entire cosmos, gently luminous, like a city seen afar at night, glimmered within the infinitude of my being... Blissful *amrita*, nectar of immortality, pulsated through me with a quicksilver like fluidity...

Suddenly the breath returned to my lungs. With a disappointment almost unbearable, I realized that my infinite immensity was lost... Like a prodigal child, I had run away from my macrocosmic home and had imprisoned myself in a narrow microcosm.[22]

The European Paul Brunton describes his first experience in superconscious bliss in a following way:

The waves of thought naturally begin to diminish. The workings of logical rational sense drop towards zero point... The reports of my bodily senses are no longer heard, felt, remembered...

Finally it happens... The brain has passed into a state of complete suspension, as it does in deep sleep, yet there is not the slightest loss of consciousness... My sense of awareness has been drawn out of the narrow confines of the separate personality; it has turned into something sublimely all-embracing. Self still exists, but it is a changed, radiant self. For something that *was* I, some deeper, diviner being rises into consciousness and *becomes* me. With it arrives an amazing new sense of absolute freedom, for thought is like a loom-shuttle, which is always going to and fro, and to be free from its tyrannical motion is to step out of the prison into the open air...

I have attained a divine liberty and an almost indescribable felicity. My arms embrace all creation with profound sympathy, for I understand in the deepest possible way that to know all is not merely to pardon all, but to love all. My heart is remolded in rapture.[23]

The last example is an experience, which I know. In this account, the feelings following immediately after the blissful state help to understand the progression of the vision by St. John. I will return to the dream, which was part of this experience, later on in chapter twenty one:

In the night, I am awakened from a dream to a feeling of indescribable happiness. I give in to this feeling, and it begins to grow more intense. In the end my normal, everyday consciousness disappears completely, I experience infinite bliss, which is absolute reality as well. It is as if I myself were this bliss and reality. The usual me is gone. There is only unbroken oneness.

Although years have passed since, I continue to feel that this experience is a deeply satisfying answer to all my inquiries about the ultimate nature of existence. Even so, immediately after the experience, having returned to my usual state of consciousness, I felt, for a time, nearly unbearable pain and disappointment regarding my return; the normal state of consciousness seemed a state of suffering compared to the bliss I had lived. Yet, in an instant, I realized my life to be as happy as a human life could reasonably expect to be. The trouble is that the entire normal, everyday existence has such duality and separateness woven into it that the sense of oneness and bliss is inevitably destroyed. I saw or rather lived out all this as an unquestionably clear, immense, intuitive vision.

Lightnings, voices, an earthquake, and hail

"And there were lightnings, voices, thunderings, an earthquake, and great hail" (Rev. 11:19). Lightnings, voices, and thundering, can be interpreted as usual to be the lights and sounds seen and heard in a deep, altered state of consciousness, or while one is returning from the deepest state. The earthquake and the hail have also appeared earlier in Revelation. This extremely powerful superconscious experience shocks St. John, and he feels himself to be pelted by hail, or in the midst of an overwhelming purification.[24]

The numbers

St. John is told in the second verse of this vision, "And they will tread the holy city underfoot for forty-two months" (Rev. 11:2). After this the vision continues with the words, "and I will give power to my two witnesses, and they will prophesy one thousand two hundred and sixty days" (Rev. 11:3). Later the bodies of the witnesses are said to lay about dead for three and a half days before the resurrection (Rev. 11:9 and 11:11). All these numbers return to the configuration of three and a half. Forty two months is three and a half years, and if we round the month to be thirty days, then one thousand two hundred sixty days adds up to three and a half years.

Figures which can be converted to three and a half appear again in the next two visions by St. John (Rev. 12:6, 12:14, 13:5). Chapters 11, 12, and 13 form a unit in their subject matter, as all of them concern the problem of evil, or the mythical beasts. Nevertheless, I have placed the eleventh chapter into the part titled *The Insufficiency of the Old Religion* because I organized the material in conformance to the different trumpet blares. I have placed the next two chapters, which form the latter part of the unit, under a separate section of its own.

I interpret "three and a half" as half of the number seven. We are concerned with a transformation process consisting of two phases. This division can be interpreted so that in the first phase, that is, in chapter eleven, St. John begins to tackle the problem of evil when the beast ascends from the bottomless pit, but he does not yet find a complete answer to the general problem of evil. His realizations will unfold only later as a result of an experience in superconscious bliss, symbolized by his seeing the ark of the covenant. In chapters twelve and thirteen, St. John then defines the answers by describing the different beasts. In this context dividing a unit into two parts is also symbolic of the conflict St. John is confronting: the omnipotent, benign God is like the thesis, and the existence of evil the antithesis.

To sum up, all numbers in chapter eleven reverting to three and a half refer to the early part of the same transformation process, although to its different aspects and stages. When the Gentiles are said to tread the holy city underfoot for three and a half years, St. John understands he will have to suffer for his old insufficient spirituality till he finds answers to his problems. When the witnesses prophesy for three and a half years, St. John is becoming aware of his problems, and when the bodies of the witnesses lie about for three and a half days, he sees clearly what his problems are, but does not yet know how to solve them. In this connection, it is easier to relate to the flow of events by counting time in days. Also, defining the length of time in this way recalls the three days which passed before the resurrection of Lord Jesus Christ.

III

SPIRITUAL REBIRTH AND THE PROBLEM OF EVIL

Chapters 12–13 of Revelation

The experience in superconscious bliss, described in the end of the Part II, renews St. John the Divine so deeply that he finds a satisfactory answer to the problem of evil. The twelfth chapter relates St. John's inner changes resulting from the superconscious experience. Chapter thirteen, which includes the most difficult theoretical speculations in Revelation, concerns the variety of forms evil can take.

12. THE BIRTH OF THE HEAVENLY CHILD AND THE DRAGON

The two important mythical images in this vision are the heavenly woman giving birth to a child and the dragon. In my interpretation, the former represents the spiritual rebirth of St. John the Divine, or the strengthening of his Self, and the latter represents evil. St. John finds a satisfactory solution for the obstructions comprised of insufficient experience of the Self and the repression of the problem of evil. These impediments have bothered him since the sixth chapter, when he heard the cries of the souls of the slain from under the altar (Rev. 6:10).

The spiritual renewal

The birth of the mythical child

"Now a great sign appeared... a woman... being with child... And she bore a male child" (Rev. 12:1–2,5).

The best known miraculous birth within Christianity is the birth of the baby Jesus, but nearly all world mythologies relate the birth of a mythical child. In the Gnostic myths, Sofia gave a parthenogenetic birth to her son Jahve, and in the Egyptian mythology, Neit, who was one of the oldest Egyptian divinities, gave birth to Ra "before such things as childbirth existed." The Chinese *Hui Ming Ching*, written during the eighteenth century, tells of Buddha's son, the radiant Julai, who, sitting on a beautiful lotus blossom, emerges out of the top of a human head. In myths, in literature, and particularly in dreams, the miraculous children are born in the most incredible ways. They come out of the heads of the gods and goddesses, off human ribs and sides, from test tubes, out of tree trunks and earth.[1]

Every miraculous childbirth is a unique and integral part of the culture it appears in. Therefore, the proper interpretation of each myth also varies from culture to culture. These myths can reflect, for example, the cyclical changes in the nature or creation of the world: the world and its different parts are, as it were, created in the vast cosmic womb. Many words associated with birth have remained in modern languages as metaphorical expressions revealing something of the interpretive dimensions of these myths. In English, for instance, we speak of ideas germinating, of something being fertile ground for introducing new practices, or of an invention being someone's brainchild.

The birth of the child in St. John's vision, may also reflect several ideas. Although I interpret the birth of the child primarily as St. John's own rebirth, I will later suggest yet another, more metaphysical interpretation.

Rebirth in the vision of St. John

The woman who gives birth in St. John's vision is his own soul, or, expressed more theoretically, that level of human consciousness which I have talked about as the subjective side of the universal Self. On this level, a person will experience superconscious bliss. The woman, however, represents this level in temporary terms, because St. John has not yet fully evolved spiritually. On the one hand, the woman is one of the embryonic forms of the Lamb's bride who appears at the end of Revelation. On the other hand, the woman continues the image of the ark from the previous vision, since both the woman's body and the ark are vessel-like images.

When St. John, at the end of the previous chapter, saw the ark of the covenant, his soul united with God, and I assume that the mythical child was conceived in that union. The blissful union of God and human soul requires absolute quietude, and therefore it cannot be depicted by ordinary sexual union. For example, Paul Brunton, quoted at the end of the previous chapter, compared one's thoughts to "a loomshuttle, which is always going to and fro," and he said that the oscillating thoughts ceased completely during an experience of superconscious bliss. Rather than using the image of an ark, Revelation could have used an image similar to that of the Holy Ghost germinating the Virgin Mary in the New Testament.[2]

In speaking of the woman, St. John uses the Greek word *gunē*. The word is used in reference to a wife, but it is also used to indicate any woman, and this is the meaning I give to it in my interpretation. The choice is important, because speaking of the wife may create an impression that the woman was impregnated by her husband. The woman in Revelation, however, does not actually have a husband. In Christian symbolism, the husband of the soul is God, Christ, or the Holy Ghost, and St. John the Divine has not yet reached the spiritual marriage. Thus, in Revelation, the conception and the birth of the child happen before the marriage.

When the child conceived in the ark of the covenant is born into the world, an ecstasy transforms St. John so deeply that he is reborn. A genuine spiritual experience always transforms a person; Paul Brunton described the effect of the experience of superconscious bliss with the words, "My heart is remoulded in rapture."

St. Teresa compares the results of the transformation brought about by the blissful union to the death of a silkworm and the birth of a butterfly:

> Let us see what comes of this little worm... When it remains in this prayerful union, completely dead to the world, it flies out as a white butterfly. Oh the greatness of God! What comes of the soul having, but for a moment, hidden itself in God's greatness, and united with Him! To tell you the truth, this soul will not recognize itself. Think of the difference between the ugly worm and the white butterfly—so it is even here.[3]

We can also find in literature certain descriptions, wherein the experience of superconscious bliss is compared specifically with the birth of a child. The following account is by an Indian man, retold to us by Paul Brunton:

> The outside world seems to disappear. He discovers the soul as a real, living being within himself; its bliss, peace, and power overwhelm him. All he needs is a single experience of this kind to obtain the proof that there is a divine and undying life in himself... When a mother gives birth to a child, is it possible that she can doubt, even for a single moment, what is happening ... In the same way, the labour of spiritual rebirth comes as such a tremendous event in one's life that it cannot be forgotten; it changes everything in a human life.[4]

Within Christianity, the birth of the child as a metaphor for the spiritual rebirth is particularly well-known from the sermons by Meister Eckhart. For example, the following quotation from him is pertinent:

> Man has two births: one in the world, and the other out of it, and the latter is a spiritual birth and a birth into God. Do you wish

to know whether your child is born... whether you have become His son? If your heart aches, you have not become the mother but are in labor and your time is near... When the heart grieves for nothing, the child is born.[5]

We could say that the child born in Revelation is St. John himself reborn. More precisely, the child is that ever-deeper state of consciousness I have called the Self; and even more specifically, the child is the objective side of the universal Self, which St. John is beginning to experience. Because the objective side of the universal Self in this vision is depicted as a child being born rather than as the Lamb, this vision emphasizes St. John's rebirth as a personal experience.

In our dreams, as well, a miraculous birth of a child fairly consistently illustrates an ever-deeper spiritual unfolding. C.G. Jung, in fact, in reference to this passage in Revelation notes, that were this a modern dream, the birth of the divine child could undoubtedly be interpreted as the awakening of the Self.[6]

Several mythical children can be born in the dreams of any one person, as various children describe the different nuances of the Self, its many levels, and the dreamer's own attitudes toward the inner changes. I will relate one of the many dreams I know involving a birth of a child. At the time of this dream, the dreamer had been overcome by such happiness she wondered what was happening, and whether she could continue her normal life in this state. In her dream, the darkness of the child reflects the strangeness of this new experience in her life:

> I see a lady of a fair complexion giving birth to a dark child. I am surprised at this, but the midwife shows the child to me and he literally radiates happiness. The midwife remarks, "Look how beautifully he smiles even while being born; this is truly a joyous occasion."

In Revelation, St. John describes further the birth of the child: "[The woman] cried out in labor and in pain to give birth" (Rev. 12:2). The labor and pain tell us that it is difficult for St. John to give up his former ways regardless of his experience in superconscious bliss. The Indian man I referred to earlier, as well as Meister Eckhart, both speak of labor in their descriptions of rebirth. We can find a similar comparison, within Christianity, also in the teachings of Theophan the Recluse, "Should we not suffer like a woman while giving birth, we would not succeed in awakening the spirit of salvation in our hearts." Labor, such as Leto's nine days and nights of pain in giving birth to Apollo and Artemis in Greek mythology, is a common mythical subject worldwide.[7]

In Revelation, the cry of the woman while in labor continues a previous mythical image, since the angel who stood with his one foot on the earth and the other on the sea, cried out with a loud voice (Rev. 10:3). At that time, St. John was not allowed to write down what the angel proclaimed, and I suggested the reason to be that mere crying out, or cognition, was not enough; St John must personally experience deeper states of consciousness. Now this required change is taking place, and it is depicted by an image relating a strongly evocative personal experience, a woman in labor.

The woman in St. John's vision

"Now a great sign appeared in heaven: a woman" (Rev. 12:1). Unlike usual dreams, the woman in St. John's vision is a vast apparition seen in the sky. I believe this to be so because the woman symbolizes St. John's state of consciousness exceeding now its normal dimensions. The expansion of consciousness during superconscious bliss was already mentioned in the quotations I presented at the end of the previous chapter. Paramahansa Yogananda described it, "My sense of identity was no longer narrowly confined to a body, but embraced the circumambient atoms... The entire cosmos... glimmered within the infinitude of my being." Similarly Paul Brunton notes, "My sense of awareness has been drawn out of the narrow confines of the separate personality; it has turned into something sublimely all-embracing ... My arms embrace all creation."

There is an important difference between the woman and the sun or the moon as a celestial symbol. Anyone can easily observe the sun and the moon just as easily as anyone can adopt general beliefs of a culture in an external way. But we cannot normally view a woman of unusual dimensions in the sky. Yet, if we have experienced expanded consciousness, the following night we may dream of enormous luminous lights, or of huge, light-emanating forms in the sky. I know of several such experiences and dreams associated with them. I relate one of them:

I still myself and turn inward, like I usually do in the evenings. Gradually, my consciousness deepens. I traverse my normal awareness quickly, passing through several layers, watching them flash by, allowing my mind to ascend on its own accord. Suddenly my own boundaries disappear completely. I experience a state of wondrous freedom, happiness, and brightness.

The following night I have a dream: I come to a huge gate. I know the gate to be normally closed, but now I am able to enter. I step into a partially subterranean room. I am told, or perhaps I simply know it in the dream, that this is a "room of mysteries." To my surprise I realize I am able to participate in these mysteries, and from underground beautiful, luminous colors begin to emerge, layer after layer. I am enchanted. I look up and see vast beautiful lights blaze across the sky. I know these celestial lights have been ignited as a result of my somehow having caused the luminous colors to flow out from underground. I feel as if never before have I done anything as good to my fellow human beings.

Although celestial lightforms as mythical and dream images depict some degree of cosmic consciousness, to see them up against the sky also most likely reflects an incomplete spiritual development. The person feels in his everyday life that he is tied down to the ground, or to his ordinary consciousness. The lightforms in the sky symbolize the occasional experience in cosmic consciousness, which is dramatically different from the ordinary consciousness symbolized by the earth.

St. John reveals more details about the woman, "a woman clothed with the sun, with the moon under her feet" (Rev. 12:1). The sun and the moon emphasize the celestial, cosmic nature of the woman. The sun and the moon, however, can be analyzed in greater detail.

A woman clothed with the sun creates an image of an extremely brilliant, shining lightform. Thus the mantle of sun in the vision expresses the brilliance and clarity of one's consciousness during the blissful state. Paul Brunton in describing his experience in ecstasy spoke of the "radiant self" in reference to his "new me," and this is what the woman is, the new, immense, and radiant Self of St. John. In Eastern symbolism, the deeper state of consciousness that the woman in John's vision represents is referred to as the diamond body, and it is said to radiate and emanate light.[8]

But the sun here may also symbolize the old God-concept based on an ethics of justice. The moon contrasts with the sun and symbolizes St. John's outward belief that God is love. This moon first appeared as the antithesis of the sun in the sixth chapter when the moon became blood while the sun turned black (Rev. 6:12). When the celestial woman gives birth to a child with both sun and moon being at least implicitly present, that child is, as it were, also their child. This birth appropriately symbolizes the solution to the problem that the sun and the moon represent, namely St. John's old concepts of God. Now that he has experienced bliss in a new way, he is transformed spiritually and finds his old beliefs alien. After the thesis and antithesis there is the synthesis, the child.

The sun and the moon were embedded also in the temple courtyard and temple symbolism of the previous chapter; at the time, while speaking of Jesus' death, I contrasted the sun and the moon with the ethics of justice and the ethics of love. But St. John must have wondered whether it is possible for God to be both justice and love itself and whether justice and love are not conceptually as different as day and night, or as sun and moon. I assume, that after experiencing cosmic consciousness, St. John feels he has finally found answers to these kinds of problems, and I will return to these answers later.

Brilliant though she is, the woman still symbolizes an insufficient spirituality. Her clothing of sun remains a symbol for the old religion. She is a more evolved symbol for the Self than would be a priest or a witness, but she is less than the Lamb's bride, or the diamond city found at the end of Revelation. Not until the diamond city appears will pure brilliance reign supreme, and only after that vision will St. John be ready to say that the sun is no longer needed (Rev. 21:23).

The moon is at the feet of the woman in St. John's vision, possibly because he feels that he had earlier trodden, unaware, on that side of religion which is symbolized by the moon. But the moon may also be at the feet of the woman because the spiritual love associated with the moon—once St. John finally experienced it personally—has impregnated the woman.

In this context, the sun and the moon can also be given quite new interpretations derived from the Oriental chakra teachings. In yoga theory, the sun and the moon are symbols for pingala and ida, or the two main energy channels wherein a person's life force ordinarily flows.[9] In the higher states of consciousness, energy, however, flows in the sushumna, located in between ida and pingala, all the way up to the top of the head into the sahasrara. In St. John's vision, the energy of the child born from the interrelationship between the sun and the moon is thus 'charged' similarly to that of an open sushumna nadi and sahasrara.

Revelation further describes the woman giving birth: "On her head a garland of twelve stars" (Rev. 12:1). The stars tell of the cosmic nature of the woman symbolizing St. John's expanding consciousness. A wreath of twelve stars can probably be seen as a reference to the twelve astronomical constellations. The star garland also continues the earlier wreath symbol, because the celestial woman expresses the victory won by human beings when they return to oneness with God, and St. John has momentarily gained this victory. He has lived in bliss, and at that time his life force has been drawn into sahasrara on the top of his head, forming a shining garland.[10]

Because the stars are emphatically twelve in number and form a garland, the stars probably do not refer to concrete beliefs, except possibly in the sense that St. John, in the light of his experience of bliss, realizes that externally acquired beliefs are insufficient in a spiritual life; a personally experienced bliss must replace them.

The celestial woman of St. John's vision compares well with the Virgin Mary of Christianity, who gives birth to the baby Jesus. Although the baby Jesus is born on earth, his birth was miraculous. As a mythical image of inner life, the Virgin Mary can be seen as a man's or a woman's purified consciousness, which makes a spiritual rebirth possible.

"The womb of creation" and the universal Self

I suggest briefly yet another complementary interpretation for the birth vision in Revelation. I assume that during his experience of superconscious bliss, or as a result of it, St. John has acquired a new understanding about the nature of reality. St. Teresa once explained that "[the soul] could not, in a thousand years, comprehend with her senses and abilities what she now grasps in a single moment [in the blissful union]."[11] Perhaps St. John also sees now with new eyes the creation and its birth, and his realizations are crystallized in the mythical images of the vision.

A celestial woman giving birth in a vision like this could represent the womb of creation, wherein the actual birthing takes place. A good parallel for the woman as the cosmic womb can be found in Plato's *Timaeus*, where Plato analyzes the birth of the world. He speaks there of the vessel, or the container—later also of the space where the creating happens. According to Plato this container is an absolute requirement for the birth of the world. And what is interesting, he compares it to a mother, "We may indeed use the metaphor of the mother and compare the container to her and the model to the father, and that which they produce together, to the children." Plato points out also that this "mother of the created" actually is invisible and has no form.[12]

Because St. John's vision of the birth of the child undoubtedly recalls the birth of the baby Jesus, and because the child in Revelation is born in the sky, I assume the child seen by St. John to be one of the forms of the Lamb, or the universal Self. Analyzed more precisely, the child being born would be that level of the universal Self which permeates creation forming its spiritual foundation. The birth of the child in St. John's vision would belong to the creation process; this becomes clearer as the vision progresses. This kind of spiritual foundation permeating all creation is similar to Kutastha Chaitanya, a concept of Indian philosophy, which I compared with the universal Self in the fifth chapter. Paramahansa Yogananda explains Kutastha Chaitanya with the help of Christian imagery in a way, which clarifies well the birth of the heavenly child in St. John's vision:

> When you feel your consciousness in every pore of creation, you have Christ Consciousness, [Kutastha Chaitanya consciousness]... When you are in tune with that Cosmic Consciousness, which is beyond this creation, you will understand that God begot His Intelligence in the womb of creation, the "Virgin Mary"; and that this Intelligence of God the Father, which is reflected or "born" in every atom of Creation, is the Christ Consciousness or "only begotten Son."[13]

In this kind of metaphysical interpretation, the birth of the celestial child is thus a part of the early stages of the creation process; his birth happens first. Whether appearing in the form of a child being born or in the form of the Lamb, the Universal Self—symbolized by both—

forms the foundation for material creation. As the Bible says, referring to Christ, "He is the first-born over all creation."[14]

I assume additionally that St. John wishes to stress with his vision that the ultimate divinity is manifested and 'functions' also in creation through the child that is being born. The child—universal love—expresses itself as love and intuition also in ego-bound individuals, although in them these feelings of love and intuitions may be strongly distorted by their ego-coverings. St. John is more specific regarding the functions of the universal Self in creation when he says the child "was to rule all nations with a rod of iron" (Rev. 12:5).

I understand the guiding function of the child to mean that the universal Self guides ego-bound women and men by working through their own loves and deep intuitions. With the help of Western and Eastern philosophies of religion, I can also suggest a more detailed interpretation of the child's iron rod. The rod of the celestial child would represent the most abstract and metaphysical law of righteousness, which could be summarized, for example, in the following words: When persons are open to universal love, they are filled with love and are happy. But when they are closed to universal love, they feel themselves without love and joy, and they suffer.

In Christian literature, Bernard of Clairvaux speaks of God's "eternal law", and he expresses it nearly the same way as was done above. Bernard explains that when man allows the love of God to guide him, he finds himself gently guided, but should he deny the love of God, he is guided by that punishment which he has brought on himself in the form of suffering. Bernard emphasizes also that according to this eternal law, righteousness inevitably manifests itself in human life.[15] Because St. John says the child will guide the nations with the rod, he is possibly emphasizing the role of suffering that derives from eternal law. That the rod is of iron may symbolize the uncompromising 'iron logic' with which the righteousness of this law plays itself out.

In Eastern philosophy, this eternal law is the law of karma. Here it is thought of in its most abstract and ethically profound sense and can be described as a metaphysical law. It is specifically the karmic law which administers righteousness in its deepest sense. Similarly in St. John's vision, the celestial character of the child would stress the high degree of abstraction of the law and its metaphysical nature.

We can conclude from the above interpretation that St. John finds out how righteousness and love are interconnected in their deeper meanings: love in itself is the reward for those who love, and persons without love unavoidably punish themselves through their lack of love. In St. John's vision righteousness and love can both be conceived as aspects of one and the same mythical image, the child guiding the nations, and therefore, the child appropriately is the child of the sun and the moon.

The problem of evil

"And another sign appeared in heaven: behold, a great, fiery red dragon" (Rev. 12:3). "The great dragon... the serpent of old, called the Devil and Satan" (Rev. 12:9). When St. John sees the dragon, I believe he understands evil in new ways, but his realizations are only alluded to in this vision. I will, however, discuss at length the problem of evil and the serpent symbolism associated with it because the problem of evil is like an essential knot or barrier in Revelation. When St. John finally in this chapter and the next unties the knot, he is able to begin his return journey in earnest. The problem of evil is also one of the central issues in any philosophy of religion. For these reasons, I will momentarily set aside St. John's vision and speak of serpents in mythology—of the serpent in the biblical Fall in particular. I will also analyze the mythical Satan and offer a theoretical solution to the problem of evil. Only after these somewhat lengthy expeditions will I return to further interpreting the visions of St. John in detail.

Mythical serpents

The serpent is often present when the original oneness in the creation myths divides into many. For example, the primal serpent in the *Pyramid Texts* of the ancient Egypt tells of itself in the following way:
My origin is in the primal flood
I am he that is born of water.
I am the giver of all qualities,
the serpent of many coils.[16]
In the Bible, the serpent does not appear in the creation myth itself, but soon afterward it allures Adam and Eve to eat from the tree of the

knowledge of good and evil. Thus begins man's worldly life banished from the oneness with God.

Some of the serpent myths reach forward to the time when the universe returns to undivided oneness. The best-known serpent in this circumstance is the cosmic Ananta-Sesha of Indian mythology, who coils itself to a ball at the ending of the grand universe. Then the god Vishnu lies in the Ananta-Sesha's embrace in the waters of the primal sea, and the serpent's many heads spread out like a fan over Vishnu to cover him.[17]

That a snake should be chosen to be included in both the creation myths and in the myths about the ending of the universe, is befitting, as it is easy to read into the snake the division of oneness, duality, and the return to oneness. The snake coiled into a ball forms a sphere, and that is, perhaps, the most natural geometric illustration of oneness. But the snake will also stretch itself open becoming a forward gliding, moving line, or a mythical image expressing the passing of time and the change it brings. Furthermore, the snake is normally born from an egg, and because of its round shape, the egg is universally used as an image for the original oneness. The tongue of the snake, split in two, is a fitting mythical illustration for the duality born of oneness, and the shedding of the skin as the snake grows depicts well the different stages of transformation. Finally, there are both harmless and fatally poisonous snakes, which is an excellent metaphor for the dualistic nature of the creation: the world includes both good and evil, vitality and death.

The mythological serpent symbolism reflects also unusual states of consciousness. Oriental teachings regarding human life energy often stress the fact that many people see the movements of this energy with their inner eye.[18] I will discuss some of the functions of the life energy, which are interesting in what they have to say regarding serpent symbolism.

According to yoga teachings, an important potential energy is hidden in an ordinary man. That potential energy is located in the lowest chakra, muladhara. It is compared to a coiled serpent, and it is called *kundalini*, which means something coiled. A central teaching of the yoga theory is that this kundalini energy can be directed up the sushumna nadi. The serpent then straightens itself, as it were, and in the higher altered states of consciousness kundalini is concentrated in the sahasrara. For these reasons the kundalini in yoga texts is talked about as the serpent force, and generally, it is depicted as a snake in Indian pictures.[19]

Serpent symbolism associated with the human life energy can be found frequently in other cultures as well, although there the symbolical meanings of the serpent are open to various interpretations. For example, the Egyptian pharaoh's headdress often had on the forehead a small serpent, and it could be seen as the kundalini energy, or the serpent force, which had been raised to ajna chakra, thus giving wisdom to the pharaoh. The great doctor in the Greek mythology, the healer and the god of health, Asclepius, was usually depicted with a staff in his hand. The serpent coiled around the staff was like those in Eastern sources where the kundalini energy is presented as a serpent climbing up sushumna. Asclepius' serpent, indeed, conveyed the meaning of the life force in ancient mythology.[20]

In Greek mythology Mercury had a staff, called caduceus, and in it, two serpents were depicted, opposite to each other, twisted around the straight staff. This symbol appeared, also, in the Mithraic religion and, later, alchemists used it. In fact, it is used even today. Although the caduceus staff has over the centuries had a variety of outward meanings, we can surmise it to have been based on the movements of the life energy. As to yoga theory, those serpents are like ida and pingala nadis, wherein the life energy flows, and the staff is like the straight sushumna nadi. Yoga literature, also, mentions this kind of interpretation of the caduceus staff.[21]

Perhaps serpent symbolism associated with the human life energy has had its impact also on the creation of the great cosmic serpents in mythology: the serpent as a symbol for energy has transferred from the level of microcosm to that of the macrocosm. The grand mythological serpents, however, reflect the cosmic energy in a few different ways. The Indian Ananta-Sesha serpent mentioned earlier symbolizes cosmic energy both in a state of rest and in activity, since it represents the whole cycle of the universe from the original coiled ball to the end when it coils itself back to a ball again. Out of the many dragons in the Chinese culture, the dragon in the *I Ching, The Book of Change*, symbolizes the universal and human active energy as an opposite to the passive rest. *I Ching* says, "The dragon flies in the heavens," for example.[22]

In the Mithraic religion, the highest divinity was depicted as a lion-headed, winged human image with a great serpent wrapped around it for its entire length. The head of the serpent was resting on the head of the god. The divinity in its deepest meaning was thought impossible to describe in words, but the god represented also the universe, and probably for this reason he sometimes stood up straight on a giant ball with the signs of the zodiac depicted on his body. Just as the spine with its sushumna nadi is man's major axis, so we can imagine this divinity as the spine or main axis of the universe. And just as human life energy flows all the way to the top of the head, so could the serpent around the divinity represent the basic energy flowing through the entire universe. On its more material levels this divinity was also the creator and the destroyer of all things expressing in this way the cosmic energy in two aspects opposite to each other. Perhaps it was for this reason that the insignia for the god was the caduceus staff with its two serpents.[23]

From these vantage points, it is possible to interpret also the Biblical serpents, of which the best known, the serpent of the Fall, can be associated with the human life energy. In Indian texts, it is clearly expressed that the serpent of the Fall symbolizes the coiled-up kundalini energy, and I examine this thought in a way that pertains to my interpretation on the whole.[24]

Kundalini in itself involves two possibilities. Kundalini can rise up sushumna to sahasrara, and that is when the person experiences bliss. But kundalini can also function—and in an ordinary human being it does—as the foundation for other energy forms. Kundalini first connects with a subtle form of life energy, and this again connects with the less subtle form of energy and so on. In this way, kundalini is seen as the foundation for man's material being, as well as, for his sense of self, that is, ahamkara or ego. In this sense, also ahamkara is a "product" of kundalini, as the Indian swami Sivananda expresses it.[25]

At the stage when the serpent first appears in the Bible, kundalini's one alternative has come to pass, because the previous biblical myths have described the first humans' innermost states. On those levels they experience paradisiacal bliss; that is, in paradise their inner serpent is able to rise up to eat the fruit from the tree of life or experience the bliss of the sahasrara. But the other alternative for kundalini has not yet manifested itself in paradise, or it has occurred only in such a small way that the first human beings have not lost their ability to know bliss and they have not yet become material, physical human beings with their own ego-consciousness.

According to the biblical Fall, when humankind comes to a new and final material level, the other alternative of the serpent force must appear in an ever-greater measure. And so in the myth, the serpent induces first the woman and then the man to eat from the tree of good and evil knowledge. The fruits of the tree of knowledge are all those experiences which are founded on the outer energy system symbolized by this tree. During the Fall, man and woman eat, that is, adopt these experiences so thoroughly that they become *tied* to them *alone* and to the energy system which is their foundation. In effect, humankind 'falls' to mere ego-consciousness and changes from an astral being to a material, physical being. The interesting thing here is that the curse on the serpent which the Lord decreed, describes this change on the level of human energy system.

The Lord God said to the serpent, "Because you have done this ... on your belly you shall go and you shall eat dust."[26] It is probably easy to read into the verse the thought that man's inner serpent is no longer able to rise up into sahasrara, and therefore, man's life force must be replenished from the dust, or from the external satisfactions, rather than from superconscious bliss.

Cursing the serpent conveys two important points. Kundalini energy must descend, or fall out of sushumna, and remain in the lowest chakra, as though coiled into a ball, at which point sushumna will be deprived of energy. This is what the yoga theory tells us. But, at the same time, the serpent's symbolical meaning changes. After the Edenic curse the serpent no longer symbolizes the coiled kundalini, because, clearly, the serpent moves about and eats the dust. In other words, after the Fall the serpent denotes the cruder forms of life energy, those which tie humankind to their ordinary consciousness and to their physical bodies and keep them from returning into oneness. Thus their falling into sin in its final outcome is the fall of their inner serpent. It, as it were, descends, changing from the serpent of Asclepius to those of Mercury.

In general, the serpent symbolism in the Bible is dualistic. The serpent functions as the metaphor for wisdom, but also as a metaphor for damnation. On the one hand, Jesus counsels his disciples, "Be wise as the serpents," yet on the other, he reproves: "Serpents, brood of vipers."[27] These general meanings of the serpents could also be associated with life energy. If we have used our life energy well, it is as if a small wise serpent could peek out of our forehead, but should we abuse this life energy, we are 'damned,' and our life energy is like a poisonous snake.

The dragon of Revelation, however, must be interpreted differently from the small biblical serpents. Because it is a grand dragon, flying up in the heaven, it must denote cosmic energy. Were the dragon to depict, like many other grand mythical serpents, the universal primal energy, it would be closely associated with the creature in Revelation which looked like the lion. That association could express itself as it did in the Mithraic religion, where a great serpent wrapped itself around the lion-headed divinity. The dragon in Revelation, however, cannot be honored with such a position, as it is clearly only an evil force; in fact, it is the mythical adversary itself, Satan and the Devil. Revelation, in fact, says just this. I assume accordingly that the dragon, in Revelation, illustrates some 'evil' form of energy similar on the macrocosmic level to what *the cursed* serpent represents on the microcosmic level.

The mythical adversary

But how can cosmic energy have evil in it? I suggest a possible explanation by using as a frame of reference the division of the original oneness into many and the subsequent return of the many into oneness.

The creation that is born from an undivided original oneness requires a force—which I define as a propelling force—to create the visible universe. Conversely, the original oneness, called God in the religious vocabulary, pulls this creation back into itself. To prevent this return from happening too quickly, the propelling (and differentiating) force creates another power or force. This opposing force which prevents the return is thus a necessary principle for the manifest universe. It is also the mythical adversary, or the Devil, as a cosmic principle. It, too, is created by God, because it results from the creative process and from the very first got its beginning from the undivided oneness like all else. But it is only one side of the cosmic energy, the side which impedes and obstructs the return of all things to oneness or God.[28]

In the Bible, the opposing force appears in the Old Testament properly named the "adversary" or "Satan." Satan appears clearly as an adversary in Chronicles, where "Satan stood up against Israel." In general, Satan in the Bible is a principle, whose opposing resistance humankind must overcome in order to return to oneness with God; indeed, Satan presumes to divert even Jesus away from God. Also the serpent of the Fall can be seen as an adversary and an opposing force after it has been cursed, for it tries to prevent human beings from finding their way back into oneness. In fact, the myth about the Fall tells us that enmity was set between the serpent and humankind after the Fall. Interpreting Satan in this way, it is a cosmic force of delusion, which manifests in a variety of actual way. In the Gospel According to John, Satan is called the "father of lies," and probably this can be interpreted to mean a primal, or basic, form of delusion.[29]

The thought of Satan's divine, or at least heavenly, origin can be inferred from the Book of Job, where Satan comes to God among the sons of God. Of course, this passage can be interpreted to mean that Satan, although not one of God's sons, arrogantly shows up anyway among them, but in literature elsewhere also, Satan is thought of as the fallen son of God. If we do not believe that Satan actually is a son of God, the Book of Job points out at least that during the time the Old Testament was written down, Satan was seen to have been a celestial being with a close relationship with God. The serpent in the myth about the Fall is, by contrast, openly said to be made by God.[30]

Calling Satan "the fallen son of God" is both poetic and theoretically relevant. During the process of the creation of all things from an original oneness, the tremendous energy involved is often described in mythologies as a grand divine serpent. Part of that energy, some sort of force, must separate or 'fall out,' and this force will begin to resist any return to oneness. As the creation evolves, this force must disperse ever deeper into the creation keeping it manifest. The 'fall' of this cosmic serpent force is then expressed in the human being in the way explained earlier: humankind's inner serpent, as well, falls during the creation.

An interesting question in interpreting the biblical Satan is, when was Satan created? The Bible does not mention this explicitly. Should Satan be identified with the serpent of the Fall, which I have not done in my interpretations, it would appear in the Bible as an active force only after the creation myth and the myth about paradise. Then it would, in effect, put an end to the harmonious paradisiacal world prevailing right after the creation.

But it is possible to see the matter differently. The Old Testament begins with the verse, "In the beginning God created the heavens and the earth," followed by the words, "And the earth was without form, and void; and darkness was on the face of the deep. And the Spirit of God was hovering over the face of the waters." If we should place Satan here, it would be as the darkness moving over the depth in contrast to the Spirit of God. Interpreted in this way, Satan would clearly refer to a cosmic force, a meaning I find essential in considering the dragon of Revelation.

An excellent comparison to the biblical Satan within the Eastern culture is one of the central concepts in the Indian philosophy called *maya*, the cosmic delusion. Literally maya means 'the measurer', and sometimes the Indians themselves equate this concept to the Christian concept of Satan.[31]

According to Indian understanding, maya enraptures humankind into her delusion so that it is difficult for them to free themselves and to return to the original oneness. Maya also entraps the entire manifest reality in a state of divergence. This explains maya's meaning as a measurer: she apportions differences where undifferentiated oneness would otherwise prevail. Consequently, maya's domain covers all of that existence where there is duality, no matter how ideally or harmoniously the duality is expressed. For example, Revelation is interpreted in the Indian literature in such a way that all other elements in St. John's heaven, namely, the elders, the creatures, even God's throne, belong to maya's domain. The enthroned alone, or God as the unmanifest oneness and the ultimate reality, is free from maya's delusion.[32] Therefore, as a concept, maya can be compared to the biblical interpretation whereby Satan entered the world when the creation process began. Satan, maya, would be, for instance, the darkness which moved over the depth.

The problem of evil

The problem of evil involves two problems, somewhat different conceptually. The first one is the conflict between the good, omnipotent God and evil. The other, closely associated with the first one, is the opposition between the righteous, omnipotent God and the unfairness of the world. I have already touched on the answer to the latter problem when I interpreted the rod of the heavenly child as the metaphysical law of righteousness. Now I will concentrate on the first mentioned problem of evil, and finally will briefly clarify the idea of righteousness.

The conflict between the benevolence and omnipotence of God and the existence of evil can be resolved on a conceptual level by discerning God as unmanifest and manifest. On the unmanifest level we are involved with oneness where there is no differentiation, neither good nor evil in the normal sense of the words. God as manifest is the total universe or creation. This level always embraces duality: birth and death, joy and suffering, good and evil. On this level, good necessarily implies evil as its opposite for the reason that human beings see these concepts as intertwined. "When everyone under heaven knows the good as good, the evil also exists."[33]

The foundation of evil, "the father of lies," is then the cosmic delusion, which is why the universe remains manifest and why mankind perceives the world through duality. Because this cosmic delusion, the father of lies, is a necessary part of the manifest divinity or the creation, it can be thought of as a work of God. In the same sense, we can say that God is responsible for the basic reason for evil, or for the cosmic delusion, although in the world, human beings themselves give concrete expressions to it through their own actions.

When we can personally and intimately experience a level of oneness, we are, at times or permanently, set free from experiencing evil. Experiencing this kind of oneness is blissful, and thus it is what we perceive as good. But on this level goodness is conceptually and perceptually separate from the opposition between good and evil, since absolute bliss is oneness and is experienced very differently from ordinary happiness. Accordingly, humankind can solve the problem of evil only by learning to experience absolute oneness. This requires that we transform ourselves inwardly, which means that the ego must die and the Self be brought to birth. Above all, we must learn to love ever more deeply and universally, because love is that magnetism which will guide us back into oneness. Love means the disappearance of the boundaries between ourselves and others. Delusion, on the other hand, appears in human life as a force which separates us from others. This force is expressed as the hatred and selfishness that we feel.

In its purest form, this kind of solution for the problem of evil can be found in Indian mythology and philosophy where the unmanifest and the manifest levels of the reality are clearly distinguished from each other. They are often aligned with the god Vishnu's breath. When Vishnu exhales, the world is born; when he inhales, the world returns to an unmanifest state from the manifest one; and when he rests, the manifest level does not exist.[34] The fact that evils like suffering and death found in the manifest world are part of the divinity is unmistakably evident in Indian mythology and philosophy. Thus evil is part of the divinity when the divinity manifests itself as the universe. For instance, in the *Bhagavadgita*, the so-called Hindu Bible, Arjuna once sees Krishna, who represents divinity, as the terrifying cosmic form of the god Vishnu:

> At the sight of your immense form
> with its many mouths and eyes,
> with its several bellies and countless horrid saber teeth,
> the earth and all the worlds tremble even as I do...
> [Men] hurry into your jaws—ah, the awful incisors!
> Others are seen caught in your fangs with crushed heads...
> while you twist your tongue,
> ready to swallow all the worlds into your flaming jaw.

When Arjuna in the *Bhagavadgita* asks for the meaning of this vision, Krishna explains his form as a manifest universe, "I am the time which destroys the world, I am the vast evolved one, I appear here to devastate all the worlds."[35]

Certain Eastern religions also stress the idea that the only final solution to suffering is that human beings, after a deep spiritual transformation, will themselves experience absolute oneness. This is the lasting samadhi or the Buddhist nirvana.

The Westerner, fond of theorizing, may argue that such an explanation as this does not dispose of the conflict between the good God and the existence of evil. The problem only shifts to another level.

Why would an unmanifest divinity want to take on a form that necessarily includes evil? The myth about Vishnu's breath tries to provide an answer. It suggests that the fluctuation from manifest to unmanifest states and vice versa is not an intentional act in the way the human intellect normally might expect an action to be. Instead, alternating sequences on a macrocosmic scale are as natural as is human respiration in the microcosmic one. Should this explanation not suffice, the Indians have many others. For example, the entire manifest level of reality is God's play, *lila*, and a play well done requires both good and evil.[36]

The general analysis of the problem of evil offers guidelines also for understanding the question of unfairness raised by religious philosophers. Why do persons' good and evil actions in the world not mete out rightful rewards and penalties, especially given God's supposed righteousness?

The answer is that God essentially is oneness, and He does not reward and penalize human beings in the way we would suppose. As ethical ideas, reward and penalty belong to the level of duality. They are part of a human sense of righteousness, that sense of righteousness with which men and women within a social structure compare merits and defaults, benefits and burdens, duties and privileges. This judgment of what is righteous differs greatly among individual appraisers, cultures and time periods. But regardless of how this sense of righteousness is measured, the world is both righteous and unfair. Applying one of these concepts in everyday life requires the other.

On the level of duality, however, a far ranging metaphysical law is in effect. This is "the eternal law" of God or the law of karma in its deepest and most abstract sense. I have earlier interpreted this law as symbolized by the rod of the child. We could say that, according to divine decree, rewards and penalties are meted out according to this law, but what really happens is that human beings reward and punish themselves through their own decisions. To reiterate: if persons open themselves up to universal love, they are filled with love, and that is their reward. But if they isolate themselves from universal love, they will suffer from the lack of love, and this is their punishment. As a result of this law justice inevitably comes to pass in any one life, and this kind of justice forms, as it were, the innermost and spiritual layer of righteousness.[37]

The problem of evil in St. John's vision

As I see it, St. John's vision about the celestial woman and the dragon reflects his inner experience. Human beings find a convincing answer for the problem of evil only in transcending duality through experiencing superconscious bliss. Then they realize intuitively and indisputably that there is such a state of consciousness and reality, one where there is no good-evil opposition. They begin to see evil in a new way: it is, at its core, the delusion which is part of ordinary existence imbued by dualism. (The last example at the end of the previous chapter discussed coming to understand this kind of delusion).

The solution I have suggested, is apparent to some degree in St. John's vision. The most important point is that St. John perceives Satan in the beginning of his vision as a cosmic principle; the dragon is, after all, a sign in heaven. As long as St. John was bound by his ordinary consciousness and the manifest creation, he thought that evil is only that which is opposite to good. For example, evil is that which arouses in him agony and a sense of unfairness. Such thinking led him to the problem-of-evil deadlock. But when he experienced absolute oneness and bliss, he comes to see the broader meaning of evil as a cosmic force and delusion.

An understanding of the metaphysical, or cosmic, law of righteousness (which I identified with the rod of the celestial child), is essential for St. John's progress. As a result of his experience of superconscious bliss, St. John is beginning to see a deeper level of righteousness. With the help of this realization he is able to resolve some of his old spiritual problems, and according to my interpretation, he returns to this effort several times in the following chapters.

Furthermore, a few other parts of the vision can be read in ways supported by the previous explanations of the mythical Satan. As it is, St. John appears to differentiate between several levels of delusion moving from the most general to the most specific as if he were following the evolution of the creation process. This movement toward more specific forms of delusion continues in the next chapter of Revelation.

The signs in heaven in the beginning of the chapter—the woman with child and the dragon—would from this vantage point disclose the very earliest stage of the process of creation. St. John now perceives this process differently due to his experience of oneness. The woman would be, as was previously suggested, the cosmic womb of creation or the platonic vessel of creating. The child that she is giving birth to would be the spiritual foundation for the creation or, in Christian terminology, "the first-born before all other creation." And finally, the dragon would be the cosmic delusion in its most general sense. The dragon, or the delusion, appearing specifically in the beginning of the vision, points to the creation process; the delusion does not exist beyond the creation. The dragon would thus, at this stage, represent the darkness in the Old Testament which moved over the primordial waters, and it would compare to the Indian maya, or cosmic delusion, which is the prerequisite for the existence of the whole creation.

My interpretation is supported by the fact that in St. John's vision the woman with the child and the dragon appear clearly in opposition to each other, "Now a great sign appeared in heaven: a woman... And another sign appeared in heaven: behold, a great... dragon... And the dragon stood before the woman who was ready to give birth, to devour her child as soon as it was born" (Rev. 12:1,3–4). Similarly, in the Indian philosophy, Kutastha Chaitanya (or the universal Self) and maya (or the cosmic delusion) are opposite forces. The universal Self guides all that exists back into oneness, whereas maya, as its opposite, serves to break it apart.[38]

After having introduced the woman, the child and the dragon, St. John describes his vision about war, and following this interpretation, through the war St. John seeks to make the creation more concrete. "And war broke in heaven: Michael... fought against the dragon; and the dragon... fought... So the great dragon... that serpent of old ... who deceives the whole world; he was cast to the earth." (Rev. 12:7,9.) Regarding the process of creation, the angel Michael would be God's creative force, which begins to create a material world. As a creative force, Michael is like God, but not the ultimate divinity beyond duality. (The name Michael means 'he who is like God.'[39]) When Michael casts the dragon to the earthly realm, it means that the creative force propels the cosmic delusion into the world so that the creation would be 'deceived,' that is, it would become manifest. Without this opposite force, 'the deceiver,' the creation would immediately return back to God, or into oneness. Casting the dragon to earth means that Satan 'falls' ever deeper into the creation.

That the casting down of Satan is pictured as war tells us of his nature as an opposing force: Satan resists also the divine creative process. The dragon fighting Michael emphasizes the point that delusion is a part of the world that results from God's creation process; it was not the dragon's, or the delusion's, own wish.

The dragon is red, probably, to stress the difference between the dragon, which severs oneness, and the universal Self, which draws everything back into oneness. The Self and other spiritually high principles in Revelation are characterized by whiteness; for example, "He who overcomes shall be clothed in white" (Rev. 3:5). Red, on the other hand, from here on is clearly associated with the mythical images representing the delusion.[40]

To continue the theoretical interpretation, I assume additionally that St. John realizes during his vision of the dragon that in the final account the solution for the problem of evil cannot be to blame humanity for its existence. Perhaps St. John had previously tried to explain the existence of evil in this way. When he had thought of God only as a good force opposite to an evil force, then evil seemed to be exclusively the fault of men and women. My interpretation is based on the fact that St. John calls the dragon in his vision "the accuser of our brethren" (Rev. 12:10).

In the Bible, Satan functions as humanity's accuser, as, for example, in Zechariah, "And he showed me Joshua the high priest standing before the angel of the Lord, and Satan standing at his right hand to resist [that is, to accuse] him." However, it turns out that Satan's accusations are false, and already in the next verse it is said, "The Lord rebuke thee, O Satan." Also, in the Book of Job, Satan accuses innocent Job.[41] It would be possible to read the dragon vision in Revelation in the same way. Perhaps St. John feels that Satan had earlier tried to shift the responsibility for his existence onto humankind. Only after having personally understood the cosmic delusion does St. John see clearly that such a small being as man cannot be the cause of an immense cosmic force, the basic form of delusion or the father of lies, for this force far surpasses ordinary human consciousness. Thus St. John is freed from false guilt. He is now ready to continue his path onward in order to be finally liberated from the power of the cosmic delusion.

The events of the vision: interpretations on the level of St. John's personal experience

If we consider the Book of Revelation as a whole, we see that the twelfth chapter stands out in the sense that nearly all mythical images in it, not just the birth of a child and the dragon, are universal. In the following I will, however, confine myself to a limited analysis of the mythical images in question.

The dragon

After St. John has, in the first two verses, introduced the woman crying out in labor, he begins to portray the dragon. The description includes details which have not yet been discussed; the dragon has "seven heads and ten horns, and seven diadems on his heads" (Rev. 12:3).

The number seven probably reflects, as mentioned earlier, cognition and change. The aspirant must, as it were, conquer the dragon's heads one at a time in order to solve the problem of evil and to become completely free of delusion. But this is difficult and creates anxiety; thus the dragon is associated with the number ten. The dragon's horns symbolize the nature of Satan as a force. But the horns may also illustrate the problem of evil pushing out to the forefront in St. John's consciousness, as that problem is no longer about to be repressed. The diadems on the dragon's head depict Satan's nature as the origin of all other forms of delusion, as "the father of lies," and perhaps they tell us also of St. John's realization that the delusion symbolized by the dragon still reigns like a king in his consciousness; he is not yet free from it. A diadem, or in Greek *diadēma*, during the biblical times was a head-dress for a king.

The dragon's actions and designs

"His tail drew a third of the stars of heaven and threw them to the earth" (Rev. 12:4). If the stars were simply celestial bodies, they might denote beliefs concerning spiritual life. The stars thrown to earth could mean that St. John's former beliefs disintegrate after his experience of bliss. But if the stars refer to the garland over the woman giving birth to the child, this description might then signify the lessening of life energy. Part of the energy moves into the lower chakras, the ones that St. John sees belonging to the earthly realm. It is appropriate for the life energy to descend when the dragon appears in the vision since the realization of the existence of delusion means that the absolute bliss has been disturbed.

"And the dragon stood before the woman who was ready to give birth, to devour her child as soon as it was born" (Rev. 12:4). Persecution of a mythical child is another universal theme in mythology; Christ and Krishna, for example, undergo persecution during their childhood. The Bible tells us how Herod ordered male children killed, and in the Indian myths, King Kamsa is told that one of his young relations was destined to kill him and so he has the children murdered.[42] In these cases the persecutor, King Herod or King Kamsa, as a mythical image represents the human ego, which does not want to undergo change. In St. John's vision, however, the child is not threatened by a king but by a dragon, and this difference reflects the special nature of St. John's experience. He realizes that the spiritual liberation of human beings is not only endangered by their own small-mindedness, but by the vastness of the cosmic delusion snaring them. St. John must feel that this delusion is about to swallow up the liberating transformation now taking place in him.

The birth of the child

"And She bore a male child who was to rule all nations with a rod of iron" (Rev. 12:5). Regardless of his fears, St. John is changed. A genuine spiritual experience, such as seeing the ark of the covenant, conveys a sense of the presence of truth, and this transforms the human spirit beyond any incertitude.

The nations that the child is said to rule are those ego-bound characteristics which St. John still possesses. The iron rod as a *general* mythical image is a symbol of power and strength. It reflects the power of the new spirituality to further transform St. John. An experience in bliss will inevitably influence a human being's wish to progress spiritually, impossible as it is to forget that supreme climactic moment. As a mythical image, the rod can be compared to the Lamb's horns which symbolize the desire of the Self to express itself freely.

The fate of the woman and the child

"And her child was caught up to God and to his throne. Then the woman fled into the wilderness where she has a place prepared by God, that they should feed her there one thousand two hundred and sixty days." (Rev. 12:5–6.) As we can see, the child and the woman who gave birth to it, have different fates: the child is raised into the center of the heaven, but the woman must leave for the earth, into the wilderness. These events, interpreted psychologically, describe St. John's return to his normal consciousness. The woman symbolizes St. John's consciousness now returned from its expanded 'heavenly' state back to its 'earthly' state. The child, or that new deeply spiritual content of his consciousness which St. John had lived with for a moment, is removed from his experiences. It is set aside as something potential into St. John's highest level of consciousness, or into heaven until he can internalize it permanently. Additionally, the expression "the child was caught up to God and to his throne" probably reflects a deeper, more thoughtful realization by St. John. A profound experience of bliss changes the meaning of divinity for St. John, so that what is divine is identified ever more clearly as being love and bliss.

Perhaps the woman in St. John's vision flees into the wilderness because during biblical times it was common for spiritual aspirants to retreat out to the desert in order to deepen their inner life. For example, the brotherhood of Qumran lived quietly in the wilderness of Judah waiting for the Messiah. Likewise, John the Baptist prepared himself for his mission in the solitude of the desert, and Jesus prayed in the wilderness for forty days. The retreat into the wilderness, or the desert, has become in the Christian literature an established symbol for spiritual preparation.[43] Certainly, St. John, after having experienced bliss, wants to withdraw into his inner world in an effort to progress spiritually and to find spiritual joy again.

The desert is often an arid place, and a desert-induced drought in St. John's consciousness would be easy to understand, since after an experience of extreme happiness, normal consciousness appears a dry desert. St. John might fall into dryness also because he must turn from a blissful experience to intellectualizing and analysis, especially regarding the problem of evil. Although the wilderness in St. John's vision may have a sense of aridity, it is only relatively so, because the vision tells us that the woman is being fed there; St. John receives spiritual nourishment during the time of his preparation. In fact, Christian literature generally acknowledges that spiritual nourishment as well as trials are part of spiritual maturation, even as the Jews, having left Egypt, received in the desert manna from the heaven.[44]

The time frame mentioned, one thousand two hundred and sixty days, the length of time the woman must stay in the wilderness, is three and a half years (when a month is thought of as consisting of thirty days). The transformation in question is, therefore, the latter part of the process which began in the previous chapter.

The war

"And war broke out in heaven: Michael and his angels fought against the dragon; and the dragon and his angels fought, but they did not prevail" (Rev. 12:7–8). Such strife between good and evil is repeatedly and variously expressed by the world mythologies. In the Indian epic, in the *Mahabharata*, the gods and the demons engage in a terrifying battle, which is eventually won by the gods. The war between good and evil appears universally also as a battle between a young hero and a beast; for example, in Greek mythology Heracles kills the nine-headed Hydra snake.[45]

Previously I interpreted the war in Revelation as a part of the creation process, but according to the psychologically oriented interpretation I am now following, the mythical war represents St. John's own internal struggle. Because, in Revelation, the war is waged in heaven, St. John's inner battle involves a high level of consciousness. In the battle, the angel Michael symbolizes St. John's intuition which guides him to what is right, and the subject of the battle is the problem expressed by the angel Michael's name 'Who is like unto God,' or what is the right 'unto God's kind' of spirituality. In his inner war, St. John tries to free himself from the old religiousness he has found to be wrong, but it is still difficult to give it up. This is revealed by the dragon fighting Michael; the dragon's offense symbolizes fittingly the power of delusion in the inner struggle.

In the war, Michael and the dragon are supported by their angels. I interpret Michael's angels to be intuitions which help St. John to become freer, but they could also represent such spiritual characteristics as courage and faith which help St. John in his inner change. The angels of the dragon, conversely, can be seen as deluded states of consciousness—like fears, agonies, and stagnant attitudes—which distort his intuitions and thus St. John must wrestle with them at the moment of his inner reckoning. I would prefer not to call the dragon's angels 'false intuitions,' as false intuition is not really intuition in the sense in which I use it; rather, it is the deluded content of consciousness.

The casting out of the dragon

"But they [the dragon and its angels] did not prevail, nor was a place found for them in heaven any longer. So the great dragon was cast out, that serpent of old, called the Devil and Satan, who deceives the whole world; he was cast to the earth, and his angels were cast out with him." (Rev. 12:8–9.) Likewise, in the previously mentioned battle in the *Mahabharata*, the demons are driven out to the earth and the sea.[46]

Interpreted psychologically, casting the dragon out to the earth expresses the return from an altered state of consciousness to a normal everyday state. St. John's state of bliss had ceased earlier, but now so does the experience of a grand cosmic power of delusion. Additionally, banishing the dragon probably reflects St. John's realizing this idea: "The problem of evil is not merely a highly abstract problem. It is a problem that is part of everyday earthly life, and it is essential to understand how that delusive power affects me and to be liberated of it." The analysis of evil—or rather of delusion—on the level of human consciousness is a subject of the next chapter, and after that, Revelation begins to describe St. John's liberation.

The expelling of the dragon is witnessed again in the vision a few verses later, "Then I heard a loud voice saying in heaven, 'Now... the accuser of our brethren... has been cast down... Woe to the inhabitant of the earth and the sea! For the devil has come down to you, having great wrath, because he knows that he has a short time.'" (Rev. 12:10,12.)

In these verses, St. John calls the dragon "the accuser" and "the devil." Both meanings are basically the same: the devil in Greek is *diabolos*, which means slanderer; it is the Greek equivalent of the accuser in the Old Testament.[47] This choice of words inspires an image of the devil accusing humankind whether on the land or at sea. In other words, St. John must examine the extent to which men and women must blame themselves for their deluded consciousness. St. John anticipates the difficulty of this prospect, and so the devil is "having great wrath." At the same time, St. John believes he will clear up the matter soon and finally be liberated from delusion, and thus the devil has only "a short time."

The woe in the exclamation "woe to the inhabitants of the land and the sea" is the third woe-cry that has been foretold. This woe-cry anticipates the difficult analysis soon gripping St. John. The woe-cries function, in a sense, as signs tying together the process of transformation which began at the start of the ninth chapter. First the bottomless pit was opened and smoke emanated from it. Out of the smoke the locusts came. Then from the depth arose the beast which killed the witnesses. And in his next vision, St. John will examine different beasts more closely.

The dragon persecutes the woman

"Now when the dragon saw that he had been cast to the earth, he persecuted the woman who gave birth to the male child. But the woman was given two wings of a great eagle that she might fly into the wilderness to her place, where she is nourished for a time and times and half a time, from the presence of the serpent. So the serpent spewed water out of his mouth like a flood after the woman, that he might cause her to be carried away by the flood. But the earth helped the woman, and the earth opened its mouth and swallowed up the flood which the dragon had spewed out of his mouth." (Rev. 12:13–16.)

We can find comparisons for these events in the myths of the world. In Greek mythology, the great snake Python persecutes Leto while she is pregnant, but Leto escapes to an island in the sea. Similarly, a woman flying as a bird in the sky is a universal mythical image. In the Egyptian Osiris myth Isis and Nephys, at times, fly in the sky as bird forms, and in the old Finnish folk poetry the same miracle is performed by Lemminkäinen's mother and Louhi, the sorceress from the North. We can find analogs even for the water spewed out from the dragon's mouth. One version of the Indian myth about the ocean churning tells how, from the mouth of the Ananta snake, who served as a pulley for the churn, a poisonous stream gushed forth, which was swallowed by the god Shiva.[48] However, I wish to interpret these mythical subjects only in so far as they have relevance for understanding Revelation.

The dragon pursues the woman both because St. John has not yet been liberated from delusion and because the problem of evil (symbolized by the dragon) is still partially unsolved. This is distressing to St. John. And so his inner happiness is in jeopardy.

The woman flying high in the sky, tells us that St. John experiences, on the level of consciousness represented by the woman, high spiritual values and intuitions. Although the problems St. John is facing are difficult, he has embraced a new heightened intuition because his consciousness has been altered. Because of this transformation he now feels he will escape the power of delusion. That is why the woman, flying like a bird, can escape the dragon. In the vision, the woman does not actually change into a bird, but she receives the wings of an eagle, a fitting symbol for humankind's return to oneness with God. Before returning to God, one must have experienced high spirituality.[49]

A mythical or dream image of a menacing body of water threatening a person is a symbol of an impending emotional state; particularly associated with this interpretation are the myths about floods. So, regardless of his sense of trust, St. John feels agony and fear. Yet he resolves to retain his rationality, which is here represented by the earth. Thus he is not swept off by emotional anxiety, or flood water, but instead the threatening feeling symbolized by the spewed out water sinks into the unconscious, or underground.

Should the extent of the time depicted by St. John, "a time and times and half a time," be interpreted to mean three and a half years, as many translations say, the report of the time the woman spends in the wilderness repeats previous material. As we remember, it was said earlier that the woman will be fed in the wilderness one thousand two hundred and sixty days, which is three and a half years (Rev. 12:6).

The dragon persecutes the other children of the woman

"And the dragon was enraged with the woman, and he went to make war with the rest of her offspring, who kept the commandments of God and have the testimony of Jesus Christ" (Rev. 12:17).

Interpreting this passage on an *individual* level, I think that the child born in the vision of St. John the Divine cannot be the firstborn, because its birth expresses a fairly high state of the return journey; other children symbolizing earlier stages of spiritual rebirth must have been born before this child. Likewise, in dreams, female figures, or the dreamer herself, may have several children, so that each child represents a different level of spirituality. The youngest child usually denotes the deepest spiritual level, and it is often in danger of being destroyed, just as newly developed spirituality is destroyed or dissipates easily.

Therefore, I assume that the other children of the woman in St. John's vision symbolize a more superficial level of spirituality than the child born in this chapter. St. John says about those children that they keep the commandments—an expression which refers to the Old Testament—and that they have the testimony of Jesus Christ; probably the testimony refers to a relatively outward way of living spirituality. When the dragon begins to wage war against the woman's other children, St. John's sense of spirituality, including its superficial levels, is ever more harshly threatened.

13. THE BEASTS

The different forms of delusion in the human consciousness

There are three central mythical images in St. John's new vision: *the beast rising out of the sea, the beast coming up out of the earth* and *an image of the beast* which has risen out of the sea. In the latter visions, the place of the beast that came up out of the earth is taken by *a false prophet*. Therefore, for the sake of clarity, that image also will be interpreted in this chapter.

The beast rising out of the sea

"Then I stood on the sand of the sea. And I saw a beast rising out of the sea" (Rev. 13:1). The sand of the sea, in this context, probably means the seashore, and the shore, as the borderline between the unconscious and the conscious, is the mythical place of cognition. Thus the beast rising out of the sea illustrates the new realization about the nature of the delusion surfacing from St. John's unconscious. But the beast rising out of the sea can be also interpreted more theoretically. Because in an evolutionary sense our conscious minds have evolved from the unconscious, the sea, as a mythical image for the unconscious, can be seen as the original or basic form of human consciousness. Then the beast would be a form of delusion that is deeply tied to human consciousness. And when the beast rises out of the sea, it, as it were, comes in view for St. John's examination.

"And the dragon gave him his power, his throne, and great authority" (Rev. 13:2). According to the previous interpretations, the dragon's throne symbolizes the concept of delusion.[1] When a new beast sits on the dragon's throne, the general concept of delusion receives new content. With his words, St. John is telling us that the delusion in human consciousness, or the beast rising out of the sea, is a manifestation of the cosmic delusion, or the dragon.

"And all the world marveled and followed the beast" (Rev. 13:3). In this verse, St. John uses the Greek word *gē*, which actually means the earth, and several translations say here that the whole earth marvelled or wondered about the beast. St. John tries to understand the nature of the beast with his conscious thinking, represented by the earth. What is it exactly like, this delusion, represented by the beast from the sea?

When human consciousness is a servant of desires and duality, I have called it ego-consciousness. When the bondage to desires and duality is so strong in human beings that they perceive their identity through these qualities, they are under the spell of delusion in their consciousness, or the beast that rose out of the sea. Thus, this mythical beast of Revelation crystallizes the central characteristics of ego-consciousness. Its beastliness emphasizes the power of these qualities and their destructiveness to human consciousness. When the beast takes over in us, the Self is superseded by the ego-consciousness: we lose the ability to experience oneness and to act in a desire-free way. Overshadowed by delusion, we see as essential that which is unessential, that is, ego-consciousness, and we experience the essential, or the Self, as unessential. In a word, the delusion symbolized by the beast of the sea means that we are identifying with our ego-consciousness.

In Indian philosophy, the delusion appearing in the human consciousness is called *avidya*, and the beast of Revelation compares well with this concept. In fact, the above description of the delusion of consciousness was based on Eastern philosophy. Indian philosophy stresses, in particular, that the avidya delusion is a part of the cosmic delusion, or maya, and similarly it is explained in Revelation that the dragon gives power to the beast.[2]

Within Christianity, the best comparison for the beast in Revelation is found in the early Gnostics, who used the term *agnōsia* to mean the opposite of *gnōsis*, or the personally experienced, spiritual wisdom of oneness; *agnōsia* was lack of *gnōsis*, and therefore, meant deception and delusion. In traditional Christianity, the closest equivalent to the beast would be original sin which began with the Fall. In my interpretations, the Fall has meant human bondage to ego-desires and to duality, and this is the chief characteristic defining the beast as well.[3]

Because the whole of ego-consciousness is saturated by delusion, the beast of Revelation can be interpreted also as a mythical image of ego-consciousness personified. (An excellent non-personified symbol for ego-consciousness is the kingdom of the beast—see verse Rev.

16:10.) When we think of the beast as ego-consciousness, we must remember that this, being in bondage to desires, is only one form of consciousness. Even during early stages of man's spiritual evolution there may also be desireless acts and momentary flashes of the consciousness of oneness.

It is easy to understand that ego-consciousness seems beastly from St. John's point of view. He has experienced absolute bliss, and after that the ordinary consciousness must seem so false to him that it appears a beast. The last example at the end of the eleventh chapter described this kind of feeling after an experience in bliss. Similarly, in Christian literature, St. John of the Cross explains that all ordinary joys are, in fact, "suffering, torment, and bitterness compared to the joy which is God."[4]

"And I saw a beast rising up out of the sea, having seven heads and ten horns, and on his horns ten crowns" (Rev. 13:1). The dragon also had seven heads and ten horns, but the dragon's crowns were on his heads whereas those of the beast are on his horns. This distinction reveals the importance of the horns in the beast. They fittingly represent human ego-desires and their consequent goal-oriented strivings. Unfulfilled desires prod us to press forward towards the object of our desires. That crowns are placed on these horns emphasizes the fact that bondage to desires is an essential part of the beastly delusion.[5]

"And it was granted to him to make war with the saints and to overcome them. And he was given authority over every tribe, tongue, and nation." (Rev. 13:7.) When the beast overcomes the saints, it means that human beings lose their intuitive contact to the Self symbolized by the saints. Then they begin to experience themselves only on the level of their ego-consciousness. All of their specific characteristics, symbolized by the tribes, tongues, and nations, become subject to their desires and to duality. According to the biblical myths, this happened at the time of the Fall when the man and the woman were overtaken by original sin.

"And all who dwell on the earth will worship him, whose names have not been written in the book of life of the Lamb slain from the foundation of the world" (Rev. 13:8). In this verse, St. John clarifies further what he said earlier. Although all human qualities are overcome by delusion—covered by the delusion, if you will—St. John is yet implying that there are also some qualities which do not completely yield to the beast's power, or worship him. These are symbolized by those whose names have been written in the book of life of the Lamb slain from the foundation of the world. These qualities express most clearly the influence of the universal Self, or the Lamb slain, on human beings.

In a previous vision, St. John saw the effect of the universal Self on creation symbolized as a mythical child. Now he explains that this impact of the Self or Lamb comes through certain human faculties; such faculties are especially our intuition and our ability to experience spiritual values. Naturally, these qualities can also be covered by delusion, as, for example, we can smother the voice of conscience. But if we cultivate these abilities even a little, they grow stronger and begin to usher us quickly away from delusion toward a more complete freedom of the Self. Because those abilities exist in every human being as innate tendencies, they have been assigned to the Lamb's domain since the foundation of the world, or since the creation of man.

St. John gives more details about the beast that rose out of the sea, and I will interpret them only later in the end of this chapter.

The beast that came up out of the earth

"Then I saw another beast coming up out of the earth... and [it] spoke like a dragon" (Rev. 13:11). Because the beast coming out of the earth speaks like a dragon, we are encountering yet another manifestation of the cosmic delusion.

The underground, from whence the beast arises, usually represents in myths the unconscious or the subconscious. Therefore, St. John realizes a new form of delusion is rising from his unconscious. But as a mythical image, the land can be seen as the opposite of the sea and sky, and then it often symbolizes conscious awareness and that which is physical.[6] These meanings point to a new form of delusion. Under its influence, human beings identify with their bodies and with that part of their ego-consciousness which they perceive and experience clearly.

A comparison to this new form of delusion is offered by Indian philosophy, which differentiates between avidiya and a narrower concept of delusion called *asmita* that emphasizes man's identification with his physical body.⁷ In Christianity, sinfulness and sin are more substantial concepts than is original sin; having inherited original sin, human beings then sin as conscious and physical beings.

The part of ego-consciousness which is experienced consciously and clearly can be called ego-awareness, although this expression is somewhat misleading. That part of the consciousness which is here spoken of as ego-awareness includes feelings that we clearly have, even though we may not particularly take notice of them.

The English language—like many others—has a word used in everyday language which describes rather well the concept I refer to as ego-awareness: the mind. The general definition of the mind is "the ability to be aware of things and to think and feel." In other words, the mind can be seen as that realm of our consciousness which we use consciously and fully experiencing the feelings contained within it. Such expressions as "bearing in mind" and "to have something in one's mind" reflect that we are "mindful" of the contents of consciousness and of their developments. When the word "mind" is used in the following with this special theoretical meaning, the reader ought to remember that the mind is part of ego-consciousness; it is marked by bondage to desires, and it is deluded. In this way it is possible to see the beast coming up out of the earth also as a mythical image personified for the ego-bound mind. Accordingly, the beast rising from the sea was interpreted as ego-consciousness personified.

When I attribute to the mind a meaning which connects it to ego-desires and thus to delusion, I am following Indian philosophy, which differentiates between the concepts of *buddhi* and *manas*. *Buddhi* means profound wisdom or intellect, and *manas* as its opposite signifies a superficial and delusory level of consciousness; *manas* is often translated with the word "mind." *Buddhi* would correspond, in Revelation, to those "whose names have been written in the book of life of the Lamb slain from the foundation of the world" (Rev. 13:8).⁸

St. John continues the description of the beast coming out of the earth, "And he had two horns like a lamb and spoke like a dragon" (Rev. 13:11). The horns of a lamb on the beast coming out of the earth are easier to understand when this beast is interpreted as a symbol for the ego-bound human mind. The Lamb's horns appeared in the fifth chapter, and at that time they were interpreted from two viewpoints, which I will now continue to develop.

To begin with, the Lamb's horns were associated with the creation of man. According to a metaphysical-mythical understanding, the Lamb, or the universal Self, is the spiritual foundation of all human beings, and upon it the levels of more tangible humanness are formed; the most superficial level being the deluded, albeit alive, thinking and feeling human mind.

Although the mind is saturated by delusion, ultimately it receives its life energy from the level of the universal Self. Therefore, the lamb's horns fit well the head of the beast seen by St. John. This idea, too, is common in Indian philosophy, which stresses that the mind receives its energy from a deeper level of the *Purusha*, or the Self.[9]

Secondly, the Lamb's horns were associated with an individual's mythical return to the oneness with God. Then the Lamb's horns express the 'desire' of the Self to manifest itself freely, that is, to experience absolute bliss. In an ordinary human being this desire, however, is distorted as it must be filtered through the ego-covering. When human beings identify with their minds, or even more narrowly with their physical bodies, they begin to seek bliss in the form of pleasures; and the objects of their desires are transitory, such as material things, other human beings or outward success. But this kind of aspiration is delusory in the sense that the transitory cannot bring lasting happiness. Yet, regardless of its delusive nature, this striving for happiness, too, reflects the Self endeavoring to express itself as eternal bliss—as religious literature often points out.[10] Thus it is fitting for the beast's horns to be like those of a lamb.

"And he exercises... the authority of the first beast" (Rev. 13:12). That is, the beast coming up out of the earth receives his power from the beast rising from the sea. This is explained also by contemporary psychology, because the conscious human mind is a later stage in human development. It is born of a diffused basic form of consciousness, wherefrom we still have the unconscious as 'a relic.' The words of St. John read well within Christianity also, because women and men are seen to commit sin as a result of original sin, or because of the influence of the beast having risen from the sea.

The false prophet

The beast that came up out of the earth does not appear in the following chapters of Revelation, but instead, a false prophet joins the dragon and the beast (Rev. 16:13, 19:20). The false prophet has essentially the same meaning as the beast which came out of the earth, that is, it is the conscious ego-bound human mind, and ultimately that delusion which leads us to identify with our desire-filled mind. These meanings are sufficient for interpreting Revelation, and when St. John later on talks about the false prophet, I take it to represent this kind of delusion. However, a false prophet has many interesting theoretical comparisons, and I will examine the image further.

A false prophet, as a mythical image, reflects the effects of delusion on human consciousness. The beast which came out of the earth, as an image for the same delusion, emphasizes the perverted quality of the delusion, or its beastliness. The phrase "a false prophet" likely refers to a person as a subject and I deduce from this that the false prophet, as a form of delusion, leads man to so identify himself with his conscious mind that he thinks that is all there is to him. Modern languages use the word "mind" as if it were a subject and they speak of the mind itself as if it were thinking or feeling something. In Revelation, there is hidden this meaning: the false prophet is the human being's identity when it is limited to being the conscious mind. But in reality, the sense of self is broader, for even when we identify ourselves with our conscious awareness, we say that we dreamt something, although dream-consciousness transcends the boundaries of the conscious mind. Thus a person functions as a false prophet only occasionally, or if the state is more lasting, it is part of one's earlier stages of maturing, when the sense of self is still relatively limited to conscious awareness. In any case, the false prophet is a form of the ego.

A good parallel for the false prophet of Revelation can be found in Eastern philosophy, where the ego is called "the false I" and "the spurious I."[11] According to this understanding, the ego is the "false I," because the "true I" would naturally be a person's deeper level or the Self. The difference between the "false I" of the Eastern philosophy and the false prophet of Revelation, however, is that the "false I" of the Eastern philosophy is a broader concept including all different forms and evolutionary stages of the ego. Perhaps St. John uses the expression "the false prophet" rather than "the false I," because in Revelation he is pondering the difference between a false and a true religion. When human beings, acting as egos limited to their minds alone, create a religion, they function erroneously as false prophets, creating their religions as would false prophets. The delusional "I" inevitably creates a delusional religion.

The false prophet of Revelation, as a sense of self limited to ego-awareness or the ego-bound human mind, can also be loosely compared to the ego-concept of Jungian psychoanalysis. According to Jung, an individual as an ego was the center of his conscious mind. Freud's ego-concept was more vague, although according to him, the ego-principle, while active, creates an experience of conscious awareness.[12] Western psychoanalytical theory admits ego's limitations, but does not view them as delusory as does Eastern philosophy and religion.

The image of the beast

"And he [the beast that came up out of the earth] deceives those who dwell on the earth... to make an image to the beast [that rose from the sea]" (Rev. 13:14). As we remember, the beast that rose from the sea represents in these interpretations the delusiveness of ego-consciousness. At the same time, the beast is a personification of the whole ego-consciousness.

When those who dwell on the earth make an image of the beast, it is the different components of human consciousness, such as the ability to think and to imagine, which are creating the image. This creation is thus a function of the human mind; that is, the image of the beast is a mental image. This mental image reflects the characteristic nature of the person's own ego-consciousness. It is a projection of the ego-consciousness. The subconscious plays an important role in the creation of this projection, as the subconscious is part of the ego-consciousness. And finally: because St. John uses the expression "an image of the *beast*", he emphasizes that the created image is delusory.

For the image of the beast, I suggest two more detailed interpretations, each complementary to the other. Both of them are important considering the subject matter of Revelation. According to the first interpretation, the image of the beast is a mental God-image created by human beings. Although it is supposed to be an image about God, human characteristics are reflected in it. Interpreted in this way, the image of the beast is an ideal type for a superficial and delusory religion.

The image of the beast reflects superficiality because it is only an image. In a superficial religion, a person actually believes in mental images and doctrines. The image of the beast is also delusory, because in it are reflected the illusions of the ego-consciousness: duality and ego-desires. Human beings create their God-images with concepts that have opposites, and they expect their God to fulfill their desires and wishes.

Furthermore, the image of the beast is an ideal type of an superficial and delusory religion, because it is a projection born *only* from the ego-consciousness. Usually the human consciousness, however, includes, along with the ego-consciousness, strains of a deeper consciousness, or the consciousness of the Self, although the boundary between the ego-consciousness and the consciousness of the Self is not always easily defined. Human spirituality is generally many-stranded, so that even a false God-image, born from the ego-consciousness, exists side by side with selfless actions and genuine spiritual experiences. The superficiality and delusion which St. John clarifies through the image of the beast, can thus be only one strand of spirituality, manifesting itself either faintly or in more well-defined ways. Another reason that the mythical image of the beast is an ideal type of a false religion is that it can include all false human images of the divine, varied as they are both in substance and in ethical value. (In their most narrow sense, the God-images have reflected the special characteristics and interests of one cultural group only. But the more elevated God-images have perhaps been created by prophets who recount a state of oneness based on their personal experiences. Their descriptions change their listeners' God-images but only according to the degree of ego-consciousness each listener retains.)

While depicting the image of the beast in Revelation, St. John may have been curious as to how the God-images come about, but the image is also an appropriate mythical image for a new stage in his spiritual progress. Having fully experienced the bliss of oneness and having at that moment overcome ego-consciousness, St. John surely sees clearly the inimical and delusory nature of his old religion. At the same time, he understands better than ever the problem of evil. Therefore, I will reiterate his solution for the problem of evil, applying it to the present context.

I assume that St. John realizes that he had earlier defined God based on his ego-consciousness. The goodness he has expected of God has been goodness on the level of ego-consciousness, and this kind of goodness has evil as its opposite. Although human beings would like to eliminate any idea of evil from their God-image, they see evil in the world, and are left to wonder about its origin. Similarly, the justice St. John expected from his God reflected the sense of righteousness which is part of life in an ordinary community, comparing merits and faults of different individuals. Maybe St. John finds that he expected God to function as would a judge mediating between individuals, rather like a person, but more powerful, enacting St. John's own ideas about goodness and righteousness. When this has not happened, St. John has perhaps asked, not unlike the prophet Habakkuk, "Why do you... hold your tongue when the wicked devours one more righteous than he?" The solution to the problem of evil in this kind of thinking is that the God-image itself, which led to the problem, is delusory and superficial. It is a mental projection based on ego-consciousness and created by the human mind.

If St. John interprets the image of the beast as a God-image created on the basis of ego-consciousness, then he is quite modern. In the philosophy, sociology, and psychology of religion, it is generally understood that persons will create for themselves a God-image as well as other religious concepts on the bases of their cultural background, the particular evolutionary stage of their community and their individual experiences. This explains the many God-images throughout the history of mankind. Likewise, the differences in individual ego-consciousness, which vary between cultures, historical periods and personal developments, elicit the great variety among the world's religions. Psychoanalytical theories offer parallels for St. John's understanding of the image of the beast. According to these theories human consciousness is vaster than the conscious mind, and it is particularly the realm beyond this conscious mind which has much affected the kind of God-images individuals create.[13]

According to my other suggestion, the image of the beast is the sense of self which is broader than the sense of self limited to the conscious mind. The false prophet represented, in previous interpretations, the narrower sense of self which covers only the ego-bound conscious mind. Because the image of the beast is born from the basis of complete, or nearly complete, ego-consciousness, it—as a sense of self—is broader than that of the false prophet. Because a person's sense of self is not limited solely to his conscious mind, I will, in the following, often simply speak of the self, when I refer to this broader, ego-bound sense of one's self.

The image of the beast, as a symbol for the self, suggests that this kind of self, too, is deluded. Although it already transcends the narrow boundaries of an ordinary human mind, it is still bound by duality and desires; women or men still experience themselves as separate entities from the rest of existence, and they still possess their own desires.

In my interpretation, the problem of the self is not at this stage as essential to St. John as the problem of his God-image. Later it will become more central in the visions, and it will be analyzed then in more detail. For now, I will simply present some parallels from literature.

The best parallel for the beast's image as a person's self is found in Eastern philosophy, according to which an individual's separate "I" in the end is simply a mental image and a delusion. For example, the Indian Ramana Maharsi explains, "Between the Self or Pure Consciousness and the inert physical body, there arises... the ego-sense or 'I' notion, the hybrid which is neither of them, and this flourishes as an individual being... Seek this and it will vanish like a phantom."[14]

In Western scientific thought, a person's sense of self is not seen as a mental image similar to that of Eastern teachings, nor is its delusory nature emphasized, but the idea of a broader self above the conscious ego is common. In Jungian psychology, in fact, a person's sense of self is thought—as a result of inner maturing—to move gradually from the center of the conscious mind, or the ego, closer to the center of the total being, or the Self. Due to inner growth, the more the sense of self expands, the closer one reaches to the Self. Freud differentiated between the ego, the id and the superego. The id refers to the instincts, and the superego, to the composite of values formed by internalizing one's parental and cultural heritage.[15] Although Freud's concept of the superego cannot be thought of as analogous to the 'broader self' as applied here, yet the superego as a concept from psychoanalysis surely speaks of the broader dimensions of man's sense of himself.

When St. John, in Revelation, analyzes and personifies the functions of consciousness with the help of the three mythical images, the beast that rises from the sea, the beast that comes up out of the earth (the false prophet) and the image of the beast, he is not much different from the theorists of our own time. For example, the way the three concepts of the Freudian psychoanalysis—id, ego, and the superego—are often used, creates an impression of living entities in the human consciousness. The metaphysical-mythical approach of Revelation and pragmatic-psychological one of the psychoanalysis, produce only somewhat differing analyses and personifications.

There are other theoretically interesting details regarding the image of the beast in St. John's vision. Because the image of the beast has been interpreted above to be both a delusory God-image and an individual's sense of self, a detailed interpretation of these concepts are explored in the following, first the aspect of the God-image and then the aspect of the self; the latter only briefly as it is examined more deeply in the seventeenth chapter.

The making of the image of the beast

"He [the beast that came up out of the earth] performs great signs so that he even makes fire come down from heaven on the earth in the sight of men. And he deceives those who dwell on the earth by those signs which he was granted to do in the sight of the beast, telling those who dwell on the earth to make an image to the beast." (Rev. 13:13–14.)[16]

In these verses, St. John mentions an important reason for creating the image of the beast, or in this case, a false God-image, and this reason has to do with the strength of the human mind. In the extreme cases man can with his conscious will direct, or at least activate, those levels of consciousness which transcend the conscious mind. During St. John's time, these phenomena were known, on the one hand, as a part of religious life—the power of prayer—and on the other hand, as witchcraft and sorcery. (Modern science has grown interested in these matters, but the research is barely in the beginning stages.)

St. John had stressed already earlier in his vision that the beast coming up out of the earth "exercises all the authority of the first beast [that rose from the sea]" (Rev. 13:12). Now the word "all," which was left out earlier, while interpreting the beast that came out of the earth, has an important meaning. The word emphasizes the fact that with the help of the conscious mind we can avail ourselves of energy which belongs to the domain of the beast that rose from the sea, or roughly, the energy which is referred to in the modern language as the unconscious. When he explains that the beast which came up out of the earth can even make fire come down from heaven onto the earth, he goes further. He seems to be saying that the power of the mind can reach to the levels which belong to the superconscious or to the higher levels of spiritual reality. Then from those levels, energy is released onto earth—that is, into such objects or events as we are capable of consciously perceiving and experiencing. This is how miraculous phenomena, or "great signs," are performed.

For an ordinary modern individual, one of the miracles easiest to grasp may be the healing of an illness through conscious autosuggestion. Should the autosuggestion be strong enough—and generally a person has a strong desire to be healthy and to live—it activates superconscious energy, or the fire from heaven. When the fire, or the energy, comes down onto the earth, or into man's body, it will heal. But St. John's worldview must certainly include also other kinds of miracles. For example, should a person pray for fulfillment of a wish to a saint no longer in a physical body, the saint may, in heaven, or in an after-death state, hear the prayer. In his great compassion, the saint may, with his spiritual power, help that person regardless of the praying individual's faults and the ego-bound nature of the wish. Then fire comes down from heaven onto the earth, as St. John describes it. The sorcery or magic mentioned in the Bible probably fits St. John's worldview because a sorcerer knows how to make use of lower cosmic energy, astral energy. St. John perhaps envisions this energy as part of heaven in this context.

Perhaps St. John now realizes a cause and effect relationship: when people as external observers see miraculous phenomena, or when they experience them themselves, they cannot help but to admit that reality includes powers which they do not fully understand. To explain these powers they create God-images. But as they are limited by their ego-consciousness, their God-images will reflect—either crudely or exquisitely—their own ego-consciousness, its dualism and desirousness.

The image of the beast speaks

"And he [the beast of the earth] was granted power to give breath to the image of the beast, that the image of the beast should both speak and cause as many as would not worship the image of the beast to be killed" (Rev. 13:15).

While interpreting this verse, it is important to remember that the image of the beast is a projection based on the ego-consciousness. Then this strange phenomenon mentioned by St. John—an image is given a breath so that it speaks—can be well understood in the light of modern psychology: when persons project their own feelings and wishes onto a false God-image, 'God's speech' is the 'speech' of their own subconscious. All this is caused by the beast that came up out of the earth, that is, it is a function of the ego-bound human mind.

The killing of people in this context possibly means that the person believing in the projected God-image is willing to kill in himself all those sides which doubt the correctness of that God-image. But killing people may also have the meaning of the dying of the ego, because even as we are able to see the delusive nature of a projected God-image, we want to give it up, and then our ego, which was bound to it, begins to die.

The image of the beast as a broader sense of self

A new sense of self is born in us when our consciousness expands so that we do not live solely as subjects of our conscious minds. The expansion of consciousness beyond its ordinary state can mean the opening of the actual parapsychological powers and their conscious control. Then the beast that came up out of the earth is performing signs, as St. John tells us. That people worship the image of the beast is easily explained by understanding that the sense of self gathers together the psyche, as it were. The concrete components of the psyche come together, or become organized under the sense of self, or the image of the beast. The image of the beast seems also to be alive, because we, as living beings, identify with our own sense of self. And the image speaks, because we all say, "I myself speak."

The killing of those people who do not worship the image of the beast can express the dying of the ego. But it can also be interpreted as the killing of doubts, because the acquisition of a new broader sense of self always means the danger of feeling superior to others since this stage of development transcends the ordinary. Under the influence of this heightened sense of self, one tends to kill in himself everything that would stir him to notice his delusional state.

Liberation from delusion

While I have been presenting the central mythical images of St. John's vision, I have taken his sequence of events out of order, and now I will return to the early parts of the vision. When St. John refers to the beast which rose from the sea, he asks, "Who is like the beast? Who is able to make war with him?" (Rev. 13:4.) With this verse, St. John is asking how human beings are able to become free of delusion in their consciousness. He answers the question a few verses later.

First St. John writes, "If anyone has an ear, let him hear" (Rev. 13:9). With these words St. John stresses the fact that the answer in this context is cognitive. To be liberated from the delusion through a personal experience will happen later.

The following tenth verse of the chapter varies in different manuscripts; basically, there are two variations of the verse.[17] The older translations generally follow one of them, the more recent translations the other. Both versions are interpreted in the following, as they both are appropriate in this context and, in fact, complement each other.

In the New King James translation, which I have been using, the tenth verse begins: "He who leads into captivity shall go into captivity; he who kills with the sword must be killed with the sword" (Rev. 13:10). These words can be associated with St. Paul's words in the Epistle to Galatians, "For whatever a man sows, that he will also reap."[18] According to Eastern philosophy, both St. John's and St. Paul's words express the law of karma. In this context, however, the law of karma is presented on a more concrete level than in the previous chapter and—instead of its metaphysical nature—man's and woman's own part is emphasized. How human beings act and think, and what their attitudes are, will change them. St. John's answer to the question about human liberation is, then: men and women can become free from delusion by gradually changing themselves.

As to the reference to leading into captivity and killing with the sword, I will suggest more specific interpretations. For example, if I should feel and express hatred for others, it is as if I tried to lock them into the prison of my hatred and negativity. But it will be I who am imprisoned, captured by my own hatred and negativity; it is I who will degenerate. Regarding killing with the sword, I think of this: all those characteristics and tendencies with which I try to force and dominate others—as if trying to kill their will—must eventually be killed in me; for this kind of liberation I will need willpower, discrimination and intuition—that is, all that which is symbolized by the sword.

The words, "He who kills with the sword must be killed with the sword" are similar to the words in the Gospel of Matthew: "For all who take the sword will perish by the sword."[19] The law of karma is clearly visible in these words: violence invites violence which eventually will turn toward the violent person himself.

To conclude the verse, St. John adds, "Here is the patience and the faith of the saints" (Rev. 13:10). That which is saintly in a human being, the Self, must wait patiently so that spiritual maturation will progress according to the law of karma. This maturation will come sooner or later as we learn that we will reap what we sow.

Interpreting the verse in this way, we can see that it comes in Revelation at an appropriate time. St. John understands that people will reward and punish themselves through their own choices and actions, so that there is no need for an outside, more or less anthropomorphic God of judgment. After this realization, St. John need no longer hold on to a false God-image, and so he can admit that it is a delusion created by the human mind. Indeed, in Revelation, after this point there follows the analyses of the beast that came out of the earth and the image of the beast.

The same tenth verse, for example, in the Today's English Version translation, reads, "Whoever is meant to be captured, will surely be captured; whoever is meant to be killed by the sword, will surely be killed by the sword. This calls for endurance and faith on the part of God's people." (Rev. 13:10.)

Expressed in Christian language, St. John emphasizes with his words the infused nature of a person's inner change and suggests the right attitude toward it. We must not try to resist change with our own will, but to surrender to it trustfully, to have faith. If we can develop this attitude, whatever is negative in us is at first pushed aside or placed in captivity, and in time, it is killed altogether. Then we will be free. Because the infused purification is a difficult inward experience, it demands endurance along with faith.

In this form, the verse has a clear connection to the Book of Jeremiah where the prophet Jeremiah predicts suffering for the Lord's people. The people have turned away from the Lord, and so He passes the dark sentence, "Such as are for death, to death; And such as are for the sword, to the sword; And such as are to the famine, to the famine; And such as are for the captivity, to the captivity."[20] One can see inner change in the Book of Jeremiah as well: the people having turned away from the Lord are like the persons bound by their ego-attachments, and they must be liberated from attachments through a severe purification.

Revelation appears to give two different answers to the question as to how human beings can become free of delusion. The first version emphasizes a person's own effort, and the second, the infused nature of the liberation irrespective of one's own endeavors. This kind of conflict is universal in religions. It is particularly well-known from speculations as to what part does men's and women's own effort and what part does God's grace play in human redemption. (Grace and infusion are comparable concepts; in grace, happiness is emphasized, and in infused purification, agony, as I explained in the eighth chapter.) One way to solve this problem has been to consider both sides. Men and women must do their own share, but the more they become free from attachments through their choices, the more room is created on a deeper level for grace and infusion.[21] In other words, in the early stages of liberation, human effort is emphasized, and later the infused nature of the change. This interpretation emphasizing infusion is also appropriate at this point in Revelation, because in the next chapters, St. John develops more deeply the changes brought about by infusion.

A further analysis of delusion in human consciousness

St. John reveals in his vision the outer form, the blasphemies, and the heads of the beast that rose from the sea, and finally, the signs of the beast and the number of the beast's name. These details support the earlier interpretations about the role of delusion in human consciousness.

The outer form of the beast

"Now the beast which I saw was like a leopard, his feet were like the feet of the bear, and his mouth like the mouth of a lion" (Rev. 13:2). This beast of Revelation has a clear connection to the Book of Daniel in the Old Testament, where the prophet Daniel saw in a vision four beasts. He compared the first beast to a lion, the second to a panther, the third to a bear, and the fourth had great teeth and ten horns.[22] In the following, the beast of Revelation is, however, interpreted only briefly without pondering its connections to other visions in the Bible.

The leopard, the bear and the lion as *general* mythical images are all beasts. The leopard and the lion, in particular, are natural predators. In this aspect, they can be associated with human ego-desires. Predators chase prey just as individuals pursue the objects of their desires, and ego-desires are an essential feature of delusion.

Leopard's fur has dark spots on a fair background, and this makes the leopard well suited to express duality since light and dark are like good and evil and right and wrong.

The bear in his broadest mythical meaning is associated with material nature. It was probably so in the early bear-worship rites, wherein we can see the close connection that early man had with nature. The bear's massive body itself as a mythical image emphasizes materiality. In his narrower meaning, the bear is one of the more common animal symbols for the unconscious. This association is possibly derived from the fact that the bear hibernates in hollows, pits, and caverns, not unlike the unconscious, which, figuratively speaking, is asleep underground. The bear has also been an important prey and source of food, and at the same time, a threat to human beings and their livestock. These features, as well, associate the bear with the unconscious, because the unconscious has two functions in human life:

on the one hand, it means nourishment and a fountain of growth, and on the other, frightening power.

Interpreted in this way, the bear's feet in St. John's vision suggest the importance that attachment to what is material has as a component in a delusory consciousness. When women and men, as living beings, must fight for their material existence, they must stand on the ground with feet like those of a bear, as it were, rather than with wings like those of a bird. Thus they must experience duality, both to be nourished and to experience want and distress. Additionally, the bear probably points out that deceptions penetrate all of the ego-consciousness, including the deep layers of the unconscious.[23]

Finally, St. John compares our human enslavement to delusion to the lion-like jaws of the beast: we are in danger of being devoured by suffering as long as we are slaves to ego-desires. Yet this suffering could help us envision our return to the original oneness and encourage us to regain the basic energy which the lion symbolizes in the Book of Revelation.[24]

The deadly wound on the beast's head

"I saw one of his heads as if it had been mortally wounded, and his deadly wound was healed" (Rev. 13:3). The different heads of the beast symbolize St. John's own delusory ways of thinking and experiencing, and that there are seven of them expresses well the process of transformation he must go through to be freed from delusion. Perhaps St. John feels he ought to be able to crush those heads one at a time. Since one of the beast's many heads has already been dead for a moment, St. John has, during that moment, felt himself to be at least partly free. For this reason I assume that the death of the beast's head was initiated by the state of bliss St. John experienced in the end of the eleventh chapter. During that state his ordinary delusory consciousness was gone, and even later the experience in bliss surely 'touched' and 'wounded' him so deeply that he felt himself partly liberated from his former state.

The original Greek text allows the interpretation that the beast's head was destroyed by a blow which caused a wound. This conveys the idea that when we first experience bliss, it actually seems like a blow because ordinary consciousness ceases altogether. We may not have even known that such a state is possible, and so we will be stunned by this experience: Paramahansa Yogananda, in fact, has called the first experience in cosmic consciousness a "liberating shock."[25] A transformed state of consciousness and its strongest effect are, however, passing, and after experiencing bliss, a return to ordinary consciousness is such a let-down that we easily feel ourselves to be again fully under the influence of a delusion. Perhaps that is why the fatally wounded head comes back to life in St. John's vision.

The beast's blasphemies

"And on his heads a blasphemous name" (Rev. 13:1). "And he was given a mouth speaking great things and blasphemies, and he was given authority against God, to blaspheme his name, his tabernacle, and those who dwell in heaven" (Rev. 13:5–6). The beast's blasphemy is essentially directed toward God and His tabernacle; the tabernacle in this context probably refers to the subjective aspect of the Self, as it did in chapter seven (Rev. 7:15). The opposition between the beast on the one hand and God and His tabernacle on the other, is expressive of the opposition between ego-consciousness and the genuinely spiritual life.

More precisely, St. John begins to understand all the more clearly—since the early part of the thirteenth chapter where these verses are presented—the significance of the ego-consciousness in the creation of a misguided religion. He realizes that human beings receive a false God-image as a projection of their ego-consciousness and a God-image like this is actually blasphemous because it reflects the beast's, or the ego-consciousness', own characteristics. As a projection of the ego-consciousness "a false I", or a wrong sense of oneself, is born. And "a false I" blasphemes God's tabernacle because a person's correct and deeper sense of I ought to be the Self, or God's dwelling.

The beast continues blaspheming for forty-two months, which is three and a half years. It is an appropriate number, because it refers to the latter part of the transformation process which I began to describe in the eleventh chapter and which St. John has expressed in different ways with the amount of "three and a half." The beast continues with its blasphemies until St. John has thoroughly understood the function of the ego-consciousness in the creation of a false religion and in his misapprehension of life. The description of this process lasts until the end of this chapter.

The sign of the beast

"And he [the beast coming up out of the earth] causes both small and great, rich and poor, free and slave, to receive a mark on their right hand or on their foreheads, and that no one may buy or sell except one who has the mark or the name of the beast, or the number of his name" (Rev. 13:16–17). In more recent translations these verses are generally divided into two separate sentences. (The translation is interpretive.) For example, the Today's English Version explains first that the beast makes everyone take the sign on their hands or foreheads, and then relates in a new sentence, "No one could buy or sell unless he had this mark, that is, the name of the beast or the number that stands for the name." Although this is a small difference, the content of the verses becomes clearer.

When the beast that comes up out of the earth is able to make everyone, great and small, put the sign on their right hands and foreheads, the vision tells us that individuals' ego-bound minds will stamp with their own special qualities all of their specific functions. In other words, man's ego-bound mind controls his thoughts and actions.

The sign referred to above is—as St. John suggests indirectly—the sign of the beast. He explains that as long as human persons are slaves to delusions, they will employ their human faculties in delusory ways. And when he associates the sign with buying and selling, he stresses the role of the ego-desires or desirousness in delusion; buying and selling are businesses, and the goal of business is to make profit. Interesting in these verses, however, is St. John's emphasis that *only* those with the sign of the beast, may buy and sell. He is probably stressing in this way that *all* thinking and acting tainted with ego-desires is delusory.

St. John probably wants to explain specifically that all spirituality which includes ego-desires in one form or another is, in the end, delusory. Perhaps St. John realizes he had expected God to intervene in the execution of goodness and righteousness in the world in the form St.

John himself thought goodness and righteousness ought to be manifested. He may, in fact, feel that he has been bargaining with God through trying to 'buy' the fulfillment of his own demands by his prayers. But now he stamps this kind of spirituality with the sign of the beast; he finds it a delusion. Although it was well-intentioned, it was bound by his own desires. The problem of ancillary desires as a fiber in well-intentioned spirituality has certainly been recognized more generally in the Christian literature. Meister Eckhart, for one, disapproves of people who try to get something, even good, with their prayers, "They bargain with our Lord."[26]

The number of the beast

"Here is wisdom. Let him who has understanding calculate the number of the beast, for it is the number of a man: His number is 666" (Rev.13:18).

The number of the beast has been interpreted, since the nineteenth century, to be a reference to Caesar Nero. When the words 'Caesar Nero' are written in Hebrew and transcribed to numbers according to the method of corresponding numbers and letters used in antiquity, we will have six hundred and sixty-six. The difficulty is that the original text of Revelation was in Greek, and in using the Hebrew version a rare form needs to be applied. During the existence of Revelation, other names, as well, have been appropriated for the beast's name—some better suited than others. For example, Father Irenaeus suggested for the number of the beast's name the Greek word *Lateinos* which meant the Roman Empire.[27] The problem with these kinds of interpretations is their non-ethical nature: the beastliness is cast onto a historical personage, institution or an empire, away from an ordinary person, away from myself.

An ethically more interesting interpretation of the beast's number can be found in Leo Tolstoy's book *War and Peace*, where Count Pierre Bezuhov ponders the riddle of the beast's number. Bezuhov has heard from a Freemason that using the number–letter correspondence the emperor Napoleon's name can be applied to the beast's number. But it occurs to Bezuhov that, likewise, his own name might fit the beast's number, and soon he actually finds the match; "This discovery was exciting to him. What connection might he have to the grand event foretold in Revelation—he did not know, yet he doubted not for a moment that there was a connection."[28]

I interpret the number of the beast according to the general symbolism of the numbers and the philosophical bases applied in this book. The number six is two times three, and therefore it describes conflicts which are part of human life and are symbolized by the number two, and the changes these conflicts bring about, symbolized by the number three. The repetition of the number six then expresses the prolonged duration of the life bound by the delusion, conflicts, and changes. In Eastern thinking this length of time, in fact, will take several consequent incarnations.[29]

Conflicts are an unavoidable part of a delusory life, because as prisoners of their desires, human beings will always experience conflict between the objects of their desires and what they have. Thus they continuously seek to satisfy their desires. But as long as they seek satisfaction in a world of deceitfulness, they find it not, nor is there an end to their seeking. They merely run in circles like hamsters on a treadmill. Apparently St. John associates the beast's number with human ego-desires, because he parallels the beast's number with the sign women and men put on their hands and foreheads while buying and selling.

These kinds of thoughts are common in religions and also in philosophies, and they have been referred to earlier. Within Christianity, a particularly good comparison for the number of the beast in Revelation is the idea of "the circle of the impious" used by Bernard of Clairvaux. This circle refers to the useless and endless seeking of persons bound by their desires. Étienne Gilson, a scholar of Bernard's works, points out that Bernhard gives nearly technical meaning to his term "the circle of the impious"; likewise, the number of the beast of Revelation as a compilation of numbers can be thought of as a kind of a technical term of the mythical language.[30]

The Buddhist symbol, the Wheel of Life, is used in Eastern cultures with a similar meaning, although it has evolved into a more detailed understanding about the power of delusion. The Wheel of Life describes the total world of delusion and a person's seemingly endless wandering, or circling, in it. The wheel has four concentric circles, of which the innermost one describes the basic reasons for desirous actions: greed, hatred, and fallacies, as well as the vicious cycle resulting from them. The second circle is divided into two halves, a light and a dark one. In the light area, a person will develop in a positive direction, in the dark area, in a negative one: toward greater attachment and accordingly toward deeper suffering. Two other circles then describe a more detailed Buddhist understanding about the world of delusion. One of them is divided in six parts, the other into twelve. The wheel itself is held by a terrible Yama monster, which represents the necessity of change; he is the deity of impermanence and death. The Wheel of Life is his mirror.[31]

When St. John says, "Here is wisdom... the number of the beast ... is the number of a man", he encourages all of us to recognize the beast in ourselves in the same way as we ought to see our own delusory life in Yama's mirror. As long as we are not free from our attachments, we are marked with the number of the beast: we go around in the circle of the impious and live in the grip of the Yama monster. The thought of the number of the beast as "the number of a man" emphasizes also that a delusory religion is our own creation, and to be liberated from it, we ourselves are to change.

IV

LIBERATION FROM THE OLD

Chapters 14–18 of Revelation

The visions in this section tell mostly about such inner transformation as leads to the death of the ego. St. John the Divine has already described this earlier, but now the change transcends the ordinary experience ever more clearly; in Christian language, the section speaks of the infused purification. The concept of infusion was presented briefly already in the eight chapter. The infused experience comes as if poured into the person undergoing it.

14. THE SINGING ON MOUNT ZION, THE THREE ANGELS, AND THE HARVEST

Experiencing the sacred

The realizations initiated by the previous vision bring such a sense of freedom to St. John that he finds life meaningful and sacred.

The Lamb and the 144,000 on Mount Zion

"Then I looked, and behold, a Lamb standing on Mount Zion and with him one hundred and forty-four thousand, having his Father's name written on their foreheads" (Rev. 14:1). The people that St. John sees are likely the same ones he noted in the seventh chapter when he saw 144,000 of the children of Israel whose foreheads were sealed with "the seal of the living God" (Rev. 7:2,4). Now these people have also received the name of the Lamb's Father on their foreheads, and they have been let up to Mount Zion where the Lamb is.

In St. John's vision, Mount Zion represents a new step toward his final goal, the New Jerusalem, because geographically Mount Zion is located in Jerusalem. In the Bible, Zion sometimes means the city of Jerusalem and its inhabitants, and yet at times, more generally, God's dwelling.[1] I interpret this new phase of the visions to mean that part of St. John has already reached Mount Zion, because he experienced bliss when he saw the ark (as mentioned at the end of the eleventh chapter). Also, on Mount Zion in Jerusalem was Solomon's temple, wherein the ark of the covenant was finally kept after the Exodus of the Jews. This temple was later destroyed.

Mount Zion is an illustration of one of the universal mythical images, the sacred mountain. Of these mountains, Mt. Sinai and the Greek Olympus were mentioned earlier, and in Christian symbolism Mount Carmel also is used to represent a holy mountain. For example, St. John of the Cross in his book *The Ascent of Mount Carmel* is actually referring to the soul's inner journey toward perfection when he writes of the ascent. In India a foremost sacred mountain is the mythical Meru, and according to this symbolism, a person's spine in India is called *Merudanda*, or Meru staff. The ascent to the inner Mt. Meru is then the ascent through the chakras all the way up to the sahasrara, or the state of bliss.[2]

The song

"And they sang as it were a new song... and no one could learn that song except the hundred and forty-four thousand" (Rev. 14:3). As was also true in the fifth chapter, singing symbolizes experiencing spirituality, and the fact that the song is a new one, emphasizes St. John is on his way from his former state of being toward a new one.

The words "and no one could learn that song except the hundred and forty-four thousand" express the universal thought that we have to experience exalted spiritual states for ourselves as a result of an inner maturing—they cannot be passed on by word of mouth. This thought appears also in the beginning of Revelation when the Spirit says, "To him who overcomes I will give some of the hidden manna to eat. And I will give him a white stone, and on the stone a new name written which no one knows except him who receives it" (Rev. 2:17). St. John of the Cross refers to the parable of a white stone in the same sense when he writes:

> It is impossible to describe the joy embracing man in this experience... Such language alone will suffice whereby the fortunate understands the events in himself, rejoices in them and keeps his silence. The soul awakens recalling... the little stone which St. John speaks of, with the name written on it known to no one but to him who receives it.[3]

The same thought about the nature of experiencing the sacred is presented in Eastern literature by stressing that one cannot know the taste of a fruit except by eating it, not from descriptions by other people.[4]

The virgins

"These [standing on Mount Zion] are the ones who were not defiled with women, for they are virgins" (Rev. 14:4). Although St. John's symbolism is stamped by strict asceticism—sexual intercourse would make one unclean—one can also read a universal meaning in it.

When we experience pleasure from satisfying ego-desires, we have intercourse, as it were, with the objects of our desires. Bound to ego-desires the consciousness, however, is not absolutely serene and resolved even during the moment of gratification, because other wishes or the desire for more of the same make the consciousness enterprising. This kind of ambition, derived from ego-desires, is fittingly symbolized through the sexual act: as if the shuttle of desires and thoughts were in perpetual motion. (Paul Brunton expressed this concept at the end of the eleventh chapter.) To achieve the highest experiences, bliss, and oneness, the consciousness must be empty, or 'clean,' from all ego-desires. And this cleanliness is symbolized in St. John's vision by virginity, which he, deviating from the usual gender symbolism, applies to a man. In Christian literature, Meister Eckhart, in particular, speaks often in his sermons of virgins and virginity using this kind of figurative meaning.[5]

A mythical understanding differentiates between several layers or levels in the human consciousness. In the outermost levels of consciousness, we are bound to our ego-desires and seek to satisfy them. The most valuable spiritual experiences occur within the inner levels which open up only after we have become liberated from our attachments. Thus the innermost levels of human consciousness have never taken part in satisfying ego-desires, here mythically expressed as sexual intercourse. For example, St. Teresa compares the human soul to a castle with many dwellings or rooms, and in the outer ones, the soul can experience intercourse which means sense pleasure, but in the inner dwellings, the soul will unite only with God. To reach the inner rooms, the soul needs to traverse the castle, and during this journey, its old habits will die off and it will experience a deep transformation.[6] Accordingly, the virgins on Mount Zion in St. John's vision symbolize these inner levels of consciousness where one experiences spiritual values 'purely.' In other words, those people are part of the Self. Meister Eckhart, too, gives this kind of meaning to the people in St. John's vision.[7]

The first-fruits and their purity

"These [who stood on Mount Zion] were redeemed from among men, being first-fruits to God and to the Lamb. And in their mouth was found no guile, for they are without fault." (Rev. 14:4–5.) The first-fruit as a mythical image says that St. John understands his spiritual transformation is incomplete. Thus all of his faculties or 'parts,' have not yet reached Mount Zion in Jerusalem. In this context, guile probably refers to delusion, the mouth as a container-like symbol relates to the consciousness, and the contents of the mouth, the content of the consciousness. With his words St. John emphasizes that those who are standing on Mount Zion symbolize the experience which is free from the delusion; on Mount Zion one experiences the sacred. Therefore, rather than guile, these people have song in their mouths.

The repetition

The vision of St. John continues: he sees three angels, each with a message to deliver. In the next verses, St. John reviews what he has already learned, but I assume that while doing so he understands matters more deeply. In the previous chapter, there were no angels, but St. John would say, for instance, "the world [or actually the earth, *gē*] followed and marveled at the beast" (Rev. 13:3); thus, St. John was at that time relying on ordinary cognition rather than intuition. In the following, I am interpreting only the more important points of the recapitulation.

The first angel

"Then I saw another angel flying in the midst of heaven, having the everlasting gospel to preach to those who dwell on the earth—to every nation, tribe, tongue, and people" (Rev. 14:6). The message of the everlasting gospel is essentially this: our own experience is what is important in a religion; what matters is that we ourselves experience love and bliss. On the contrary, externalized beliefs like different God-images are unessential. They reflect ego-consciousness and the cultural differences it creates among different groups: nations, tribes, tongues, and people. A religion, however, cannot be built on ego-consciousness, because in the core of a genuine, deeply spiritual life is the transcending of that consciousness, which means the death of ego.

Another angel

"And another angel followed, saying, 'Babylon is fallen, is fallen, that great city, because she has made all nations drink of the wine of the wrath of her fornication'" (Rev. 14:8). Later on Babylon has an important place in Revelation, but it cannot yet be interpreted in detail as St. John mentions it only briefly.

The symbolism of Babylon in the Bible comes from a historical event, the forced transfer of the Jews into Babylon from Jerusalem and Judea during the 590s and 580s B.C. As a general mythical image Babylon, which was the capital of the ancient Babylonia, is comparable to Egypt and Assyria. It symbolizes the estranged side of the human consciousness, or the ego-consciousness, as this form of consciousness is the state of the mythical exile.[8] Because St. John has in the previous chapter explained ego-consciousness and the delusiveness of the religions based on it, it can be tentatively assumed that Babylon as a mythical image represents a delusory sense of life, formed by ego-consciousness, and a spirituality based on this consciousness.

In Christian literature, Babylon and Babylonia generally have a negative meaning. For example, in the following passage the Orthodox bishop Theophan the Recluse uses Babylonia as a symbol for outward spirituality. He speaks here of the right "prayer of the heart" eventually reached through a more outward one, "In this case the understanding is no longer like the captive who was taken from Jerusalem to Assyria, but it is like the returner from Babylonia home to Zion."[9]

The angel's words, "Babylon is fallen, is fallen" reiterates St. John's realization that his old religion and sense of life have been permeated by ego-consciousness, and he must give them up. Later on we find out that Babylon's defeat takes a long time. It is difficult to detach oneself thoroughly from old habits and feelings, although St. John has already understood that they are delusory.

Babylon, symbolizing a false religion and an improper attitude in life, has meant intercourse with wrong values. Therefore, it has represented fornication.[10] Acting on the wrong sense of values has also been like a drug, as it has given satisfaction to the ego-consciousness. Because satisfaction like this is not fulfilling, one who partakes in it will eventually be disappointed and so he will suffer. That is why the wine from Babylon is for St. John that of the wrath of fornication.

The third angel

"Then a third angel followed them, saying with a loud voice, 'If anyone worships the beast and his image, and receives his mark on his forehead or on his hand, he himself shall also drink of the wine of the wrath of God, which is poured out full strength into the cup of his indignation. And he shall be tormented with fire and brimstone in the presence of the holy angels and in the presence of the Lamb.'" (Rev. 14:9–10.)

In these verses St. John emphasizes again that his old religion has been delusory. He explains that, in the end, everyone who has fallen into a false religion, must come to realize his delusion; and to face one's own delusion is as painful as it is to drink the wine of wrath and to be scorched by fire and brimstone. But the agony leads to release from the delusion, and so it is good. Thus the wine of the wrath one must drink, is the wine of *God's* wrath, and therefore the one who suffers is tormented in the presence of the holy angels and the Lamb. At the end of this vision St. John describes a change that causes pain but is beneficial. The words of the third angel may, however, refer also more broadly to the visions of this section (that is, to chapters 14–18), which all illustrate infused purification.

Inner transformation: agony and liberation

Reaping the earth's harvest

"And I looked, and behold, a white cloud, and on the cloud sat one like the Son of Man, having on his head a golden crown, and in his hand a sharp sickle. And another angel came out of the temple, crying with a loud voice to him who sat on the cloud, 'Thrust in your sickle and reap, for the time has come for you to reap, for the harvest of the earth is ripe.' So he who sat on the cloud thrust in his sickle on the earth, and the earth was reaped." (Rev. 14:14–16.)

During a strong transformation, it seems to us we are losing our previous foundation, as if we were cut off from our roots. I feel that this is the kind of an experience St. John is describing when he explains that the earth's harvest has been reaped.

As a mythical image, grain represents a person's energy, or both the psychic and physical functioning that produces a harvest. The roots—which give grain its strength—are the motives for activity. Until the ego's death these motives are ego-desires, because the person is striving to satisfy his wants. Since the deepest roots of the motives are in the subconscious, they are figuratively underground, even as the roots of the grain are. Until the death of the ego, human activity and personal identity are bound by ego-desires. That is why in St. John's vision the grain is attached to its roots before the mythical harvest.

But the transformation is beginning to take place, and St. John has been prepared for it by the introspection he has described in his previous visions. In this vision, he hears the words, "The harvest of the earth is ripe," and, like the grain, he has matured. Spiritual maturation means turning inward, and the earlier, more outward attachments begin to be discarded by St. John.

On the inner road, during the different stages of our development, we must often experience the harvest described by St. John. In the early stages we will notice the change, perhaps, only in the sense that we simply have no more motivation for the actions that previously were normal. But when the severance is experienced on a deeper, intuitive level of spiritual internalizing, it can be an intensive and even a frightening experience; and I believe that St. John in his vision is describing this kind of transformation. I will compare the harvest in Revelation to excerpts from *The Dark Night* by St. John of the Cross, which in itself is a profound and detailed description of infused purification.

St. John of the Cross says the purification involves a stage wherein "the soul... separates from all that has been created," and in this separation "the roots of the sins and every imperfection are cut off." St. John of the Cross explains the meaning of the change in the following way, "To be able to listen to God the soul must be... separated from his attachments and senses." He gives also advice for someone living through this stage, "Should its own powers cease, the soul must not be disturbed, but rather, she has a reason to rejoice." It is difficult, however, to retain a cheerful attitude during the standstill, and so the change is generally experienced to be "bitter and terrible." The writings by St. John of the Cross reveal that he, too, experienced these stages as terrifying.[11]

St. John the Divine finds that his previous attitudes and spiritual beliefs have been cut off at their roots. Whereas previously he had drawn in both internal and external energy from them, now he fully realizes that these roots were formed in delusion and permeated by ego-consciousness. He sees he is in the midst of a transformation.

In the vision, the reaper of the earth's harvest is "one like the Son of Man." The expression "the Son of Man" is used in the Bible to refer to Jesus, particularly in such connections as have to do with the fulfillment of justice such as when Jesus is said to act as a judge. For example, in the Gospel of John, God gives Jesus "authority to execute judgment, because he is the Son of Man." In the Gospel of Luke, Jesus recalls the punishments which were passed in the days of Noah and Lot, and he says, "Even so will it be in the day when the Son of Man is revealed." While relating this judgement day of the Son of Man, he adds, "Whoever seeks to save his life will lose it, and whoever loses his life will preserve it."[12]

The quote from the Gospel of Luke, is particularly interesting because it seems to point out that the judgment passed by the Son of Man is, in fact, based on the inner law of human life: he who clings to his ego will suffer, but he who lets go of his ego will find a deeper life. And this law is that "eternal law" of God, or the law of karma, which earlier was read into the rod of the heavenly child; in the Gospel of Luke this law is just expressed in slightly different words. For this reason I interpret St. John's reference to the Son of Man to emphasize his earlier realization, "An anthropomorphic God outside human beings, allotting punishment and rewards, is not necessary for the fulfillment of justice, which will come to pass in its deepest meaning according to the inner law at work in human life itself."

Although God's eternal law, or the law of karma, functions in individual lives, the law itself surpasses the individual and as such is a fitting target for a mythical personification. Therefore, I interpret here the one like the Son of Man as a personification of the eternal law of God, or the law of karma. St. John's narrative has developed in such a way that the child of the twelfth chapter who was said to guide the nations with his rod now has another mythical personification representing especially his guidance. Both mythical images—the child and the one like the Son of Man—however, are associated with Jesus.

In the Bible, the law of karma is expressed also in an even more concrete way, as presented earlier, "Man will reap what he sows." And now, in Revelation, the time to reap has arrived: a transformation follows the inner maturation.

Because the harvest in Revelation is reaped by the one who sits on the cloud thrusting his sickle onto the earth, the sense of rootlessness resulting from the reaping befalls on St. John from heaven, as it were. St. John must feel that these things are infused or poured into him, although, at the same time, according to the law of karma they result from that which he has sown earlier. Apparently a deep intuition about the necessity of the transformation initiates this purification in St. John, because in the vision it is an angel who calls for the harvest to be reaped.

But why should it be one like the Son of Man sitting on the cloud? In many places in the Bible when the Son of Man and his coming judgment is talked about, the Son of Man is said to come "with the clouds of heaven."[13] Here, however, I interpret the cloud to continue the previous cloud symbols in Revelation. The reader might remember that a great angel who stood on the earth and the sea was clothed with a cloud, and the two witnesses ascended into heaven in a cloud (Rev. 10:1 and 11:12). At that time, the cloud was interpreted to be a cover concealing secrets. The one like the Son of Man sitting on the cloud, on the other hand, has emerged from the cloud cover.

This transformation can be understood in the following way. A central problem in St. John's previous religion was: How could a just God allow injustice in the world. This problem began to clear up for St. John when, after his rebirth, he understood justice in a new way as being expressed through the law of karma. And now, in the reaping of the harvest, he himself experiences a spiritual transformation according to the law of karma, and thus he knows from a personal experience how justice in its spiritual and innermost meaning comes to pass. This clearing up of matters, or the victory gained over the problems, is perhaps enhanced by the wreath-crown which the one like the Son of Man has on his head. (The word *stephanos* used by St. John is the same word which he used earlier for the crowns of the locusts and the garland of the heavenly woman.[14])

Reaping the grapes

"Then another angel came out of the temple which is in heaven, he also having a sharp sickle. Another angel came out from the altar, who had power over fire, and he cried with a loud cry to him who had the sharp sickle, saying, 'Thrust in your sharp sickle and gather the clusters of the vine of the earth, for her grapes are fully ripe.' So the angel thrust his sickle into the earth and gathered the vine of the earth." (Rev. 14:17–19.) Reaping the grapes from the vine of the earth expresses a change similar to the reaping of the harvest of the earth, but instead of affecting behaviors, the change affects experiencing values (the symbolism of the grapes in the Bible is connected to the value experience.[15])

A value experience is usually awakened by some source. In a religious life, a value experience can be initiated by a church ritual or it can be created by the praying person's spiritual imagery; in a more worldly setting, the beauty of a work of art or nature can be a source for a value experience. In the symbolism in Revelation, this connection between the source and the value experience initiated by it is expressed as the vine: the vine brings nourishment to the grapes, and similarly the individual receives joy from some source. But now that the grapes are cut off the vine, St. John feels himself cut off from the things which earlier had been a source of joy.

In the case of the grapes, the reaping is a result of St. John's inner maturation, because in his vision he hears the words "her grapes are fully ripe." A new way to experience values is ripening in St. John, a way that is not tied to external sources. (In this connection, the word *external* is relative, because even a mental image can be an outward source of a value experience.) In the interim, when the new way—independent of outer sources—to experience values has not yet opened up, this change, too, brings agony: St. John in the midst of the change finds himself cut off and without nourishment, joy and love.

St. John of the Cross describes this kind of an experience as a part of infused purification, wherein the soul is dissevered from its attachments. He writes:

God... weans it [the soul] from the breast milk and the child's mild and sweet food... so that it would reach for the nourishment of the strong... In this purification of the wants, God has taken from the soul all enjoyment.[16]

Even as a child is weaned from her mother's breast which had provided her with nourishment, the grapes of the vision in Revelation are severed from the vine that nourished them. In this context, St. John of the Cross describes specifically a preliminary transition from meditative prayer to contemplation, and this could well be the meaning of the gathering of the earth's vine clusters in St. John the Divine's spiritual transformation. The accounts of the two saints are, in fact, combined in the following.

In Christianity, meditative prayer refers to concentrating on some religious thought or image. The one who prays draws from them spiritual joy, in the same way as in Revelation the grapes receive nourishment through the vine. According to St. John of the Cross, man in his spiritual development, however, comes to a stage where he finds himself unable to pray in this way, and it will not nourish him, no matter how he tries to concentrate. Applying the symbolism in Revelation, this is when the grapes are cut off from the vine. St. John of the Cross explains further that the experience may feel dreadful, but in reality the soul is going through a transition to contemplative prayer, in which she starts to experience inner quiet without any images.[17]

St. John of the Cross calls the first stage of infused purification "the purification of the senses." When the soul does not get satisfaction from what the senses and the imagination can give, the sense desires fade, and, in the words of St. John of the Cross, the "palate of the soul" is cleansed for the more internal spiritual nurishment.[18] I feel that the harvesting and the reaping of the grapes in Revelation could reflect such a purification of the senses.

Because the clusters of the vine are reaped by a sickle thrust from heaven onto earth, St. John the Divine experiences infused purification, which comes over him as if poured from heaven. That angels too are in his vision emphasizes the intuitive or infused nature of his progress.

In the vision, the angel that calls for the gathering of the grapes, comes out from the altar and has power over fire. I assume this to be the same altar fire as that which was interpreted to be universal love in the eighth chapter (Rev. 8:5). Indeed, St. John is to learn ever deeper and more universal love during the closing events of the vision.

Trampling of the winepress

"So the angel thrust... it [the grapes] into the great winepress of the wrath of God. And the winepress was trampled outside the city, and blood came out of the winepress, up to the horses' bridles, for one thousand six hundred furlongs." (Rev. 14:19–20.)

As a symbol, the winepress creates an image of pressure, compression, and anguish. In the northern cultures, similar images are a press and a mangle. Having endured the difficult circumstances in our lives, we feel ourselves to have survived exceeding pressure. The events described by St. John in this vision culminates thus in a sense of deep anguish before his liberation.

When St. John has been severed from his previous sources of joy during the gathering of the clusters of the vine of the earth, he is left so disconnected that he finds it terrifying. St. John of the Cross describes this feeling emphasizing the sense of pressure, "Under the stress of this oppression and weight, the soul feels so much a stranger to being favored that she thinks, and so it is, that even that which previously upheld her has vanished along with everything else."[19]

In the winepress, the grapes are in between two forces—on the one hand, there is the winepress, and on the other, the trampling. This image means that St. John the Divine is in the midst of an inner conflict which he finds crushing. We must face inner conflicts in many forms at different stages of our lives, but here the winepress experience is analyzed so that it serves to explain a deep spiritual transformation.

One crushing force is human attachments, ego-desires. Individual persons would, at least in some ways, want to continue to live as before; they would like to draw satisfaction from the previous sources of joy. In St. John's case the attachment in question is probably his former religion and the enjoyment and comfort he derived from his religious ideas. But now he is in a state where he understands the defects in his previous condition. He realizes that he must change. The other force distressing St. John—as it would anyone in the midst of a winepress experience—is the new life he feels waiting for him. But before the transition has truly happened, the new situation is unknown and therefore, frightening, even agonizing.

Although in the end, the change will lead to good, St. John lives through such throes that he feels himself to be the target of God's wrath. Perhaps he believes the foot crushing him in the press to be the foot of God Himself. In the words of St. John of the Cross, "Although the hand of God is truly gentle and sweet, the soul finds it heavy and wrathful."[20]

Why does St. John the Divine experience a change so terrible that it manifests itself as God's wrath? The question can be answered by further studying St. John of the Cross. That the change should be oppressive can come from heightened self-knowledge. As our spiritual development progresses, we see ourselves suddenly in a new light, such as we are with all of our attachments. In Revelation, St. John, based on his earlier analyses, realizes now, in the bright light of intuition, the shortcomings of his former religious life—he feels ashamed and he suffers. It may also seem impossible to be freed from all his previous failings. This moment of realization is described by St. John of the Cross through a parable of pure light, but his parable includes also a similar inner conflict expressed in the winepress symbolism, "When this pure light falls on the soul to dispel impurity, the soul finds herself so unclean and miserable she feels God to be against her, and she feels herself having stood up against God."[21]

St. John of the Cross explains also that the anguish comes from the "soul's natural moral and spiritual weakness." We don't normally take inner changes easily, but they are especially difficult during the culmination of the change. In the words of St. John of the Cross, "The soul suffers in her weakness so much that she is nearly exhausted; this is so, in particular, at the times the light is cast on it brighter than usual. Both the senses and the spirit seem under some enormous, dark burden."[22]

Constrained by the two forces, we might feel we have come to a dead end. We are unable to see how we could move forward in any direction. Although part of us would like to return to our old ways of life, we understand it is not possible. The former life has irrevocably proved itself inadequate. But we do not know how we can go onward.

We cannot visualize ourselves without the ego-desires and enjoyments which so far have provided us with our goals as well as the entire sense of identity. St. John the Divine must wonder anxiously what spiritual life there is left for him should his religious imagery no longer satisfy him.

This dead-end situation can develop to terrifying dimensions. The aspirant in the winepress may feel: "Should I lose myself as I am now, what will be left of me? How can I live? What will motivate me to continue to live?" On the deeper levels of spiritual development this fear is not an ordinary everyday fear, but something deeply rooted in the human psyche. For years—or considering the Eastern understanding of reincarnation, even for thousands of years—we have identified ourselves through our attachments. When those attachments fall away, we resist the change; we fear a feeling of emptiness. In our distress, we feel like crushed grapes. Often it takes utmost anguish to bring us finally to feel so helpless there is nothing to do but to surrender. And when we have no more strength to fight, a transformation occurs.

In the grape parable, the skin and the flesh of the grape symbolize the level of the ego-consciousness. In agony, we are so badly crushed that finally we surrender ourselves. Then a deeper level of consciousness, the Self, will course out. The Self is presented in this vision as the core-extract of the grape; and because the Self means a new, ever deeper love and joy, it brings a solution to the conflict symbolized by the winepress. It is like a synthesis emerging from the thesis and antithesis. St. John need not cling to his ego nor step into a dead emptiness, but in the crush of the winepress and the trampling, out of himself, or the grape, a new life comes gushing forth.

In Revelation, the core-extract of the grapes is blood, because the grapes are we ourselves and blood symbolizes our core-extract, core-essence, love.[23] Thus the winepress experience is a kind of a crucifixion of the ego. When the ego dies, the blood, or the Self, springs forth, as the blood flowed from Jesus on the Cross.

After his winepress experience, St. John—like anyone having lived often enough through such an experience—is able to live that joy and love which have no source in the outer world or in his own mental images. He finds within himself an ability to feel joy regardless of outer factors and conditions. This change is explained by St. Teresa's parable wherein she says the superficial joys come to us, as if through a water pipe from a distance, but spiritual joy flows forth directly from the spring which is the innermost part of the soul.[24] The first situation is comparable to the event in Revelation where the grapes receive nourishment through the vine, and the latter, to the blood gushing forth from inside the grapes.

Having survived the winepress, we are able to enjoy again those joys brought to us by our senses which we consider good. But the difference is that our attachment to outer enjoyment has weakened. We do not suffer when some outer joy is kept from us, because the ability to draw from the inward joy has begun to ripen.

There are a few more details to interpret in the trampling of the winepress in Revelation.

The winepress was trampled "outside the city" (Rev. 14:20). The reason for this is probably a state of consciousness alienated from the normal life: in our deep agony, we are 'outsiders.' We are separated even from our own everyday feeling for life, and so the experience takes place outside the normal life, or the bustle of the city.

St. John writes that "blood came out of the winepress, up to the horses' bridles" (Rev. 14:20). Apparently so much blood streams out that it reaches from the ground up to the horses' bridles covering them in blood. Essential in this illustration is that St. John uses the soaking of the horses' bridles in blood as one of his mythical images.

St. John is likely to feel that his consciousness with its attachments up until now has been like an unmanageable horse. Without the bridles, or a sense of righteousness and willpower, it would run off wherever it should please. A good comparison here is the parable by St. Teresa wherein she says that some people have such a chaotic consciousness that it is like a wild horse, and that only a skillful rider can spare one from accidents.[25]

When blood foams up to the horses' bridles in St. John's vision, it means that love is replacing a sense of righteousness and willpower to an ever-greater extent. As a result of his winepress experience, St. John moves ever more clearly from the ethics of justice to the ethics of love, although the change is not yet complete. At the same time, his whole attitude toward life lightens, because his thinking, feeling and actions stem more spontaneously from unconditional love. Perhaps he feels that from now on he can continue his mythical journey, as it were, riding a horse immersed in blood, or love, and thus quickly reach his destiny.

St. John notes that blood came out of the winepress for one thousand six hundred furlongs. One thousand six hundred is formed from the number "one thousand" and the number "six hundred," or essentially, from one and six. I suggest these numbers symbolize the twofold meaning of St. John's winepress experience. When blood came out from the grapes, he felt liberation, which was an experience in love, joy, and oneness. The number one, like the number one thousand derived from it, describes this kind of experience in oneness. On the other hand, the love pouring out affected St. John's behavior and his attitude, freeing him to get a new lease on life, symbolized by the number six which is associated with action and change.

In reality, one thousand six hundred furlongs is almost two hundred miles. Thus the field of blood rushing out of the winepress has a diameter of hundreds of miles and it rises from the ground to a height of about five feet. This unbelievable amount of blood probably reflects the enormity of St. John's winepress experience and its transforming effect.

15. THE VICTORY OVER THE BEAST AND THE DECLARATION OF THE FINAL PLAGUES

The liberation

St. John's purification continues, but in this chapter, it is lightened by joy. His relief is the result of the winepress experience in the previous chapter, wherein the core-extract of the grapes, or love, flowed forth. St. John of the Cross explains that along with agony, the purification sent by God includes joy. "In the midst of dry periods and anguish, God... often allows the soul, when she least expects it, sweetness, pure love and spiritual knowledge which, at times, are particularly exquisite."[1]

The sea of glass and the victory over the beast

"And I saw something like a sea of glass mingled with fire, and those who have the victory over the beast, over his image and over his mark and over the number of his name, standing on the sea of glass" (Rev. 15:2). The victory over the beast illustrates the sense of freedom spreading over St. John: he feels that he has gained a partial victory over delusion in its many manifest forms.

In the fourth chapter the sea of glass represented that which is unconscious, potential, and even chaotic, and it has the same general meaning here. Only those matters which seem unconscious, potential, and chaotic to St. John, are different. The change is natural, because he has long traveled the inner road, and his understanding of reality has changed.

I assume that the sea of glass symbolizes in this vision the realm of ego-consciousness or man's delusory existence. It is the world of the beast, of the image and the name of the beast, or the world of delusion. Even as St. John has been changing, he has begun to see reality in a new way. With the opening up of a new state of consciousness, that which he had previously considered normal awareness now appears as uninformed, subconscious chaos—or at best, a mere dream. The idea of normal consciousness being but a dream is common both in Western and Eastern literature. It was, in fact, used as an example earlier in Ludwig Wittgenstein's words, "In our best moments we wake up just enough to realize that we are dreaming... Most of the time we are fast asleep." In the *Bhagavadgita,* the thought is expressed in these words, "What is the time of awakening to an ordinary man, is night to a yogi." St. John's sea of glass in this vision can be compared to the well-known concept of the sea of *samsara,* or the sea of delusion in Eastern philosophy, which generally refers to delusory existence.[2]

Perhaps the sea in Revelation is of glass because one can see through glass, and surely St. John feels by now that he has seen through his deceitful human consciousness. One can also stand on the surface of the sea of glass, and so St. John can express his partial victory over delusion through a mythical image of "those who have the victory over the beast... standing on the sea of glass."

And why is the sea of glass mingled with fire? Fire is a mythical image for energy, but energy can present itself both in its noble form as a fire of love and wisdom, and in its ignoble form such as a caustic passion. Fire carries negative symbolism, for example, in the *Bhagavadgita* where desire is said to be "a constant enemy" and "a fire never satisfied."[3] The same meaning of desire fits well this section of Revelation, as human bondage to desires is a characteristic property of ego-consciousness. In ego-consciousness, or in the sea of delusion, men and women live as if burning with desire and passion. We might recall that the dragon or the cosmic delusion, which gave the power to the other forms of delusion, was "fiery red" (Rev. 12:3).

However, the positive meaning of fire is also appropriate here if we assume that fire purifies women and men with its flame of love and wisdom. As long as they are prisoners of their desires, they will also be subject to a purifying fire. Thus the sea of glass would mean ordinary consciousness, which may already include, along with the ego-consciousness, intuitive wisdom and love.

The region above the sea of glass where those victorious over the beast are, represents a pure consciousness of the Self, or that consciousness which is free from desires and where even the purifying aspect of fire is no longer needed.

The song of Moses and the Lamb

"And I saw [them]... having harps of God. And they sing the song of Moses, the servant of God, and the song of the Lamb, saying, 'Great and marvelous are your works... Just and true are your ways... For your judgments have been manifested.'" (Rev. 15:2–3.)

The song sung by the victorious is not only the song of the Lamb as it was earlier, but also the song of Moses, and here God's righteousness in his judgments is stressed. Moses, as a symbol, generally refers to the Old Testament religion, where God is the God of righteousness; he gave Moses the tablets of law, the laws of right and wrong. That Moses is brought into the song tells us, that after his significant spiritual experience at the end of the last chapter, St. John has thoroughly and personally understood how righteousness in its deepest sense shows itself in human life. It comes to pass according to the law, "Whoever seeks to save his life will lose it, and whoever loses his life will preserve it." And now in the agony of the winepress, St. John himself has lost some of his ego and must have felt he has received a righteous 'judgment.' Therefore, he can say that God's judgment has been made manifest. But more than that happened in the winepress. St. John's Self, blood or love, gushed forth, whereby he began to find his genuine life. Thus he understands from a personal experience how righteousness and love are deeply connected to each other, and so the song is both that of Moses *and* that of the Lamb.

The temple of the tabernacle of the testimony

"After these things I looked, and behold, the temple of the tabernacle of the testimony in heaven was opened" (Rev. 15:5). The opening of the temple in heaven symbolizes—as it did in the end of the eleventh chapter—the opening of an exalted state of consciousness. St. John's spiritual experience, which began in this chapter with the song of Moses and the Lamb, and the playing of the harps, heightens thus to an ever more heavenly experience.

The word "testimony," in the temple of the tabernacle of the testimony, probably points out, that in this experience, keen intuitive realization is central. Similarly, St. John of the Cross explained in the passage quoted at the beginning of this chapter, that "God... allows the soul... spiritual knowledge which, at times, is particularly exquisite." The opening of the temple of the tabernacle of the testimony probably is not as absolute an experience in bliss as is the opening of the temple at the end of the eleventh chapter when the ark of the covenant was visible. In fact, St. John of the Cross stresses that one does not always notice clearly the love flaming in the soul during an infused purification.[4]

The word "testimony" in this connection suggests also that the exalted spiritual states are like a testimony for the individual who experiences them: the individual is changed by the power of his experience. This change is soon described in Revelation.

The new change begins

The present vision by St. John begins with a verse which I have not yet interpreted, "Then I saw another sign in heaven, great and marvelous; seven angels having the seven last plagues, for in them the wrath of God is complete" (Rev. 15:1). In this verse, St. John anticipates his new intuitive transformation with its different phases symbolized by the seven angels. This change, too, involves a purification filled with agony, and that is why the angels have plagues. But at the same time, the change is good, and so the plagues are *God's* wrath.

St. John continues his description of the angels toward the end of the chapter, after the temple of the tabernacle of the testimony in heaven has been opened, "And out of the temple came the seven angels having the seven plagues" (Rev. 15:6). Continual spiritual intuitions change individuals, and I feel it is this transformation that the angels coming out of the temple describe. St. John, however, traces the source of this change to a loftier reality than human intuition.

He writes, "Then one of the four living creatures gave to the seven angels golden bowls full of the wrath of God who lives for ever and ever" (Rev. 15:7). Although "God's wrath" is a projective expression, the phrase informs us that St. John thinks of God as the origin of his purification. A good comparison can be found in St. John of the Cross, who speaks of purification saying that it is "God's influence flowing to the soul."[5] When, in Revelation, one of the creatures gives the angel the bowls of God's wrath, the outpouring mentioned by St. John of the

Cross is pictured as a series of metaphors that move from God to creature to angel.

A bowl, as a symbol, emphasizes the nature of purification as an actual experience. While St. John's purification progresses, he must as if drink, or experience, the contents of the bowls.[6]

"The temple was filled with smoke from the glory of God and from his power" (Rev. 15:8). When St. John says the temple is filled with smoke from the glory of God, he is using a paradoxical mythical image. Because smoke creates poor visibility and even darkness, the glory that is usually associated with brightness functions to obscure the vision. A brightness which obscures, however, is possible in the inner life. When the temple in heaven opened, St. John surely felt himself to taste God's glory or brightness, and now this spiritual experience begins to change him. But, during the transition, he feels confusion and even anxiety, and these feelings are depicted as smoke and obscurity and as the darkness created by the smoke.

St. John of the Cross, likewise, combines light and darkness in his description of infused purification; he speaks about the "divine and dark light." He compares God to pure light, which creates in man "a dark night", and by the dark night he means specifically agony and confusion.[7] St. John of the Cross asks also, "If it is a divine light, why does the soul call it a dark night?" And he answers, "For one thing, the reason is the height of the divine wisdom, which surpasses the soul's comprehension and thus it is darkness to it. Another reason is the soul's lowliness and impurity, and that is why this divine wisdom is painful for it, bringing agony and even darkness."[8]

Furthermore, St. John of the Cross points out, "When the soul is truly facing this kind of divine light, it feels utmost pain for its own impurity."[9] Also St. John the Divine is in a transformation. A new life is opening to him, but he does not yet experience it to the point that the new would wipe away all the old.

This chapter of Revelation ends with words: "And no one was able to enter the temple till the seven plagues of the seven angels were completed" (Rev. 15:8). Before the inner transformation of St. John the Divine has fully taken place, he cannot experience those blissful superconscious states symbolized by the temple in heaven. On the contrary, during the transformation he must feel agony: he feels himself a target for plagues.

16. THE PLAGUES FROM THE BOWLS AND THE BATTLE OF ARMAGEDDON

The infused purification

"Then I heard a loud voice from the temple saying to the seven angels, 'Go and pour out the bowls of wrath of God on the earth'" (Rev. 16:1). The exalted spiritual experience of the previous chapter, symbolized by the opening of the temple in heaven, begins to influence St. John's ordinary consciousness, the earth, and changes it. During the transformation St. John feels that something painful is as if poured or infused into him; the transformation is painful but purifying.

During a purification, one encounters several similar inner trials and likewise feelings of mercy, but always in different degrees of intensity and with different overtones and on different levels of consciousness. In Revelation, purification has occurred during the trumpet blasts and the harvest; the trumpet blasts have structural similarities with St. John's new plagues. In both cases, during the first plague, something is thrown down onto the earth; as a result of the second and third plagues, the sea and the rivers and the springs of the waters are changed. The fourth plague concerns the sun, and during the fifth, the darkness descends and men are in agony. In the sixth plague the river Euphrates is mentioned, and after the last trumpet blare and pouring out the last bowlful, there are lightning, thunder, hails and earthquake.[1]

While St. John of the Cross describes infused purification in his book *The Dark Night*, he interprets the same verses twice. His first interpretation of the verses portrays the purification of the senses, but the second time he describes a deep spiritual purification.[2] In the following, I will choose excerpts from the works of St. John of the Cross so that they will clarify the images in Revelation without paying attention to the depth of the purification.

The first angel

"So the first [angel] went and poured out his bowl upon the earth, and foul and loathsome sores came upon the men who had the mark of the beast and those who worshipped his image" (Rev. 16:2). In this verse, the word *helchos* of the original manuscript has been translated as 'sore.' The original word refers to suppurating sores, abscesses, and ulcers. If it were abscesses, they could be easily interpreted, as the kind of ego-inflation mentioned in the sixth chapter or as the dominance of the ego in human consciousness. St. John's remaining ego would appear like an abscess to him, and he would see it as an illness and suffer from it. An ulcer, on the other hand, is a deeper symbolic image than an abscess, and therefore, it is more appropriate in this context. An ulcer opens up a passage into the deeper layers of the human body, analogous to St. John's opening to experience the deeper layers of his consciousness. As he becomes more inwardly directed, St. John sees his previous outwardness, or his ego-bound state, ever more clearly, and this awareness causes him to suffer. Therefore, the ulcers are painful. While they are infected and filled with puss, what they secrete is agony, as it were.

St. John of the Cross, likewise, uses ulcers and wounding as symbols in his descriptions of purification, and he is explicit regarding the painfulness of purification:

> The Holy Ghost wounds the soul in order to destroy and to bring an end to its bad habits... This is called by the spiritual aspirants "the path of the purification." On this path, a person suffers severe trials and feels immense torment in his spirit, which is usually reflected also in his senses and brings deep agony.[3]

The second angel

"Then the second angel poured out his bowl on the sea, and it became as blood as of a dead man; and every living creature in the sea died" (Rev. 16:3). The ulcers mentioned in the previous verse have deepened St. John's sense of life, and now this deepening continues so that he experiences a transformation on the level of the sea, or the subconscious. When the sea becomes blood, St. John experiences spiritual love. From the power of this ever-deeper love, St. John's subconscious ego-desires die. The creatures of the sea probably symbolize these subconscious, although relatively structured, desires.

Because the verse speaks specifically about the blood of the dead—and the expression is oppressive—it is also frightening for St. John to have his previous sense of self die, and it brings him anxiety. In inner transformations, even the experience of love can be terrifying, if it is overwhelming in its power. Also, regardless of its wonder, love may be painful if the person does not yet experience true spiritual bliss which is the fulfillment of love. So it is that he feels love as a painful longing for fulfillment.[4]

St. John of the Cross stresses the fact that love and anxiety are intertwined during the purification process. He speaks about "the dark and beloved plagues" and uses the expression "the darkness of love." He says:

> The soul loves in many ways... She finds rest nowhere, but is driven by longing, because she is aflame and wounded by love ... The world becomes narrow for such a soul... She is filled with agony unto darkness... Her anxiety and writhing are even greater when the love has ignited, because the pain has increased multifold for two reasons. The first reason is the spiritual darkness, wherein the soul finds herself, and the doubts and fears rising from it bring her anxiety. The other reason is the love of God, which ignites the soul and encourages her and leads her to an awesome fear with the wounds of love.[5]

The third angel

"Then the third angel poured out the bowl on the rivers and springs of water, and they became blood" (Rev. 16:4). St. John feels that the transformation takes place also on those levels of his consciousness, symbolized by the rivers and the springs, which are deeper than the mythical sea.[6] Having been wounded, St. John's consciousness opens to ever deeper inner levels. The springs are those levels of consciousness which do not have even relatively organized subconscious contents or the mythical creatures of the sea; in these depths of consciousness, there is only pure feeling, or water. Perhaps that is why St. John does not, in this verse, mention anything about the deaths of the creatures of the sea. Because there is no death, the experience related by this verse probably emphasizes the joy of love more than did the previous verse. In the words of St. John of the Cross, "The soul feels she has received, in the midst of these dark agonies, a deep-cut wound from God's powerful love, and along with it, a certain sense and foretaste of God."[7]

Using yoga theory, I suggest that the rivers symbolize the lesser energy channels, and the springs the chakras. Their waters changing to blood corresponds in yoga theory to the cleansing of the nadis, which is thought necessary for a bliss experience. That is why yoga teaches the variety of pranayama exercises which I mentioned in the ninth chapter. But during purification, general goodness and truthfulness also have an important place. In fact, in the well-known eightfold yoga path of Patanjali, the first steps, *yama* and *niyama*, mean this kind of general virtuousness. It is said that practicing yama and niyama will cleanse our consciousness so that we will be freed from ego-desires and will be able to feel compassion toward everything. (From here on, I will compare, at times, the events in Revelation to the Patanjali's eightfold yoga path. Yama and niyama are the first two steps on this path. The third is *asana* or the correct meditation posture, but that has no clear correspondence in Revelation, and the fourth is the above-mentioned pranayama practice. The yoga sutras of Patanjali are generally considered to be a classic account of Eastern yoga, although it is not known with certainty when Patanjali himself lived.[8])

The fourth angel

"Then the fourth angel poured out his bowl on the sun, and power was given to him to scorch men with fire" (Rev. 16:8). Before the pouring out of the fourth bowl, the angel of the waters and another from the altar have spoken, but their speech involves merely clarifying comments and reiteration, and therefore, I interpret them only in the notes.[9]

As mentioned, the fourth bowl is poured on the sun. This is a little unusual, because in the beginning of the vision the angels were said to pour the bowls out on the earth. Yet the sun as a celestial object, of course, is in the sky. The mythical sun of Revelation, however, is part of the mythical earth, since the sun in this interpretation represents a former God-concept, which St. John had created with the help of his conscious thinking, and conscious thinking is, in the mythical worldview, part of the earth.

When fire scorches men, St. John the Divine feels pain for finding some superficial spirituality still left in himself. St. John of the Cross also describes anxiety through scorching heat by saying that the infused purification is "cleansing with fire," wherein the soul is parched "on embers, so that she will scorch... and the impurities within her disappear."[10]

"And men were scorched with great heat, and they blasphemed the name of God who has power over these plagues and they did not repent and give him glory" (Rev. 16:9). St. John the Divine has already concluded that his previous religion was so incomplete that it seems to him blasphemous. And yet he is not able to fully liberate his feelings from it. Certainly many of us have experienced a similar situation, where one understands the old attitudes and habits to be wrong, and yet cannot let go of them.

The fifth angel

"Then the fifth angel poured out his bowl on the throne of the beast, and his kingdom became full of darkness" (Rev. 16:9). St. John suffers when he realizes how powerful the delusion, or the beast, is. He understands that the delusion reaches far beyond conscious thinking, covering all of ego-consciousness, or the domain of the beast. Perhaps he understands at the same time that he cannot become fully free of his former religion as long as he is bound by his ego-consciousness, because delusory religion rises from delusory consciousness.

When the kingdom of the beast darkens, it seems to St. John that darkness is taking over all of his ego-consciousness. Perhaps he wonders anxiously: "How is it possible at all to be liberated from delusion and a delusory religion when they are so deeply rooted in consciousness?"

The mythical image of darkness was particularly close to St. John of the Cross, who called infused purification the dark night. He explained that in this night "the understanding [is] in darkness."[11]

"And they [men] gnawed their tongues because of the pain. And they blasphemed the God of heaven because of their pains and their sores, and did not repent of their deeds" (Rev. 16:10–11). In this verse, the conflict between becoming aware of something and the actual transformation is described again. St. John the Divine even gnaws his tongue in trying to assure himself of his delusory consciousness, but being convinced and aware of something is not enough; he will need to transform emotionally as well. However, he is not able to do so, and therefore, men will not repent.

The sixth angel

"Then the sixth angel poured out his bowl on the great river Euphrates, and its water was dried up, so that the way of the kings from the East might be prepared" (Rev. 16:12). In the verse, St. John describes two results from the pouring out of the bowl: the drying of the river Euphrates and the anticipation of the new kings.

I have earlier interpreted the river Euphrates to be a river of life force, of a kind where the energy still flows on relatively superficial levels.[12] When Euphrates dries, St. John feels that the life force which he has relied on up until now dries up. On the psychological level, the drying up of the life energy can be compared to the drying up of feelings. Dryness is a natural result of the impasse St. John has found himself in. St. John of the Cross, as well, often explains the sense of dryness to be part of the dark night. For example, the quotation related above says, in its more complete form, "The understanding [is] in darkness, the will in dryness, the memory in emptiness, and the affections in supreme anquish." A good comparison for the drying of the river Euphrates is also St. John of the Cross' expression "the dryness and emptiness of the abilities of the soul."[13]

The kings of the earth of Revelation have been, until now, associated with the ego, because in acting like the old kings of the earth, human beings use their abilities in an organized and desire-filled way. There is, however, another path open for them, a selfless way of acting, and I feel that the new kings anticipated by St. John symbolize this kind of saintly behavior.

St. John expects the new kings from the East, or the direction of the dawn: he hopes that along with his new intuitive realizations, he will begin a new and selfless way of behaving. Because the coming of the new kings is prepared for by the drying of the river Euphrates, the transformation from desirousness to selflessness is preceded by a difficult period of dryness.

A certain change from a greedy to a selfless way of acting happened already after the winepress experience when the blood gushed forth up onto the horses' bridles. These two transformation processes are similar to each other regardless of the differences in the mythical images. The flowing of blood from the winepress was preceded with the reaping of the harvest by its roots and cutting of the grapes from the vines. Then the grain and the grapes were cut off from the nourishment previously brought to them through the roots and the vine. Assyria and Babylonia, through which the river Euphrates flows, are left without the refreshing waters when the river dries. Both cases illustrate a feeling of oppressive emptiness, rootlessness, and dryness. Additionally, the roots of the grain and the vine as well as the river Euphrates itself all can be seen as symbols for the streams of life force. Of course, the river Euphrates is a much more powerful image than the two previous ones; this difference is natural because St. John's transformation in this vision happens on a more essential energy level.

Dryness is an important stage in the spiritual life. It precedes a change, because during it, a previous desirous attitude in life and its corresponding life force will die out. When the usual ego-desires and the feelings of satisfaction that follow their fulfillment no longer motivate our actions, we will have to learn new attitudes in order to act.

The following words from St. John of the Cross are fitting here, although he does not speak of life force: "The soul loses the power of her desires, and she feels dried out as she finds no satisfaction."[14] St. John of the Cross explains also that in this dryness, the senses will be purified, and he tells of "the newness of sense" resulting from the drying out. This newness of sense refers to our ability to use our senses and other faculties in a new, selfless way. St. John of the Cross says of men who have accomplished this transformation that "their actions and faculties are then more divine than human."[15] The newness of sense is symbolized by the new kings of the earth in Revelation. According to St. John of the Cross, this new attitude will not be fulfilled completely until the soul has "reached perfection," because it requires a "soul's union with God."[16] Similarly, St. John of Revelation at this stage only anticipates the arrival of the new kings.

On the yoga path of Patanjali, the step following the pranayama, or the fifth step, is *pratyahara*. Pratyahara means that the life force becomes more inward, and this is gained through the practice of pranayama. The yogi experiences the withdrawal of the life force so that the ordinary feeling of the body disappears and the senses cease to function. Then the more superficial energy streams have 'dried out,' and the yogi is ready for concentration of the consciousness.[17] Through mastering the pratyahara yogis actually feel that they are something other than their sense perceptions, as these die off during the withdrawal of energy. This kind of experience will begin to change their sense of themselves, and they will gradually break away from their superficial attachments. In this way also the foundation for new selfless acting is created.

Because pratyahara means the ability to internalize and externalize prana at will, the drying up of the outward energy streams in yoga is intended to be a humanly controlled process. Contrarily, in Revelation, the drying up is part of infused purification.

The inner battle

The spirits of demons

"And I saw three unclean spirits like frogs coming out of the mouth of the dragon, out of the mouth of the beast, and out of the mouth of the false prophet. For they are spirits of demons, performing signs" (Rev. 16:13–14). When St. John sees the spirits of demons, he feels that he has become a target for the demon's attacks. Thus his dead-end, dried-up situation is resolved—yet, it does not lead to liberation but to a terrible torment.

Famous torments are included in St. Anthony's biography, written during the 4th century by Athanasius, archbishop of Alexandria, who knew St. Anthony personally. At one time Anthony's whole cell was filled with creatures: lions, bears, leopards, oxen, snakes, scorpions, and wolves—and all these creatures together created a horrible commotion and their rage was terrible. But St. Anthony did not back off, and the demons disappeared.[18]

St. John of the Cross, for his part, describes torments by the demons thus: "Satan... will attack... the soul creating spiritual terror and chaos." He tells also about different "spirits," which harass individuals. During the early stages of purification such spirits are "the spirit of immorality," "the spirit of blasphemy," and "the spirit of chaos." St. John of the Cross describes, for example, the effects of the spirit of blasphemy in the following way: "[It] will mix intolerable disrespect into all of man's beliefs and thoughts. And it will bring these things into man's mind with such a force that they will be almost voiced; this is a terrible torment for the soul."[19]

Outside Christianity, Tibetan literature, in particular, is laden with descriptions of demons, about meeting them and about the possibility of gaining victory over them. For example, we can read in the biography of the Tibet's great yogi Milarepa that evil spirits came to mock him. Milarepa, however, tamed those spirits, and they became his disciples and followers.[20]

Modern persons may tend to describe their experiences of torment as a sudden confusion or a strong sense that their consciousness has been somehow fragmented. During these states they may, for instance, hear voices in their heads, which repeat relentlessly seemingly strange, unfamiliar matters to them. But in the most extreme cases, even modern persons can feel they have met with demons or tormentors, whose presence they feel in psychic reality as forces with personal powers.[21]

This kind of experience, as a part of spiritual evolution, suggests that human beings must, during their transformative experiences, uncover their consciousness, as it were, layer by layer. In every new stage of development, they must experience ever deeper levels of consciousness, both in delusion and in bliss; during the culminating moments of the change, the unfolding of new levels of consciousness—whether it be delusion or bliss—can become forceful.

In the eleventh chapter St. John saw the beast, which rose up out of the depths. Now, in St. John's tormenting experience, his level of consciousness has descended even deeper than in meeting the beast, because from the beast's, the dragon's and the false prophet's mouths, or from deep inside them, spirits of demons come out. Only after St. John has lived through these levels of consciousness will he be free to continue his journey along the path of the tree of life. The spirits of demons, like the beast in the eleventh chapter, are, as it were, guards that St. John is to pass. A frog is a particularly good mythical image for the spirits of demons, because the tormenting experiences come leaping like frogs out of the waters of the unconscious into the clearly felt experiences. It is not possible to say what the torments felt by St. John were like exactly, but I will suggest guidelines based on literature.

The torments coming out of the mouth of the dragon, or the cosmic delusion, could well be doubt and lack of faith. St. John may feel: "There is no deep meaning to life, and all that I have experienced has been nothing but imagination." Or, if he cannot doubt in this way, he may feel that he will never be able to become free from delusion. The delusion keeping him a prisoner, seems eternal, and compared to a small human being which he himself is, it appears an immense cosmic power. In Christian literature, St. Teresa has described the torments of disbelief, "The Devil... leads [the soul] to think that God has forsaken her... and it seems to [the soul] that she has not dedicated one thought for God and never will do so either." St. Teresa compares the torment brought with this kind of state to the agony of hell.[22]

The spirit coming out of the mouth of the beast can probably be compared to the spirits of immorality, blasphemy, and chaos mentioned by St. John of the Cross. As the beast represents the delusion belonging to all of human ego-consciousness, we can probably assume that many forms of confusion colored by the aspirant's own personality now pour out from his unconscious. St. John of the Cross describes the spirits of immorality and chaos in this way:

> Some are approached by the Satan's angel, the spirit of immorality, to whip their senses with hideous and powerful temptations and to afflict them with ugly thoughts and extremely vivid images; sometimes this is more difficult for them than death.
>
> At other times they are attacked by another appalling spirit, which Isaiah calls *Spiritus vertiginis* (the spirit of chaos)... This spirit will darken their consciousness by filling them with thousands of trivial worries and problems... This belongs to the most severe tests and horrors of the dark night.[23]

The false prophet, as a form of delusion, causes man to identify with his conscious mind and physicality, and the torment coming out of the mouth of the false prophet could convince its victim that he would become permanently happy by satisfying all his ego-desires. Typical expressions of this torment are the desire for omnipotence and a delusory state of megalomania. A well-known example of this kind of demon is also presented by the biblical passage where the devil approaches Jesus after he has fasted forty days and nights. The devil shows Jesus "all the kingdoms of the world and their glory" and says, "All these things I will give you if you will fall down and worship me."[24]

That the spirits of the demons, according to Revelation, perform signs tells us of the nature of St. John's torment. He is likely to feel himself living on a parapsychological plane which surpasses ordinary states of consciousness.

The battle of Armageddon

"[The spirits of demons] go out to the kings of the earth and of the whole world, to gather them to the battle of that great day of God Almighty... And they gathered them together to the place called in Hebrew, Armageddon." (Rev. 16:14,16.) The words tell us that St. John recognizes the components of his own ego, the kings of the earth, to be his actual opponents. Although the spirits of demons have seemed outsiders, they had power over St. John because they resonated in his consciousness. The demons' attack culminates then in a great inner battle.

The name Armageddon means 'Hill of Megiddo,' and Megiddo is a historical city mentioned in the Bible. Many battles were waged in its surroundings, and according to the Bible, the kings Josiah and Ahasja were killed in these battles.[25] The battle of Armageddon in Revelation also has kings in it as the spirits of demons gather the kings of the earth to wage war. In the war, the kings represent the powers of the ego, and they form one of the opponents in the war. The other formation is not mentioned clearly. I believe, however, because the battle of Armageddon is executed on "that great day of God Almighty," that the other side is God, or more theoretically the Self.

As was true of the winepress experience, two forces are opposed to each other in an inner battle. Unlike the winepress, in a battle man feels the two forces in him fighting each other actively; he is not just compressed by them as he was in the winepress. Because the experience is still part of the infused purification, man feels the battle waged in himself as if he were only a battlefield for the war.

St. John of the Cross describes the inner battle as a part of the infused purification in the following way:

How marvelous! At this stage the opposites rise against each other: the power of the soul confronts the power of God which attacks the soul, and... they wage war in this soul, trying to drive each other out in order to take charge... and the soul must suffer this opposition in herself.

This contemplation infused by God has many extremely good characteristics and the soul receiving them has many bad ones, as she has not yet been purified. Because both of these opposites cannot exist side by side in the soul, inevitably she will suffer. Because the mentioned contemplation purifies the soul of her imperfections, she becomes the site where these oppositions fight each other.[26]

Of the many battles in the world mythology, we can compare the battle of Armageddon with the battle in the *Mahabharata*, which the Hindu Bible, the *Bhagavadgita*, is a part of. The *Bhagavadgita* describes a time when two armies, the Kurus and the Pandavas, are opposed to each other, prepared to begin a battle. One of the soldiers, Arjuna, is supposed to fight, but he hesitates. Then Krishna begins to advise Arjuna, and the *Bhagavadgita* includes the counsel given by Krishna in this situation.

According to the commonly used interpretation in India, the soldiers of the Kurus' army are man's characteristics, which keep him bound to his ego, and the chief of the Kuru's army, Bhishma, is the ego itself. "Protect Bhishma," the soldiers of the Kurus' army are told.[27] The army of the Pandavas, on the other hand, illustrates man's good qualities which will help him gradually to be liberated spiritually. With the army of the Pandavas is also Krishna, who symbolizes the Self or the divinity, and he is Arjuna's charioteer representing thus also man's guide or spiritual intuition.

"I am coming as a thief"

"Behold, I am coming as a thief. Blessed is he who watches, and keeps his garments, least he should walk naked and they see his shame" (Rev. 16:15). St. John has presented this remark, apparently out of context, right before the verse about Armageddon. The shame warned about in the verse is the male sexual organ—although one can read the verse also in a more general sense. As a mythical image, one of the most essential characteristics of the male sexual organ is its pushing outward; the organ tries to reach its goal, as it were, and so it can be interpreted to be a symbol for desires, and in general, for ego-consciousness. The garments in Revelation symbolize different levels of human consciousness.[28]

The parable used by St. John reflects the New Testament words, "The day of the Lord so comes as a thief in the night," as the battle of Armageddon happens "on the great day of God Almighty."[29] As a general symbol, a thief suggest that we cannot consciously decide the content of our consciousness. It comes to us like a thief, as a surprise. Interpreted in this way, the words are here appropriate, because spontaneity is an essential feature of the infusion, whether the infused experience is characterized by agony or happiness. Because St. John has presented his remark right before the battle of Armageddon, he may refer to both, first agony and then the liberating sense of mercy.

During the distressful phase of the infused transformation we feel that the old attachments which had given us a sense of comforting and familiar identities, have been suddenly stolen from us. Then we are left in such an aloof, dry state, that it is agonizing for us. St. John described this kind of experience earlier in the mythical harvest and in this chapter in the drying of the river Euphrates. A good comparison for the inner condition caused by the thief is the Christian condition of "poverty of the spirit," as the thief leaves its victim poor. Mythical poverty, the poverty of the spirit, however, means lack of attachments and therefore readiness for higher spiritual experience. In the infused transformation, this higher spiritual experience is grace or 'outpouring of mercy' and that, too, comes 'as a surprise' without us being able to invoke it through our own will.[30] We can, however, prepare ourselves for such stages in the spiritual life, and I believe this is what St. John wants to stress with his remark. We should tend to our deeper states of consciousness, and we ought to put our superficial desires aside. In this way, spiritual change can progress to the depths that Revelation now describes.

The seventh angel

"Then the seventh angel poured out his bowl into the air, and a loud voice came out of the temple of heaven, from the throne, saying, "It is done!" (Rev. 16:17.) We can assume that the words "it is done" declare victory at the battle of Armageddon. The kings who took part in the battle have been killed, meaning that St. John's ego has further decreased. The seventh step thus represents also in connection with the bowl plagues the culmination of the inner transformation process, the liberation. Because the voice declaring the victory comes from the temple and the throne, St. John perhaps experiences also a significant spiritual advance. Applying the chakra symbolism, it could be said that his life force has reached the seventh chakra, the sahasrara, which is the center for experiencing bliss.

Pouring the bowl out into the air probably reveals that the victory gained in the battle is an infused grace-filled experience. (As interpreted earlier, the air represents value experiences, and the earth, as its opposite, symbolize cognition). As ego-driven persons, using just our own power we cannot win such a difficult inner battle as this, because victory would mean the ego's ever deeper death. Nevertheless, it is perhaps correct to say that we could also use our own will, but only to make the choice. We leave our own ego-desires, or shame, aside and choose to surrender. During these moments, a religious person says, "Thy will be done." Someone else with a philosophical orientation may decide, "Come what may, I will accept it." Surrender brings a sense of liberation, and a feeling of joy and love will overcome the anxiety.

The following quotation of St. Teresa tells how she gained victory in an inner spiritual battle. St. Teresa's battle was like that of Armageddon; in it, St. Teresa was tormented by the "devil."

> The only help in this torment is to wait for God's mercy. Suddenly, with but one word, or through an unexpected event, God liberates the soul from all agony so quickly it seems the soul had never been shadowed by clouds... And like one who has survived a battle and gained victory, the soul praises the Lord, because it is He that has fought the victory for her. The soul sees clearly that she did not fight herself but all the weapons with

which she could have defended herself, seem to be in the hands of the enemy.[31]

The results of the battle

"And there was a great earthquake, such a mighty and great earthquake as had not occurred since men were on earth" (Rev. 16:18). St. John's shattering is so violent that he has never before experienced one like it. Perhaps he feels for a moment that his ego has died completely, as might be revealed by the words "it is done." It turns out, however, that this feeling is premature.

"Now the great city was divided into three parts, and the cities of the nations fell" (Rev. 16:19). I interpreted, in the eleventh chapter, the city to depict a general state of human consciousness. In this connection, I interpret "the great city" to be St. John's ego-consciousness such as he now experiences it. I believe St. John to realize that the victory in the battle of Armageddon was only one step in a larger transformation process, symbolized by the number three. Because this transformation process means gradual death of the ego, the cities that fall are those parts of the ego which died in the battle of Armageddon.

"And great Babylon was remembered before God, to give her the cup of the wine of the fierceness of his wrath" (Rev. 16:19). The dying of the ego must continue, and Babylon symbolizes St. John's new, upcoming phase of evolution. Accordingly, the two following visions deal with Babylon.

"Then every island fled away, and the mountains were not found" (Rev. 16:20). A similar change happened in the sixth chapter, where the mountains and the island moved out of their place (Rev. 6:14). Now the change is even more thorough, as St. John feels that the beliefs symbolized by the mountains and islands disappear.

"And great hail from heaven fell upon men, every hailstone about the weight of a talent" (Rev. 16:21). The hail symbolizes the plague-like nature of the infused purification, because after the earthquake St. John is so deeply overcome by confusion that he falls into agony again.[32]

A hail parable can be found also in the works of St. John of the Cross as a symbol for the infused purification, or "the dark contemplation." He tells of the beneficial agony sent by God overtaking the soul, and he writes, "He sends hail—or contemplation—like bread crumbs."[33]

In Revelation, the hail, however, rather than bread crumbs, are big rocks; a talent weighs several pounds. Clearly, St. John at this stage feels merely the weight of agony, and not yet its beneficial effect.

"And men blasphemed God because of the plague of the hail, since that plague was exceedingly great" (Rev. 16:21). Blaspheming God emphasizes the fact that St. John's ego has not yet died completely, and so his transformation must continue.

17. THE PROSTITUTE OF BABYLON

Introduction to the riddle of Babylon

"Come and I will show you the judgment of the great prostitute... And I saw a woman sitting on a... beast which was full of names of blasphemy, having seven heads and ten horns... And on her forehead a name was written: 'Mystery, Babylon the Great, the mother of prostitutes... of the earth.'" (Rev. 17:1,3,5.) In the fourteenth chapter, Babylon was a city that I associated tentatively with the mythical exile, or ego-consciousness. Now that St. John reveals more about Babylon, I will continue its interpretation.

I will begin with the similarity of the prostitute of Babylon to the image of the beast. The same beast is the basis of both the earlier beast's image and that of the prostitute of Babylon, because the prostitute sits on its back. Therefore, both the image of the beast and the prostitute of Babylon can be interpreted as images born from the delusory human consciousness; they both are projections of ego-consciousness.

First of all, the image of the beast in my interpretation was a projected God-image and a model of a delusory religion. Secondly, the image of the beast symbolizes a wider sense of self than a human being consciously perceives, but still, a desire-filled one. The prostitute of Babylon illustrates all this well. Yet, in these interpretations, I give more importance to the sense of self, because I feel that St. John has resolved his problems with the delusory religion satisfactorily, but he has only scratched the surface when it comes to the problem of the self. Also, the self is a more basic concept in our lives than our religious images, because the kind of self we have and all the consciousness that goes with it, determine the quality of our religious attitudes. Although I place the self in the foreground in my study, I will present the prostitute briefly also as a false religion.

Babylon as the wrong religion

The historical interpretations of Revelation take Babylon most often as a pseudonym for Rome, and in that case, the prostitute would symbolize some religion practiced in Rome during the time Revelation was written, such as Caesar worship. But the prostitute of Babylon has carried the meaning of pagan worship also as a universal symbol. For example, when the Indian swami Vivekananda explains that we should not see paganism in the Indian image worship, he uses the metaphor, "Idolatry in India... is not the mother of harlots." (Vivekananda's thought is that the images in the worship are symbols, not gods.)[1]

Additionally, the prostitute of Babylon illustrates well any delusory religion, a religion tied to dualism and desires. As a grandiose individual mythical image, the prostitute riding on the back of a beast is an ideal model for this kind of religion created through mythical thinking. I feel that St. John emphasizes with the prostitute especially the desirousness in a delusory religion. And, in using the image of the prostitute specifically, he gives a severe judgment on this kind of religion. Apparently St. John feels that the human being overcome by a delusory religion is like a man who strives to satisfy his desires, and his delusory image of god is like a grand prostitute that will satisfy them. The prostitute will satisfy the man only for a fee, and likewise, a human being perhaps tries to do good to have his wishes granted in return.

The higher the viewpoint from which a person's spiritual life is viewed, the more clear it becomes that even the slightest strain of disaffection, greed, and dualism in one's religion, is enough to prevent a genuine, deeply spiritual life in its most demanding sense. For example, in Christian literature, St. John of the Cross speaks of the cataract of desire. He explains, that as the cataract clouds the eyes of the soul, she thinks that the cataract is God, because she only sees the cataract. St. John of the Cross stresses that even the smallest desire prevents the soul from receiving those gifts of God which are beyond the desires.[2] This cataract of desire which the soul thinks is God can well be compared to the prostitute of Babylon when the prostitute is interpreted as the God-image tied to desires.

Paramahansa Yogananda of India writes:
 To remove the veil of *maya* is to uncover the secret of creation. He who thus denudes the universe is the only true monotheist.

All others are worshiping heathen images. So long as man remains subject to the dualistic illusions of Nature, the Janus-faced *Maya* is his goddess; he cannot know the one true God.[3]

Should we compare the gist of the above quote with Revelation, the heathen images would justly parallel the image of the beast in Revelation; and the Janus-faced *Maya*-goddess is like the prostitute of Babylon when the latter is seen as the false God-image tied to dualism.

Religions often, however, regard the different forms and stages of development of spiritual life with a gentle acceptance. For example, Indian literature—like the teaching of the earlier mentioned Paramahansa Yogananda—emphasizes that human consciousness is at first inevitably tied to mental images and desires, and therefore, a person is allowed to create both outer and inner images of God. We may also pray for the fulfillment of our own good desires, because prayer has a great power. But, at the same time, it is stressed that we are to strive to move toward ever more spiritual and noble mental images and ever more selfless prayer. In this way, we are able to climb step by step ever higher on our spiritual paths; we will be freed from bondage and finally gain the peak that is "the direct and immediate experience of the supreme Truth." Once free, we may continue to enjoy inner and outer images, but we are no longer tied to them in a desirous way.[4]

If the prostitute of Babylon in the Book of Revelation is interpreted as a false God-image, the message revealed in Revelation is severely judgmental. St. John's strictness would come from him wanting, once and for all, to go beyond images and a religion tied to greed. And this requires from him, and from anyone else, inner transformation and the death of the ego.

Babylon as a sense of self

Concisely, the prostitute is that self which all high religions ask us to give up. More theoretically, Babylon is one of ego's stages of development. This stage of development lies between the sense of self limited to the conscious mind and that of the saint who has given up his own self completely. A saint says, "Not I but Christ in me."[5] The Babylon stage represents a somewhat later stage of the ego's development: at that stage we have already overcome our narrow consciousness but we still have ego-desires left. Because it is impossible to draw a definite line between the ego and the Self, it would be possible to say that the Babylon stage is characterized by the Self being already largely free of the ego covering, but yet, we have a sense of separate self in our consciousness, and this is what the prostitute illustrates.

The interpretation I suggest for Babylon is based also on historical events in the sense that the exile of the Israelites in Babylon takes place at a later date than the slavery in Egypt. Egypt in these interpretations, symbolizes the early stages of human ego-bondage, as was explained in the eleventh chapter which examined the mythical meaning of the city of Egypt.

As a whole, the Babylon stage of development is multifaceted and it lasts a long time in a human life. During it, occasional states of inspired creativity cross the boundaries of narrow consciousness, and at its strongest the Babylon stage is characterized by a surge of altered states of consciousness.

St. John had already crossed the boundaries of a narrow conscious mind before the beginning of Revelation; the visionary nature of Revelation alone testifies this. In these interpretations I have, however, assumed that St. John's consciousness has gradually expanded: over the course of Revelation, he has moved more clearly into the Babylon stage of development and ever farther from a sense of self limited merely to an everyday conscious mind. I believe this is the reason why the king of the earth, as a singular individual image, is missing in Revelation. The king of the earth would, as one grand mythical image, depict the sense of self that is limited to conscious mind: the human being, as a king and a man, would feel himself to rule his own conscious mind, the earth. But St. John speaks of the kings of the earth always in plural. This shows that when he functions as the ruler over his conscious mind, or the king of the earth, he feels he is the king and user of some of his abilities and characteristics only. Instead, the prostitute of Babylon, as a grand mythical image of an individual personality, represents the individual and personal sense of St. John's self. This symbolic representation fits anyone who has reached this stage of the development.

I have found two sources in literature wherein the Babylon of Revelation is interpreted as the human desire-bound self. The first one is the work by J.E. Irion, *Interpreting the Revelation with Edgar Cayce*, which includes Cayce's interpretations of Revelation during trance states. Cayce was asked once, "Does Babylon symbolize the self?" And Cayce answered, "Babylon symbolizes the self." He explained also that the destruction of Babylon in Revelation depicts man's "purification."[6]

The second source is the work by the Jungian psychoanalyst Edward Edinger, *The Bible and the Psyche*, wherein Edinger interprets briefly the Israelite's captivity in Babylon and mentions at the same time the prostitute of Babylon from Revelation. He writes:

> The immediate reference is to Rome but she is presented as a manifestation of the archetype, Babylon. The symbolism of Babylon is very similar to that of Egypt, signifying secular, fleshly existence oblivious to God. Psychologically it represents secular egohood living unconsciously at the expense of transpersonal energies ("drunk with the blood of the saints"). Although, at one phase of development, the "captivity" of Egypt and Babylon is a necessary coagulation, at a later phase it becomes bestial and blasphemous.[7]

Within Christianity I know of no similar clear interpretations, yet Babylon—either in general or specifically as the Babylon of Revelation—is used as a metaphor in connection to the bondage of desires. For example, St. John of the Cross in his work, *The Ascent of Mount Carmel*, describes the suffering caused by desires in the following way:

> Man, overcome by desires, manifests already in this life that which is said of Babylon in Revelation, "In the measure that she glorified herself and lived luxuriously, in the same measure give her torment and sorrow" (Rev. 18:7).[8]

Bernard of Clairvaux writes disapprovingly, in one of his letters, of men returning from a crusade to Jerusalem engaging in a tournament once back home, "How fittingly can we say of these men, 'We sought improvement for Babylon, yet there was no cure for her.'"[9]

I will mention also Gregory the Great, for he makes use of yet another grand prostitute of the Bible, the prostitute of Ezekiel's visions, as an image for man who has grown proud of his own greatness.[10] This fits well my interpretation, because the Babylon stage means the danger of hubris, as in it persons have already crossed the normal boundaries of their narrow everyday consciousness.

The Babylon stage of development in literature

The best comparisons for the Babylon stage are found in Christian literature which describes the higher levels of inner life, although the descriptions have not been linked with Babylon symbolism.

St. John of the Cross divides infused purification in two parts, the sensuous and the spiritual, or the night of the senses and the night of the spirit.[11] His way of seeing could, perhaps, be crystallized in the following way. When the soul has experienced the purification of the senses, an ever higher and expanded inner life opens for her. Then the spiritual realm of the soul, the spirit, is made free, but first it is in bondage to her desires, so that it must withstand purification. If we look at it in this way, the prostitute of Babylon would be the spiritual part of the soul before purification, that is, she would be an unpurified spirit. The destruction of Babylon in Revelation would then correspond to the purification of the spirit, the night of the spirit, depicted by St. John of the Cross. I find the above analogy between Revelation and the writings by St. John of the Cross so excellent that I use the works by St. John of the Cross as the major source for comparisons in interpreting Babylon.

In the eleventh chapter I had already borrowed from St. Teresa the parable wherein the death of an ugly worm will release a beautiful butterfly. According to St. Teresa, this transformation happens when the soul experiences bliss while the ordinary state of consciousness is suspended. In Revelation, that transformation happened when St. John saw the ark of the covenant. The ugly worm is, therefore, like the human being that is tied to the earth, that is, to the everyday consciousness and physical being. But while the worm is dying, the state of bondage begins to disappear, and when the freely flying butterfly unfolds from the worm, the soul feels she is born again with an ever-freer state of consciousness. St. Teresa, however, continues her parable explaining that the butterfly must die before the soul may unite with God in a spiritual marriage.[12] Even the butterfly represents a level of an incomplete spiritual development, symbolizing the fact that men and women are still somewhat in bondage.

I compare the prostitute of Babylon with this butterfly stage of development, although St. Teresa's butterfly and the prostitute of Babylon clearly differ from each other as mythical images. St. Teresa was well aware of the danger of elevating herself, so that even a more liberated stage of the development of the self is only a small butterfly in her descriptions. The grand prostitute of Babylon, on the other hand, glows with the symbolism of conceit and self-exaltation.

Outside religious literature, the best comparison for the Babylon stage of development known to me can be found in Jungian psychology; I explained briefly some of its theory of individuation in the fifth chapter. The core of this theory was that during individuation we deepen our sense of self so that it transfers from the center of the ordinary consciousness—in Jungian terminology "the conscious"— to the center of our whole being.

Jung explained further that during individuation we can become aware of and live out, to an ever-greater degree, those contents of the consciousness which have previously belonged only to the unconscious. In the final stages of our development we see deeply into the secrets of the consciousness. Jung also said he had discovered that shortly before realizing one's Self, an archetype is activated in consciousness, expressing itself as such "collective ideas" as the hero, the magician, the saint, the ruler of men and spirits, friend of God, and the Merciful Great Mother. We begin, for example, to see those images in our dreams, and begin, as an ego, to identify with this archetypal *mana*-personality, as Jung called it. As we identify with the mana-personality, we appropriate the deep subconscious charge attached to it to our own ego, and so the ego becomes inflated. Jung stressed that we are to undo this wrong identification and to find the harmony between the outer and inner factors, and the center of our total being, the Self. Jung explained the inflation of the ego in identifying with the mana-personality also so that at this stage "man knows and wants more than men generally do" and cannot avoid admiring himself at least a little for having seen deeper than others.[13]

Applying Jung's theory, the prostitute of Babylon would then be such a sense of one's self, wherein man, as an ego, experiences himself as a powerful mana-personality. In Revelation, the stage is pictured as the grand prostitute rather that the great magician or the Great Mother, since the delusory nature of this kind of self is emphasized in the vision of St. John.

The prostitute of the Bible and the women of Revelation

A good comparison for the prostitute of Babylon in the Bible is found in Ezekiel's vision, where Ezekiel describes Jerusalem as a woman. The Lord favors this Jerusalem woman, "'I swore an oath to you and entered into a covenant with you, and you became mine,' says the Lord God." But the woman is unfaithful to the Lord, and so the Lord gives the woman a prostitute's verdict:
"You also committed prostitution with the Egyptians, your very fleshly neighbours... You also played with the Assyrians, because you were insatiable... Moreover you multiplied your acts of prostitution as far as the land of the trader, Chaldea; and even then you were not satisfied. How degenerate is your heart!" says the Lord God, "seeing you do all these things, the deeds of a brazen prostitute."
In the end the Lord, however, forgives the Jerusalem prostitute: "And I will establish my covenant with you. Then you shall know that I am the Lord... I provide you an atonement for all you have done."[14]
I interpret the events in these visions of Ezekiel to mean that he initially is describing man's fall from union with God into ego-consciousness. Then, at the end of the vision, Ezekiel foretells man's return back to union with God, which means, theoretically, consciousness of the Self. Prostitution, in Ezekiel's vision, is the stage of ego-consciousness. Because Chaldea means Babylonia in the Bible, the prostitute of Babylon identifies herself with only one stage out of all those symbolized in Ezekiel's vision. That stage represents a later stage in the ego's development; the prostitute in Ezekiel's vision had practiced prostitution first with the sons of Egypt and Assyria and only later with the traders of Chaldea. Ezekiel's vision and Revelation parallel each other also in that at the end of Revelation the prostitute of Babylon is replaced by Jerusalem, the Lamb's wife, when St. John enters the spiritual marriage.

There are three grand female forms in Revelation: the heavenly woman who gives birth to a child; the prostitute of Babylon; and the holy city, Jerusalem, which is the bride and the wife of the Lamb. All these three grand women represent in my interpretation various forms, levels or stages of development that occur in human consciousness.

Having for a moment been like a heavenly woman that gives birth to a child, St. John's consciousness has greatly expanded. But he still has his self left and he has ego-desires which he longs to satisfy: he still feels himself to be a prostitute compared to the completely selfless saint, the bride of the Lamb whom he would wish to resemble.

The problem of the self

Religion's demands for extinguishing one's own self or "I" is difficult to comply with—in fact, it is difficult even to understand. What is self or "I"? How could we give up our self? And why should we give this self up?

A general answer to these questions is that "the I" we are to give up is "the I" that is bound to desires. It is the image and feeling created by our desires. It is because of these desires that we feel ourselves separate from others and even partly opposite to them. When our desires vanish, our whole attitude toward life will change. We will experience ourselves in others, and their happiness is our happiness. A difficult theoretical problem is then created as to whether we can at this stage speak of "I" at all, and if we can, in what specific sense. As far as I understand, according to Christianity individuals retain their sense of I-ness as individual souls even after their purification, but their souls are now seen as having returned back to the original state created by God in the beginning. An absolute melting into the omnipresence can be seen more clearly in pantheism.[15] Fortunately, I need not analyze these metaphysical questions more extensively, because, for my interpretation, the following general assumption is enough: when we give up our own "I" it means that our consciousness is not desirous any more.

Also the following perception of the self helps to understand the progression in Revelation. According to this thinking, the self is like a boundary between immanence and transcendence; that is, as a concept, it is transcendental. Immanent levels, in ourselves, are all those abilities through which we function, and those desires that we seek to satisfy. The transcendent refers to a sense of oneness that is completely free of ego, and in religious thinking corresponds to the transcendent God. The sense of a separate self forms then a door, if you will, from immanent to transcendent. As long as that door exists, one can glimpse transcendent light through it, and for a moment, the door may fly open, but generally the door closes the doorway, and so we are held captive by immanence. On our inner path we are, therefore, to capture our self or I, give it up, and then the road is open into transcendence.[16]

The problem of I has crystallized universally as the question, "Who am I?" For example, St. Teresa explained, "We have much to grieve and feel shame for when it is our own fault that we do not understand ourselves and know not who we are." According to St. Teresa, the inner life begins when we contemplate these questions.[17] The Indian Ramana Maharshi for his part taught, "Everyone is aware that he is. Yet one ignores that awareness and goes about in search of God... But the method of realization is the enquiry 'Who am I?'"[18] According to Maharshi, as man inquires "Who am I?" he first follows his thoughts into his sense of self but continues further:

> Of all thoughts, the thought "I" is the root... Whence does this thought "I" arise? Seek for it within; it then vanishes... That which remains on seeing that the "I" does not exist is... [a] vivid Realization, as a direct and immediate experience of the supreme Truth.[19]

In Revelation, St. John has now reached a moment in his spiritual development when he finally must be able to enter through the transcendental door of the self into the union with God which is his goal. That is why resolving the problem of self is so important to him that he dedicates a whole vision to it.

St. John tells us in the beginning of the vision where it happens, "So he [the angel] carried me away in the Spirit into the wilderness. And I saw a woman" (Rev. 17:3). St. John contemplates the riddle of self so deeply that he detaches from his normal state of mind and finds himself again in the wilderness, in the state of inward "spiritual preparation."[20]

Babylon in the vision of St. John

The wealth and femininity of the prostitute

"The woman was... adorned with gold and precious stones and pearls, having in her hand a golden cup" (Rev. 17:4). The prostitute's magnificence and wealth come from the expansion and deepening of the consciousness that is characteristic of the Babylon stage. Once the ego has already died partially, a deeper state of consciousness is opened, and so the aspirant, who has come to the Babylon stage, feels he enjoys previously unknown dimensions of consciousness in their many new nuances. Spiritual joy and happiness will, perhaps, become transformed states of consciousness, intuitive understanding will deepen and become clearer, and the sharp boundary between sleep and the waking state will disappear. Individuals may have visions while they are awake, even as St. John did in Revelation, or they may allow visual images to pass spontaneously through their consciousness. Should the parapsychological abilities open up, they will notice their lives to follow new laws, so that the boundaries of time and place can be traversed.

St. John of the Cross describes a soul which has experienced the dark night of the senses and the inner change brought by it, in the following way:

> Like one who is set free from a confining prison, she roams now with a much more spacious spirit... enjoying a more satisfying and inward joy... Her imagination and abilities are no longer tied to discursive thinking... She receives... much spiritual communication and understanding through her senses and her spirit, and she then often has pictorial and spiritual visions.[21]

A wealth of perceptional experiences is well symbolized by the gold, jewels, and pearls that the prostitute has. Gold is a precious metal, telling us that the consciousness has become more noble, as it were. The luster and brilliance of the jewels, similarly, tell us of the radiant happiness and clear intuition of the new perceptional life. Additionally, a jewel as a stone symbolizes that deepest state of consciousness that is now opening, and the hardness and lasting quality of a jewel speak of inner strength that the opening of these levels of consciousness means. And a seeker finds the pearl when he dives into the depths of the sea, brings up a pearl-oyster and opens it. Similarly, men and women find new spiritual experiences and happiness when they dive into the sea of their consciousness and open up new dimensions there.

At this point, persons are particularly open to receive and they surrender freely. They open up to all the riches of the inner life whether they are visions, parapsychological experiences, clear spiritual intuitions, or ever deeper feelings of love. They receive all these with abandon. This receptivity of the consciousness is symbolized as a woman, because anatomically a woman's body can take something into itself. Additionally, receptivity is emphasized regarding the prostitute of Babylon in that in her hand is a golden cup, the cup duplicating the woman's vessel-like body; it, too, represents human consciousness opened to new experiences. In the symbolic Babylon stage of development, man no longer feels himself to be an active performer in charge of his consciousness, or a masculine king of the earth, but a receptive and surrendering woman.

The prostitution and the clothing of the prostitute

As rewarding as the Babylon stage is, a person experiencing it is still tied to ego-desires and he still has left a sense of separate self. The prostitute as a mythical image expresses succinctly the characteristics of this stage of development: the prostitute gives the inner space of her body for men to use and in intercourse man's sexual organ moves inside the prostitute. Even so is movement brought about in man's consciousness during the Babylon stage by ego-desires, and he is not able to quiet his consciousness as fully as an absolute spiritual experience would require. Also, a prostitute receives a payment for her services, and the payment is the enjoyment that man as a separate self feels in satisfying his ego-desires.

Because St. John wants to progress to the highest states of consciousness—and these require complete lack of ego-desires—he condemns this stage as prostitution. Compared to those higher stages, even the Babylon stage is still imperfect. St. John of the Cross stresses the same idea, for no sooner has he described the inner riches the soul receives after the sensuous night than he adds, "These who have come so far, are still, nevertheless, on a quite low and natural level in their union with God... because the gold of their spirit has not yet been purified nor illumined."[22]

"The woman was arrayed in purple and scarlet" (Rev. 17:4). The red color is here associated—as it is also more generally in Revelation—with delusion and ego, and has the color white as its opposite. A comparison elsewhere in the Bible can be found in the words of the prophet Isaiah, "Though your sins are like scarlet, they shall be as white as snow."[23] During biblical times certain shellfishes were the source for the color purple. The prostitute's clothing is red signifying delusion befitting the delusionary Babylon stage. But it is also purple, a color which came from shellfishes of the sea. This suggests that St. John is richly perceptive, for the potential of the unconscious, the sea, has already become actual for him in an abundant measure.

The intercourse between the prostitute and the kings

"With [the prostitute] the kings of the earth committed fornication" (Rev. 17:2). The general meaning of the prostitute's fornication is already clear, but I will analyze the picture in yet greater detail. When the kings of the earth and the prostitute have had intercourse, the components from different levels of consciousness have united. (As I explained earlier, according to my interpretation, the king of the earth is one of the lower centers of the ego, for example, man as the performer of his thinking, acting or imagining, and the prostitute offers a deeper, more lasting sense of self than those abilities.) Within modern psychological terminology the Babylon stage means gaining a sense of personal wholeness and integrity.

St. John described such renewal earlier. When he met with the beast rising out of the depth (in the eleventh chapter), he was freed from repressions, and this made him more whole. The sense of wholeness in the Babylon stage, rather than the deterioration that accompanies repressions, comes from persons beginning to use all of their abilities ever more freely to progress inwardly: this stage is a later or higher stage of personal healing. Earlier the aspirants perhaps had to make themselves concentrate on spiritual matters and the inner experiences because more superficial and outward enjoyments attracted them. But now forcing is no longer needed, because they, as thinkers, and as those who act and will—or within the symbolism of Revelation, as the kings of the earth—enjoy spiritual matters more. But, as is characteristic of the Babylon stage, they still have also desirousness left in them, and for this reason the kings of the earth enjoy intercourse with the prostitute or with the spirit not yet purified.

St. John of the Cross describes this healing that happens in those who have progressed spiritually: "Both parts of the soul enjoy then—

both in their own way—one and the same spiritual nourishment... as one single individual and person... The purpose is that... the sensuous part of the soul would unite with the spirit."[24] The image of the union of the spirit and the sensuous part of the soul, presented by St. John of the Cross in the above quotation, compares quite accurately with the intercourse between the prostitute and the kings of Revelation.

Only personal wholeness can guarantee progress into ever deeper states of consciousness. Any fracture in the personality, be it conflict or tension, can become a threat in an intensive transformation process and can cause the human psyche to shatter. St. John of the Cross writes about this also, "So they [both parts of the soul], united and harmonious in a certain way, are together prepared to endure the severe and difficult purgation of the spirit waiting them."[25]

The drunkenness of the inhabitants of the earth

"The inhabitants of the earth were made drunk with the wine of her fornication" (Rev. 17:2). These words tell us: from the joy, or wine, that St. John has experienced on the level of unpurified spirit, some has overflowed to the inhabitants of the earth. That is, St. John has experienced joy also on the more superficial levels of his personality. This is characteristic of spiritual experiences, and surely well-known to many who observe themselves. When we experience feelings of strong spiritual joy and happiness, those feelings can activate or waken also sensual enjoyment. St. John of the Cross says about this, "The enjoyment and the inner satisfaction that those who have progressed embrace in their spirit, comes to them in ever more overflowing measure, pouring out from here to their senses."[26]

But this kind of diffusion dilutes and makes the experience more superficial. In the words of St. John of the Cross, "Because the lower part of the soul has been part of these communications, they cannot be so powerful, pure, or strong as is required for [a genuine] union."[27] According to St. John of the Cross, this is so because "the sensuous part is weak and unable to realize the powerful experiences of the spirit."[28] I assume that St. John of Revelation has also come to see the same thing, and for this reason the wine of the prostitute, which has made the inhabitants of the earth drunk, is the wine of fornication.

Yoga literature has descriptions of similar phenomena. Until the yogi through step by step exercises has learned to control the movements of the kundalini energy, that energy may rise upward spontaneously as a result of some emotionally based incitement. An elevated state will follow, but it is not lasting; and when the kundalini energy in this kind of situation returns quickly downward, the flood may even appear as a strengthened sensuality.[29]

The drunkenness of the prostitute

"And I saw the woman, drunk with the blood of the saints and with the blood of the martyrs of Jesus" (Rev. 17:6). The blood of the saints and the martyrs is that deep happiness and love which has been released in St. John in ever greater measure. As to the drunkenness of the prostitute, it is a clearly felt experience: persons in the Babylon stage may actually feel themselves becoming drunk from the sheer happiness of living.

But now St. John awakens to see that he has experienced his happiness in an incomplete way. He has felt himself to be an ego, a separate, personal self experiencing everything. And this attachment to his own "I" has kept happiness from expanding across the boundaries of the "I" to a cosmic state of consciousness and a genuine spiritual bliss. The joy has been swallowed within the boundaries of his own "I," as it were, into the belly of the prostitute. Christian literature stresses the danger of false ecstasy. It is called spiritual drunkenness and its opposite is soberness of the mind and the spirit.[30]

The prostitute on the mountains

"The seven heads [of the beast] are seven mountains on which the woman sits" (Rev. 17:9). The prostitute does not sit just on the back of the beast, but she sits on its seven heads and those heads are also the seven mountains. This verse has generally led to thinking that the Babylon of Revelation is a pseudonym for Rome, because Rome was known in ancient times as the city of the seven hills. Apparently the symbolism of the Book of Revelation has, indeed, been influenced by historic Rome; in fact, in the historical setting of Revelation, it is difficult to think of a better mythical image for an ego than the Roman

Empire. However, I interpret the prostitute sitting on the mountains as a more universal mythical image, and then it means self-glorification.

A human being's sense of self as a separate self is strictly speaking a self-glorification, because according to religious understanding, anyone should be only a medium for God, and such a saint as one of whom St. Paul could say, "Not I, but Christ in me." The prostitute, then, on the heads of the beast and on the mountains, reveals what St. John has realized: he has put his own self in a wrong, elevated place, having been misguided by the heads of the beast, or his own ego-consciousness.

But we can read also other forms of self-glorification in the prostitute on the mountains, and they, too, fit well this section of Revelation. During the Babylon-stage, St. John has already understood the falseness of his old God-concept, and he has tried to give it up as much as possible. He does not believe in an alienating God-concept any longer, but he does not yet experience the highest spirituality either. He is only striving toward it. So, the questions as to how he can change and what he should be experiencing personally have become the center of his spiritual life. St. John, perhaps, realizes now, that in this intermediate stage, he has elevated his own self to being the most valuable being in his life; his own self has become to him like a god. (As I explained earlier, the mountain in Revelation is associated with the God-concept, and it is also generally in mythology associated with gods.[31])

Additionally, sitting on the mountain, may reflect self-conceit, presumption, and pride. Presumption would be a natural interpretation, because in the Babylon stage one's inner life is very rich. St. John of the Cross also cautions about the danger of presumption. He explains that some, who have progressed, "experience these spiritual blessings in a very outward and sensual way." (According to him, seeing visions is an outward experience). And he goes on to say that these people are easily filled "with presumption and pride."[32]

In the Bible, the Book of Isaiah identifies sitting on the mountains as meaning self-glorification. There the king of Babylon brags, "I will ascend into heaven, I will exalt my throne above the stars of God; I will also sit on the mount of the congregation." The king of Babylon in the Bible is generally interpreted as Satan, but I find also the human ego a fitting interpretation; then the bragging of the king of Babylon is similar to the self-glorification which is a peril in the Babylon-stage.[33]

It would be easier to understand the strict judgmental language of St. John the Divine in this chapter, if we assume that he has fallen into self-conceit, pride, and spiritual vanity. The expression of the prostitute being "adorned with gold and precious stones and pearls," might refer to self-conceit and vanity. St. John would have adorned his own self with the riches of his inner life, as it were, and he himself would have taken credit for them as an ego. Perhaps, for this reason, he is now so horrified regarding his own state that in the cup of the prostitute, or in St. John's consciousness, are "abominations and the filthiness of her fornication" (Rev. 17:40). St. John of the Cross says of presumption that it is difficult to correct, and in some people "illusions ... are so deeply etched... that their return to the way of virtue and true spirituality is rather doubtful."[34]

The reign over the kings of the earth

It is clear from St. John's vision that the seven heads on which the prostitute sits are also the seven kings (Rev. 17:9). Additionally, it is said of the prostitute of Babylon that she is "that great city which reigns over the kings of the earth" (Rev.17:18). I view these descriptions of the prostitute from the basis of the unifying function of the self. The human self functions as a center which overarches the more specific faculties of consciousness. The kings of the earth are those lower centers of the personality through which a person functions as the performer of different abilities, but the actual center of the personality is the self. The prostitute, therefore, reigns over all the kings of the earth.

The mother of abominations

"And on her forehead a name was written: 'Mystery, Babylon the Great, the mother of prostitutes and of the abominations of the earth'" (Rev. 17:5). Babylon as the mother of the earth's prostitutes and abominations compares well with the general understanding in Eastern philosophy that a sense of a separate self is the root of all ego-based experiencing and the source of all human troubles. In the words of Ramana Maharshi, "This ego or individual being is at the root of all that is futile and undesirable in life... All unhappiness is due to ego. With it comes all your trouble... If the ego is, everything else also is."[35]

We can understand the concept of the separate self as the source of all troubles thus: the human bondage which is created by desires crystallizes, as it were, into one's own self. Do I not want to feel that it is *I* myself who receive pleasure from satisfying my desires? In the *Bhagavadgita*, inner liberation is often defined by saying that a person, once free, will lack a sense of I and mine.[36]

St. John of the Cross expresses the same idea saying that "the roots of all imperfections of the sensuous part are in the spirit." For this reason, St. John of the Cross emphasizes that purification of the sensuous part is never finished until the spirit has been purified.[37]

Those who bear the prostitute

Throughout the vision, the prostitute sits on something. In the beginning of the chapter, the prostitute "sits on many waters" (Rev. 17:1). Next, she sits on the beast (Rev. 17:3), then on the heads of the beast, the mountains and the kings (Rev. 17:9), and finally, the angel explains to St. John, "The waters which you saw where the prostitute sits, are peoples, multitudes, nations, and tongues" (Rev. 17:15).

The changing of the image which bears the prostitute reflects the progress of St. John's understanding. First, he realizes that self is a projection of the unconscious, borne by the many waters, but he does not yet analyze the more specific nature or cause of the projection. Next, his thinking becomes more specific. The prostitute is an idea sustained by a person's delusory consciousness: she sits on the beast. After this he defines the nature of the delusory sense of one's self more specifically. The prostitute sits on the heads of the beast, on the mountains and kings, because St. John sees that the self is born through the influence of the delusory consciousness, self-glorification, and the lower centers of the consciousness. Finally, he realizes that the self is also created by a person's specific abilities. When we use our abilities symbolized by peoples, nations, and tongues, we feel ourselves to be the owners and the performers of these abilities.

That the prostitute sits on so many different mythical images, probably reflects the general nature of the self. It is an image born from the basis of total human ego-consciousness: the unconscious or the many waters, the lower centers of the consciousness or the kings, and the specific conscious abilities or peoples, nations, and tongues.

St. John describes also the color of the beast bearing the prostitute, "I saw a woman sitting on a scarlet beast" (Rev. 17:3). With the redness of the beast, St. John emphasizes the delusory character of the ego-consciousness; earlier the dragon, or the cosmic delusion, was scarlet. This seven-headed and ten-horned beast does not, however, wear crowns any longer as it did in the thirteenth chapter. The change probably comes from St. John having already sundered so many of his delusions that he feels the beast does not reign over his consciousness fully any more.

Liberation from one's own "I"

The angel in the vision foretells the path St. John is to follow to become fully liberated from his ego. Foretelling is natural, because in the Babylon stage the intuition has cleared and so foretelling is possible. Because the matters announced by the angel do not bring new content to the events in Revelation—they will repeat later—I will consider here only the most essential parts.

The seven kings

The angel says to St. John, "Why did you marvel? I will tell you the mystery of the woman and of the beast that carries her, which has the seven heads and the ten horns... The seven heads are seven mountains ... They are also seven kings. Five have fallen, one is, and the other has not yet come." (Rev. 17:7,9–10.) In the verse, the seven kings are used in the same way as the seven seals, seven trumpet blows, and seven bowls of wrath of God were presented earlier in order to express the process of growing awareness and transformation. Now the subject of transformation is the death of the ego, and, therefore, kings are appropriate mythical images. Because St. John's self-glorification dies with the death of his ego, the kings and the mountains are easily equal to each other.

When five of the kings have fallen, St. John realizes that he has progressed five steps toward ego's death. As it is, part of the ego has died already in the battle of Armageddon and also earlier. One king remains, however, and this stage is the Babylon stage. One part of it is the understanding of the delusory nature of self, represented by this seventeenth chapter, and the other part is liberation from Babylon described in the next chapter. But one more stage is yet to come in its entirety, because "the other has not yet come." It turns out that St. John will have to meet kings even after the eighteenth chapter. The complete death of the ego is a long process, and the victory won in the battle of Armageddon was only a partial victory. This is what the angel now declares to St. John.

Destruction of the prostitute

"And the ten horns which you saw on the beast, these will hate the prostitute, make her desolate and naked, eat her flesh and burn her with fire" (Rev. 17:16). The verse clarifies how one can let go of the ego. Giving up requires both an ever-deeper awareness of humankind's situation and also an inner personal transformation. Therefore, I interpret the verse from both viewpoints.

As to the dawning awareness, the prostitute representing the self must be revealed to be a projection of ego-consciousness, a mere mental image, a phantom. In other words, the prostitute must be naked, undressed so as to show what she or it really is. After men and women have realized deeply the projected phantom-nature of their own selves, they must discontinue the projection: they must treat it as just another delusion of the ego-consciousness. The core of this delusion is the ego-desires, symbolized by the horns of the beast. Therefore, the beast with its horns will have to "eat up" the prostitute. That the prostitute ends up in the beast's stomach, as it were, is an excellent mythical image for destroying a projection, or returning it to its origin. When the prostitute is burnt, individuals are burning away that sense of self that is merely a projected delusive image.

In these events foretelling the future, St. John is again reminiscent of Oriental philosophy. A good comparison here is with Ramana Maharsi's words, which I already quoted partially earlier, "If one then earnestly inquires 'Who am I?' one will see that there is no such thing as 'I' or 'me'... Seek this [I] and it will vanish like a phantom."[38]

As to the interpretation of the passage on the level of inner experience, the prostitute's nakedness refers to the nakedness of life which overcomes persons who are in the midst of inner transformation. It is as if all the ornaments the prostitute was adorned with are taken off of her; during this deep inner change, we lose those rewarding spiritual experiences which we enjoyed previously. St. John of the Cross often uses this kind of parable of undressing to refer to a person's inner cleansing. When he writes about the dark night of the spirit, he says, "God wants to undress the old person... seizing from the soul those pleasures she previously derived from spiritual blessings." He explains also that the soul will come to "nakedness and poverty of the spirit," and speaking of the purification of the senses, he describes the same feelings thus, "God... told them to unclothe themselves and to set aside the festive raiment and ornaments they were normally wearing."[39]

The eating of the prostitute, also, can be interpreted as a feeling experienced during a time of overpowering inner transformation. Human beings suffer in realizing they have been so overcome by delusion that even their sense of self has been a delusion, and in their suffering, they feel swallowed completely by delusion, or the beast. But this state of anguish also implies a realization which brings good in its wake, and so the self begins to disappear as if it were digested in the beast's stomach. This kind of a parable, too, is found in St. John of the Cross, "Seeing her wretchedness, the soul feels herself being destroyed and melting away in a cruel spiritual death. She feels as if she were swallowed into a beast's stomach, being digested there and suffering the same agonies as Jonah suffered in the belly of the sea monster."[40]

Finally, the burning of the prostitute illustrates that feeling of inner scorching and burning common during an intensive transformation. If the burning were complete, St. John the Divine would be fully liberated from his own self. Complete burning of the prostitute turns out, however, to be difficult in the dark night of the spirit, a topic which the next, the eighteenth, chapter addresses.[41]

18. DESTRUCTION OF BABYLON

Desire-filled human nature and purification of the spirit

Having realized clearly (as seen in the previous chapter) the desire-filled, even prostitute-like nature of his own self, St. John the Divine is ready for a deeper purification, the one St. John of the Cross calls "the night of the spirit." The previous visions of Revelation, particularly the winepress experience and plagues from the bowls, have prepared the way for this purification. During the earlier experiences St. John was already partly freed from desirousness, and he learned to still his consciousness from the mental images that are tied to the senses. But the transformation is not yet complete. As explained by St. John of the Cross, not even the purification of the senses is completed without the deeper purification of the spirit.[1] Thus St. John of Revelation must free himself more thoroughly from desires and from bondage to his mental images.

The destruction of Babylon described in Revelation compares so clearly with the analysis of the inner life of St. John of the Cross that I will use his works again as the main source for comparisons. Before interpreting the events of the vision in detail, I will, for the sake of clarity, introduce the characters in the vision, their interrelationships and the problem of desirousness represented by them.

The characters in the vision

The main character in the new vision of St. John is undeniably the prostitute of Babylon, who represents a desire-filled transcendental self, or, in the language of St. John of the Cross, the spiritual part of the soul before its purification. (In his vision St. John of Revelation often speaks of Babylon as a city, by which he probably means the general state of consciousness corresponding to the sense of self that is characterized by desirousness.[2])

Other images in the vision are the kings, the merchants and the seafarers. The merchants symbolize, like the kings, those centers of consciousness through which we act as the performers of our different abilities. Unlike the kings, the merchants as a mythical image emphasize desirousness, because a merchant seeks profit. In Christian literature, the merchants are used with this kind of meaning, for example, by Meister Eckhart when he interprets the episode in the Bible where Jesus drives the merchants away from the temple. Eckhart explains that the temple is the human soul, and it must be completely empty of merchants, or desirousness, so that God alone might dwell there.[3]

We can infer from the events of the vision that the seafarers, as well, function as merchants, but unlike the other merchants their 'basis' is the sea, or the unconscious. Therefore, they, more strongly than the merchants, symbolize the human being as a feeling individual acting from an emotional unconscious basis. In these interpretations I will not, however, greatly stress the difference between the merchants and the seafarers.

All these characters—the kings, the merchants and the seafarers—belong, unlike the prostitute, to the immanent level of human consciousness. In the terminology of St. John of the Cross, they belong to the lower part of the soul, or the sensuous part, and compared to it, the unpurified spirit of the prostitute is a higher part.

The last group of characters in the vision is comprised of the saints, the apostles and the prophets, who being holy are associated with experiencing genuine spiritual values and possibly with non-desirous action. The saints, the apostles, and the prophets belong to the level of the Self, and when they represent experiencing oneness and bliss, they are already, at least partially, transcendent. In St. John of the Cross' inner world, they represent the more thoroughly purified spiritual part of the soul. In this vision, the saints, the apostles, and the prophets are, nevertheless, merely subordinate characters.

Interrelationships

The main characters in this vision—the prostitute, the kings, the merchants and the seafarers—are closely interrelated. St. John of the Cross stresses the connection between the spiritual and the sensuous parts of the soul, "Because the soul is one single individual entity, its both parts affect each other."[4] St. John of Revelation describes these interrelationships between the different parts of human consciousness by repeating some of the things he has said before. He describes the intercourse between the kings and the prostitute with these words: "The kings of the earth who committed fornication and lived luxuriously with her" (Rev. 18:9). Here, as in other descriptions of the interrelationships, he begins to realize the superficiality and desirousness of his earlier perceptions and feelings; that is why the intercourse is fornication.[5]

St. John describes the relationship between the prostitute and the merchants with these words: "The merchants of the earth have become rich through the abundance of her luxury" (Rev. 18:3). The prostitute's luxury is that joy of living and sense of freedom which anyone experiences as a separate, personal self, once he has become more whole and opened up more blockages in his consciousness. Joy and freedom reflect a transformation also in the lower levels of the consciousness, in the levels symbolized by the merchants, because along with his sense of integration, new psychic abilities may open up; perhaps his creativity will blossom and his energy will increase. Such an integration may change him so strongly that he is healed from physical illnesses, should he have them. All this means the enriching of the 'lower' levels of the personality. But now St. John begins to see his own desirousness. He has greedily reached for the riches of the lower part of the soul; in this he has been like a merchant who has become rich through the abundance of the prostitute's luxury.

The seafarers, as well, have profited from the prostitute, for St. John writes: "All who had ships on the sea became rich by her wealth" (Rev. 18:19). This could mean that spiritual joy which St. John has experienced as a self, has spread also into his lower, more sensuous levels, and so the seafarers have profited from the wealth of the prostitute. (This phenomenon was discussed in the previous chapter while interpreting the inhabitants of the earth getting drunk from the wine of the prostitute.)

The interrelationship between the prostitute, the merchants and the seafarers functions also in the opposite direction, because the vision reveals that Babylon has bought their goods (for example, Rev. 18:11). This relationship tells us that the way human beings function as the performers of their abilities, has an effect on their spiritual, higher experiences. I will analyze these effects more closely by interpreting the prostitute's merchandise.

The merchandise

The vision spares two full verses to count out the goods the merchants have sold to the prostitute, "Gold and silver, precious stones and pearls, fine linen and purple, silk and scarlet, every kind of citron wood, every kind of object of ivory, every kind of object of most precious wood, bronze, iron and marble; and cinnamon and incense, fragrant oil and frankincense, wine and oil, fine flour and wheat, cattle and sheep, horses and chariots, and bodies and souls of men" (Rev. 18:12-13).

To reiterate, the goods the merchants have sold to the prostitute, represent the different ways that the lower experiences, feelings, actions and so on, can transfer into the content of the experiences lived on a higher level of consciousness, or on the level of the personal self. These ways are the ones that St. John has used to move his inner development forward. But in them he now detects a trace of desirousness. Because the items are merely listed, their interpretation is mostly left to the reader's own intuition. In my interpretation, I assume that St. John has already partially recovered from the shock of realizing his own desirousness. Now he is able to look at matters more calmly and understand that the stage represented by Babylon has taken him forward on the spiritual path regardless of remaining traces of desirousness.

St. John begins his list with these words, "Merchandise of gold and silver, precious stones and pearls." Additionally, there is wine and oil among the goods. All these refer to sacred experiences. While St. John has concentrated on experiencing what is holy on those levels of consciousness possible for him, he had expected the experience to move to a higher spiritual level, that of the prostitute; that is why gold and silver and other treasures have been offered for sale to the prostitute. In Christian language, St. John has strived to practice contemplation, but now he finds that his contemplation has been imperfect; it has had a trace of desirousness.

The list of goods contains also artefacts, "Every kind of object of ivory, every kind of object of most precious wood, bronze, iron, and marble." I interpret the objects to be mental images St. John has concentrated on to bring about and intensify spiritual experiences in his own consciousness. In Christian language, this has been meditative prayer, and the objects have been made of many materials, even as mental images are of many different types, some more valuable, some less so.

A portion of the goods is associated with incense and pleasing fragrances. These are incense, fragrant oil, citron wood, frankincense, and perhaps also cinnamon. Earlier, I already interpreted incense as a mythical image for prayer.[6] This kind of prayer, however, has desirousness left in it, because the smoke from the incense rises upward. Nevertheless, the fragrance from the incense is pleasing. Perhaps St. John wants to tell us with this, as with other images associated with fragrances, that his old religion gave fragrance and spice to his life, even though it also contained desirousness.

Fragrant oil was used in biblical times for beautifying hair, and thus, as a mythical image, it can express enhancement of thoughts. (As I explained earlier in the ninth chapter, hairs are like thoughts coming forth from the mind.) Even as St. John has sincerely tried to tend his inner life, he has also strived to make his thoughts beautiful, but again, in a desirous way.

The chariots, as a mythical image, probably represent the inner journey, or striving to progress spiritually. Because the merchants have offered the chariots to the prostitute, St. John realizes that his striving to progress spiritually has contained desirousness. He has expected a payment for his striving, that is, he has wanted satisfaction and happiness for himself.

St. John counts out also animals: cattle, sheep, and horses. The horses can be easily associated with the inner journey. All animals mentioned by St. John are domestic animals, indicating that he has already tamed his instincts on his spiritual path. Of the animals, the sheep probably represents the sheep-like quality a person needs in order to transform from ego to the Self, the slain Lamb. St. John has wanted to be ready for this, but he has not understood earlier that he has expected a reward for his attitude.

Flour and wheat refer to human actions and its productivity, or good works. Perhaps St. John understands that his good works have actually been for him like the merchandise for the merchant. He has wanted a payment for them in the form of happiness and joy.

Furthermore, the goods contain fabric: linen and purple and silk and scarlet. Purple and scarlet are red—they were already mentioned as the prostitute's clothing—and being red, they are associated with delusion. Some pieces of linen, on the other hand, are probably white or a light color, and should they be white, they are, in Revelation, associated with the level of the Self. This chapter tells of Babylon that it is clothed also in linen: "... was clothed in fine linen, purple and scarlet" (Rev. 18:16). Perhaps the linen reveals St. John's realization that he is nevertheless on his way out of the red of delusion to the white of the Self.

Perhaps the most descriptive is the last section of the list, bodies and souls of men, for bodies in this context refer to slaves. With a desirous attitude a woman or a man is, indeed, a slave without a deeper freedom. One lives in slavery dictated by the ego-desires, as it were, or in the words of St. John of the Cross:

> Should the soul be attached to something... the will becomes a slave and loses its freedom, and then the movements of the mind will incite and propel the soul to follow along.[7]

Other desirousness

In the vision by St. John the Divine, the merchants' and seafarers' desirousness is revealed also in the merchants' weeping "for no one buys the merchandise any more" and in the seafarers', who had grown rich by Babylon's wealth, grieving for its destruction (Rev. 18:11,19). The prostitute's desirousness is clearly expressed in the words addressed to her, "And the fruit that your soul longed for" (Rev. 18:14). St. John tells us with these mythical images, that he has wanted all those riches—pleasure, creativity and energy—that a human being experiences on the 'lower' levels, or as merchants and seafarers, and that he has also longed to be happy as the separate self, or the prostitute. Certainly, among the fruits the prostitute has longed for, has also been happiness, in fact, even bliss. Having lived in a state of bliss while seeing the ark of the covenant, St. John must have wanted to experience it again.

The problem of desirousness

Longing to feel happiness is a propelling force on the inner path, for it is a powerful motive for spiritual deepening. But now St. John has reach a point where he must realize this subtle paradox: that he can gain what he desires only by giving up desires. The deepest experience of holiness requires complete surrender.

This thought is like spiritual mathematics and vastly different religions and philosophical texts express it. St. John of the Cross explained the matter in this way:

> The soul may not be attached to any particular knowledge, neither to a heavenly nor to an earthly one, nor to striving for any kind of enjoyment or pleasure nor to anything that can be thought of. She must be quite empty... God... will enter the empty soul and fill it with his divine gifts.[8]

Particularly, St. John of the Cross stressed the prayer without desires:

> Some think that one sets out to pray to gain sensuous pleasure and devotion, and they strive for spiritual enjoyment and comfort. Then, true surrender disappears.[9]

Also the *Bhagavadgita*, the essence of Indian philosophy, emphasizes a lack of desire as one of its central messages. For example:

> You have a right to perform your prescribed duty,
> but you are not entitled to the fruits of action...
> Those who want to enjoy the fruits of their work are misers...
> By renouncing the fruits of action the wise attain bliss.[10]

St. Teresa defines two forms of union which clarify well St. John the Divine's present problem. First, there is the union wherein the will of the soul and that of God unite. The second union is "the joyous union," because in it, human beings experience ecstasy. St. Teresa emphasizes again and again that "the highest perfection" on the spiritual path forms from the first union: the soul must give up her own will and submit to God's will, and she may not expect any reward from God. St. Teresa explains further that a joyous union can arise only from the foundation of the union of the wills.[11]

St. Teresa's thought is clearly that the union of wills means complete lack of desire. But if man strives for joyous union, he still has desirousness left in him, because he wants happiness. I assume that St.

John in this stage of his visions realizes that he lacks the most important thing, the union of wills. Therefore, he must give up his own self, or the prostitute of Babylon and all of his desirousness.

We can elucidate the destructiveness of desires in a spiritual life in yet another way. Even when one is deeply engaged inwardly, attachments will lead the human consciousness toward the objects of the desires. Then the prostitute, the merchants and the seafarers are bartering, and the more superficial levels of the consciousness, the merchants and the seafarers, partake in the inner experience. Fragmentation and superficiality of consciousness will follow, and they will keep the experience from deepening to a state of bliss: desires and the fragmentation of the consciousness go hand in hand. To counteract the desires, we must learn a new attitude: an absolute selflessness and surrender. The opposite of fragmentation, in Christian language, is recollection, and more generally, the ability to concentrate. The destruction of the prostitute of Babylon means thus destruction of desires and fragmentation, as well as learning desirelessness, recollection, and concentration.

St. John of the Cross writes about this:

Those who strive onward are also plagued by... natural crudeness which every human being contracts from sin, and by the fragmentation of the spirit and by superficiality. Therefore, it is necessary for the soul to experience illumination, purification and gathering together in the midst of the trials and agony during this night of the spirit.[12]

In the practice of yoga, concentration of the consciousness is called *dharana*, and as the sixth step, it follows pratyahara on Patanjali's eightfold yoga path. Although in pratyahara the body's normal sensations and the perceptions which are derived from the outer world disappear, or at least begin to fade, a yogi's consciousness can still wander from one object to another: it can be fragmented. In the next step, dharana, the yogi learns through practice to keep his consciousness concentrated on one object. When the concentration is practiced in an early stage of yoga, the object of concentration can be chosen freely; common objects of concentration are the breath, mantras and the higher chakras. Additionally, in yoga theory, dharana is said to purify the consciousness, and in teaching concentration, the meaning of desirelessness is emphasized.[13] According to yoga, the destruction of Babylon would thus compare to dharana, or the stage of concentration.

The events of the night of the spirit

The angel and the voice from heaven

St. John begins his vision with words, "After these things I saw another angel coming down from heaven, having great authority, and the earth was illuminated with his glory. And he cried mightily with a loud voice, saying, 'Babylon the great is fallen, is fallen.'" (Rev. 18:1,2.) With these words, St. John tells us that in one moment of realization he experiences all that he has gradually understood in the previous chapter. This is an exalted spiritual intuition, for the angel comes from heaven. But the angel illuminates earth, and therefore St. John understands also clearly and consciously the nature of his previous stage of development and his self. The early part of the vision contains much repetition, and so I will discuss only the essential points.

"And I heard another voice from heaven saying, 'Come out of her, my people, lest you share in her sins, and lest you receive of her plagues'" (Rev. 18:4). This voice, too, expresses St. John's intuition. The voice continues, "Render to her... according to her works; in the cup which she has mixed, mix for her double. In the measure that she glorified herself... in the same measure give her torment and sorrow." (Rev. 18:6–7.) The verses tell us, that the change St. John is facing, is still infused purification. The cup can be seen as human consciousness, which has been earlier 'contaminated' by the prostitute, or the desirous self, and the feeling of infusion is expressed in such a way that what St. John must now experience will be poured into the cup.[14]

The agony of the night of the spirit is also revealed in the words heard by St. John the Divine: the voice uses the words render, torment and sorrow. St. John of the Cross, for his part, writes about the agony of the night of the spirit that it "cannot be compared to anything, because it is terrifying and stupefying to the spirit."[15]

In Revelation, the voice justifies the torment to be given to the prostitute, "for she says in her heart, 'I sit as queen, and am not a widow, and will not see sorrow'" (Rev. 18:7). The prostitute continues to boast; it is not easy to free ourselves emotionally. The words, "I sit as queen," reveal the power of a delusory self; the prostitute claims to be the queen or the most important part of our human consciousness. The words, "I am not a widow and will not see sorrow," express our stubborn belief that we gain pleasure from satisfying our ego-desires. In mythical thinking, a self bound to ego-desires—or rather the corresponding state of consciousness—is like a woman who is satisfied by her husband. However, consciousness should first become a widow. This widowhood means it would be empty of the movements created by the ego-desires; it could then withdraw inward to those levels which are symbolized by virgins. Only then would we be ready to experience higher and more spiritual values, or in the words of St. John of the Cross, "God... will enter the empty soul and fill it with his divine gifts."[16]

The intuitions symbolized by the angel descending from heaven and the voice coming from heaven trigger the emotional transformation of St. John the Divine. When the voice from heaven has ceased, St. John becomes the speaker. I assume that from here on he embodies the purification of the spirit at the same time as he is describing it.

The destruction of the prostitute

Babylon is destroyed. It burns, for St. John relates in different verses of the vision that the merchants and the seafarers see "the smoke of her burning" (Rev. 18:9,18). Revelation has foretold the prostitute's burning in the early part of the vision with the words, "She will be utterly burned with fire" (Rev. 18:8) and in the previous vision, where it was said, "The ten horns... on the beast... will... burn her with fire" (Rev. 17:16). The destruction of Babylon was prophesied also in the Old Testament, "And Babylon, the glory of kingdoms, the beauty of the Chaldeans' pride, will be as when God overthrew Sodom and Gomorrah. It will never be inhabited, nor will it be settled from generation to generation."[17]

When Babylon burns in Revelation, St. John is liberated from his desirous self. The general meaning of burning—burning off of the old—is a well-known mythical image, but I will clarify the idea with a few relevant quotations. St. John of the Cross explains that "the same fire of love, which later unites with the soul and illuminates it, will first attack it and purify it." And he continues:

"[In this purification] the flame is not sweet for the soul, but painful... and the flame will not bring refreshment nor peace for the soul, but wear her out and ignite her, tiring her and making her suffer with self-knowledge.[18]

Using Eastern phrasing, we could say that karma is burning away in the fire of wisdom when Babylon burns. Eastern literature offers also parables which describe the burning off of the previous sense of self that was bound to desires. In the following quotation from Paramahansa Yogananda, the emotional impact of the event is different from Revelation; instead of agony, it communicates a sense of liberation and joy:

Wisdom's fire is burning. I am feeding the flame. No use sorrowing more! All perishable pleasures, all temporary aspirations I am using as fagots to feed the eternal fire of knowledge ... Ah, my myriad ambitions are crackling joyously at the touch of God's flame. My ancient home of passions, of possessions, of incarnations, of many kingdoms of my fancy, of many air castles of my dreams—all are being consumed by this fire of my own kindling.[19]

"The smoke of her burning," the expression used by St. John the Divine, creates an impression that he first sees only the smoke created by the burning, while the fire is yet covered. That is, St. John is at first confused by his experience. Perhaps he does not realize right away that the burning of Babylon means liberation. St. John of the Cross, as well, emphasizes the fact that darkening of the understanding and the spirit are part of the purification phase. For this reason, the purifying fire is according to him also "dark light" and "dark fire," which are comparable to "the smoke of burning."[20]

The prostitute's torment, or the agony that St. John the Divine feels during the night of the spirit, appears in many verses, particularly in the following, "The merchants... stand at a distance for fear of her torment" (Rev. 18:15). The expression, "stand at a distance," probably illustrates alienation in the sense of self-observation; St. John consciously recognizes his change and the agony brought about by it.

The destruction of the prostitute is also described in the words addressed to her in the vision, "And the fruit that your soul longed for has gone from you, and all the things which are rich and splendid have gone from you, and you shall find them no more at all" (Rev. 18:14). The verse describes the loss of joy and inner wealth, and this is agony for anyone experiencing profound transformation. The state described in the verse is also well expressed as "poverty of spirit," of which St. John of the Cross says in connection with the night of the spirit, "this blessed night... renders the spirit poor and empties it of all possessions and natural attachments."[21]

The additional words in Revelation, "you shall find them no more at all," perhaps reflect St. John the Divine's subjective feeling about the continuation of the agony. St. John of the Cross also says that the soul feels, in the midst of deep agony, that she can never again feel any joy.[22] But the words of Revelation probably have another meaning as well. Perhaps St. John believes that his realization about his own desirousness has created such an absolute transformation in him that he will never again wish to adorn his own self, or the prostitute, with the feelings of happiness and joy which are symbolized as riches.

Agony and poverty of spirit can also be seen in the next verse in Revelation, "Alas, alas, that great city, that was clothed in fine linen, purple, and scarlet, and adorned with gold and precious stones and pearls! For in one hour such great riches came to nothing" (Rev. 18:16–17). In the words of St. John of the Cross, "She is... indeed poor in spirit and stripped of the old self."[23]

The torment of the kings, the merchants, and the seafarers

"And the kings of the earth... will weep and lament for her" (Rev. 18:9). "And the merchants of the earth will weep and mourn over her, for no one buys their merchandise any more" (Rev.18:11). "The merchants... who became rich by her, will stand at the distance for the fear of her torment, weeping and wailing" (Rev. 18:15). "And every shipowner, all who travel by ship, sailors, and as many as trade on the sea, stood at the distance and cried out when they saw the smoke of her burning" (Rev. 18:17–18). "[The seafarers] threw dust on their heads and cried out, weeping and wailing, and saying, 'Alas, Alas, that great city, in which all who had ships on the sea became rich by her wealth! For in one hour she is made desolate'" (Rev. 18:19).

When the kings, the merchants, and the seafarers are having difficulties, St. John feels agony in the lower, or more sensuous levels of his soul, to use the language of St. John of the Cross. In fact, I will refer once more to the latter's teaching according to which purification of the sensuous part of the soul will not be complete before the spirit has been purified. Thus, during the night of the spirit, different parts of the soul are to be purified at the same time. St. John of the Cross expresses this by saying that "in a severe and difficult purification of the spirit... both parts of the soul, the spiritual and the sensuous, must experience complete purification."[24]

The torment that the merchants and the seafarers feel for the prostitute's destruction and the loss of her riches, is comparable to St. John of the Cross' imagery. He speaks of "torment that is felt for the emptiness and poverty of the soul's sensuous and spiritual being." Speaking of the different troubles accompanying the night of the spirit, St. John of the Cross uses the same images as Revelation, that is, crying and wailing:

> This is a painful disorder involving many inner fears, imaginings and struggles of the soul... She feels such deep agony and sorrow in her spirit that she bursts into a powerful spiritual crying and wailing. At times she cries out loud and melts into tears, should she have enough strength and ability for it.[25]

The vision in Revelation about the destruction of Babylon develops in such a way that St. John first describes the events from the merchants' angle and then from the seafarers'. Here we can see the transformation process evolving from a more superficial level to a deeper one, although the deepest level is the prostitute, and she apparently is burning all the while. St. John of the Cross wrote about the deepening of the transformation during the night of the spirit in the following way:

> When the soul has been purified from the mostly outward imperfections, the fire of love begins anew and gnaws at the soul ever deeper inward, to wear out and purify what is still left.[26]

In Revelation the seafarers ask, while watching the destruction of Babylon, "What is like this great city?" (Rev. 18:18.) Perhaps St. John wonders in the middle of the transformation, "If I let go of my own self, what will be left of me? What could replace my self?"

The joy of the holy

"Rejoice over her, O heaven, and you holy apostles and prophets, for God has avenged you on her!" (Rev.18:20.) When St. John is ever more fully liberated from his attachments during the burning of Babylon, his spirit is emptier and poorer so that he may experience genuine spirituality. St. John of the Cross describes the liberation in this way:
> When those [imperfections of the soul] have burnt completely ...soul's torment is over, and only joy remains... When the soul is purified from dirt with this fire of love, she will ignite into ever greater love yet.[27]

At the end of the chapter, the destruction of Babylon is celebrated with the words, "The sound of harpists, musicians, flautists, and trumpeters shall not be heard in you any more... And the light of a lamp shall not shine in you any more. And the voice of bridegroom and bride shall not be heard in you any more." (Rev. 18:22–23.) The singing and the playing symbolize spiritual experience which, St. John realizes, he has earlier experienced in a wrong and imperfect way, as an ego or a separate self.[28] The light and the symbolism of the bride and the bridegroom, which I will return to in the following chapters, are also associated with spiritual experiences representing their higher, blissful forms. In this connection, the words mean that St. John has tried to live through even the highest experiences as an ego, as an "I" tied to desires, without realizing that he must surrender completely and give up his own self.

St. John rejoices over the destruction of Babylon in the following way, "And no craftsman of any craft shall be found in you any more. And the sound of a millstone shall not be heard in you any more." (Rev. 18:22.) The craftsmen symbolize fittingly human abilities, and the turning of the millstone, which I will soon return to, symbolizes generally movement and man's physical and mental activity. With his words, St. John tells us that he wants to separate the use of his skills, and more generally, his ability to function, from his desire-filled self. Thus he will be able to begin desireless, saintlike action which represents, along with experiencing spiritual values, the other side of the Self.[29]

The incompleteness of the transformation

Babylon is thrown into the sea

"Then a mighty angel took up a stone like a great millstone and threw it into the sea, saying, 'Thus with violence the great city of Babylon shall be thrown down, and shall not be found any more'" (Rev. 18:21). Up until now, Revelation has told us about the burning of Babylon, but in the end of the chapter Babylon is thrown into the sea. This surprising turn can be interpreted both psychologically and philosophically. In a myth, both levels can serve to complete each other.

In the psychological interpretation, the sea is the unconscious, and throwing something into the sea symbolizes some state of consciousness 'sinking' into the unconscious. More theoretically, once in the sea, the actual state of consciousness becomes only potential. Throwing something into the sea does not, however, need to mean outright suppression, but rather a change in the degree of clarity and solidity of the state of consciousness. Nevertheless, we must ask: why can St. John not rid himself completely of the prostitute of Babylon, or his own self?

The sense of a separate self is connected to ego-desires, so that only a complete freedom from the ego-desires down to the last seed and sprout can liberate us entirely from the sense of a separate self. As long as we have even unconscious seeds of ego-desires, the self is potentially present. Should we, for one reason or another, strengthen those seeds and begin to satisfy our ego-desires, a renewed sense of self is born in us. Then Babylon would rise from the sea of potentiality and become actual. St. John believes, however, that this will not happen, because he says about the millstone, "[It] shall not be heard in you any more" (Rev. 18:21).

Interpreted in this way, the throwing into the sea agrees with the image of the previous chapter, where the beast eats the prostitute (Rev. 17:16). The eating of the prostitute was predicted in the previous vision, and in this chapter the prediction is fulfilled, but through a different metaphor. The beast, or the delusory ego-consciousness, is now pictured as the sea with Babylon being thrown into its depths. Although St. John is freed from his self as Babylon is destroyed, he is left, with unconscious seeds of desires, and so the beast or St. John's ego-consciousness exists. Because St. John's liberation from delusion is not complete, the purification must continue. In the later chapters of Revelation, St. John indeed must wrestle further with his ego-desires as well as with the beast.

These thoughts reveal that St. John of the Cross' concept of the night of the spirit, or the purification of the spirit, is in its entirety broader than the destruction of Babylon described in this chapter. The scope of Babylon's destruction, however, compares very well with that of dharana, the stage of concentration of the yoga path, because dharana is a step toward the actual meditation, wherein the deeper purification will happen.

According to a philosophical interpretation, throwing of Babylon into the sea would be conceptual reckoning. The human self, Babylon, belongs to the realm of delusion, and there it must be placed. The sea that Babylon is thrown into would then be conceptually the same sea of delusion that those victorious over the beast stood upon in the fifteenth chapter. This interpretation of the throwing of Babylon into the sea is supported by the words in the following chapter which say of the prostitute of Babylon, "And her smoke rises up for ever and ever!" (Rev. 19:3.) The sense of a separate self, or the prostitute of Babylon, as an essential part of the sea of delusion keeps an individual a prisoner of delusion. This form of delusion will persist as long as there is humankind. The smoke of delusion women and men wrap themselves into will thus rise for ever and ever; Eastern literature, in fact, often makes use of the expression "the smokescreen of delusion."[30] Yet, all must find their way into freedom from the darkness of the smoke and the sea of delusion.

The millstone

And why does St. John compare Babylon to a millstone which is thrown into the sea? The Old Testament has a similar image wherein the prophet Jeremiah concludes a chapter characterizing the destruction of Babylon with these words, "Now it shall be, when you have finished reading this book, that you shall tie a stone to it and throw it out into the Euphrates. Then you shall say, 'Thus Babylon shall sink and not rise from the catastrophe that I will bring upon her. And they shall be weary.'"[31]

A thorough interpretation of a mythical image would always require approaching it from many different directions. The mythical worldview is a network of countless analogies, where one mythical image will settle into the complex of many different analogical relationships. Measured with the yardstick of conscious thinking, a mythical way of seeing is incredibly expressive. Different sides of a mythical image tell their own tale which serve to complete the total picture. How, then, the totality reveals itself to the interpreter's intuition is another matter. Because of the broadness of Revelation, I have generally presented only one, or at the most, a few viewpoints for each mythical image, but now I will interpret the millstone more extensively.

The modern person probably first thinks of the saying "millstone around one's neck." This common metaphor appears already in the Bible, in the Gospel of Mark where it is said, "And whoever causes one of these little ones who believe in Me to stumble, it would be better for him if a millstone were hung around his neck, and he were thrown into the sea."[32] The saying fits well also in Revelation: the self is like a millstone around our neck, because it is the source of suffering, "the mother of prostitutes and of the abominations of the earth."

Many parables associated with the grinding of the grain can also be read into the millstone analogy. The millstone, being used for grinding, is in motion—and, similarly, human consciousness is in motion, when, steeped in desires, it reaches out for its goals. We are, however, unable to stop the perpetual motion of our consciousness until we are inwardly ready for it. And so we need to use the millstone of our consciousness as well as possible to understand matters more deeply and to change in a better direction. St. Teresa says about the early stages of the spiritual path, "Let us allow this millstone to turn and grind the wheat; our will and understanding must not cease their toiling."[33]

But St. John has already progressed beyond the early stages of the inner transformation, and during the infused purification he perhaps feels himself in the embrace of a supraindividual transformation process, as it were. In the terminology of modern psychology, he has passed the personal level and moved in ever greater degree into the 'program' belonging to the realm of the collective unconscious. Applying the millstone parable, St. John perhaps feels that some power, independent of him, turns the transformation mill of his life, or at least, that the transformation happening in him is in continuous movement, progressing revolution by revolution.

The grains that are ground between the millstones are different attachments. When St. John allowed the inner transformation to evolve, his grains of wheat died one after another, and so he has become freer from attachments. At times this transformation has been terrifying; at those times the attachments were broken as if they were crushed by the heavy millstones.

The geometric form and the revolving movement of the millstone also may have awakened associations in St. John's mind. If the millstone is assumed to be round—millstones with other forms were also used during the ancient times—it is like a mandala. And the closer to the center of the millstone the movement takes place, the smaller the centrifugal force; in the ideal center point of the millstone the movement has ceased all together. In this way of seeing, the millstone would also image the inner world, where we are to journey once we have become ego-bound individuals. This world, too, is a kind of a mandala, but it turns continuously, and keeps us in its tight grip. A millstone is indeed an appropriate illustration for the world of delusion, because in seeking the way to the center of a revolving millstone, we must move against the centrifugal force, and that force can be seen as the power of delusion. The millstone can, also, be loosely compared with the wheel of life, or the wheel of karma of Eastern philosophy, because in these wheels we must wander as prisoners of delusion and seek the way to freedom.[34]

By this stage, St. John has already walked for a long time in the world of the millstone, spiraling closer to its center, revolution by revolution. During the journey, his attachments have been ground down; he has become more inward and learned to quiet his consciousness. Now that he has, in this vision, finally progressed close enough to the center, he can throw his 'vehicle,' or his heavy millstone, his own self, away. Thus he is able to move to higher and deeper spiritual levels in the following visions.

V

THE HIGHEST LEVELS OF SPIRITUAL LIFE

Chapters 19–22 of Revelation

In the last chapters of Revelation, the transformation of St. John the Divine culminates in spiritual liberation. This means living bliss and love in ever higher degrees. The states of consciousness described in Revelation are higher possibilities available for man, and only few—like Jesus and Buddha—have lived them in full measure. Literature has, nevertheless, many descriptions about these states, and even the little insights that many of us have of them, will help to understand them partially.

19. THE ANNOUNCEMENT OF THE WEDDING OF THE LAMB, THE RIDER, AND THE LORD'S GREAT SUPPER

The new phase of evolution

St. John of the Cross divides the night of the spirit into two phases: during the first phase, a purifying fire causes agony, but later the fire gives also warmth and light. Then it is both a purifying and loving fire.[1] I feel that the nineteenth chapter of Revelation describes this kind of latter phase of the night of the spirit. The issue is still purification, or breaking of the ego-bondage. As it is, St. John the Divine is not yet fully free from all bondage, although he has given up his sense of a separate self. The killing of the kings in this vision illustrates the destruction of the bondage. But the images of the vision also describe happy states of consciousness paralleling the loving fire mentioned by St. John of the Cross. The wedding symbolism and part of the description of the rider on a white horse illustrate the happy states, although the wedding is merely anticipated. This chapter could have been placed in the previous section which discussed the infused purification, but the higher transformed states of consciousness are emphasized so much in this vision that I include it with the final chapters.

Wedding symbolism appears also in the final chapters of Revelation, and therefore I associate the events of these chapters with the wedding between the soul and God. In St. Teresa's bride symbolism, the nineteenth chapter would be placed within the preparation for the engagement. The revealing of the ark of the covenant was, in the eleventh chapter, compared to the first "face to face" meeting between the bride and the Bridegroom, which, according to St. Teresa, is a preparation for the wedding between the soul and God. After this face-to-face meeting, the soul "makes a firm decision that she will not accept another husband" than God, but "the Lord ignores her intense wishes for engagement," because the soul must prepare herself more thoroughly. St. Teresa explains further that during the time of preparation, the soul will receive many gifts from the Lord, but must also bear difficult trials.[2] Indeed, these two features, the trials and the gifts, can be seen in this vision of St. John the Divine as well.

Strengthening of the sense of oneness

The announcement of the wedding of the Lamb

"And I heard, as it were, the voice of a great multitude as the sound of many waters and as the sound of mighty thunderings, saying, 'Alleluia! For the Lord God Omnipotent reigns! Let us be glad and rejoice and give him glory, for the marriage of the Lamb has come, and his wife has made herself ready.' And to her it was granted to be arrayed in fine linen, clean and bright, for the linen represents the righteous acts of the saints." (Rev. 19:6–8.)

Although the verses announce the wedding of the Lamb, the wedding apparently takes place later, because in the twenty-first chapter St. John sees the holy city descending from heaven, and he calls the city the bride and the wife of the Lamb (Rev. 21:2,9). We can probably assume that the wedding of the Lamb, in its entirety, lasts a long time, and the preparations for the wedding get under way in this chapter.

The wedding in myths and in religious literature

Mythology is rich in wedding themes and richer yet in union of the female and male principles. The Assyrian-Babylonian lore has a myth about the wedding between the god Niurta and the goddess Bau, which was observed in rituals in the beginning of the new year. Also the cult of the Babylonian god Marduk presumably included a wedding ritual. In Greek mythology, the union of the female and male principles can be found, for example, in the *Iliad*, which describes the union of Zeus and Hera on top of Mount Ida.[3]

Depending on the distinguishing features of the myth, the culture it is part of, the historic period, and the participating individual's perception, the wedding and the union between the female and the male reflect the union and harmony of a variety of ideas. These ideas may be, for example, an attuning of the cosmic forces—like the universal spirit and nature—or simply the harmony in nature. If, for example, the masculine heaven and the feminine earth celebrate their wedding, people may be trustful of the coming year: in time, heaven with its rain will make the earth fertile, and the earth will bear harvest. Experienced on the individual level, the wedding and the union may support an individual's sense of regained wholeness on physical, mental, and even spiritual levels. Depending on the context, the mythical image of the wedding and the union can be experienced as expressions of physical pleasure, or the union of different mental characteristics—for example, intellect and feeling. On the highest spiritual level and as a part of religious symbolism, the mythical wedding depicts living in the consciousness of oneness or bliss; this is also how I interpreted the marriage of the soul and God in the eleventh chapter.

In Christianity, the bride symbolism is perhaps best known from the Song of Solomon, or the Song of Songs, of the Old Testament. In it, the bride expresses her sense of oneness with her bridegroom with these words, "I am my beloved's and my beloved is mine."[4] Later, the Christian mystics have used the symbolism of the Song of Solomon in describing their own ecstatic experiences. For example, St. John of the Cross writes, "The soul feels...joy and celebration, enjoys God and praises him...she acknowledges like the bride in the Song of Solomon: *Dilectus meus mihi et ego illi* ('My beloved is mine and I am his')."[5] Also the poem by St. John of the Cross which forms the core of his book *The Living Flame of Love* offers an example of the bride symbolism. The name alone reveals the essential content of the poem: "The verses the soul speaks as she unites intimately with God, her beloved bridegroom."[6]

Similar symbolism can be found in Indian religious literature and yoga theory, because in India the union between man and his mythical husband, or God, means spiritual bliss and the ultimate union, samadhi. For example, the Indian swami Vivekananda writes, "Who in this universe is more fit to become the husband than He? Who in this universe is fitter to be loved than He? So let Him be the husband, let Him be the Beloved... When man has this love in him, he becomes eternally blessed, eternally happy...In the presence of this Light of Love...he realizes...at last the beautiful and inspiring truth that Love, the Lover, and the Beloved are One."[7] In yoga theory, a person's kundalini energy is seen as feminine. When the yogi has brought the kundalini energy through the chakras to the sahasrara on top of the head, the feminine kundalini is said to unite with the masculine Shiva, and the yogi will experience the bliss of samadhi.[8]

The wedding of the Lamb and the bride of the Lamb

In Christian interpretations of Revelation, the wedding of the Lamb is seen, most often, as the union between God's congregation and God, and in that connection the bride of the Lamb is the congregation, or the church. But Christianity includes also interpretations of Revelation which incorporate the bride symbolism. For example, Bernard of Clairvaux, in speaking of the bride in Revelation who has prepared herself, emphasizes that only the one who behaves and loves as the Bridegroom behaved and loved can become His bride.[9]

More generally—without a clear reference to Revelation—the expressions "the bride of the Lamb" and "the wedding of the Lamb" appear in Christian literature in many different associations in the meaning of the purified soul and the spiritual bliss that will be her lot. For example, a source compiled during the Middle Ages and containing biographies of German nuns portrays the death of a devout nun by saying that she had left for the heavenly wedding of the Lamb for which she had, already on earth, prepared herself. In modern times, Basilea Schlink writes in her autobiography, "To make me a true bride of the Lamb, the Lord wanted to ignite my heart with love for Him."[10]

C.G. Jung saw the wedding of the Lamb in Revelation as a version of the archetypal sacred marriage, *hieros gamos*. Usually, he saw human integration in this image; this meant, in the first place, a more solid connection between the unconscious and the conscious, and a smoothing out of opposites. He explained that the visions of St. John, similarly to the "classical individuation process," end with the wedding. Nevertheless, he found the wedding of the Lamb described by St. John unusual. According to Jung, the vision does not describe smoothing out the opposites, but in it, simply "light unites with light." As far as I understand Jung's interpretation, he saw the wedding of the Lamb as a grand metaphysical vision about the world's spiritual development rather than as an illustration about a personal wholeness.[11]

In my interpretation, I follow the Christian bride symbolism, which I will analyze theoretically. Expressed theoretically, the Lamb of Revelation (or the Bridegroom of the bride symbolism) is the universal Self. More specifically, the Lamb is the objective side of the universal Self or that level of spiritual reality which man experiences as the content of his consciousness. The wife of the Lamb is the subjective side of the universal Self. The subjective side refers to the level of consciousness where that content is actually experienced. Thus, in the wedding, a person actually experiences the significant reality symbolized by the Lamb.

The words, "His wife has made herself ready," mean that St. John's deep level of consciousness has, in an inner transformation, prepared itself to experience spiritual reality which exceed the narrow boundaries of the self. The preparation has meant that St. John's consciousness has been liberated from attachments and the separate sense of self. The bright clean linen that the wife of the Lamb is dressed in (Rev. 19:7–8) also reflects this level of consciousness, now 'clean' from attachments. In Christian literature Catherine of Siena, a 14th century mystic, speaks about the wedding raiment of love that the soul is dressed in—after undressing her own will.[12]

The thought that the bride of the Lamb has prepared herself has its place also in Eastern yoga theory because in order to live in spiritual bliss, the yogi is to prepare his feminine kundalini energy by drawing it up through the sushumna nadi, or through the different chakras.[13]

The marriage supper

"Then he said to me, 'Write: blessed are those who are called to the marriage supper of the Lamb!'"(Rev. 19:9). The essential features of the bride symbolism are repeated in the marriage supper parable. A person's mouth and stomach, reminiscent of a vessel, are comparable to the wife of the bride symbolism; and the food and drink, which are in the mouth and in the stomach, are comparable to the bridegroom. In other words, the mouth and the stomach symbolize human consciousness, and the food and the drink, the content of consciousness. The marriage supper itself as a mythical image, besides symbolizing union, emphasizes the idea that the high spiritual values nourish us only when we experience them, or eat them. Thus those are blessed who can partake in the marriage supper.

In the Bible, the marriage supper or dinner is also more generally used to symbolize the experience of spiritual values. For example, in the Gospel of Matthew, Jesus characterizes the heavenly kingdom with these words, "The kingdom of heaven is like a certain king who arranged a marriage for his son... saying, 'Tell those who are invited: See, I have prepared my dinner; my oxen and fatted cattle are killed, and all things are ready. Come to the wedding.'" The dining parable is also used in the beginning of Revelation where we read, "Behold, I stand at the door and knock. If anyone hears my voice and opens the door, I will come in to him and dine with him, and he with me" (Rev. 3:20). St. John of the Cross interprets these words to mean the union between God and the human soul.[14]

The sacred supper and, more broadly, sacred foods are also universal symbols; I have earlier referred to the sacred supper of Mithraism. In Indian symbolism drinking of the *amrita* nectar often means living in spiritual bliss.[15]

Worshiping God

"And I fell at his feet to worship him. But he said to me, 'See that you do not do that! I am your fellow servant, and of your brethren who have the testimony of Jesus. Worship God! For the testimony of Jesus is the spirit of prophecy.'" (Rev. 19:10.) He at whose feet St. John is about to fall is apparently the angel who spoke about the wedding feast. I use the words of the angel to focus on an important philosophical problem, although other interpretations are also possible.[16]

St. John has come to a realization during his visions: what man experiences himself is essential in a spiritual life, not what he thinks God to be as a separate entity. This realization inevitably leads to the question: if what an individual experiences is essential, will God then be reduced to a form in the human consciousness? According to my interpretation, this problem confused St. John already in the ninth chapter, when smoke covered the sun and the air. Now St. John returns to his problem and he finds a satisfactory answer for it.

When St. John wants to fall at the angel's feet to worship him, he is about to experience as holy something which is part of human consciousness. As I have explained earlier, in my interpretation of Revelation, angels, the Lamb's bride, prophets, witnesses, priests, the holy, and so on, are symbols for deep levels of human consciousness. Analyzed philosophically, consciousness and its various levels must be differentiated from the content of consciousness that is being experienced at any one time. And, what is being experienced is, in religious life, God or Spirit, and according to a religious worldview, these exist objectively. "The spirit of prophecy," the expression used by the angel, is indeed descriptive, because it differentiates between human consciousness, or a prophet who prophesies and the objective content of the consciousness, or the spirit of prophecy. When, in Revelation, the angel tells St. John to worship God instead of the angel, perhaps St. John understands these things intuitively. Giving up an alienating religion does not necessarily lead to regarding human consciousness as a most sacred object, or in other words, God cannot be reduced to a form of human consciousness.

Interpreted in this way, the angel's words in Revelation can be compared to the platonic view, which maintains that there is an objective world of ideas and values. I assume additionally that, based on his own experience, St. John comes to a 'platonic' outlook. It is characteristic of the highest spiritual states of consciousness that the person experiencing them feels he finds a new level of spiritual reality as already existing; he does not feel that he creates it through his own experience.

It is also characteristic of high spiritual states that during them a person feels himself clearly to cross boundaries of his own self. In Revelation, St. John has already destroyed the prostitute of Babylon, and in this vision the angel's words, "I am your fellow servant and of your brethren," might refer to a feeling of universal brotherhood. When St. John has crossed the boundaries of his narrow self, he feels on a deeply spiritual level that he is one with all. He lives also in his fellow human beings, and therefore everyone is God's servant and brethren to each other.[17]

It is important to keep in mind the special character of exalted spiritual experiences, particularly now that the events in Revelation concentrate on describing them. For lack of better expressions, we are left to use the word "experience" for transformed states of consciousness, although the word in its normal meaning elicits the idea that the corresponding state of consciousness is limited to the person's own self, even to the inside of his body. As I explained earlier, this is not so with exalted spiritual experiences. For this reason, Eastern literature, in particular, emphasizes the idea that a saint's spiritual experiences always have a far-reaching power to do good. Although the saint may not act outwardly, his high state of consciousness as such is "action without acting," helping the world.[18]

I emphasize the fact that it is difficult to describe the transformed states of consciousness at all. The difficulty is that our language does not have words for them because it is those words that are utilized to communicate common experiences which become rooted into usage, and the transformed states deviate from the common experiences. When I discuss St. John's exalted spiritual states of consciousness in the following, I do not attempt to offer a vivid impression. I rather concentrate on analyzing the mythical images of Revelation according to the nature of my book. The reader who is interested in these states of consciousness, might look for more detailed descriptions of them, for example, in the works which I have used as sources for the final chapters.

Infusion of the Holy Spirit or merging into the Om-vibration

The heavenly rider

"Then I saw heaven opened, and behold, a white horse. And he who sat on him." (Rev. 19:11.) The opening of heaven tells us that a high level of consciousness opens for St. John. Heaven, the rider and the horse form together the mythical image of this new perception. Heaven is the exalted level of consciousness, "the other heaven," or the superconscious. The rider seen in the opened heaven is the content of consciousness, and the horse is the energy base of this state of consciousness. (Later on, however, I will often speak simply of the rider as the symbol of this new state of consciousness.)

Earlier, when the wedding of the Lamb was announced, it was said that the wife of the Lamb had prepared herself and dressed in bright, clean linen, and this cloth expressed, according to my interpretation,

St. John's purified consciousness. The white horse suggests that the energy level comparable to that state of consciousness has been purified, or become white.

The white horse and the one who rides on it appeared in the sixth chapter, where they were the first to be sent off and where the rider was said to go out "conquering and to conquer" (Rev. 6:2). St. John, after many trials, has broken out of his bondage, and is returning to the original pure, or white, state which in Revelation means victory. The reappearance of the white horse and its rider in St. John's visions means, therefore, a step forward in St. John's mythical return journey.

The rider can be also compared to the male child whose birth was mentioned in the twelfth chapter and who represented an exalted spiritual state of consciousness. At the time it was said about the child that he will rule all nations with a rod of iron, and in this vision the same words are said about the rider, "He himself will rule them [the nations] with a rod of iron" (Rev. 19:15). We can infer that the rider is the same male child grown up. In the twelfth chapter, the child was "caught up to the throne" and St. John's vision continued on earth, because St. John was not yet ready to permanently experience the high spiritual state symbolized by the child.

Now he has, however, become the bride of the Lamb and has 'made himself ready,' and therefore, the male child reappearing in the visions can come in a grown-up form. In theoretical terminology the rider is the Self, and more specifically, its objective side. St. John experiences this state ever more fully because he has been further liberated from his attachments during his inner transformation. The details of the vision describe more clearly what St. John's new experience is like.

The faithful and true Word of God

"And he who sat on him was called Faithful and True" (Rev. 19:11). Two verses later St. John tells of the rider, that "his name is called the Word of God" (Rev. 19:13). In the Bible, the Word of God is Amen, and Amen means 'verily,' 'truly,' or roughly the same as faithful and true. The identity between Amen and "Faithful and True," is made clear in the third chapter of Revelation, where it says, "These things, says the Amen, the faithful and true witness, the beginning of the Creation of God" (Rev. 3:14). Earlier I have explained that, transferred into the Eastern tradition, Amen is the Om-sound, which in that culture is the word of God, or God's voice.[19]

The reader might remember that in the sixth chapter the first creature, one that looked like a lion, sent off a white horse and its rider. At that time, I interpreted the lion to be the basic universal energy, or in the Eastern worldview, the Om-vibration. When the rider, "Faithful and True," on his white horse appears in St. John's vision, St. John has come to a stage on his return journey where he connects with this basic energy, "the beginning of God's creation" or the Om-vibration. St. John has, throughout Revelation, heard the roar of many waters, thunder and trumpet blows, but I assume that in this chapter he begins to hear the sound of Om in a new way. Having walked along the path of the tree of life from the base upward many times, he now identifies with the Om-sound more fully than earlier. A comparison with Eastern yoga will help to understand this clearly.

On Patanjali's eightfold yoga path, after concentration, dharana, follows the actual meditation, *dhyana*. Then the yogi detaches himself even more from outward and image-like objects of concentration, striving to sustain a clear, completely inward state of consciousness. (In other words, the meditation of the yoga theory, dhyana, is roughly the same as Christian contemplation.) At this stage, the yogi can also use Om-sound and Om-light as an object of meditation. The stage following dhyana is samadhi, bliss.[20] For example, Ramana Maharshi wrote about the Om-sound, or the *nada* meditation, in the following way:

Meditation on *nada* is one of the various approved methods... Just as a child is lulled to sleep by lullabies, so *nada* soothes one to the state of *samadhi*. Again, just as a king sends his state musicians to welcome his son on his return from a long journey, so also *nada* takes the devotee into the Lord's abode in a pleasing manner.[21]

Identifying with the Om-sound varies in intensity, and it can involve different experiences; this is a long stage in a human life. Essentially, however, a person experiences the identification with the Om-sound as a state of liberation, one which expands consciousness and heightens spirituality and thereby changes him. He begins to feel himself increasingly in everything that exists, because the Om-vibration penetrates everything. It exists in the entire creation, because it is, as it is said in Revelation, "the beginning of the creation."[22] Therefore, I assume the rider Faithful and True appears in the vision because St. John is identifying with the Om-sound to the point that his consciousness expands beyond its previous boundaries.

In Christian language, St. John's new stage of development is caused by an infusion of the Holy Spirit, or by baptism in the Holy Spirit. Becoming absorbed in the Om-vibration and baptized in the Holy Spirit is, in fact, in the yoga literature thought of as one and the same thing. St. John of the Cross, for his part, explains similarly that the sound the apostles heard when the Holy Spirit descended upon them was the same sound which appears in Revelation as the sound of many waters and of thunder.[23] In the Bible, the descent of the Holy Spirit upon the disciples is described in the following manner, which well illustrates the characteristics of the Om-vibration:

And suddenly there came a sound from heaven, as of a rushing mighty wind, and filled the whole house where they were sitting. Then there appeared to them divided tongues, as of fire, and one sat upon each of them. And they were filled with the Holy Spirit.[24]

In India, Om-meditation is regarded highly, because the meditator, in becoming one with the Om-sound, is thought of as attaining contact with God himself. Similarly, St. John of the Cross explains that God communicates himself by creating this voice in the soul.[25] This same idea is presented in Revelation in that the rider seen by St. John the Divine is called the Word of *God*.

The sword of the rider

"Now out of his mouth goes a sharp sword" (Rev. 19:15). The rider represents St. John's state of consciousness when he identifies with the Om-sound. But the Om-sound itself aptly takes the form of a sword coming out of the mouth of the rider. The word of God as a sword appears also elsewhere in the Bible; Paul in his Epistle to the Ephesians, encourages us to receive the sword of the Spirit, "which is the word of God."[26]

The sword coming out of the mouth of the rider may also express that sublime intuition which St. John experiences in this stage of development. We could, perhaps, think that he experiences his new spiritual intuitions as God's talking to him. In Christianity, exalted spiritual experiences are often referred to as spiritual communications, and even locutions. For example, according to St. Teresa, God speaks to the soul in a new way in these experiences. She writes, "Some locutions come from deep inside the soul... Some are so outward that they can be heard with ears, and in those cases, they seem plainly spoken words."[27]

St. Teresa describes elevated spiritual experiences also in the following way:

> His Majesty awakens her in a way that resembles a shooting star or a thunderclap appearing suddenly. Although the soul hears no sound, she understands unmistakably that she has received an invitation from God... The Beloved makes it clear that He is with the soul, and... calls her with such a definite sign the soul cannot doubt. He whistles so penetratingly and distinctly, that the soul cannot but hear it.[28]

In St. Teresa's description the penetrating whistle is comparable to the sharp sword coming out of the mouth of the rider.

In St. John's stage of development, the intuitive state of consciousness may express itself as a sharp sword also because he is still, to some degree, tied to his ordinary consciousness. In this stage, the powerful and bright intuitive experience suddenly, as it were, pierces his ordinary consciousness, and the experience moves into a deeper level. Both St. Teresa and St. John of the Cross describe such moments of penetration, and thus their descriptions are fitting in understanding the meaning of the rider's sword in Revelation. In the following quotation, St. Teresa tells about an angel with a flaming face and a spear she saw in a vision, "He seemed to pierce my heart with it several times, so that the spear penetrated inside me. When he withdrew it, I felt like he tore my heart and my insides with it. An all-encompassing love for God ignited in me."[29]

St. John of the Cross describes an experience in piercing in the following way:

> It happens that the soul realizes how she has been attacked by a seraph with a raised arrow in his hand—an arrow aflame with the fire of love... And when he burns the soul by piercing it

with the arrow, the flame of the soul enkindles and flares... She feels herself burning powerfully and melting in love.[30]

The sword in St. John's vision can be interpreted also in a more everyday manner, when it would represent all that with which we overcome obstacles and progress on the inner journey—in this stage, through intuition. Interpreted in this way, the rider with its sword would be like the miraculous youth of ancient legends who gains victory over the beast with his sword. Soon it will be revealed that the rider seen by St. John wages war against evil. In later Christianity this youth fighting the beast is crystallized in St. George, who in the visual arts is depicted on a white horse with a sword or a spear in hand. The iconic illustrations of St. George are legendary. He may fly through the air with his horse and often his weapons are thin as hair. Perhaps the icon painters wished to emphasize the symbolical meaning of St. George as an image for a human being's inner victoriousness.

One more example, a personal experience known to me, will help to explain the meaning of the youth with the sword in a modern person's life:

> In a deeply inward state, I experience suddenly an extremely bright state of consciousness. It seems to reach into the core of my being. The following night I have a dream. I see a cross-section of a well; its water becomes crystal clear. A youth with a shining sword in his hand comes to it. He dips the sword deep into the well, and a brilliant, huge jewel rises out of the well.

The rider's robe, eyes, and the crowns

St. John explains further that the rider of the white horse "was clothed with a robe dipped in blood" (Rev. 19:13). We can think that this mythical image culminates the earlier stages of development in Revelation, because in the seventh chapter people appeared, dressed in white clothing purified in the Lamb's blood, and so much blood flowed out of the press after the winepress experience that it rose up to the horse's bridles (Rev. 7:14 and 14:20). The robe dipped in blood which St. John now sees illustrates a state of consciousness saturated in love.

The previous examples from St. Teresa and St. John of the Cross already spoke about love. St. John of the Cross used the expression, "the soul... feels herself... melting in love." In Indian literature, Sri Yukteswar describes the merging into the Om-sound as a spiritual baptism, and according to him, this baptism is also *bhakti yoga*, or yoga of love, because it means living love. He uses the following words which compare well with the blood-dipped robe of St. John's vision, "Man... becomes baptized or absorbed in the holy stream of the sound."[31]

In Revelation, St. John continues the description of the rider: "His eyes were like a flame of fire" (Rev. 19:12). As an experience, the fire probably is the light, the light of Om that may be seen in the transformed states of consciousness; the light can be seen also in other forms than circular.[32] Interpreted in a more ordinary way, the rider's fiery eyes are our intuitive vision, because with intuition we see matters in the light of wisdom, or with the fire of *Logos*. When St. John's consciousness during this chapter has expanded, his intuition has brightened, and then his eyes have begun to flame with the fire of Logos. Additionally, the flames of the rider's eyes can be compared to the flaming tongues the disciples saw, according to the Bible, in the descent of the Holy Spirit, and to the previous expressions from St. Teresa about "the angel with a flaming face" and "a shooting star."

"And on his head were many crowns" (Rev. 19:12). This means that the spiritually deeper way of experiencing, symbolized by the rider, is beginning to have the ruling position in St. John's consciousness.

The names of the rider

"He had a name written that no one knew except himself" (Rev. 19:12). The claim is paradoxical in the sense that St. John mentions the rider's names; as we know, they are "Faithful and True" and "The Word of God." Additionally, St. John writes, "And he has on his robe and on his thigh a name written: King of kings and Lord of lords" (Rev. 19:16). The vision, however, is paradoxical only on the level of conceptual thinking. In the mythical reality both the rider's names which are told us and the claim that only he himself knows the names express essential aspects of the rider. The name, "King of kings and Lord of lords," suggests that—as an illustration of an exalted spiritual state of consciousness—the rider is far above normal consciousness.

That no one else knows the rider's name but he himself is comparable to an earlier mythical image of St. John, the psalm, which could be learned only by those who sang it on Mount Zion (Rev. 14:3). The issue is again a special characteristic of sublime spiritual experiences: the knowledge of them cannot be given to others in words—only he who lives through them understands their nature.

The warring nature of the rider

St. John portrays the rider's warring nature with many details, "And in righteousness he judges and makes war" (Rev. 19:11). "And the armies in heaven, clothed in fine linen, white and clean, followed him on white horses" (Rev. 19:14). "And he himself will rule them with a rod of iron. He himself treads the winepress of the fierceness and wrath of Almighty God." (Rev. 19:15.) Furthermore, St. John describes the rider's sword by saying that "with it he should strike the nations" (Rev. 19:15). All this judging, warring, striking, and treading the winepress describes those inner trials which St. John, at this stage, experiences alongside happy intuitions and love. Because he is not even yet fully free from his attachments, the rider, or St. John's deeper state of consciousness, must still judge and wage war.

Judging means differentiating between right and wrong; St. John must be able to tell the difference between what will take him forward, and what will delay his transformation. He must also be able to let go of his attachments or wage war against the nations and rule them. In Christianity, the heavenly army means the angels, and therefore St. John wages war against the different forms of delusion with the help of elevated intuitions. I have, in the twelfth chapter, interpreted the iron rod as the law of karma, or God's eternal law, according to which human spiritual evolution happens; additionally, the rod may have meanings similar to that of the sword. And in God's winepress of wrath, the spiritual love or St. John's essence pours out again—St. John must endure even the winepress experience anew.

St. Teresa, also, speaks about the difficulties the soul must withstand when she has already progressed far on the spiritual path:

> My God, what inner and outer trials the soul must endure before she can enter the seventh dwelling! Truly, thinking of it, I fear sometimes, that should we know this beforehand, it would be

difficult for our weak nature to be able to suffer these trials and decidedly withstand them regardless of all the good they represent.

After this, St. Teresa counts out many trials, inner agonies and battles, some of which I have already used as examples.[33]

Liberation from attachments and delusion

The fate of the beast and the false prophet

"And I saw the beast, the kings of the earth, and their armies, gathered together to make war against him who sat on the horse and against his army. Then the beast was captured, and with him the false prophet who worked signs in his presence, by which he deceived those who received the mark of the beast and those who worshipped his image. These two were cast alive into the lake of fire burning with brimstone." (Rev. 19:19–20.)

St. John does not tell us how the beast and the false prophet are won, but probably we can assume that the rider with his armies gains victory in some way. To understand the victory, we must first, however, solve the meaning of the fiery lake that the beast and the false prophet are thrown into.

The sea mixed with fire, which according to my interpretation depicted human ego-consciousness and a delusory form of existence, appeared in the fifteenth chapter. I compared that sea loosely to the Eastern concept of the sea of delusion or the sea of *samsara*. Now I assume that the sea mixed with fire has become openly fiery and, at the same time, it has diminished from a sea to a lake. Thus, a mythical image, "lake of fire" has formed. I assume also that the changing of the sea mixed with fire to the fiery lake reflects St. John's inner transformation. When his consciousness has expanded from its previous state, he sees ego-consciousness as nothing but a small lake compared to the new spiritual dimensions which have opened for him. At the same time, he experiences ego-consciousness as all the more delusory. Under it, persons are the slaves of their attachments, of fiery desires and wishes which make them captives of delusion. St. John might perhaps wish to say, according to the Eastern tradition, that this is a tragic world, that the soul is burnt here in the fire of delusion.[34] But the fire of the fiery lake in his vision can also be "purifying fire," because in a state of ego-consciousness persons must, in different ways, free themselves from desires.

To be more exact, St. John uses the expression, "the lake of fire burning with brimstone" (Rev. 19:20). Later on he speaks of "the lake which burns with fire and brimstone" (Rev. 21:8). Earlier I associated brimstone, or sulphur-rich stone, with repression, and the same interpretation fits well here also.[35] When we try to free ourselves from our desires only by repressing them, such heat forms on the bottom of our consciousness that even the stones, the symbols of the deeper levels of the unconscious, burn in it. This kind of state is unfortunately common as long as human beings are prisoners of delusion.

According to the more common biblical interpretations, the fiery lake of Revelation is usually associated with hell. But the hell of the Bible need not be interpreted in one way only. It can be seen as a state of consciousness, wherein man burns in the fire of his own desires. Additionally, this state can be understood as prevailing just as well during the physical life as after death.[36]

Based on these ideas, we can now interpret the throwing of the beast and the false prophet into the fiery lake. I interpret this action both as a conceptual reckoning and as an emotional experience. On a conceptual level, the throwing means that the beast and the false prophet belong to the sea of delusion, a person's ego-bound existence. Expressed in modern language, the beast and the false prophet are principles which define a delusory way of living. As principles, they cannot be killed; they exist, that is, they live as long as humankind exists. Therefore, they need to be thrown alive into the fiery lake. Only the more specific forms they manifest in, like the kings and the captains, can be killed, and they will be killed, as we shall soon see.

Interpreted as an experience, throwing the beast and the false prophet into the fiery lake means that St. John is liberated. He identifies with the Om-sound and Om-light, and experiences ever more exalted spiritual intuitions. St. John then sees that a consciousness stamped by the beast and the false prophet are so delusory and insignificant that he is emotionally liberated from these forms of delusion. They belong only to the ego-consciousness, or to the fiery lake, whereas he himself already identifies with a higher form of consciousness. The Indian Sri Yukteswar describes liberation in the following way, "[When] man becomes again baptized or absorbed in the stream of Spiritual Light... man is saved for ever and ever from the bondage of Darkness."[37]

C.G. Jung, however, interpreted the fate of the beast and the false prophet differently. The false prophet was according to him St. John's "shadow", and when the beast and the false prophet are, in Revelation, thrown into the fiery lake, St. John is repressing his shadow. Jung explained that Revelation's solution to "the terrible conflict of existence" does not mean agreement between the opposites but their final separation: to be saved, one is to identify with God's light aspect only. At the same time, Jung stressed that the meaning of the apocalyptic visions is not to point out to the common man "how much shadow there is under his light form, but to open the seer's eyes for God's immensity."[38]

Jung's interpretation is natural on a psychological level, but I have made use of the openness of the myth and chosen to look at it differently in order to present, based on literature, the higher levels of a spiritual life; we cannot experience them if we simply repress the dark sides of our beings.

The fate of the beast's allies

"Then I saw an angel... and he cried with a loud voice, saying to all the birds that fly in the midst of heaven, 'Come and gather together for the supper of the great God, that you may eat the flesh of kings, the flesh of captains, the flesh of mighty men, the flesh of horses and those who sit on them, and the flesh of all people, free and slave, both small and great'" (Rev. 19:17–18).[39] After this St. John describes the fate of the beast and the false prophet and continues, "And the rest were killed with the sword which proceeded from the mouth of him who sat on the horse. And all the birds were filled with their flesh." (Rev. 19:21.)

I interpret the kings, the captains, the free and the slaves to be such parts of St. John's consciousness which still have attachments left; they are specific manifestations of the beast and the false prophet. When the rider kills them, St. John is freed from attachments. Because the weapon used for the killing is a sword coming out of the mouth of the rider, St. John's liberation is induced by his new high states of consciousness. As the ever more spacious and beautiful dimensions open up, the old attachments, now unnecessary, die off.

That the birds eat the flesh of the slain reveals something more about St. John's transformation. The flesh probably symbolizes either directly human physicality or a general attitude that is attached to the physical existence. The birds illustrate some state of consciousness free from ties to the earth, or physicality. When the birds eat the flesh of the slain, St. John begins to experience physicality in a new way—both his own material being and possibly the whole material reality. Because St. John uses the expression "the birds were filled with their flesh," he suggests that the energy previously tied to physicality transfers into a new way of experiencing, symbolized by the birds.

I believe that the new way of experiencing physicality opening up to St. John means a feeling of freedom from physicality, not repression of physicality. Should it mean repression, St. John would have to return to those earlier phases of Revelation which describe confronting the repressions. Particularly the Eastern sages have described the sense of freedom from physicality—sometimes quite dramatically. The following quotation is from Ramana Maharshi:

Just as a man who is drunk is not conscious whether his upper cloth is on his body or has slipped away from it, the *jnani* is hardly conscious of his body, and it makes no difference to him whether the body remains or has dropped off.[40]

The feeling of freedom from physicality—even when not as dramatic as in the previous quotation—is a natural development from the characteristic features of this stage. In this state a person reaches deep meditation, or in Christian terminology, contemplation. During this state, consciousness turns so much inward that the sensations of the body cease, and it expands beyond normal boundaries. Then, the individual's sense of identity transfers from the body to a wider and more spiritual state of consciousness symbolized by the birds. In Christianity, the soul is often said to "fly with the wings of contemplation."[41]

Besides contemplation, the sense of freedom from physicality can be produced also by other experiences differing from the usual ones, if they are strong enough. St. Teresa discusses many such experiences. In one description, she relates "the flight of the spirit" in the following words:

It is an experience where the spirit, indeed, seems to leave the body. On the one hand, it is clear that the person is not dead. On the other, at least at times, she cannot tell whether she is in the body or not. She feels with her whole being that she has visited a foreign land which is completely different from where we live. There the light reveals itself to her.[42]

When she describes these experiences and their effects, St. Teresa uses bird parables: as if "a mighty eagle would lift [the soul] and would carry her on its wings," and the soul "grows wings with which she flies easily."[43]

Some parapsychological experiences may have similar effects, although they don't always include the sense of spiritual heightening. For example, in the so called out-of-body experience persons actually feel their conscious minds transferred to the outside of their bodies, and this kind of experience beyond question changes their relationship to physicality. In fact, I know a case where, after a clear out-of-body experience, the person repeatedly dreamt of being transformed into a bird. This kind of mythical thinking is close to Egyptian mythology, where the bird represented the soul free of the physical body. In Eastern yoga, the ability to produce the experience under discussion is one of the higher practices.[44]

The birds of St. John's vision fit in well with the eagle symbolism in Revelation, because while the birds eat men's flesh, St. John's soul is being freed from material captivity and is soon ready to return to its original state like a magnificent eagle.[45]

20. IMPRISONMENT OF THE DRAGON

The spiritual engagement or sabikalpa samadhi

St. John does not apply bride symbolism in this vision, but I feel that the contents of the vision are comparable to the stage called by Christian mystics the spiritual engagement. Characteristic of this stage are the spiritual ecstasies which happen frequently. During the ecstasy, normal consciousness has been completely set aside and the body is dead, as it were, so that to an outsider the person appears to be in a deep trance. During the stage of spiritual engagement, bliss, however, is not permanent, because the wanderers on their inward journey still have a few attachments left. For this reason, they must endure tests during the engagement. But if they will pass the tests, they will be freed even from the last few attachments and will be ready for the spiritual marriage.

St. Teresa writes:
And now you will see what His Majesty does to bring about this engagement. As I understand it, it has to happen when He showers his charms onto the soul severing her free from her senses ...I believe this stage is such that the soul has never been so open to the divine matters, and never before has she had such great light and knowledge about His Majesty... The abilities of the soul have sunk so deep that we can say they are dead even as the senses are dead.

When He [the Bridegroom of the soul]... wants to pull this soul to himself, her breath is cut off so that although, at times, the other senses continue to function a little longer, she is unable to speak. Yet, at times, everything disappears suddenly, and the hands and the body grow so cold the body seems to have no soul, and sometimes, not even breath. This lasts only a short while—each time—because the minute this great rising subsides even a little, the body appears to return to itself somewhat, drawing in some breath only to die again to give a more complete life to the soul in this way. Nevertheless, such great ecstasy does not last long.[1]

In Eastern tradition, the ecstasies of spiritual engagement are called the states of samadhi. On Patanjali's eightfold yogapath, samadhi follows meditation, that is, samadhi is the eighth, or the highest stage of yoga.[2] But Eastern literature differentiates between several kinds of samadhis and their stages which are classified differently depending on the source. The lower samadhi is called *sabikalpa samadhi*, and I feel it compares well to the Christian mystic's spiritual engagement. In sabikalpa samadhi, the normal consciousness and the corporal feeling disappear during the bliss experience. Paramahansa Yogananda writes about this stage, "In the initial states of God-communion (*sabikalpa samadhi*) the devotee's consciousness merges in the Cosmic Spirit; his life force is withdrawn from the body, which appears 'dead,' or motionless and rigid." According to Yogananda, the name *sabikalpa* comes from the Sanskrit word *bikalpa*, meaning separation, and he explains that there is a slight sense of separation left in sabikalpa samadhi because of remaining attachments.[3]

Casting the dragon into the bottomless pit

"Then I saw an angel coming down from heaven, having the key to the bottomless pit and a great chain in his hand. He laid hold of the dragon, that serpent of old, who is the Devil and Satan, and bound him... and ...cast him into the bottomless pit, so that he should deceive the nations no more." (Rev. 20:1–3.) In the previous chapter, St. John won the victory over the lower forms of delusion, the false prophet and the beast. The dragon, the father of delusion, will be next. Casting the dragon into the bottomless pit, however, is only the first step in his final bout with the dragon.

In samadhi, all the change and movement brought on by delusions quiet down, and the binding of the dragon reflects this stillness of consciousness. The words, "that he should deceive the nations no more," speak of the same thing, as human beings, having fully quieted themselves, will no longer use their different abilities in delusory ways to seek satisfaction for their ego-desires.

Entering the state of ecstasy may happen so spontaneously, suddenly, and strongly that persons would not be able to stop it if they tried; St. Teresa has described such experiences.[4] But the withdrawal can also happen more gradually. Paramahansa Yogananda tells about withdrawing into sabikalpa samadhi, "But if you sit still and persist long enough, you will begin to feel that wonderful silence of God. When your mind is withdrawn, centered in Him, the world is forgotten and you find in that silence a happiness greater than any worldly pleasure."[5]

Sri Daya Mata, a disciple and successor of Paramahansa Yogananda, describes her withdrawal into trance-like samadhi:

With deep feeling and devotion, I was practicing what we call in India Japa Yoga, repeating the name of the Divine again and again... In this practice, the whole consciousness gradually becomes absorbed in one thought to the exclusion of everything else... My heart was bursting with a thrill indescribable. Suddenly, I lost all awareness of this world. My mind was completely withdrawn into another state of consciousness.[6]

I find the binding of the dragon to parallel these more gradual withdrawals into samadhi very well. In concentrating through silence or some helpful medium like a mantra or the sound of Om, a devotee binds, as it were, the movements caused by delusion. In the end, a complete silence comes, and with it, bliss.

The bottomless pit, wherein the dragon is cast, means in my interpretations St. John's unconscious, or that level of consciousness which he is not fully aware of. When the dragon is shut up into the bottomless pit, the entire delusory form of existence tied to duality and represented by the dragon is barred from the level of consciousness actually experienced by St. John. Then, he remains in a state of oneness and bliss.

Because the angel captures the dragon, it is St. John's intuition that guides him into samadhi. The seal with which the angel locks the bottomless pit can be interpreted as the light of the third eye, because the light experience can precede samadhi. As I explained earlier, this circular, seal-like light is seen in a deeply withdrawn state.

The power to judge

"And I saw thrones, and they sat on them, and judgment was committed to them" (Rev. 20:4). St. John does not tell us who "they" are, which gives more freedom to the interpreter. I make use of this freedom, and assume, that St. John describes the withdrawal into samadhi.

Particularly when the withdrawal into samadhi happens gradually, we can probably say that it involves 'judgment.' The meditator shuts out all outward experiencing and movements of consciousness and surrenders to ever deeper silence and spiritual awareness. Tools like a mantra or Om-sound function as the object of concentration while all else is left aside. For example, Daya Mata, quoted above, aptly described this kind of discriminating judgment: "In this practice, the whole consciousness gradually becomes absorbed in one thought to the exclusion of everything else."

The discriminating judgment practiced during the "engagement" stage of the spiritual life is more than making choices, striving and using will power. It means surrendering to experience spirituality, and this ability to surrender has gradually matured as intuition has been strengthened and attachments fallen away. This kind of power to judge is invisible, if you will. Maybe this 'invisibility' is the reason why St. John does not define in any way who "they" are to whom the judgment was committed. Perhaps in saying that "they" sat on the thrones, St. John is emphasizing the idea that a state has taken over in his consciousness where this withdrawal into a deep ecstasy happens with ever greater abandon.

Thousand years

"And [the angel] bound him [the dragon] for a thousand years" (Rev. 20:2). St. John's state of bliss, during which the delusion symbolized by the dragon is removed from his experience, lasts for the mythical thousand years. Because the first number of a thousand is one, a thousand years as a mythical numerical amount describes fittingly the experience in oneness characteristic of the samadhi state. For example, Paramahansa Yogananda in speaking of sabikalpa samadhi uses the expression "oneness with God."[7] In ordinary life, a thousand years, as a period of time, extends far beyond the individual's personal experience, and this reflects well the cessation of the sense of time during the experience in oneness innate to samadhi. Afterwards the person experiencing the samadhi feels, perhaps, that he has during the samadhi lived an eternity, or has been completely outside time.

The resurrection

"And I saw the souls of those who had been beheaded for their witness to Jesus and for the word of God, who had not worshipped the beast or his image, and had not received his mark on their foreheads or on their hands. And they lived and reigned with Christ for a thousand years. But the rest of the dead did not live again until the thousand years were finished. This is the first resurrection. Blessed and holy is he who has part in the first resurrection... they shall be priests of God and of Christ, and shall reign with him a thousand years." (Rev. 20:4–6.)

St. John uses the universal mythical images of death and resurrection in characterizing his deep transformation; the same images appeared in the eleventh chapter, where two witnesses died, were resurrected, and rose up into heaven. In St. John's new vision, the resurrected are those who "had been beheaded for their witness to Jesus and for the word of God" (Rev. 20:4). These beheaded ones symbolize well those parts of St. John's consciousness which earlier were ego-bound but whose bonds have now been broken. Among the resurrected are, however, also some who "had not worshipped the beast or his image, and had not received his mark on their foreheads or on their hands." These are those parts of St. John's consciousness through which he had earlier experienced oneness, but they, too, are refined in samadhi, or are resurrected.

Bliss in St. John's vision is pictured as a spiritual resurrection, which makes sense, because there is a vast difference between the normal delusory state of consciousness and samadhi. For example, Paramahansa Yogananda uses resurrection in this meaning of leaving delusion for bliss in the following prayer where he speaks about Jesus, "As thou didst attain the joy of resurrection, so may we know that same joy in the resurrection of our consciousness from the tomb of delusion into the freedom of God's presence."[8]

St. John emphasizes also the blissfulness of the resurrection with his words, "Blessed and holy is he who has part in the first resurrection" (Rev. 20:6). St. John refers to the same blissful and spiritually exalted state of consciousness in explaining that the resurrected "shall be the priests of God and Christ, and shall reign with him a thousand years" (Rev. 20:6).

Not all dead, however, will experience resurrection, because St. John says, "the rest of the dead did not live again" (Rev. 20:5). This is because during the spiritual engagement, or sabikalpa samadhi stage, part of a person's spiritual energy is still latent, as it were, held down by the remaining attachments.

The return of the dragon

"Till the thousand years were finished. But after these things he must be released for a little while" (Rev. 20:3). "Now when the thousand years have expired, Satan will be released from his prison" (Rev. 20:7). When the experience in oneness has passed in a thousand mythical years, the individual returns to his ordinary, delusory consciousness. This is symbolized in the release of the dragon or the delusion. Paramahansa Yogananda describes the ending of the sabikalpa samadhi state in following words, "When you return to ordinary consciousness, the delusions of the world will again somewhat affect you, unless you are highly evolved and free of all desires and attachments."[9]

St. John describes in his vision only one trance-like samadhi from the beginning till the end, although during the stage of the spiritual engagement a person experiences these bliss states many times and with different characteristics. Once again St. John concentrates the essential features of one long stage in a human life into the mythical images of the vision.

Liberation from the last attachments

The dragon deceives the nations

"[Satan] will go out to deceive the nations which are in the four corners of the earth, Gog and Magog, to gather them together to battle, whose number is as the sand of the sea. They went up on the breadth of the earth and surrounded the camp of the saints and the beloved city." (Rev. 20:8–9.)

In Indian literature, the lower level of samadhi is also called samadhi with seeds. The name comes from the fact that in this stage of spiritual evolution the human consciousness is thought of as containing seeds of desires, or karma. In right conditions these seeds can begin to sprout and grow, and man becomes a prisoner of his desires.[10]

In modern language, the karmic seeds are the most latent desires of the unconscious which can become active. When they awaken, persons begin to use their abilities in desirous, or delusory, ways, and I assume that this is what happens in Revelation when the dragon deceives the nations. The image used by St. John, "the sand of the sea," is truly a fitting expression for the karmic seeds activated from a latent state. Sand grains are like tiny seeds, and the sea symbolizes the unconscious or potential state wherefrom the desires arise. Because Babylon was finally cast into the sea, the hostile nations compared to the sand of the sea can be seen also as the unburnt remains of Babylon. Apparently, St. John feels that there are endless desires awakening in him, as he compares the number of the nations specifically to the sand of the sea.

In the Old Testament's Book of Ezekiel, Gog is the prince of Magog, and Ezekiel prophesies that in the end of days Gog will attack the nation of God, Israel, but he will be destroyed.[11] If the Book of Ezekiel is interpreted mythically, Israel is the Self, which in this vision by St. John is represented by "the camp of saints and the beloved city." Gog represents, both in Ezekiel's and St. John's visions, attachments, and the events of both visions can be seen as an inner test and battle similar to Armageddon. Opposite each other in the battle are, on the one hand, St. John's deeper level of consciousness, the Self, and on the other, the different desires. When St. John uses the expression, "they surround the camp of the saints," he probably feels his newly exposed attachments choking his sublime spiritual experiences.

In the Book of Ezekiel, Gog is a king, whereas in Revelation he is not mentioned as a king. Although the earlier hidden attachments are activated in St. John's consciousness, perhaps they no longer organize even into lower grade ego-feelings, which in Revelation are symbolized by the kings, or more accurately, by the kings of the *old* earth. In using the proper names Gog and Magog, which in the Bible have a troubled sound, St. John may, nevertheless, stress the meaning of Gog and Magog as the remains of the prostitute of Babylon, or one's personal sense of self bound to desires.

Swami Vivekananda explains that because of the last seeds of karma we experience the universe to be such as we see it outwardly.[12] In the last stage of spiritual evolution the seeds of karma are the human desires to experience reality as tied to time and place. Generally, we are not even aware of these desires, because we take our normal understanding of reality so much for granted. But such a sense of reality disappears in altered states of consciousness, because, during them, we feel ourselves to live beyond the reach of time and place. Because of the repeated states of samadhi we then grow aware of this desire and at the same time realize ourselves to be subjects to attachments: we are not, after all, ready to bear the sense of complete freedom, timelessness, and spacelessness, regardless of its blissfulness. But the last attachments could be also other kinds, such as a desire to experience bliss in which there is a trace of attachment left. That desire will prevent the feeling of bliss while it keeps one from fully giving in to it.

The fire comes down out of the heaven

"And fire came down from God out of heaven and devoured them" (Rev. 20:9). St. John describes the feeling created by his experience as the last attachments disappear, and this feeling is generally compared to the burning fire.

In the Eastern literature, the matter is expressed in such a way that even the last seeds of karma must be burnt before one can move into the highest, "seedless" form of samadhi. And the burning happens with the help of intuitive wisdom, meditation, and repeated samadhi-states.[13]

In the language of St. John of the Cross, the fire falling from heaven is infused purification. The fire of ever higher spiritual experiences illuminates the soul, and in the light of these experiences, the soul sees even the last fragments of "her own darkness and wretchedness." Then she will be purified in her introspection. "The soul is purified in receiving illumination in the fire of loving wisdom."[14]

We can find a more detailed comparison for the fire falling from heaven from St. Teresa's book *The Interior Castle*, where St. Teresa relates the events taking place just before the spiritual marriage:

> The more she [the soul] learns to know God's greatness... the more her desire for the Lord grows. Also, love increases in the

measure the soul discovers how much this great God and the Lord deserves to be loved. So this desire grows little by little over time, until it ends... in great torment... (Her intellect is in such a state that the soul is not the master of it, nor can the soul think anything but the cause of the suffering. When the soul is separated from Him who is her Good, why should she wish to live?)

When the soul now wonders in this state and inwardly remains in fire, it happens often that some slight absentminded thought or heard word... will deliver to her from some place—wherefrom and how, this is not known—a kind of a blow, or a fiery arrow strikes her. I don't mean that this is actually an arrow, but be it whatever, it is obvious that it could not come from our own nature. It leaves a deep scar... into the innermost being of the soul. Like a lightning bolt, it burns to dust everything that is worldly in our own nature.[15]

In St. Teresa's description the fiery arrow and the burning lightning bolt are much the same mythical images as the "fire falling from heaven" of Revelation, and St. Teresa's expression "burns to dust" compares well with the "devouring by fire" of Revelation.

Additionally, the following excerpts from St. Teresa help to explain the inner meaning of the fire falling from heaven. In these quotations, St. Teresa emphasizes the purifying and deadening effect of love's agony, and its infused nature:

It is right that the precious is expensive, particularly in purification of the soul... Nevertheless, the soul is quite happy to suffer it [the agony]... even though it is not a question of dying once and for all, but continually, because nothing less, indeed, is in question... How could anyone think that one could keep this from happening! It is as impossible as someone thrown into a fire would wish to stop the flames from being hot and burning her... This is painful, but its effect on the soul is strong... The soul... realizes that nothing worldly could help her in her agony, and she has, more than ever, let go of all that is created, because she now realizes that the Creator alone can comfort her and give her satisfaction.[16]

Interpreted in this way, the armies of Gog and Magog in Revelation are devoured by the "fire of loving wisdom." At the same time, even the last fragments of Babylon are burnt away. When the ability to experience inner bliss opens for a devotee, the attachments to the old sources of pleasure finally disappear completely—the attachments do not simply sink into the unconscious nor are they repressed there. In the Book of Ezekiel of the Old Testament, on the other hand, Gog and his armies are buried in the ground, that is, the Bible offers a deeper solution for the difficult problem of the death of the ego in Revelation than in the Old Testament.[17]

The fate of the dragon

"And the devil, who deceived them, was cast into the lake of fire and brimstone where the beast and the false prophet are. And they will be tormented day and night for ever and ever." (Rev. 20:10.) I interpret the casting of the dragon into the fire and brimstone lake in the same way as the casting of the false prophet and the beast into the same place in the previous chapter. The issue is conceptual reckoning. The dragon belongs in the sea of samsara, the world of duality and delusion. As long as there is the manifest world, there will be the dragon as well, because as a counter force, it upholds the manifest universe. Secondly, casting the dragon into the fiery lake reflects St. John's liberation: he must feel himself freed even from the father of delusion.

And why are the dragon, the beast, and the false prophet tormented night and day, for ever and ever? As abstract principles of delusion, the dragon, the beast, and the false prophet cannot feel pain and trouble. But material or mental forms of delusion exist throughout manifest reality. The entire manifest reality is characterized by change, and clearly and symbolically, change means trouble. Additionally, St. John's words can be seen as a projected expression characteristic of mythical language. The different principles of delusion cause trouble and suffering *in human lives*, because in the lake of delusion, we experience our existence through duality—birth and death, growth and destruction, union and separation—and thus we suffer.

St. John's spiritual outlook

When St. John has been liberated from even the last form of delusion, the dragon, he feels he sees reality in the right way. At the end of the chapter, he gathers together the basic principles of his new spiritual outlook.

The enthroned

"Then I saw a great white throne and him who sat on it, from whose face the earth and the heaven fled away. And there was found no place for them." (Rev. 20:11.) In this verse, St. John presents his new understanding about God, or expressed more philosophically, the most fundamental reality. It is now clearly transcendent.

A transcendent God cannot be grasped or defined by ordinary thinking, symbolized by the earth, and therefore the earth flees from the face of the enthroned. But the fleeing of the earth may also reflect an earlier interpretation I gave about similar situations: perhaps St. John's old everyday consciousness with its attachments, symbolized by the old earth, disappears once and for all.

Heaven, in my interpretations, has had two meanings. In the first place, it has symbolized the superconscious and those significant spiritual experiences and intuitions which occur at that level of consciousness. This kind of superconscious experiencing has in St. John's case changed radically during the course of the Book of Revelation. A new form of consciousness, samadhi, has opened up for him, and it is so unlike his earlier spiritual experiences that he does not wish to associate God with his old way of experiencing. Thus the old heaven must flee from the face of the enthroned. Additionally, the fleeing heaven probably emphasizes—similarly to the fleeing of the earth—St. John's inner change.

Secondly, heaven, in my interpretations, has symbolized the higher levels of spiritual reality. Now St. John defines divinity in a new way. In the beginning of Revelation, along with the enthroned in the heaven, there were other basic principles, specifically twenty-four elders and four creatures which, regardless of their abstractness, represent duality. According to an Indian view three of the four creatures belong to the domain of duality, as I explained in the fourth chapter: *anu* (atom or physicality), space, and time. St. John has exposed physicality, space, and time as manifest forms of delusion, and he has been freed from attachments to them during this vision and the preceding one. When the old heaven in this vision flees from the face of the enthroned, St. John severs the transcendent divinity completely from duality.

The judgment

"And I saw the dead, small and great, standing before God, and books were opened. And another book was opened, which is the book of life. And the dead were judged according to their works, by the things which were written in the books. The sea gave up the dead who were in it, Death and Hades delivered up the dead who were in them. And they were judged, each one according to his works. Then Death and Hades were cast into the lake of fire... And anyone not found written in the book of life was cast into the lake of fire." (Rev. 20:12–15.)

In these verses, St. John extends the law of karma to a metaphysical law of cause and effect involving *all* different levels of human existence. The law of karma is clearly expressed in the words, "The dead were judged according to their works." Man reaps what he sows. I will analyze St. John's descriptions in greater detail from the basis of Eastern teachings about reincarnation and the reality it serves to create, because interpreted in this way St. John's words agree with the overall interpretation I have presented.

According to Eastern theory, when the physical body dies, we move on to the astral level to which our spiritual characteristics direct us. In Eastern thinking, the astral levels belong to the domain of delusion: even there, we are prisoners of our desires. From the astral level, we eventually move either drawn by our desires back to physical existence, or if we have been able to free ourselves either partially or completely from our desires, to a higher astral level or into complete freedom. This transition is death on the astral level and birth into the new level. We move on in this way in the wheel of karma and the cycle of birth and death until we reach the final liberation.[18]

In Revelation, Death perhaps parallels physical death and Hades, the astral levels. I take St. John's words, "Death and Hades were cast into the lake of fire," as conceptual reckoning: the realm of physical death and Hades are all part of delusion, the fiery lake. Only complete liberation is freedom from delusion, and thus, from Death and Hades.

St. John's words, "Death...delivered up the dead who were in them. And they were judged, each according to his works," can be understood to mean that we dying physically are guided to a new level according to our desires and liberation. When St. John applies the same words to Hades, he tells us that the same thing happens when we, in the wheel of karma, move away from an astral level. For example, in what form and into which circumstances we reincarnate into physical reality depends on what we have been like on the astral level. St. John says also, "The sea gave up the dead who were in it." This probably means that our unconscious affects our fate in the wheel of karma.

St. John differentiates between two kinds of dead in his vision: those who have been written into the book of life and those who have not. Those written into the book of life are the fully liberated ones. They will not reincarnate any more. The latter are individuals who are not completely free from attachments. They will be cast into the fiery lake, or according to Eastern theory, they are to move into some new level of deluded existence according to their own karma. And in that wheel of karma they will then be burned, on the one hand, by their own desires, and on the other, by the purifying fire, until they become fully liberated from their desires.

Besides the book of life, other books appear in St. John's vision, "And I saw the dead...and books were opened" (Rev. 10:12). I assume that these books belong to people's personal lives. The book is like each one's individual consciousness, or more accurately, the traces of memories left in one's consciousness from different lives. The nature of this book determines each person's place in the wheel of karma. There are many of these books, because there are many people. There is only one book of life, however, in St. John's vision, and the reason may be that the final liberation, which the book of life speaks of, is the same for everyone, regardless of the name used for liberation.

The second death

St. John uses the expression "the second death" twice in this vision. "Blessed and holy is he who has part in the first resurrection. Over such, the second death has no power, but they shall be priests of God and of Christ, and shall reign with him a thousand years." (Rev. 20:6.) "This [the lake of fire] is the second death" (Rev. 20:14). St. John mentions the second death in the next chapter, "all liars shall have their part in the lake which burns with fire and brimstone, which is the second death" (Rev. 21:8). The second death appears also in the early chapters of Revelation, where St. John writes, "He who overcomes shall not be hurt by the second death" (Rev. 2:11).

In these verses, St. John says specifically that the second death is the lake of fire. In my interpretation the lake of fire means the domain of delusion, and one is liberated from delusion in experiencing the spiritual resurrection. In other words, blessed is anyone who "has part in the first resurrection," because "over such the second death has no power." Because the lake of fire, or the sea of delusion, at this stage, includes everything else except the state of final liberation, only he who has found the absolute liberation, is free from the second death. Or, in the words of St. John, "He who overcomes shall not be hurt by the second death." I understand that St. John emphasizes with the term "second death" that human beings must continue to die, or move to new levels of delusion, time after time, until they experience resurrection and are fully liberated.

In using the name "death" for the lake of fire, the domain of delusion, St. John sharpens again the judgment he passes on a delusory life. The more exalted the spiritual states of consciousness he has lived through, the more delusory, stuporous, and downright dead has ordinary life begun to appear to him. Jesus' famous words, "Let the dead bury the dead," similarly may refer to the death-like existence of the living men. St. John of the Cross expressed the matter with a verse, "By killing you have changed death to life," and he explains its meaning in the following way, "You have killed everything that kept me dead and without the life of God, wherein I now find myself to live."[19] Likewise, in the beginning of Revelation, the likeness unto death of the ordinary attitude in life, is presented succinctly, "you are alive, but you are dead" (Rev. 3:1).

21. THE WEDDING OF THE LAMB AND THE NEW JERUSALEM

The spiritual marriage or nirbikalpa samadhi

The last two chapters of Revelation describe the highest state of consciousness possible for human beings. This state will become manifest when all attachments have disappeared. Then individuals become perfect saints and they experience continuous bliss. They can, at times, withdraw their consciousness from the outer world into a trance-like inner state of bliss, but they can also experience bliss while being conscious about the outer world and functioning in it. In Christian language, this state is the spiritual marriage between the soul and God; the word "marriage" signifies the lasting nature of the union with God. According to Eastern terminology, this is the highest form of samadhi called *nirbikalpa samadhi*. The word "nirbikalpa" means that all separation has ended. Sometimes nirbikalpa samadhi, however, is used to mean samadhi experienced during trance, and *sahaja nirbikalpa samadhi* is used for samadhi wherein the saint is, at the same time, aware of the outer world.[1] In the following, I will generally use the term "nirbikalpa samadhi" to describe the highest samadhi.

Only a few persons have entered a spiritual marriage or manifested nirbikalpa samadhi in themselves. St. Teresa of Avila and St. John of the Cross, who lived during the 16th century and whom I have used as my examples, have described their spiritual marriages based on their personal experiences. In our own times, several women and men, particularly of Indian origin, are known to have lived in that state. These include Ramana Maharshi (1879–1950), Paramahansa Yogananda (1893–1952), and Anandamayi Ma (1896–1982).

Besides saints, ordinary human beings, as well, have momentarily lived in a state where an exceptional bliss—or at least a deep sense of spiritual meaning—merges with more normal awareness so that functioning in the outer world is possible during that state. I will first present examples from such more common experiences, because they, too, are likely to help us to understand the possibilities of spiritual marriage. To prepare the ground, I have chosen examples with different levels of intensity and varying lengths of duration.

The author Mika Waltari recounts:

I have, perhaps, several times had a mystical experience. And the strongest of them happened in Rome... I had, at that time, lived through a specific period of religious problems... I think I had meditated a lot. In any case, during those times, I was very happy... As I stepped out into the bright sunshine, a happy, odd, charmed feeling would rise in me....

It could be called a kind of an expansion of awareness where in an unexplained, incomprehensible moment, one would realize something, something about God's being... It embraced a very strong sense of brightness and light, which was not just because of the sparkling sunshine in the autumn of Rome. All problems were resolved in such a way that in general I had no problems, but rather understood something of life: how everything that happened resulted from something incomprehensible, an intellect so supernatural—intellect, perhaps, is a wrong word—something invincible... unreachable... the only thing that can be called perfect... But it is impossible for me to explain this, no matter how I try.[2]

Another example is a dream and an experience known to me:

I had dreamt of the birth of a magical child. In the dream, the child led me to a high mountain. When I reached the peak of the mountain, I was overcome by perfect bliss. I had never before lived through anything like it—I had not even suspected such a state to be possible for anyone.

I woke up, but the bliss did not go away. It seemed I had become an immense cloud of bliss. What I was normally, my ordinary consciousness, was present, but it was only a slightest strand in my new being. My new being, bliss, regarded my small "I" with kind understanding; this is how I might try to express the matter. It 'knew' that my little "I" had her own responsibilities she needed to fulfill, and so I accomplished my usual duties that day. Toward the evening, the state grew weaker, but its recession did not bring disappointment; rather it left a peaceful conviction in my mind: this is how I ought to live always.

The next description is an experience by an American woman, an experience which overtook her soon after she had met Paramahansa Yogananda who had come to the United States. (She wrote about her experience in the third person, describing it as though it happened to a man.)

He was conscious of a great peace within himself. He felt that in some deep fundamental way, he had become a different person... The floodgates of joy broke in his soul; he was inundated with waves of indescribable ecstasy. Words that had been merely words to him before—bliss, immortality, eternity, truth, divine love—became, in the twinkling of an eye, the core of his being... the only possible reality... The whole universe was to him bathed in a sea of love; he said to himself many times, "Now at last I know what *love* is!"... He felt his mind expand ... endlessly widening, growing, touching everything in the universe....

During these weeks, he went about his daily duties as usual, but with a hitherto unknown efficiency and speed... his work seemed like child's play, happy and carefree... his inward joy covered every action and circumstance with a cosmic significance... This state of illumination was present with the man for about two months and then gradually wore away.[3]

Those who have lived in a lasting state of bliss have generally been unwilling to describe it. For example, Ramana Maharshi answered to inquirers, "It is impossible to describe *samadhi* since it transcends the mind."[4] Yet, he did give some guidelines:

People are afraid that when the ego or the mind is killed, the result may be a mere blank and not happiness. What really happens is that the thinker, the object of thought and thinking all merge in the one Source which is Consciousness and Bliss itself, and thus that state is neither inert nor blank... You can have, or rather you will yourself be, the highest imaginable kind of happiness. All other kinds of happiness which you have spoken of as "pleasure," "joy," "happiness," "bliss," are only reflections of the *Ananda* which, in your true nature, you are.

In this state you remain calm and composed during activity. You realize that you are moved by the deeper Real Self within and are unaffected by what you do or say or think... You realize that there is nothing that belongs to you as ego and that everything is being done by something with which you are in conscious union.[5]

Within Christianity, we can find an example of the spiritual marriage from St. Teresa. During the latter part of her life the state was permanent. The state would recede "at most, for one day or a little longer," as she writes.[6] According to St. Teresa, the spiritual marriage began from an experience she describes in the following way:

> The Lord revealed himself to the person we have been talking about, as she was about to partake in a Holy Communion. He came in the form of a great brightness and beauty and majesty, even as He was following the resurrection, and the Lord told her that now was the time for her to consider as her own what was His, and that He would look after her. Additionally, He said things that are easier to comprehend than express in words.[7]

In another place, St. Teresa describes the same event and says the Lord, in a vision, spoke the words, "My honor is yours and yours mine."[8]

The basic principles of the spiritual marriage are conveyed in St. Teresa's narrative—the complete death of the ego, bliss, the permanency of the bliss and retention of the ability to function:

> This butterfly is now dead: it died full of joy for having found peace, and Christ lives in her... Truly, it seems to the soul that she no longer exists... In this temple of God, in his dwelling, only He and the soul rejoice together in complete silence... In this Lord's mercy, that we now speak of, there is no more separation, because the soul stays always with God in the mentioned center... It must seem to you, based on this, that the soul must no longer exist in herself, but rather is in such a deep withdrawal that she cannot direct her attention to anything. On the contrary, in everything that has to do with serving God, she is much more alert than before.[9]

The spiritual marriage in Revelation

Renewal

"And I saw a new heaven and a new earth, for the first heaven and the first earth had passed away. Also there was no more sea" (Rev. 21:1). In these verses, St. John continues his description of the inner renewal that he spoke of in the previous chapter in saying that the earth and the heaven fled away from the face of the enthroned (Rev. 20:11). The first heaven symbolizes St. John's former way of experiencing high spirituality, which has proved insufficient for him. Now it is replaced by nirbikalpa samadhi, wherein he feels himself to fully experience ultimate reality as bliss. This is the new heaven. The first earth refers to St. John's old awareness and sense of physicality, which included attachment to desires, and the new earth symbolizes awareness and physicality free of attachments. Expressed in another way, the new earth refers to the unselfish actions of the saints and that desireless dualistic consciousness which they use in performing actions.[10] The words, "there was no more sea," indicate that there is no more unconscious, or potential. Even the last unconscious seeds of karma have been burnt away, and St. John has now made actual what was potential. The secret of the sea of glass that was in front of the throne in the fourth chapter has been completely exposed while St. John has experienced lasting bliss.

A few verses later, the Book of Revelation underscores the totality of the renewal. "Then he who sat on the throne said, 'Behold, I make all things new'" (Rev. 21:5).

Returning home and the bride symbolism

"Then I, John, saw the holy city, new Jerusalem, coming down out of heaven from God, prepared as a bride adorned for her husband. And I heard a loud voice from heaven saying, 'Behold, the tabernacle of God is with men!'" (Rev. 21:2–3.) The tabernacle of God can also be translated as a dwelling of God. A little later, the same thoughts are repeated. The angel says to St. John, "Come, I will show you the bride, the Lamb's wife... and [he] showed me the great city, the holy Jerusalem, descending out of heaven from God" (Rev. 21:9–10).

The holy city, Jerusalem, is the goal of St. John's inner journey and his spiritual home, which he has been striving toward during his exile. When Jerusalem appears in the visions, St. John has reached his goal, the spiritual perfection symbolized by the holy city. A city that is holy, like many other symbols in Revelation, is a universal mythical image; for example, in India, the holy city is Benares, and within Islamic tradition, it is Mecca. The pilgrimages directed to these geographical holy cities—Jerusalem, Benares, and Mecca—are like mythical images lived out in external reality, inspiring the traveler to engage in a journey into the inner holy city as well. The expression *"new* Jerusalem" in Revelation discloses that the holy city in St. John's vision is the inner Jerusalem.

According to the bride symbolism, the new Jerusalem is the bride and the wife of the Lamb; Jerusalem is that inner level of St. John's consciousness with which he experiences ultimate reality, bliss, or God. As a level of human consciousness, the holy city corresponds, in Revelation, to the earlier vessel-like, and therefore, feminine images like the white robes (Rev. 6:11), the temple (Rev. 7:15), and the woman giving birth to the heavenly child. God, or the Lamb, within the symbolism of Revelation, is then the content of this feminine city, or the Bridegroom of the bride. In his vision, these relationships—consciousness and the content of the consciousness—are expressed by naming the holy city as God's dwelling, and God as the content of that dwelling.

When the holy city descends from heaven, the descent reflects both the feeling of infused grace and the ending of alienation. The holiness which to St. John during the early part of his journey seemed to be outside him becomes his own experience in a deeply spiritual way.

The wedding?

It would be natural to expect St. John's transformation in Revelation to culminate in a mythical wedding, because the wedding of the Lamb had been foretold earlier (Rev. 19:7). But the wedding is not described in Revelation. The reason may be that St. John only intuits that there are higher possibilities available for a human being although he does not yet experience them himself. In my interpretation, I assume, however, that the wedding is celebrated, and I believe this happens between the two descents from heaven. When St. John sees the holy city descending from heaven twice, in verses two and ten, this may not be simply rhythmic repetition. Perhaps St. John is experiencing such an intensified inner change that it indicates he is celebrating the mythical wedding. Be that as it may, between the verses that describe the two descents from heaven it is possible to find out some details about the state of the spiritual marriage. These verses anticipate the union between humankind and God, our final liberation and return to our spiritual home, and I interpret them from these perspectives. The marriage itself would follow the mention of the latter descent.

"And he [God] will dwell with them, and they shall be his people, and God himself will be with them and be their God" (Rev. 21:3). It is not difficult to read into this verse the union between God and man. The words parallel St. Teresa's earlier quoted description of her own wedding, wherein the Lord told St. Teresa that now was the time for her to consider as her own what was His, and He would look after her. The same union between God and the human soul is echoed in the words coming forth from the throne, where the soul is like the wayward son returning home, "He who overcomes shall inherit all things, and I will be his God and he shall be my son" (Rev. 21:7).

"And God will wipe away every tear from their eyes; there shall be no more sorrow, nor crying; and there shall be no more pain, for the former things have passed away" (Rev. 21:4). The saints who have described their own experience of spiritual marriage, or nirbikalpa samadhi, have described lasting joy which means an end to sorrow and pain. For example, St. Teresa says about the souls who have entered the spiritual marriage, "No dryness nor inner trials trouble them any longer." In fact, she writes, "When such souls are persecuted, they feel great inner joy and much deeper peace than in the previously mentioned states, nor do they feel any need for retaliation toward those who harm them or wish to do so."[11]

St. John of the Cross speaks of the joy of "the perfect life" paraphrasing the psalms, "You changed my sorrow to joy, you undressed my cloak of mourning and wrapped me in joy." And Ramana Maharshi's account of the sahaja nirbikalpa samadhi includes the words, "You have no worries, anxieties or cares."[12]

In nirbikalpa samadhi, a person can avoid the sensation of pain by withdrawing to a deeper level into a trance, or he can feel pain, but it will mean nothing to him. Ramana Maharshi wrote about this in the following way, "The unrealized man identifies himself with the body that feels it [pleasure or pain], whereas the Self-realized man knows that all this is Self, all this is Brahman. If there is pain let it be; it is also part of the Self and the Self is perfect."[13]

The verse of Revelation I quoted above includes also the sentence, "There shall be no more death" (Rev. 21:4). This sentence may speak of human liberation from the cycle of birth and death, which I discussed in the previous chapter. But the sentence may also refer to a new attitude toward physical death, of which I gave an example from Ramana Maharshi in the nineteenth chapter. I will add here one more example, this one from St. Teresa who talks about the effects of a spiritual marriage on souls, "They have no more fear of death than they would of a gentle rapture."[14]

St. John hears also the words, "It is done" (Rev. 21:6). He heard the same words in the sixteenth chapter after the battle of Armageddon, but his liberation was not complete at that time. Now, however, the words refer to the final victory, homecoming, and union with God, and perhaps they also refer to the mythical wedding.

The words spoken by the enthroned, "I am the Alpha and the Omega, the Beginning and the End. I will give of the fountain of the water of life freely to him who thirsts" (Rev. 21:6), refer to the spiritual marriage as a homecoming and its blissfulness. The Alpha and the Omega are the first and the last letters of the Greek alphabet—therefore the saying A and O, the beginning and the end. Those who have come so far have reached the end, which is also the beginning. They have found their way back to their spiritual home, God-union, wherefrom they fell in the beginning of time.

The verse presents also the thought that the thirsty will receive the water of life to drink. A more common expression in Christianity is, perhaps, "living water," which actually means spring water or groundwater from a well. Figuratively, living water, as well as the water of life in this verse, means God's blessing, peace, grace, and so on. For example, St. Teresa explains that drinking living water means "perfect contemplation," and it is the goal of the soul's inner journey. She describes the joy of the spiritual marriage paraphrasing the psalm, "Here the wounded deer will receive water in an overflowing measure."[15] Expressed more philosophically, the water of life is a spiritual joy and bliss that a saint experiences in the present.

The verse emphasizes that the water of life is given freely. Within the ethics of love that St. John has permanently entered, we need not 'buy' or earn what we want through good works. It is given to us freely, as a gift, when we open ourselves to love.

The holy city

In this vision, St. John describes the new Jerusalem, and his description tells us more about the spiritual marriage, the nirbikalpa samadhi state.

The city of precious stones

"And [the angel] showed me the great city, the holy Jerusalem... having the glory of God. And her light was like a most precious stone, like a jasper stone, clear as crystal" (Rev. 21:10–11). The holy city, Jerusalem, is St. John's purified consciousness, and the content of the city, which in the verse has been expressed with the words "the glory of God," is that high spirituality, or God, which St. John lives after he has entered the spiritual marriage.

The Christian mystic, Meister Eckhart, says plainly that the holy city of Revelation is every spiritual soul who has returned to her original purity. Other mystics offer many parallels in which the purified soul is a jewel, a diamond castle, or a beautiful city. St. John of the Cross speaks of "the jewel of the soul" when he discusses the highest spiritual states of consciousness, and St. Teresa explains that "the soul can be thought of as a castle made of a single diamond or a brightest crystal." St. Teresa also calls it "this sparkling and beautiful castle, this pearl of the Orient," and the name of her well-known book *The Interior Castle* refers to the same diamond castle metaphor. According to St. Teresa, God lives in the innermost rooms of this castle.[16]

The English Mother Julian of Norwich (1342–1416) speaks of the human soul as a city, and she explains that God waits for that city to return to "her native beauty." City symbolism appears, for example, in her vision:

Then the Lord opened my spiritual vision and showed me my soul which was in the center of my heart. I saw my soul to be as big as an infinite world or a blissful kingdom. Its condition showed it to be an honorable city. In the center of this city sits our Lord Jesus... Once Jesus has taken his place in the soul, he will never leave... because in us he has his dearest home and everlasting dwelling.[17]

In Eastern symbolism, as in the *Bhagavadgita*, the human physical body is the city with nine gates, its openings being the gates of the city. But according to Eastern understanding, our physical body is not our only body; different states of consciousness are also 'bodies' which are called, among other names, the astral body and the spiritual body. With the symbolism of Revelation in mind, the interesting thing is that the deepest level of consciousness is often called the diamond body. The name appears, for example, in the Old Chinese text *Hui Ming Ching*.[18] Additionally, this level of consciousness has other names such as "the nephrite-city" and "the dwelling of the heavenly heart" which correspond well to the holy city of Revelation. The following descriptions come from the Chinese book *Tai I Ching Hua Tsung Chih*, *The Secret of the Golden Flower*, "The God of utter void and life lives in the purple hall of the nephrite-city... The heavenly heart resembles a dwelling; the light, the master of the house."[19]

A good comparison for the jewel city of Revelation can be found in the Tibetan mandalas, their center being presented symbolically as a palace. It is the pure and sacred palace, the crystal palace of clear Awareness, and it symbolizes a human being's highest level of consciousness, the state of clear Awareness.[20]

The clarity of the holy city is emphasized also in St. John's vision when he says the city is made of crystal clear jasper. Today, jasper is the name for a pink semiprecious stone, but here it probably refers to a transparent stone, since St. John says it is crystal clear. The transparency of the city is further stressed when it and its street are compared to clear glass: "And the city was... like clear glass" (Rev. 21:18), "And the street of the city was... like transparent glass" (Rev. 21:21). The clarity of the holy city is understandable because during his inner journey St. John has freed himself gradually from the tarnished layers covering up his pure soul. In this way, he has come to the deepest level of consciousness that expresses itself as a stone. At the same time, his consciousness has become clear, pure, and transparent. Previously the prostitute of Babylon was adorned with jewels, but now the human consciousness itself, or the holy city, is of clear precious stone, because St. John is completely liberated from his ego.

The clarity of the holy city St. John speaks of is undoubtedly an actual, experienced state of consciousness. In fact, even a beginning meditator can feel, at times, the normal restlessness of the mind cease, the cloudiness dissolve, and the consciousness left crystal clear.

When the holy city, the human consciousness, is crystal clear, the content of the city—or the spiritual value, divinity, and God's glory that a person enjoys as the content of his consciousness—can shine through unobstructed. St. John thus has a reason to say that the light of the city is "like a most precious stone" (Rev. 21:11).

The crystalline clarity and transparency of the purified soul, which allow God to shine through it, are common metaphors in religious literature. St. John of the Cross, in describing the highest states of consciousness, explains, "In this state the soul is like a pure clear crystal struck by light."[21] And Mother Teresa of Calcutta says, "Our souls should be like a clear glass through which God can be seen."[22]

There are numerous similar comparisons within the Eastern culture. In Patanjali's yoga sutras the purified consciousness of the yogi is compared to a crystal, and similarly the Indian Paramahansa Yogananda prays, "Make me transparent with purity, that I manifest Thy healing light within me."[23]

When St. John in Revelation uses the metaphor "crystal clear," the crystal may also allude to concentration and intensification, or crystallization. In this meaning, St. John could be speaking of the inner change that has happened in him regarding his energy level—which I have discussed in earlier chapters. For a person to experience bliss, life energy must concentrate from its dispersed state so that the energy flowing in the sushumna nadi is strengthened. For this reason, the Chinese text, *The Secret of the Golden Flower*, speaks about the crystallization of the life energy, or "light," that happens during yoga practice. The book says, for example, "The shining of the light crystallizes gradually."[24]

"And the city was pure gold" (Rev. 21:18). "And the street of the city was pure gold" (Rev. 21:21). Gold has appeared earlier as the wealth of the prostitute of Babylon, but I applied to her the words of

St. John of the Cross, "The gold of their spirit has not been purified."[25] St. John the Divine emphasizes in the present verses that now the gold is pure. St. John's consciousness has been purified from all attachments, and so it has become like pure gold. (I will return to the street symbol in the next chapter.)

In the Christian visual arts, the head of a saint is often encircled with a golden halo, and this halo is the golden radiance of the pure soul, or, as it were, of the inner holy city. It is also the golden aura said to be seen by spiritually sensitive people.[26]

In the West, during the times following Revelation, gold was a central symbol for alchemists, and we can probably say that the alchemist's dream of turning metal into gold has come to pass in the holy city. (The alchemists themselves can be so interpreted as to suggest that for some of them, refining metals meant also refining the human consciousness.[27]) In Eastern literature, gold is a central symbol in the earlier mentioned Chinese work, *The Secret of the Golden Flower*. This text uses numerous alchemistic symbolism, and the book makes the connection between this symbolism and refining of human consciousness explicitly clear. Like the diamond body, the golden flower symbolizes a human being's deepest level of consciousness, and this golden flower is "opened" with the help of the yoga exercises. A yellow castle appears also as a symbol for the spiritual body in the same book. The yellowness of the castle means, in fact, the yellowness of gold.[28]

Similar images—jewels, gold, wondrous castles, beautiful cities, diamond bodies, and golden flowers—appear also in dreams. We need only to pay some attention to our own dreams to notice a regular pattern. During a happy phase in life we dream of lovely rooms, castles, palaces, and cities. The dreams may also include diamonds and shimmering gold. All these rooms, castles, and cities are the dreamer's own inner dwellings, or we ourselves. On the other hand, during difficult times, the events in our dreams often happen in gloomy, dismal places. As a dream symbol, the nature of the human body changes also. A diamond body, which corresponds to the jewel city of Revelation, can be seen in the dream connected to a bliss experience. Such a symbol appears in the following dream that preceded the bliss experience described in the eleventh chapter; the wedding feast, part of the dream,

also belongs to the symbolism of Revelation. That the dream was dreamt by a woman is reflected in the dream images:
> I see a calm and grand woman standing. Another, smaller female figure separates from her belly. This woman, radiating wondrous light, comes dancing toward me. When she is in front of me, I see that she is made entirely of diamonds. I look into her eyes; they too shine as jewels. Next I sit down at a feast. I am at a wedding, and this is the wedding feast. A man sits by my side. He is my bridegroom, but he is no one I know in reality. I don't even see him; I only feel a wonderful happiness spreading from him, and I wake up overwhelmed by unexplainable bliss.

The form and the measurements of the city

"And he who talked with me had a gold reed to measure the city, its gates, and its wall. And the city is laid out as a square, and its length is as great as its breath. And he measured the city with the reed: twelve thousand furlongs. Its length, breath, and height are equal. Then he measured its wall: one hundred and forty-four cubits, according to the measure of a man, that is, of an angel." (Rev. 21:15–17.) Thus, St. John's holy city is a cube with a square floor plan.

In the biblical tradition, the holy city can be compared to the holy of the holies in the Old Testament Salomon temple, since that holy of the holies had a square floor plan. As a geometric shape, the holy city can be interpreted to be a mandala. Although the mandalas used in Eastern rituals and meditations are generally circular, within the circle, there is often a concentric square. This pattern appears in particular in the Tibetan mandalas with a sacred palace pictured at their centers. Because the palace is drawn as a square, the holy city of Revelation and the palace of the Tibetan mandalas parallel each other also as figures.[29]

The circle and the square as general mythical images can be interpreted from the basis of the theme of alienation and return that I have used as a central guideline in my interpretations. Then, the circle describes original wholeness, or a lack of differentiation, which in myths is symbolized, for example, as the original egg. The division of the circle into segments—the mandalas are often divided into segments—

illustrates the differentiation of the original state; here the mythical original egg is broken. Also, the paradise of Eden in the beginning of the Bible is still a kind of a mythical original state, although it does already have differentiation in it. The paradise of Eden is, indeed, sometimes presented as circular in the Christian visual arts, although the Bible does not mention its roundness.[30] In the Bible, differentiation begins clearly when Adam and Eve are exiled from the paradise. All biblical references to human efforts to realize themselves and their relationship with God belong to this stage of differentiation. When the traveler, finally, on the path of the tree of life returns to union with God, the goal is expressed as a square, because a square fittingly illustrates the new wholeness gained through differentiation.

The transition from a circle to a square can be found also in Revelation when the heaven in the fourth chapter is seen as a circular but already differentiated picture of the original state—as I have previously suggested. The square holy city appearing at the end of Revelation would be the new wholeness of perfection one has gained while travelling through differentiation back into union with God. C.G. Jung applied this kind of interpretation of the circle and the square to the symbolism of the medieval alchemists. He explained that the problem of squaring the circle the alchemists were concerned with reflected psychic efforts to find the way from an undifferentiated original state through differentiation to a new, higher wholeness.[31]

In the earlier mentioned Tibetan Buddhist mandalas, the circle outside the palace has, however, a different meaning. Usually it is multi-layered, and its different layers symbolize the steps of spiritual development aspirants must accomplish before they can enter the palace of clear Awareness. Nevertheless, it has similarity with Revelation in it that these steps include some that are described also in Revelation. Circles symbolize, for example, purification by fire and spiritual rebirth.[32]

In St. John's vision, the measurer of the city is an angel, and when St. John dictates the measurements of the wall, he uses the expression "the measure of an angel." This probably tells us that the measurements of the holy city—twelve thousand furlongs by height, length, and breath—are to be understood symbolically, or with the sense of an angel, if you will. In a realistic way of measuring, the height of the city would probably not be given, particularly not, if it were more than one thousand miles as it is in the case of the holy city.[33]

The central measurement of the holy city, twelve, as a mythical number, illustrates the perfection St. John has reached once his exile is over. When twelve appears in thousands, it describes, as a large number, the long duration of the change, and the great value of what is gained. The same number symbolism based on the number twelve occurs again in the case of the wall, as its measurement is one hundred and forty-four cubits; the symbolism of the number twelve is emphasized when it is raised to the second power.

The foundation

"Now the wall of the city had twelve foundations, and on them were the names of the twelve apostles of the Lamb" (Rev. 21:4). "And the construction of its wall was of jasper... and the foundations of the wall of the city were adorned with all kinds of precious stones; the first foundation was jasper, the second sapphire, the third chalcedony, the fourth emerald, the fifth sardonyx, the sixth sardius, the seventh chrysolite, the eighth beryl, the ninth topaz, the tenth chrysoprase, the eleventh jacinth, and the twelfth amethyst" (Rev. 21:18–20).

I interpret the foundations of the holy city to be the foundations of human spiritual life. The Bible offers a parallel, for example, in Jesus' words, "Whoever comes to me, and hears my sayings and does them, I will show you whom he is like: He is like a man building a house, who dug deep and laid the foundation on the rock." That the names of the apostles are associated with the foundation is probably a fitting mythical image of Christian tradition, as one of the apostles was, in fact, a foundation for Jesus' congregation, "And I also say to you that you are Peter, and on this rock I will build my church."[34] In Revelation, the names of the apostles written into the foundation of the holy city are mythical images and refer to internalizing Jesus' teachings.

In Eastern culture, the spiritual path is often presented as specific steps as in Patanjali's yoga sutras which I have used as a comparison to Revelation. In yoga, the steps preceding samadhi are the foundation on which samadhi is built. Buddhism, on the other hand, speaks of the eightfold path, whose seven first steps mean mainly ethical, right kinds of living, and the eighth, concentration. When all these steps have been experienced and learned, liberation, or nirvana, will follow.[35]

In Eastern symbolism, a foundation and its construction seem to be popular metaphors. In the Chinese work *The Secret of the Golden Flower*, creating the foundation for enlightenment is explained in the following way:

> The second paragraph [of the text under study] means construction of the foundation... The shining of the light crystallizes gradually. Therefore, a great terrace forms, and on it, in a while, Buddha appears. When this golden being appears, who else could he be than Buddha, for Buddha is the golden saint of the great enlightenment.[36]

In the text, the crystallization of the light, or the concentration and purification of the life energy, means the creation of the foundation for enlightenment. The appearance of the Buddha refers to enlightenment. In Mahayana Buddhism, the *Amitayur Dhyana Sutra* presents a complicated meditation practice including the visualization of the following figure, "You will see a base of lapis lazuli. It is transparent and shining inside and outside. Below the base you will see... a golden banner with seven jewels, diamonds, and other precious stones supporting the base. The base reaches to the eight areas."[37] The base mentioned in the text corresponds well to the layout of the holy city, and the jewels supporting the base are like the jeweled foundation of the holy city.

I suggest additionally a more detailed interpretation for the jeweled foundations in St. John's vision: according to yoga theory they can be seen as chakras. In the chakra teachings, samadhi is experienced when the energy has traveled to the top of the head, into sahasrara. Before this, however, the six chakras below the sahasrara must have been opened. This opening of the chakras constructs the foundation for samadhi. This interpretation is especially fitting because the yogi is said to see with his inner eyes the opened chakras shine as brilliant, radiant lights.[38] Thus, the opened chakras are appropriately illustrated as shining jewels. I suggest that the jewels supporting the lapis lazuli base in the above quoted Buddhist meditation exercise refer to the chakras.

It is also possible to find parallels in yoga theory for the number of foundations of the holy city, which were said to be twelve. Because the opening of the six lower chakras is necessary before reaching the sahasrara center the yoga theory uses the expression "sixfold path," and should the chakras be differentiated as to inner and outer parts—this is often done while speaking of the petals and the pericarp of the lotus—we end up with the number twelve.[39] Sometimes the lower chakras are also seen polarized so that their number then is twelve.

With the chakra theory in mind, the holy city of Revelation could be interpreted to be the highest energy center, sahasrara, where the energy is during samadhi. But another interpretation based on yoga theory is possible, and I prefer this one. During samadhi, yogis and saints are said to experience the center of their being around their hearts, although the life energy is in sahasrara. The heart is talked about as the seat of the Self also more commonly in Eastern literature —as in the *Chandogya Upanishad*—and I feel that this so-called spiritual heart corresponds best to the holy Jerusalem.[40] Also in Christian symbolism, the holy city, Jerusalem, is found in the heart: Serafim of Sarov speaks of "the interior Jerusalem of the heart," and Bonaventure explains, "No one can enter the heavenly Jerusalem before, by grace, it has descended to his own heart, even as St. John saw it happen in Revelation."[41]

The colors of the jewels, as the foundations for the holy city in Revelation, are difficult to trace because during biblical times the names of the jewels may have been different from those of today. Additionally, the name of chalcedony was derived simply from the city of Chalcedon wherefrom different precious stones were imported. The Eastern texts, on the other hand, are explicit as to the colors of each chakra although a chakra can include more than one color. Particularly the petals and the pericarps of the lotus can generally be of different colors. The colors vary also because the chakras are different in different stages of development. I have found no clear correlation between the assumed colors of the jewels in Revelation and the colors in the above mentioned Eastern sources.

The walls and the gates

"Also she had a great and high wall with twelve gates, and twelve angels at the gates, and names written on them, which are the names of the twelve tribes of the children of Israel: three gates on the east, three gates on the north, three gates on the south, and three gates on the west" (Rev. 21:12–13). "And the twelve gates were twelve pearls: each individual gate was of one pearl" (Rev. 21:21). "Its gates shall not be shut at all by day (there shall be no night there)" (Rev. 21:25).

If the holy city is seen, as I have suggested, as a state of consciousness, the wall surrounding it symbolizes generally the boundary between the more outward and the more inward states. We can find this kind of understanding in the speeches by Abba Dorotheus, a Christian monk from the 6th century:

> We are...all like travelers journeying toward the holy city... Therefore, let each and every one find out where he is... Has he covered a short distance or gone far... has he reached the city and entered through Jerusalem's gate, or once near the city, was he unable to step in.[42]

Analyzed more specifically, the inside of the city represents, in this vision, the pure consciousness of oneness, and the outside, purified dualistic consciousness. Should the saint's consciousness reside only inside the city, he experiences trance-like samadhi which he enters by diving into the depths of his consciousness. A pearl well represents the state of oneness and bliss found in the depths of consciousness, and therefore the gates of the city can well be described as pearls. The saint can, however, also ascend out of those depths and travel through the gates of the city to the outside. As explained earlier, the saint can, in the state of the spiritual marriage, function also in the outer world when he wants to. Because one experiences continuous bliss in the spiritual marriage, part of his consciousness remains inside the city.

Once the saint moves through the gates to act, he uses skills that have been dormant in the trance-like samadhi. In St. John's vision, these skills are, according to the general symbolism of Revelation, represented by people and classes of people. In this case, those people have the family names of the children of Israel which are written into the gates.[43] Those skills, as it were, wait on the gates to be taken into use, and accordingly they are also removed and left at the gates when the saint re-enters the trance-like samadhi. The names of the tribes of Israel, written on the gates of the holy city, and apparently arranged symmetrically on the sides of a square, probably symbolize also the inner harmony that is manifested in the spiritual marriage.

Because the saint experiences samadhi bliss also during action, the connection between bliss and the more outward action is continuously 'open.' This is suggested by saying that the gates of the holy city are not shut by day; the mythical day expresses well the time of action when the saint is at the same time both inside and outside the wall. St. Teresa describes this kind of dual state in saying that during the spiritual marriage she felt like her soul was "somehow divided." Sometimes she even "chided her soul, because this [soul] constantly and endlessly just enjoyed the quietude, leaving herself in the midst of many trials and errands."[44] In this aspect, the spiritual marriage is clearly different from engagement when samadhi is experienced only in a trance-like state, or while the gates of the city are closed. In fact, St. Teresa describes the engagement stage, "the Lord orders the gates of the city and the wall closed. When He wants to cease this soul, her breathing stops... Sometimes everything disappears suddenly."[45]

According to Eastern sources, nirbikalpa samadhi is a state of continuous Awareness which does not cease even during sleep.[46] The saint does not have an unconscious state, or mythical night, and therefore, in the holy city of Revelation "there shall be no night there" (Rev. 21:25).

That angels are the gate keepers of the holy city tells us that the relationship between the inner and outer is guided by intuition. The intuition, or the angels, guard the life energy, or the inward and outward movement of the person's consciousness. While acting in a state of nirbikalpa samadhi, the saint may experience troubles caused by the outward world, but they do not disturb his inner peace; the angels on the gates of the wall do not allow anything disturbing to enter the innermost parts of the soul. St. Teresa summarizes the peace of the spiritual marriage: "thus the soul does not worry about anything that happens."[47] Also, the actual transfer of the consciousness away from the outer world is guided by intuition, the angels.

The Tibetan mandalas which have a square palace inside a circle also place a gate at every side of the square. It is possible to enter into the palace through the gates, but first the aspirant comes to the inner courtyard of the palace. Therefore, the gates can be seen to be located in the surrounding wall as they are in Revelation. Similar to Revelation also are the gate keepers in front of the palace gates. In Buddhism, usually, the gates of the palace describe different paths to enlightenment.[48]

The nations and the kings of the earth

"And the nations... shall walk in its light" (Rev. 21:24). This verse describes the way a saint acts. The nations are different human characteristics and skills. When they wander in the light of the holy city, the saintly acts receive their motives and inner guidance from universal love and wisdom, the light of the holy city. The modern saint-like 'activist' Mother Teresa emphasizes the importance of divine love in acting rightly: "Our work is only the expression of the love we have for God.... It is not how much you do, but how much love you put into the action."[49]

"And the kings of the earth bring their glory and honor into it" (Rev. 21:24). "And they shall bring the glory and the honor of the nations into it" (Rev. 21:26). The kings of the earth mentioned here are the kings of the new earth St. John saw at the beginning of this chapter, and these kings symbolize consciousness and physicality purified of all desires, or "the newness of sense." There are many kings, because St. John, typical of Revelation, differentiates between several forms or centers of activity in human beings. Yet, there is no longer a separate sense of self because saints do not feel themselves to act as a separate self and do not expect a reward. Expressed in religious language, saints give the credit for their actions to God, and therefore, in Revelation, the kings bring their glory into the holy city, or where God lives. Mother Teresa speaks of these things in the following way, "I am only a small instrument in God's hand. Our Lord and our Lady gave all the glory to God the Father. Like them, in a very, very small way, I want to give all the glory to God the Father."[50]

St. Teresa describes the attitude of those souls who have entered spiritual marriage, "Now they have... a great desire to serve and praise Him and, according to their abilities, to be helpful to other souls... if only Lord could receive even the slightest praise through it."[51]

In Eastern culture, desireless action is well-known, particularly from the *Bhagavadgita* whose thoughts on desirelessness I have quoted in connection with the destruction of Babylon. Additionally, the following verses shed light on the principles of correct action—we must act without attachment and give the credit for our actions to God—ideas which can be found in Revelation also.

> Having denounced attachments,
> the yogi performs actions
> with his body, mind, intellect
> and even with the senses.
> Dedicating all action to me [Krishna or God],
> contemplating the higher Self,
> without greed for gain, without selfishness,
> fight vigorously![52]

The temple, the sun, and the moon are missing

"But I saw no temple in it, for the Lord God Almighty and the Lamb are its temple. And the city had no need of the sun or of the moon to shine in it, for the glory of God illuminated it, and the Lamb is its light" (Rev. 21:22–23). More accurately, St. John calls the Lamb the lamp, *luchnos,* of the city. This is important because the lamp appears also in the following chapter. When God's glory and Lamb light the holy city, the saint feels bliss, or in the Eastern language, he is enlightened. Because in nirbikalpa samadhi the bliss, or God-contact, is permanent, he does not need a separate high state of consciousness, previously symbolized by the temple, to experience bliss.

For the sun and the moon I have given interpretations in which both represent, in different ways, superficial religion, or more generally, an alienated worldview and sense of life. Now the alienation is over, as St. John himself lives in bliss, or God's glory, and so, the holy city does not need the sun and the moon to light it. The lack of the sun and the moon as a description for an inwardly illumined state of consciousness is also found in the following words by Krishna in the *Bhagavadgita*.

> Without pride and delusion,
> those who have defeated the evil of attachment
> remain within themselves,
> turned away from desires;
> liberated from oppositions felt as happiness and suffering,
> they will go without erring into this everlasting place.
> And it is not illumined by sun nor moon nor fire.
> Having gone in, they will not return:
> this is my highest dwelling.[53]

22. THE PARADISE OF THE NEW JERUSALEM

The paradise

"And he showed me a pure river of the water of life, clear as crystal, proceeding from the throne of God and of the Lamb. In the middle of its street, and on either side of the river, was the tree of life, which bore twelve fruits, each tree yielding its fruit every month. And the leaves of the tree were for the healing of the nations. And there shall be no more curse." (Rev. 22:1–3.)

The mythical paradise described in these verses is probably inside the holy city, although it is not explicitly so stated; thus the traveler has finally returned to the paradise from whence he was exiled at the beginning of the Bible. St. John's account of paradise completes the description of the highest states of human consciousness imparted by Revelation.

Paradise in myths, in religious literature, and in dreams

In mythology, paradise is often the abode of dead good men, as was the Greek Elysium described by Homer in the *Odyssey*:
Man's life is light there, passing gently and carefree;
no snow, no freezing winds, no torrential rains, trouble him
but rather an everlasting zephyr
wafts and murmurs there always.[1]

A description of the paradisiacal state is also found in the myths of the lost golden age, which the Roman poet, Ovid, used in his collection of poems *Metamorphoses*. In his poems, Ovid wrote that during the past golden age there was an eternal spring; honey dripped from trees, the fields produced harvest of themselves and the streams flowed milk and nectar. Paradise has also gleamed in the minds of men and women as a distant dream image of happiness, difficult to reach, like an island-paradise far away. For example, the Hesperides of the Greek mythology, the daughters of night, lived on the other side of the ocean in the far West, in a beautiful garden. Golden apples grew there, which they, together with a terrifying dragon, guarded.[2]

In the light of my subject, more interesting are the descriptions which associate paradise with personally experienced bliss. St. John of the Cross writes about the spiritualized soul in this way:

She drinks deeply sheer brightness and love, and realizes even her innermost parts to be filled with the currents of illumination brimming with joy. She feels the streams of the living water to spring forth from within—streams which according to the Son of God will flow from such souls.

You will concentrate and sink into this knowledge [the spiritual, personal experience] so completely that you are a well of those living waters flowing so powerfully... out of God. In that current, you will receive a wondrous joy which becomes a harmonious part of your soul, as well as of your body. This becomes completely a paradise, watered by the divine spring, so that you will witness the words of the psalm, "The power of the stream will make God's city happy."

Should the soul now... gain spiritual freedom, she gains the twelve fruits of the Holy Spirit.[3]

St. Teresa writes about the soul in a state of grace:

As you know, all the streams flowing from a very pure spring are as pure as the spring, and similarly, the works that spring forth from a soul in a state of grace are pleasing to God and in the eyes of men, because they come from the spring of life wherein the soul has been planted like a tree. She would offer no protection nor fruits unless her roots were in the spring which maintains her, keep her from drying and causes her to produce good fruits.

St. Teresa also calls the soul "this tree of life which has been planted into the living waters, or God."[4]

The metaphors used by St. John of the Cross and St. Teresa are used widely in Christianity; St. Bernard also explains that the believing soul has in herself a spiritual paradise.[5]

In Eastern culture, a good example of paradise is Amitabha Buddha's Western land, one of the four lands inside the gates of the mandala palace; this paradise depicts the enlightened human consciousness. In the *Amitayur Dhyana Sutra*, this "land of highest happiness" is described as having endless precious stones, jewel trees, flowers and fruits. The water in its streams is the color of seven jewels, there is a golden channel and eight lakes, and Amitabha Buddha himself lives there. Indian yoga literature, also, includes paradise symbolism, as the rising of the kundalini energy into sahasrara is described as the ascent to "the island of gems surrounded by the kalpa trees in the ocean of nectar."[6]

Similar paradisiacal mythical images—lovely trees, water, springs, jewels, and brightness—appear also in dreams which reflect happy states of consciousness. For example, the writer Mika Waltari related a dream he dreamt after a mystical experience he had had, one which I used as an example in the previous chapter:

I experienced something in that dream. I was lying under an extremely beautiful big tree in paradise. I cannot use another name for it. And in my dream, I had cried so that there were salt crystals in my eye corners... When I woke up from the dream I was overcome by the thought that after this I can never doubt again. So strong and powerful was this experience.[7]

The following dream was told to me by someone who had been very happy before dreaming it:

I am in a beautiful park, under the shade of huge trees. I see a fountain, and from it rises a flower formed of jewels. The flower begins to radiate wondrous white light, and exquisite happiness overtakes me.

The paradise in Revelation

In the paradise of Revelation, there is "a river of the water of life ... proceeding from the throne of God and of the Lamb," and "the tree of life, which bore twelve fruits, each tree yielding its fruit every month" (Rev. 22:1–2). Water and fruits are mythical drink and food. They are fitting for paradise because the saint's high spiritual states of consciousness refresh and nourish him.

In connection with these symbols, an apt interpretation of the water of life is that it stands for perfect contemplation, a meaning St. Teresa used, or more generally, it refers to experiencing something of great spiritual value. The saint drinks this living water during the spiritual marriage as if from an unceasing stream, and dryness will not disturb her any longer. St. Teresa says that in the seventh dwelling where the soul lives married to God "there is hardly ever such dryness... that there was, at times, in other dwellings." The traveler has finally arrived at the "fountains of living waters," as the seventh chapter of Revelation foretold, and there God gives her freely "of the fountain of the water of life," as was promised in the previous chapter (Rev. 7:17 and 21:6). Also, Jesus' words in the Gospel of John are now fulfilled, "He who believes in me... out of his heart will flow rivers of living water."[8]

The tree of life, as a general mythical image, is the saint's purified soul, and therefore, the fruits of the tree are first and foremost the states of bliss the saint experiences and which nourish him—and others through him. The fruits, however, can be also the external deeds the saint 'produces' while acting in the world. That the fruits of the tree of life ripen every month probably illustrates a permanent state of bliss and a continuation of the good actions. Because St. John uses the expression "twelve fruits," he probably emphasizes the perfection of the saint.

According to the Bible, the Lord God said after the Fall as He explained why He exiled man from paradise, "And now, lest he put out his hand and take also from the tree of life, and eat, and live forever."[9] By the end of Revelation man has, however, transformed himself to a tree of life, and so he is allowed to enjoy its fruits.

St. John says about the leaves of the tree of life in his description of paradise, "And the leaves of the tree were for the healing of the nations" (Rev. 22:2). The leaves of a tree appear as mythical images, for example, in the Bible when man and woman resorted to the big leaves of the fig tree right after the Fall.[10] Generally, the leaves of a tree represent in myths something of lesser and more external value than its fruits. The leaves of the tree of life in St. John's vision can thus symbolize, for example, knowledge acquired through the senses and practical wisdom which the saint uses while acting in the world.

St. John emphasizes, "And there shall be no more curse... and his servants shall serve him" (Rev. 22:3). The curse mentioned in the verse came to pass when man and woman fell in the beginning of the Bible and when they were exiled from paradise. God said at that time, "Cursed is the ground for your sake."[11] Now the curse and the sin of separation have ended, as the exiled ones have found their way back into union with God. The latter part of the verse stresses the idea that specific human abilities and characteristics that individuals have symbolized in Revelation have been liberated from their attachments and thus they have become God's servants.

The paradise of Revelation and yoga theory

Applying yoga theory, the paradise in Revelation is a mythical image of the energy system of a perfected human being, and therefore I will explain the details of the paradise once more from this viewpoint.

The river of the water of life which flows "from the throne of God and of the Lamb," parallels the sushumna nadi. It has opened completely in the state of nirbikalpa samadhi, so that life energy flows in it. The throne, where the river begins from, is sahasrara, the thousand-petaled lotus, which is the ending point of sushumna. When St. John says that the river of the water of life flows "clear as crystal," this is comparable to the occasion when the yogi sees the sushumna nadi as a bright thread of light with his inner eyes. The angel showing the river of the water of life to St. John (Rev. 22:2), also refers to the inner eyes of intuition.

Other details of paradise which I have not yet interpreted and which would be difficult to do outside yoga theory can be understood from its basis. St. John's description includes an odd detail: a tree grows in the middle of the street in paradise. "In the middle of its street... was the tree of life" (Rev. 22:2). I interpret this to mean that the tree and the street itself, in fact, merge, or more specifically, the street is the trunk of the tree of life. At this stage, the tree of life symbolizes appropriately the entire human prana energy system, as all of it has been purified by now. And the most important part of this system, the trunk of the tree, is also the street, because perfected saints and yogis can 'transport' life energy along the nadis depending on whether they act in outward reality or have consciousness withdrawn inward into the trance-like samadhi. In his previous vision, St. John described the street of the city to be "pure gold, like transparent glass," which corresponds well to the purified state of ida and pingala nadis and the brightness of the opened sushumna.

The verse about the street and the tree of life reads, in the biblical translation which I have used here, in its entirety, "In the middle of the street, and on either side of the river, was the tree of life" (Rev. 22:2).

The content of the verse is difficult to apply to reality because the verse does not explain how the river, the street and the tree of life relate to each other. Are there actually three trees of life in the paradise, one in the middle of the street and one on each side of the river? Due to the ambiguity of the verse, it has been translated in various ways; also the original text is open to interpretations. Most commonly in the English translations, the matter has been so envisioned that the river of life flows in the middle of the street and on both sides of the river there grows a tree of life; here there are apparently two trees of life.[12]

The verse is, however, easily understood from the basis of yoga theory, when we see it describing a situation where the opened sushumna is in the middle of ida and pingala, and from ida and pingala depart smaller nadis, and all of these are purified. In other words, sushumna is the river of the water of life, and in the case of three trees of life, it is also the trunk of the tree in middle. This tree would not have branches. The trunks of the two outer trees would again be the ida and pingala nadis. Should there be two trees of life, ida and pingala would form the trunks of these trees. In both views, the lesser energy channels departing from ida and pingala would be the branches of the trees.

The twelve fruits of the tree of life correspond to the energy centers or chakras of the 'prana tree.' As mythical images, the fruits can be fittingly seen to be round as the chakras are often explained to be round. Additionally, according to yoga theory, once opened, every center bestows upon the yogi new strengths, abilities and spiritual states of consciousness, so that the opened chakras affect the person like nourishing fruits. A tree bearing wondrous fruits is one of the universal mythical images, and here I suspect it to be based on experiences of the movements of the life energy. For example, the Hesperides' golden apples growing in the far West may reflect this kind of inner experience, although those apples apparently are also clouds gilded by the evening sun.[13] Also, the Christmas tree candles, familiar to modern persons, are like opened chakras, and the topmost star is like sahasrara, or rather the guiding star of the spiritual eye of intuition showing the way to the travelers. (As it is, Christmas celebrates the birth of the mythical child, and after that, aspirants still have the journey to crucifixion and resurrection ahead of them.)

The leaves of the tree of life, which according to Revelation "were for the healing of the nations," form the outer surface of the tree of life. The outer points of the energy system can be seen as acupuncture points through which the physical body can indeed be healed as has been proved in practice. There are many acupuncture points in the human body, even as there are countless leaves in a tree.

The highest enlightenment

"And there shall be no night there: They need no lamp nor light of the sun, for the Lord God gives them light. And they shall reign for ever and ever" (Rev. 22:5). The most important thought in the verse is expressed in the words "The Lord God gives them light." This expression can be interpreted to refer to the highest state of consciousness, experiencing utmost reality or divinity, which has often been described simply as radiance, light, and brightness.

St. John of the Cross ends his work, *The Living Flame of Love*, with a description of enlightenment. This work is the culmination of St. John of the Cross' account of the journey of the soul. Enlightenment is, according to him, the destination of the spiritual path, similarly to Revelation. St. John of the Cross writes:

But when the Bridegroom wakes in the perfected soul... the soul feels strange joy as the Holy Spirit breathes in God where the soul itself is illuminated and ignites in love. Therefore, she utters the following verses:
And in your sweet breathing,
which is full of goodness and brightness,
how gently you awaken my love! [14]

The Indian text, *Sat Chakra Nirupana*, says that sahasrara shines constantly like lightning and inside sahasrara shines the Great Void. Similar light symbolism is used in *The Tibetan Book of the Dead* where humankind's highest state of consciousness is described: "Your consciousness is... brightness and emptiness in the form of vast light. It has no birth, no death; therefore it is the Buddha of the Immortal Light." In Eastern religious literature, this state is generally the highest spiritual enlightenment. The above mentioned *Tibetan Book of the Dead* also uses the words "complete enlightenment." There are only a few descriptions about this state, but the Indian Paramahansa Yogananda offers such expressions as "ever-new joy" and "unending bliss." He explains also that a person's highest possible experience is to know God as Bliss, "in which every other aspect of Divinity—love, wisdom, immortality—is fully contained."[15]

In mandalas, the central point usually illustrates the state of enlightenment, just as the center of the holy city in Revelation is the Lord God who "gives them light." In the center of Buddhist mandalas, there is often a so-called central Buddha in the middle of the meditation Buddhas; but some other symbol can be, as well, in the center of these mandalas, like a jewel lightning, or *vajra*.[16]

Because the Lord God gives light in the holy city, there is no night and "They need no lamp nor light of the sun" as St. John tells us (Rev. 22:5). The absence of both night and the light of the sun was already presented in the previous chapter, but the words "They need no lamp" bring us a new detail. In his previous vision, St. John said that the Lamb is the lamp of the holy city, and therefore we need to ask why the Lamb-lamp has disappeared from the holy city. I understand the change described by St. John to mean that at the moment of reaching the highest state, one goes even beyond the Lamb, the level of the universal Self, and (expressed in religious language) the soul unites with God, the utmost divinity.

The understanding wherein even the state of consciousness symbolized by the Lamb, or Christ, is past, appears, I believe, also elsewhere in the Bible. In the first Epistle to the Corinthians, Paul explains that the Son, the Christ, will defeat all enemies—the last of them being Death—and "then comes the end, when he delivers the kingdom to God the Father."[17] I believe that Paul speaks of "the end" in a general sense, considering the whole world, but in my book I have followed mainly the development of one individual only. Thus the end, when the Lamb delivers the kingdom to God, means the final, or highest, enlightenment of one individual. Once enlightened, man has "overcome," and then, according to the words in Revelation, he will be made "a pillar in the temple of my God, and he shall go out no more" (Rev. 3:12). Because I have interpreted these words according to the Eastern tradition to mean that the enlightened one must no longer incarnate into the world, the world 'ends' for this person.[18] Interpreted in this way, Revelation can be read as a description of the final times as it is generally understood.

The actual content of Revelation ends with the important words of the fifth verse, "The Lord God gives them light," which I interpreted above. The concluding verses are comprised of repetitions, warnings and encouragements only.[19] Because Revelation is the last text in the Bible, it is possible to see spiritual enlightenment, which has been the ultimate meaning of human life in religions and partly also in philosophies, as the destination of the entire Bible.

The last words of Revelation resound, "Amen. Even so, come, Lord Jesus! The grace of our Lord Jesus Christ be with you all. Amen."

ABOUT THE BOOK
NOTES
BIBLIOGRAPHY

ABOUT THE BOOK

This book was first published in Finnish in 1993 by Helsinki University Press. It was then translated into English by Tarja Sagar and published in Finland by Inner Kingdom (inner.kingdom@saunalahti.fi) in 2001.

When the time came to produce the second printing of the book Tarja suggested that the main text of the book would be reviewed and edited by an American-born expert, because Finnish and English are surprisingly different languages. (Finnish belongs to rare Finno-Ugric languages and English is Indo-European.) Tarja Sagar recommended Patricia Taylor, Ph.D., and to my delight Patricia kindly assumed the task.

Although many years have passed since this book was first published in Finland, its message is still valid: it is possible to read man's inner spiritual path and some basic problems in religion in the images of the Book of Revelation. Most sources I have used to support this thesis are timeless classics in their own fields. I have retained also some of the more encyclopedic sources I originally used, though today people who would like to find more information about these topics would probably search it from internet.

The Bible verses quoted are taken from the New King James Bible, unless otherwise mentioned. The other quotations were translated by Tarja Sagar from Finnish into English, but those quotations which were originally in English have been mostly quoted in their published English form. I thank sincerely Self-Realization Fellowship for permitting me to use direct quotations from their books.

I present my heartfelt gratitude to Tarja Sagar and Patricia Taylor who did such a great and wonderful work to get this book into its present English form.

Espoo, Finland
November 2019
Irma Korte

NOTES

In the notes, I will mention only the name of the author or the name of the work (either the complete name or an abbreviation). The full account of the sources can be found in the bibliography. When I have used more than one work from an author, the number in parenthesis after the author's name will disclose the particular work in question.

I have availed myself to several biblical and general encyclopedias, but they are not always mentioned in the notes.

Of the Greek versions of the New Testament, I have used the work by Nestle–Aland Novum Testamentum Graece (26th ed.), and in researching the Greek words, I have relied mainly on A Greek–English Lexicon of the New Testament by William Arndt and Wilbur Gingrich (for more specific information on the work see bibliography under Arndt). I will not mention these works again in the notes).

Since the quotes not originally in English have been translated from Finnish, the quotes in the text are slightly different from those in published English translations. Yet, in the notes the references are given, for readers' convenience, to the published English translations.

In transcribing the names of the Chinese books, I have followed in the text the forms used in English language. In the notes and in the bibliography, the names appear in the forms printed in the source books.

For the sake of clarity, I mention here that in the main text of this book I have taken some small liberties in the quotations I have presented. In places, I have left out the beginning of the sentence of the original quote, and yet used a capital letter in the beginning of the quote. Similarly, I have sometimes ended the quote in the middle of the original sentence, and yet closed it with a period. I have occasionally added a word or two in brackets within a quote for clarity. I have not shown the paragraph divisions in the quotes except in very long quotes where the original text already shows them. I have followed the same principle in the Bible quotes where I have not shown the divisions between the verses.

Introduction

1. For the identity of St. John the Divine see, for example, Bowman (1), pp. 59–60.

2. For example, Julian of Norwich sometimes saw her visions "by physical sight" (Julian of Norwich, chapter 10, p. 76, chapter 73, p. 191). St. Teresa of Avila told that she saw her pictorial visions always "in a very inward way" (St. Teresa of Avila (1), p. 402; St. Teresa of Avila (2), pp. 411–412). St. Teresa's pictorial visions were, in general, flashes of religious subjects like Christ (St. Teresa of Avila (3), pp. 237–242). Another form of visions besides the pictorial visions, expressed in modern language, is a strong and bright intuition. St. Teresa of Avila called these "intellectual visions" (St. Teresa of Avila (2), pp. 405–406).

3. For more information on such views see Court, pp. 15–17, 164.

4. See Court, pp. 16, 109, 161; compare also to my text in chapter 12.

5. Concentration on images, for example, in meditation is, however, only the first stage on the inner path, as becomes clear in my text in chapter 14 and in the concluding chapters.

6. A short general overview of the theological interpretations can be found, for example, in Court, pp. 2–19.

7. Brontë, pp. 532–533, 578–579; Tolstoy, pp. 337–339 (see also my text in chapter 13 where I briefly speak of Tolstoy's reference to Revelation); Dostoevski, pp. 210–211, 256, 391–393, 400; Mann, pp. 539–578, partic. pp. 543–543, 547, 569, 573.

8. Swedenborg wrote, along with the shorter works, two extensive interpretations of Revelation in Latin. The broader one of these was Apocalypsis explicata, but he did not finish it. The narrower version was Apocalypsis revelata. After Swedenborg's passing, these were translated and printed supplementing the unfinished work with the interpretations from the Apocalypsis revelata. (Swedenborg (1), editor's foreword, p. vi.) Of the interpretations I mention in the text, see for example Swedenborg (2), p. 9; Swedenborg (3), pp. 164, 198.

9. Engels (1), pp. 463–468; Engels (2), pp. 13–15.

10. Lawrence, pp. 87–88.

11. The most complete interpretation of Revelation by Jung is included in his book Answer to Job, Jung (1), §§ 698–744, pp. 435–459.

12. The interpretations by Sri Yukteswar are included in his work The Holy Science. The interpretations by Paramahansa Yogananda are essentially same, and they are dispersed throughout his works. I will refer to them more specifically in places where I have used them as my sources.

13. The book I mention is Irion: Interpreting the Revelation with Edgar Cayce.

14. The purpose of my book is not to discuss Christian theological problems. I must refer to theological problems at times, because Revelation is unquestionably a religious text. Often, however, I pass those problems with a brief mention regardless that they may have been at some point over their historical past the subjects of even fierce debates. I do not strive to insist through my interpretation that some theological problem ought to be solved in the manner I suggest, but rather, I present the problems as I see them transmitted by the Book of Revelation.

15. For example, Bowman (1), pp. 60–61, 70.

16. Op. cit., pp. 70–71; Rist, p. 441; Chester Beatty p^{47}-papyrus includes the verses 9:10–17:2 of Revelation.

4th chapter

1. St. Teresa of Avila (2), p. 428. I use the words 'macrocosm' and 'microcosm' in a broad sense so that they include also the more spiritual levels of man and reality, not only the visible and superficial levels.

2. Tao Tê Ching, § 1, p. 17, § 42, p. 67. For Indian philosophy see, for example, Yukteswar, pp. 11–12.

3. Spinoza, part I, def. III–IV, p. 45. Hegel, § 6, p. 4, § 16, p. 9, § 20, p. 11. Hegel's understanding of the Absolute was naturally in its entirety much more multifaceted than simply equating the Absolute with oneness.

4. New Larousse Encyclopedia, p. 90 (the Orfian myths); Finnish Folk Poems (1), for example, poem no. 1, p. 3; Gen. 1:7; Anandamayi Ma, p. 86.

5. Seyce, pp. 148, 206–207, 176. We know, however, that the names of months used by the Hebrews were partly borrowed from Babylon (for example, Harper's Bible Dictionary, pp. 1072–1073).

6. For example, Harzer, pp. 657–658; Yukteswar, pp. 12, x–xii. Harzer translates Purusha as contentless consciousness.

7. I rely here on the information given by the Greek historian and philosopher Plutarch. He tells of the Persian creation story, according to which Oromazes (or Ormazd) who was born of light, created first six deities, and Areimanius (or Ahriman) created the other six deities. After this, both original deities created yet 24 other deities. (Plutarch, p. 115.) See also New Larousse Encyclopedia, pp. 310, 316, 318.

8. Plato (1), 31b–32c, pp. 56–61; Yukteswar, pp. 3–5.

9. For beliefs of antiquity see, for example, Hesiod, pp. 101–105; for Indian beliefs, Yukteswar, pp. xiii–xiv; for Persian beliefs, New Larousse Encyclopedia, p. 318.

10. For mandalas, see for example Cirlot, pp. 199–203.

11. Plato (1), 33b, pp. 60–63; Cowen, p. 85. The mandala-like figure illustrating the manuscripts by Hildegard of Bingen has been published in Grof, p. 44; the illustration is from the 12th century. In the figure, the circle is formed from the round central light and the nine layers of angels surrounding it. The figure reminiscent of a circle from Jacob Boehm's works has been presented in Purge, figure 30.

12. Jung (2), pp. 213, 220–221; Jung (3), §§ 627–712, pp. 355–384 (includes illustrations), § 714, pp. 387–388, § 718, pp. 389–390; Jung (4), §§ 329–331, pp. 221–223.

13. The English Bible translation I mention is Today's English Version, also called Good News for Modern Man. In my mind, the translation "in the circle" is, however, already an interpretation. The expressions used by St. John are *kuklothen tou thronou* (in the case of the elders' throne, Rev. 4:4) and *kuklō tou thronou* (in the case of the creatures, Rev. 4:6)

14. A photograph of the Saint-Denis window can be found, for example, in Cowen, p. 51. See also pictures op. cit., pp. 38, 50.

15. For the stonealtar of Tarakeswar see, for example, Yogananda (1), pp. 134–136.

16. Ezek. 1:10.

17. For the history of the signs of the zodiac see, for example, Gossner, pp. 787–788.

18. See New Larousse Encyclopedia, illustrations pp. 49, 59, 60, 62, 69–70. For the eagle star see Seyce, pp. 171, 173, 204–205.

19. New Larousse Encyclopedia, p. 40.

20. Biblical reference John 1:1. For Indian beliefs see Yogananda (2), p. 167; Yogananda (3), p. 300; Vivekananda (1), p. 56. I will return to the Word in the visions of St. John in chapter 19.

21. For Gnostics see Pagels, pp. 59, 64–65, 68–70. For Indian philosophy see Yukteswar, p. 3, and the figure p. 8.

22. For example, New Larousse Encyclopedia, p. 362. I refer also to the book The Hero with a Thousand Faces by Joseph Campbell. Campbell writes about myths using the cyclic nature of change as his main approach (Campbell, e.g. pp. 36–40).

23. E.g. Isa. 46:11.

24. For eagle, see Cirlot, pp. 91–93.

25. For more information see Wheelwright, pp. 37–57, 71, 96, 100. Hegel, §§ 484–487, pp. 294–297, § 808, pp. 492–493; see also the summary of the last mentioned work written by J.N. Findlay, particularly p. 491.

26. Seyce, pp. 167–174 (the astronomy in Babylon). Yukteswar, pp. 12–14.

27. Gen. 1:27. Plato (1), e.g. 41d–43a, pp. 88–95; see also Plato (2), p. 59 and the introduction for the same work, p. 9. For Indian philosophy see Yukteswar, pp. 2–12. As I explain in chapter 6, I interpret the verse Gen. 1:27 so that man created as an image of God forms the 'essence' of man. The thought of man as an image of God can be interpreted also in a broader sense. According to this view the visible universe is, as if, God's body, and is, on the level of microcosm, comparable to man's body. The different levels of spiritual reality assumed to exist in religious worldviews would compare to man's psychic levels. Within Christianity, the thought of man as an image of God in a broader sense, appears in the source Bonaventure (1), particularly on pages 79–84, where Bonaventure describes the abilities of man's soul as an image of God.

28. Augustine spoke of God's eternal thought as the prerequisite for creation, Augustine (1), book XI, § 8, p. 151; see also Augustine (2), book XII, chapter 26, pp. 505–506; Eckhart (2), p. 62.

29. Yukteswar, pp. 14–15; Avalon, p. 1.

30. Yogananda (3), p. 300; Yogananda (1), p. 19n.

31. For concentration on the Om-vibration see, for example, Ramana Maharsi, p. 148, and my text in chapter 19. The descriptions of the Om-vibration belong to the teachings by Paramahansa Yogananda, and can be found, among others, in the article titled Science Says in the magazine published by the organization established by Yogananda (Science Says, p. 54n).

32. St. John of the Cross (1), pp. 466–467.

33. St. Teresa of Avila (2), pp. 281, 320–321.

34. Marja-Leena Teivonen writes in her book, Under the Bodhi Tree, how a man who practiced meditation explained her, "A strange thing happens to me sometimes. It is different from anything else that I have experienced and felt. I am not crazy, but sometimes I hear a strange sound. It is like a train was approaching incredibly fast. It has happened a few times. And I don't know what it is." Teivonen associates the sound with chackras and particularly to the throat chackra (Bodhipuun juurella, Under the Bodhi Tree, p. 150).

35. The Om-vibration in association with death: Moody (1), pp. 5, 15; Moody (2), pp. 30, 121. See also the article Science Says mentioned above in the note 31. The article presents the results of Moody's research comparing them to the Indian yoga teachings.

36. The rapids of Tuonela are called Rutja and Turja. Rutja rapids: for example, Finnish Folk Poems (2), poem 2846, p. 476. Turja rapids: for example, op. cit., poem 2880, p. 499. In placing the Rutja rapids into the Tuonela stream I am simplifying the matters, as in the poems the rapids can be located in the North or in Lappland. Interpreting on the psychological level, the North can be seen as the subconscious or the basis of consciousness. Lappland can be compared to the North because it is a northern country, and the poems often use the North and the Underworld interchangeably. For the use of drums see, for example, Allione, p. 148.

37. E.g. Exod. 19:16–19; John 12:29.

38. Yogananda (1), p. 277.

39. Yogananda (3), pp. 44, 15, 15n.

40. Loyola, § 99, p. 126; Yogananda (3), p. 285. The general meanings of the Greek word *haplous* are single, simple, sincere, and the specific meanings, as pertaining to eye, are clear and healthy. I believe that in the verse Matt. 6:22, and similarly in Luke 11:34, the eye in question is 'the inner eye' or the intuitive wisdom, or perhaps, in fact, the light of the spiritual eye. The verse in the Gospel of Matthew speaks in a positive sense of the 'one-eyed' concentration on spiritual life. I believe this is so because the verse is preceded by the words, "For where your treasure is, there your heart will be also", soon followed by a warning that no one can worship *two* masters, God and mammon (Matt. 6:21–24).

41. Light in association with death: Moody (2), pp. 58–59. Whirling sphere of light: Finnish Folk Poems (2), poem no. 2863, p. 486. Shooting of the star: Finnish Folk Poems (3), for example, poem 414, p. 291.

42. Bible research has recognized that differentiating between colors is scarce in the Bible (for example, Corney, pp. 657–658). St. John uses the word *stephanos* for the elders' crowns, which means a wreath, a crown, and more generally, a reward, adornment, and magnificence.

43. A type of organization of the original sea takes place in the beginning of the Bible when God separates the waters under and above the firmament (Gen. 1:6). A mountain rises from the original sea, for example, in the Egyptian mythology (Clark, pp. 37–38).

44. Probably everyone who has paid attention to his dreams is familiar with the mythical image of existing in two places at once. I present an example of such a dream. "I am outside with a childhood friend. The atmosphere of the dream is lovely, reminiscent of the times when we played together as children, although, in the dream, we are adults. A third person comes to us. He unlocks the door to a cellar or a cave. I know that my childhood friend and I myself are in the cave and have been there a long time, locked up. Now I am curious to see how my friend and I have fared during our long imprisonment." Particularly common in dreams is a situation where the dreamer is at the same time the observer of the dream and the person acting in the dream.

45. The expression "on each side of the throne" is found in Today's English Version. The expression "in front of the throne" is found in the official present-day Finnish Bible translation.

46. John 1:1.

5th chapter

1. Bonaventure (1), p. 109.

2. Court, pp. 55–56.

3. The expressions "the sensuous part of the soul," "the lower part of the soul," and "the center of the senses" are found in St. John of the Cross (for example, St John of the Cross (2), pp. 330, 332–333; St. John of the Cross (3), p. 582; in the English translation of the works of St. John of the Cross the term "sensory" is used instead of "sensuous"). The expression "the old man" can be found, for example, in the Bible (Eph. 4:22). The Indian expressions: Bhagavadgita (1), III:27, p. 192; Yukteswar, p. 7.

4. For example, St. Teresa of Avila (2), pp. 433, 437 (the center of the soul); St. John of the Cross (3), p. 582 (the deepest center of the soul); St. Teresa of Avila (2), p. 435 (interior of the soul); Eckhart (1), pp. 3, 15 (the ground of the soul); St. John of the Cross (2), p. 332 (the spiritual part of the soul); op.cit., p. 358 (the higher part of the soul).

The expression "the real self" comes from Immanuel Kant; the original expression was "eigentliche Selbst" (Kant, p. 98). Kant's understanding of man's "real self" was cautious; the real self was the realm of freedom and conscience, but it could not be known directly. Jung, in his psychology, used the term "Selbst", and I will shortly return to its meaning (see the notes 12 and 22 of this chapter with respective sections of the text). The Western literature that is based on the Oriental thought applies the term Self, which is also used to translate the Indian expressions describing man's deeper level. For Indian philosophical terminology see, for example, Yukteswar, p. 6.

5. Eckhart (1), e.g. p. 3.

6. E.g. Eckhart (1), pp. xli–xlii, xxxvi–xxxvii, 237–238.

7. Hesse, p. 123; Gal. 2:20.

8. Hesse, p. 123.

9. In the sense that I speak of love in my book, it has two aspects. On the one hand, love means a state of surrendering, happiness and bliss or value experience, and on the other, ambitious striving for happiness and completeness. This dualism is clearly apparent in Greek mythology where Aphrodite expresses the aspect of surrendering love and Eros the goal oriented one. (Woman as a mythical image is associated with surrendering and man with ambition.) I do not always specify which form of love is in question, but probably this is clear from the context. Naturally, both kinds of love can be present in the same experience.

10. 1 Cor. 15:10.

11. This kind of thinking is common in the religious literature; see e.g. Julian of Norwich, chapter 10, pp. 77–79; Eckhart (1), p. 187; Ramana Maharsi, p. 23; Gilson, p. 54.

12. Jung (5), § 706, p. 425, §§ 789–791, pp. 460–461.

13. Col. 1:15–17; John 8:58; see also John 1:15; 1:30; 6:62.

14. Yukteswar, pp. 5–7. Ramana Maharsi, p. 24.

15. Matt. 10:39; 16:25. The same idea can be found also in the verses Luke 17:33 and John 12:25.

16. 1 Cor. 15:22.

17. Vivekananda (3), pp. 197–198; Bhagavadgita (1), VII:4–7, pp. 366–371, VIII:28, p.75; Yogananda (3), pp. 437–438; Yogananda (4), pp. 19–21.

18. Ramana Maharsi, p. 58, p. 119.

19. Yogananda (3), pp. 332–334. Swami Sri Yukteswar equates Kutastha Chaitanya with the Holy Spirit of Christianity (Yukteswar, p. 6).

20. Plato (1), 41d–42d, pp. 88–93.

21. Hegel, e.g. § 486, p. 296, §§ 788–808, pp. 479–493.

22. Individuation in Jung's theories: Jung (6), §§ 266–269, pp. 171–172; Jung (5), §§ 757–762, pp. 448–450; individuation in the analytical psychology: Edinger (1), pp. 4–7; God in us: Jung (6), § 399, p. 236; detachment from emotional ties: Jung (2), 327–328. Jung's interpretations on religion can be found in nearly all of his writings which I use as my sources. The same theme appears also in both works by Edinger which are listed in the bibliography.

23. The expression "the root of David" actually means 'the scion or the branch from the root.' Other Bible translations, in fact, instead of the expression "the Root of David" use, for example, expressions "the great descendent of David" (Today's English Version), and "the Scion of David" (The New English Bible). The expression is probably derived from the many instances in the Old Testament, particularly Isa 11:1. Jesus was descendant of David and he was called the son of David: Matt. 1:1–3, 6, 17. Lion in the Indian symbolism: Bhagavadgita (1), X:30, p. 527, and e.g. Vivekananda (2), p. 253.

24. The meanings of the universal Self and the basic vibrations of the universe will become more clear toward the end of Revelation through different symbols, the universal Self in the forms of the child and the Lamb, and the basic vibration in the form of the rider of the white horse (see particularly chapters 12 and 19).

25. John 1:29; 1:36; 1 Cor. 5:7.

26. The Lamb symbolism in Revelation as part of the creation act can perhaps be understood also through the more general mythical associations in Christianity. The Lamb in Revelation, as a mythical image, is, because of its horns, much like the ram, which in mythical associations is the male sheep with horns and capable of impregnation.

The ram, in ancient myths, was held in high regard, as it was associated with impregnation and therefore with creative power in general. For example, in the ancient Egyptian mythology, the highest divinity, which varied over time, was along with other forms depicted as a man with a ram's head. This was so also in the case of the sun-god Ra, which is probably easy to understand because of sun's power to create life. Additionally, death and resurrection were closely associated with Ra's form, even as they are associated with Christ as Lamb. Ra was thought of being a small child in the morning, a grown up at noon, and an elder in the evening, dying at the approach of the night. At night he wandered in the kingdom of death, and then he was depicted as a human figure with a ram's head, Efu Ra, traveling in a boat. But in the morning he was born again, rising up to the sky again. At times, the god Amon would blend into the sun-god. He, too, was sometimes depicted as a figure with a ram's head. (New Larousse Encyclopedia, pp. 11, 45, 48, and illustrations pp. 19, 32; Clark, pp. 256, 265; Jung (7), § 357, p. 240.)

In Christianity, Christ and ram have been associated in the sense that Augustine interpreted the ram with horns sacrificed by Abraham instead of Isaac to be Christ (Augustine (2) book XIV, chapter 32, p. 695; Gen. 22:13).

27. Isa. 53:7. The symbolism of the sacrificed Lamb in Revelation probably derives also from the ancient use of lambs as sacrificial animals, which is mentioned in the Old Testament, for example, Exod. 12:3; 12:5; 29:38.

28. For example, Yogananda (2), p. 144.

29. The shepherd parable: Matt. 18:12–13; inner Guru: Yukteswar, pp. 38–41.

30. Jung (5), §§ 748–754, pp. 443–447; Jung (8), §§ 1271–1273, pp. 540–541; Jung (9), §§ 1488–1495, pp. 656–659; Jung (10), §§ 234–235, p. 130; Jung (11), § 1641, p. 727; Jung (12), § 125, p. 70.

31. St. John of the Cross (2), pp. 327, 361–362.

32. Instead of the kings the word "kingdom," *basileia*, is used.

33. A translation of the verses Rev. 5:9–10 more faithful to the original language would be, "You [the Lamb]... have bought men for God by your blood out of every tribe and tongue and people and nation and have made them a kingdom and priests to our God, and they shall reign on the earth." In my interpretation I follow this translation.

In the original language, a kingdom is called *basileia*. The ruler of a *basileia* need not, however, be a king, but the word *basileia* is used in the New Testament, for example, for the kingdom of God. Similarly, Revelation speaks of the kingdom of Jesus and the kingdom of the beast, and in both places the kingdom is *basileia* (Rev. 1:9 and 16:10).

Interpreting on the psychological level, a kingdom refers to human consciousness in general, and that who reigns and lives in the kingdom at any particular time, reveals what kind of and what level of human consciousness is in question. In this vision, the kingdom apparently consists of priests who are devoted to God; probably this is how we are to interpret St. John's words about the Lamb having made men kingdom and priests to God. St. John uses in the first chapter of Revelation the same expression, but in the original Greek without the word 'and' (Rev. 1:6). He explains that Jesus Christ has made men *basileian, hiereis,* or a kingdom, priests, to God; that is, the kingdom and the priests here apparently refer to the same thing. This kind of kingdom of the priests appears also in another place in the Bible, as in the Exodus the Israelites are said to be "a kingdom of priests and a holy nation" of God, should they keep their covenant with Him (Exod. 19:5–6).

The kingdom of priests would symbolize the human consciousness in a pure and holy state. Expressed in the mythical language of the Bible, the human consciousness is like this before the Fall. The kingdom of priests, as a form of human consciousness, can also refer to spiritual perfection which is fulfilled in the final stages of man's cyclical evolution when he becomes a saint. In both cases, all man's characteristics—or those that he has at any particular time—are fully free from desirousness. In the symbolism of Revelation, all men are priests at that time, and the human consciousness in its totality is the kingdom of the priests.

When St. John says that the Lamb has bought men by his blood, made them priests and set them to reign the earth, he is stressing the meaning of the universal Self as the most important level of the human existence. The words are given in the vision as the reason for the Lamb to be allowed to open the seals of the scroll. In this way, St. John is pointing out that the secrets of the human existence must be solved from the basis of the most fundamental level, the universal Self. Additionally, I believe that St. John has phrased his words so that they suit specifically to this place in Revelation: his words reflect the early stages of man's creation, and due to the cyclic nature of man's evolution, the corresponding stages of the return journey. Part of the words fit better to the creation act and part of them to the return journey.

Applied to the creation act, the fact that the Lamb has made man a kingdom and priests, emphasizes the importance of Lamb in the creation of man, even as according to Paul all things were created through Christ. The reference to Lamb's blood means the assumption in the metaphysical-mythical human image that the universal Self through its power gives life to man's other levels of being: man's superficial side receives its strength from the level of the universal Self. (This thought becomes more evident in the 13th chapter.) The 'power,' or blood, of the universal Self is love, and the meaning of blood as love becomes clear already in the next chapter.

Applied to the return journey, the same words emphasize that the Lamb or the universal Self has an important liberating and guiding role on man's return journey in the form of intuition and spiritual love. (This thought will become more clear later, among others, in chapters 12 and 13.) Buying from the land means, in this context, liberation from desirous conscious thinking and activity, and reigning on the earth refers to the new land which St. John sees in the end of the Book of Revelation and which symbolizes "the newness of sense" or man's consciousness and physical being purified from desirousness. (I will return to these thoughts in the concluding chapters.)

34. New Larousse Encyclopedia, p. 369 (Krishna's play). *Kantele* is an old Finnish instrument resembling a psaltery and a zither.

35. See note 31 of chapter 4 and my interpretation of angels in the end of this chapter.

36. Matarasso, p. 9.

37. Moody (2), pp. 58–63.

38. See note 31 in chapter 4.

39. Because Revelation is a religious myth, the angels in St. John's worldview probably have also a metaphysical side independent of man's experiences. In other words, the angels are spirits included in religious worldviews. In my interpretation, I try to focus as much as possible on the level of experience, and therefore I interpret the angels as intuition.

40. The second form of intuition I mention is called in Christian literature, among others, an intellectual vision (see note 2 of the introduction). The kind of experience I mention last is described, for example, in Yogananda (1), p. 272; see also op. cit., p. 476.

6th chapter

1. For example, Vivekananda (3), pp. 160–163; Yogananda (3), p. 264; Sivananda, pp. 30–34, 36–38, 52–54. These matters will become more clear in following chapters, particularly in chapters 9, 12, 16, and 22.

2. Sivananda, pp. 32, 36–38; Yogananda (3), pp. 263–265; Yogananda (1), pp. 401–412; Avalon, pp. 54–56, 115. There are a number of variations on the theories I touch on in the text. At times, also an etheric or energy body is differentiated between the physical and astral bodies. Then the astral body denotes mainly that level of human being through which man experiences feelings.

3. Vivekananda (4), p. 45; Avalon, pp. 253, 295; Yogananda (3), p. 164.

4. Gen. 1:26–27; 2:7.

5. Origen, pp. 24–25.

6. Gen. 2:8–10; The Art of Prayer, p. 180.

7. Gen. 3:17.

8. Gen. 3:7 (figtree); Gen. 3:24 (the way to the tree of life); the interpretation of the Fall will become more clear in chapters 9 and 12.

9. Yogananda (1), pp. 169–170; Yogananda (4), p. 4n.

10. Smend, pp. 86–87.

11. For example, Yogananda (1), pp. 158n, 358n.

12. Yukteswar, pp. 14–15; Yogananda (1), p. 158n. Cayce spoke of glands and not of energy centers, but the glands he referred to, compare closely to the energy centers of the Oriental yoga theory (see e.g. Irion, pp. 11–14). Chakras as keys to interpreting Revelation are also mentioned briefly in Tansley, pp. 84–85.

13. We might expect that St. John would see seven riders and thus parallel the cosmic energy or the number of the torches in heaven, but he does not. He describes the descent of the cosmic energy down to the microcosm or to man's chakras through four 'elements.' This is how the matter is presented also in the Oriental theory, where five or four (see the following note under Yogananda) cosmic energies are differentiated, but according to how strongly these energy forms are represented on different levels, there are seven energy *levels* which are differentiated in the macrocosm and microcosm. Physical man must, of course, draw energy also from 'earthly' sources or food.

14. For the Indian symbolism see Yogananda (3), p. 264n, and for Chinese beliefs, for example, Tibetan Yoga and Secret Doctrines, p. xxviii n.

15. The rider of the white horse appears in chapter 19.

16. Sivananda, p. 46.

17. The meaning of red and white can be found, for example, in Isa. 1:18. For the kings see chapter 5 and for the colors of the chakras Sivananda, pp. 41, 44.

18. Gen. 3:17. The mythical meaning of the sword appearing in the chapter becomes clearer and also more multifaceted partly already in this chapter, and later in chapters 13 and 19.

19. Zech. 9:17. The symbolism of the crushing of the fruit will become more clear in chapter 14. I referred to the mythical meanings of woman and man in chapter 5.

20. Sivananda, pp. 43–44.

21. The ethics of power, justice, and love have been presented, for example, in the work Tillich: Love, Power and Justice. In the Oriental religion, the four paths of liberation are more specifically karma yoga or the path of action; jnana yoga or the path of wisdom or knowledge; bhakti yoga or the path of love; and raja yoga or the path of yoga or the royal path. Each path has different stages of evolution and different characteristics. I assume here in a general sense that will power is essential on the path of action, discrimination on the path of wisdom, love on the path of love. The actual yoga path will become more clear toward the end of my book when I use Patanjali's raja yoga as a parallel to the events in Revelation.

22. Gen. 3:19.

23. St. John of the Cross (4), p. 95.

24. St. John of the Cross (3), p. 607; see also St. John of the Cross (4), pp. 98–99.

25. The idea that purification continues in the purgatory is clearly evident, for example, in the teachings of Catherine of Genoa (Catherine of Genoa, pp. 71–72, 76).

26. Yogananda (3), p. 305.

27. Bible references: Mal. 4:5; Matt. 11:14. For Gnostics see, for example, Walker, p. 63. Plato (1), 41e–42d, pp. 90–93; Plato (3), 617d–621d, pp. 504–521; Plato (4), 81–83, pp. 282–291; 107–108, pp. 368–375.

28. The sword will be interpreted as an image of intuition in chapter 19.

29. St. John of the Cross (4), p. 85.

30. For example, The Art of Prayer, p. 207.

31. Court, p. 64.

32. Sivananda, p. 41.

33. Sri Yukteswar, as well, interprets the verse in question in this way (Yukteswar, p. 32). The basic human conditions I present are common knowledge within world's religions and philosophies, for example, in the Buddhist teachings about suffering.

34. Hab. 1:13.
35. Augustine (1), book VII, § 5, pp. 76–77.
36. Eph. 4:24.
37. St. John of the Cross (2), p. 379; see also Rom. 13:12–14.
38. E.g. Jung (13), § 522, pp. 240–241, where Jung associates an earthquake dream with mental illness. Earthquake can, however, occur in dreams also more generally during times of powerful transformations.
39. Clark, pp. 41, 98.
40. E.g. New Larousse Encyclopedia, pp. 27–28.
41. As a mythical image, the moon is often associated with a woman, as the phases of the moon are like the monthly changes in a woman's body. The researchers often maintain that the moon is one of the basic images in a matriarchal culture (for example, Erich Neumann, pp. 55–57). The connection between the moon and the woman strengthens the meanings of subconscious and value experience associated with the moon, because a woman's womb is like the subconscious, giving birth to new experiences and realizations even as a child is born into the world from the womb. A woman as a mythical image represents also a value experience because woman's vessel-like body can open and receive, even as a human being engrossed in a value experience must remain open and receptive.
42. Matt. 21:19; Jer. 24:1–10; 29:17. Prov. 27:18.
43. Bhagavadgita (1), II:67, p. 153.
44. Exod. 19:18–20; 24:16–18.
45. New Larousse Encyclopedia, p. 172.
46. St. John of the Cross (3), p. 587.

7th chapter

1. Bhagavadgita (1), VI:19, p. 328. Wind as the movement of the mind appeared in the previous chapter.
2. Tree and plant symbolism was explained in chapters 4 and 6.
3. For mandala symbolism see chapter 4.
4. St. Teresa of Avila (2), p. 346.

5. St. Teresa of Avila (2), pp. 317, 345, 439; see also e.g. Gilson, pp. 45, 133. St. John of the Cross (4), p. 98. I explain the meaning of a divine union in chapter 11.

6. Ezek. 40:16, 26, 31, 34, 37; 41:18–20, 25–26. There were palms as ornaments also in Salomon's temple (1 Kgs. 6:29; 7:36; 2 Chr. 3:5). For palms as a symbol of victory see, for example, Cirlot, p. 249.

7. See also e.g. Jung (14), § 128, pp. 74–75.

8. The saying in the original language is *apo anatolēs hēliou*.

9. E.g. Brother Lawrence, pp. 36, 41.

10. Eckhart (2), p. 13; see also op. cit., p. 66. St. Thérèse of Lisieux compares the soul to a tent which must remain empty so that God can enter (St. Thérèse of Liseux, p. 202).

11. The tabernacle: Exod. chapters 25–40, esp. Exod. chapter 36, 40:36–38.

8th chapter

1. Julian of Norwich, chapter 56, p. 161 (lofty deeps); Eckhart (2), pp. 332–333 (superessential nothingness). Yogananda (1), p. 412 uses the expression "lightless light, darkless dark."

2. For Gregory the Great and William of Saint-Thierry see Gilson, pp. 104 (note 147), 208, 219 (note 21). The original writings by Gregory the Great and William of Saint-Thierry are included in the series Patrologia latina, the work by Gregory the Great in the part 76 (II:14, p. 957), and the work by William of Saint-Thierry in part 184 (IV:10, p. 372).

3. Gilson, pp. 104–105. The original source: St. Bernard of Clairvaux (1), VII:21, p. 953; compare 2. Cor. 12:4. The quote would fit in better with the later events in Revelation, but I present it here because St. Bernard applies in it the symbolism of this chapter of Revelation. It may be strange to think that the level of consciousness symbolized by heaven, or the superconscious, would not always be in a silent state. This probably has a natural explanation: persons experience the high states first, as if, mixed in with the duality of the ego-consciousness. Not before the movements of the ego-consciousness calm down completely will there be silence also on the level of the superconscious.

4. St. Teresa of Avila (2), pp. 418–420.

5. Op. cit., p. 419.

6. Wittgenstein, § 6.45, pp. 148–149.

7. Engelmann, p. 6. I emphasize that this is my own interpretation. The quote is from a letter Wittgenstein sent to Paul Engelmann on April 9, 1917. In the letter, Wittgenstein first discusses briefly what cannot be expressed in words. In the end, Wittgenstein refers to Engelmann's changing states of mind and explains that life is but a dream. I understand this so that the normal life, which is composed of changing states of mind, is a dream, whereas 'mystical' cannot be expressed in words. Tractatus is based on the notes from the period during which the letter was written (Kenny, p. 3).

8. Humphreys, pp. 104–105.

9. Blyth, pp. 53, 63; see also op cit., pp. 46, 56.

10. The sound of the trumpet: e.g. Exod. 19:16–19. Artemidorus, book I, § 56, p. 45.

11. See note 31 in chapter 4. The chakra theory may help to explain also the expression "there was silence in heaven," used by St. John in Rev. 8:1, which I interpreted to describe a high state of consciousness. Because only the chakras lower than sahasrara are understood to emanate the Om-sound, there is a literal soundlessness in the consciousness during such strongly transformed states wherein the life energy has moved into the sahasrara. Within Christianity, St. Teresa of Avila tells that the "disturbing sounds" she hears in her head cease when the prayer includes suspension of the abilities of the soul, in other words, in a strongly transformed state of consciousness (St. Teresa of Avila (2), pp. 320–321).

12. The incense smoke appears already in chapter 5. The smoke rising to God, which happens in this eighth chapter, also symbolizes well the thought that God hears the prayer.

13. Exod. 9:24.

14. St. John of the Cross (2), p. 355. Bhagavadgita (1), IV:19, p. 242.

15. Sivananda, pp. xx–xxi; Yogananda (3), pp. 363–369.

16. Bhagavadgita (1), IV:36, p. 265. For the boat see also Jung (4), § 305, p. 202.

17. The stars were interpreted toward the end of chapter 6. They appear in the verse Rev. 6:13.

18. Jer. 23:15; Lam. 3:15; Amos 5:7.

19. The eagle was Zeus' insignia, and sometimes Zeus himself became an eagle in myths. Because Zeus carried out his will with the help of the eagle, we can probably say that the eagle functioned also as Zeus' messenger or mediator. I believe, however, that the eagle in Greek myths associated with Zeus symbolizes more broadly high value experiences rather than just intuition. For example, New Larousse Encyclopedia, pp. 98, 101, 138. For eagle see more generally, for example, Cirlot, p. 91, and Jung (4), § 305, pp. 201–202.

20. For example, in the Finnish Folk Poems Louhi has a threatening meaning when she, as a black eagle, steals the Sampo (for example, Finnish Folk Poems (3), poem 680, p. 496). There are, however, several variations of these poems; not all of them involve a black eagle. Interpreting in a more general way, black represents that which man is not conscious of; and foreign, unknown things are often experienced threatening. Here the eagle illustrates that St. John must realize and experience more: he must change, and the change is painful.

9th chapter

1. For symbolism of air see chapter 4.

2. Bonaventure (2), p. 277; Yogananda (1), pp. 108–109.

3. Jung (12), § 291, p. 186.

4. E.g. Exod. 10:1–19.

5. Dante, p. 11 (canto 3).

6. For Greek mythology see, e.g. Murray, pp. 290, 298; for Egypt, e.g. New Larousse Encyclopedia, p. 19. The Bible reference Gen. 3:15. Jung has researched the two first mentioned myths in Jung (7), §§ 450–456, pp. 293–298.

7. Scorpion's meaning as a whip with spikes, a lash, can be found in the English Bible translations. King James translation says, "I will chastise you with scorpions", but The New English Bible says in the same place, "I will use the lash" (1 Kgs. 12:11, 14).

8. Jer. 46:23.

9. St. John of the Cross (4), p. 92.

10. Samson's long hair was also a cultural symbol. He was a Nazirite who was not supposed to cut his hair (Judg. 13:5; 16:17).

11. Ps. 40:12.

12. Homer (1) book 1, verse 47 and verses 49–52, p. 2; New Larousse Encyclopedia, p. 109 (the origin of the name Apollo).

13. Encyclopedia Britannica, p. 120. According to this tradition, joy is associated with Apollo differently from the Apollyon of Revelation.

14. Encyclopedia Britannica, p. 121.

15. For the altar symbolism see chapters 6 and 8.

16. Gen. 2:10–14.

17. Jer. 2:13; 2:18; see also Isa. 8:7. The meaning of a strange land as a symbol for ego-consciousness was explained briefly in chapter 7. Sihor appears to occur as Nile in the verse Isa. 23:3. Sihor, in the Old Testament, is clearly associated with Egypt, but Bible researchers do not agree about the exact meaning of Sihor.

18. Bible reference Gen. 15:18. River symbolism in yoga theory: Sivananda, p. 34.

19. See chapter 4, note 31; and Science Says, p. 26; Moody (2), pp. 30–33; Yogananda (3), p. 214n.

20. Yogananda (1), p. 238; Sivananda, pp. 71–72, 75.

21. Bible reference Isa. 34:9. St. John of the Cross (3), p. 587.

22. St. John of the Cross (4), p. 83.

23. Disapproving attitude: Gal. 5:20. Accepting attitude: Exod. 7:3–12.

24. Hos. 1:2.

25. St. Teresa of Avila (2), p. 338.

26. John 10:10.

10th chapter

1. Gen. 9:9–17.

2. Heb. 8:10–11.

3. The idea that speaking about the deepest secrets of life is not sufficient nor is it possible, is universal. I referred to it already in chapter 8. The old Chinese Tao Tê Ching points that out in the first few lines, "The Tao, that can be expressed is not the eternal Tao" (Tao Tê Ching, § 1, p.17).

4. Cumont, pp. 26, 190–191. For example, St. Teresa of Avila often uses eating as a parable; see e.g. Teresa of Avila (3), pp. 128, 130, 165.

5. St. John uses in this vision mostly the word *biblaridion*, the little book, whereas in the fifth chapter he used the word *biblion*, scroll. In the verse 10:8 he, however, uses the word *biblion* again, indicating that he apparently does not think of the book and the scroll very different from each other. In using the word *biblaridion*, the little book, St. John perhaps emphasizes that the level now in question is only the microcosm not the macrocosm, which is the alternative meaning I gave for the scroll in the fifth chapter. The smallness of the book may be due also to St. John already having read some of the scroll while the seals were being opened. Therefore, the contents of the scroll have been, as if, reduced.

6. The Indian literature presents several variations of the subject; sometimes honey can mean also more sensual enjoyment. Variations on the parable can be found, among others, in Yogananda (2), pp. 125, 132, 149.

11th chapter

1. Sackcloth: e.g. Gen 37:34; Jonah 3:5–8; Matt. 11:21.

2. Oil symbolism was discussed in chapter 6.

3. For lampstands see chapter 6.

4. John 2:1–11.

5. E.g. New Larousse Encyclopedia, pp. 16–20; Gen. 4:1–8.

6. Steiner, pp. 182–185; Jung (12), §§ 13–14, p. 8.

7. Gen. 19:1–25.

8. New Larousse Encyclopedia, pp. 16–17 (Osiris myth); op. cit., pp. 152–155 (Kore myth).

9. E.g. Räisänen, pp. 45, 67–69.

10. Jung (1), § 661, p. 418, § 689, p. 430.

11. Eckhart (1), p. 138; Teresa of Calcutta (1), pp. 73–74. In their entirety, Eckhart's and Mother Teresa's understandings of the meaning of Jesus' death are of course multifaceted; see e.g. Eckhart (2), pp. 140–141.

12. For the symbolism of the number ten see chapters 4 and 9. A tenth of the city can also depict just a small portion of St. John's general attitude in life.

Revelation describes later the destruction of the city of Babylon, which according to my interpretation means the death of St. John's own self or ego. The destruction of the city described here denotes the beginning of this death of the ego.

13. St. John of the Cross (3), pp. 582–584.

14. Exod. 30:6; Num. 7:89.

15. 1 Kgs. 8:4.

16. The new covenant in the New Testament is described with the words I already quoted in chapter 10, "None of them shall teach his neighbour, and none his brother, saying, 'Know the Lord,' for all shall know Me, from the least of them to the greatest of them'" (Heb. 8:11).

17. Spinoza, part V, prop. 33, prop. 35, and prop. 36, pp. 263–265. I am not certain that the way Spinoza speaks of intellectual loving of God should compare exactly to the state of bliss I speak of, but Spinoza does explain that intellectual loving of God is same love with which God loves himself, and that God rejoices in his infinite perfection. I will return to the Indian samadhi terminology in the concluding chapters. The expression, "an experience in cosmic consciousness," is used, for example, by Paramahansa Yogananda in relating a personal experience, Yogananda (1), pp. 141–145.

18. Bonaventure (1), pp. 94, 106–109.

19. St. John of the Cross (2), p. 338 (the quote from Jonah: Jonah 2:5); St. John of the Cross (4), p. 84 (the arc of the covenant).

20. St. Teresa of Avila (2), pp. 336–337, and after the last ellipsis, p. 339.

21. St. Teresa of Avila (2), p. 355.

22. Yogananda (1), pp. 142–143.

23. Brunton, pp. 304–305.

24. The earthquake has appeared earlier in the verses Rev. 6:12; 8:5; 11:13. I interpreted the earthquake more specifically in chapter 6. I interpreted hail when it appeared in the verse Rev. 8:7.

12th chapter

1. For example, Pagels, pp. 64–65 (Gnostics); New Larousse Encyclopedia, p. 37 (Egyptian mythology); Liu Hua Yang, pp. 122–123 (Chinese text). The latter work, in fact, says in the same place that a child being born is not physical but is composed of man's higher and more spiritual life energy.

2. The quote from Brunton appeared in the end of the previous, or 11th, chapter. The conception of Virgin Mary is described in the Bible in Matt. 1:18–20 and Luke 1:34–35.

3. St. Teresa of Avila (2), p. 343.

4. Brunton, pp. 217–218.

5. Eckhart (1), p. 67.

6. Jung (1), § 714, p. 442.

7. The Art of Prayer, p. 117 (Theophan the Recluse); New Larousse Encyclopedia, p. 116 (Leto myth).

8. Diamond body as a mythical image will be discussed in greater detail in chapter 21.

9. Sivananda, p. 34; see also chapter 6.

10. For yoga theory see Vivekananda (4), pp. 46, 52. Among the Christian mystics, at least St. Teresa of Avila explained that the most spiritual part of the soul is located on top of the head (St. Teresa of Avila (2), p. 320). Compare this place in Revelation to the earlier verses Rev. 6:2; 9:7; 10:1.

11. I used this saying from St. Teresa as an example in chapter 11 (see note 21, chapter 11).

12. Plato (1), 49a, pp. 112–113, 50d, pp. 116–119. The images about the creation of the world imparted by St. John's vision and Plato's Timaeus are not completely comparable, although they have many similarities.

13. Yogananda (3), p. 334.

14. Col. 1:15; see also chapter 5.

15. St. Bernard of Clairvaux (2), pp. 44–46; see also Gilson, pp. 95–96.

16. Clark, p. 50. The Egyptian original snake does not, however, yield a single explanation; over time, in different texts, it appears from highest divinity to the enemy of divinity (see op. cit., pp. 50–52).

17. Purge, pp. 31–32; New Larousse Encyclopedia, p. 362; for mythical snakes more generally see, for example, Huxley's work The Dragon, and New Larousse Encyclopedia, pp. 49, 340, 363.

18. See note 3 chapter 6, and additionally, among others, Vivekananda (2), p. 253, and Avalon, pp. 20–21.

19. Vivekananda (3), p. 164; Sivananda, pp. 52–54; Avalon, p. 1. Avalon speaks also of the connections between kundalini energy and cosmic energy, op. cit., pp. 36–39.

20. The snake in the head-dresses of the Egyptian pharaohs and also more generally in the head-dresses of the royalty, appears to have been a rule at least during the years 1580–1200 B.C., see for example the illustrations in Lange and Hirmer. See also Purce, illustration no. 8; Purce gives in the caption a similar explanation for the snake coming out of the pharaoh's head-dress as I do. For Asclepius see e.g. New Larousse Encyclopedia, p. 162 (illustration) and p. 163, also Murray pp. 178–180 and illustration XXXI. Asclepius' staff would be, as if, the tree of life depicted with the help of the snake.

21. New Larousse Encyclopedia, p. 207; Jung (4), illustration 165, p. 326; Purce, illustration 11 with its caption; Avalon, pp. 21, 21n. Caduceus staff has been a widely used symbol, see for example, Cook, pp. 114–115.

22. I Ching, pp. 85, 87; see also Huxley, p. 54.

23. Cumont, pp. 105–110. The interpretations I present in the text are, however, my own.

24. Sri Yukteswar's interpretation has been presented in Yogananda (1), pp. 169–171. Its basic idea is that the coiled kundalini stimulates the sexual energy. This interpretation does not involve the ideas about the Fall of the snake and its curse, which I suggest in the text.

25. Sivananda, pp. 52–54.

26. Gen. 3:14.

27. Matt. 10:16; 23:33. See also e.g. John 3:14.

28. My suggestion is loosely based on the Oriental philosophy, see for example Yogananda (3), p. 280; compare also Jung (15), § 290, p. 196.

29. For example, Harper's Bible Dictionary, pp. 908–909; 1 Chr. 21:11 (adversary); Gen. 3:15 (enmity, more precisely, persecution is placed between the snake and the wife); John 8:44.

30. Job 1:6; Jung (1), §§ 649–654, pp. 409–412; Davidson, pp. 261–262 (the origin of Satan). Gen. 3:1 (the origin of the snake).

31. Yogananda (3), p. 280; Yogananda (1), p. 275n.

32. Yukteswar, p. 4.

33. Tao Tê Ching, § 2, p. 18.

34. Bhagavadgita (1), II:28, p. 109; Purge, illustration 1.

35. Bhagavadgita (1), XI:23–30, 32, pp. 557–563. Apparently, Gnostics also had similar emphasis as the Indian philosophical beliefs I present in the text. They differentiated between the original divinity and the creator, possibly in an effort to make a difference, on the one hand, between the act of creating and the creation, which include differentiation between good and bad, and on the other, the original divinity. The Gnostics expressed this idea, among others, so that sometimes the God of Israel was seen as a creator next to the mother Sofia, but at the same time it was pointed out that he was a lower god and not the original divinity (Pagels, pp. 3–39, 59, 64–65, 69–70).

This viewpoint may partly explain also the well-known concept maintained by some of the Gnostics that Satan, archangel Satanael, was the creator of the world (e.g. Walker, pp. 38, 41). Additionally, the core of Gnostics' teachings was the thought that man is to manifest in himself a deeply spiritual wisdom based on experience, *gnōsis*, which would mean, at the same time, living divinity (Pagels, pp. 161–162). I feel that the Gnostics, who lived during the times Revelation was written, pondering the nature of the original divinity, the creation of the world, and Satan's character, supports my interpretation of these matters being important to St. John.

36. Vivekananda (5), pp. 463–474, esp. pp. 464, 470; Vivekananda (1), pp. 94–95; Yogananda (1), pp. 474–477.

37. The meaning of the "eternal law", or the Oriental law of karma, as the innermost level of righteousness comes from the idea that it concerns—in the sense that I have presented it in this chapter—specifically man's inner life. The Oriental literature, however, uses the law of karma often to explain also man's outward life. But I take this to mean that man first changes himself inwardly, and this inner change will have an outward effect, for example, so that man will be able to create new circumstances for himself, or that man will, in the next life, incarnate into new circumstances according to his inner karma (see chapter 20). These two kinds of righteousness—outer and inner—are connected in many ways. Should someone, for example, explain his indifference to social justice by saying that those with difficulties are only dealing with their own karma, he will unequivocally change himself to a cold and

thus to an unhappy human being according to the law of karma. The Oriental law of karma is many-sided, including also the concept of mass karma.

38. Yukteswar, p. 6, and illustration p. 8.

39. For example, Gaster, p. 373.

40. For redness see also Court, pp. 146–147.

41. Zech. 3:1; Job 2:1.

42. Matt. 2:1–16; New Larousse Encyclopedia, p. 369.

43. E.g. Luke 1:80; 3:2; Mark 1:13; St. John of the Cross (2), p. 314.

44. Exod. 16; see also e.g. St. John of the Cross (2), p. 314.

45. Hindu Myths, pp. 278–280; for Heracles see New Larousse Encyclopedia, p. 170 (Hercules is the Latinised form of Heracles).

46. Hindu Myths, p. 280; the sea that the demons in this Hindu myth are exiled into, is the sea surrounding the mythical land, op. cit., p. 273.

47. For example, Hammer, p. 838.

48. New Larousse Encyclopedia, p. 116 (Leto myth). Haavio parallels the events in the Egyptian Osiris myth and in the Lemminkäinen tale, Haavio, pp. 240, 250, 259. The flight of Louhi or the Old Hag of the North, e.g. Finnish Folk Poems (1), poem 22, p. 45; poem 54, p. 79; for Ananta snake see New Larousse Encyclopedia, p. 367.

49. For bird and eagle symbolism see chapters 4, 6, and 8.

13th chapter

1. To reiterate, the throne is the concept and the 'content' of the throne is the content of the concept, as explained in chapter 4.

2. Yukteswar, pp. 27–29, 63.

3. For Gnostics see Pagels, p. 149; Walker, pp. 46, 164; Walker parallels the Oriental concept of avidya and the Gnostics' concept of *agnōsia*. The myth of the Fall was interpreted in chapters 6 and 12.

4. St. John of the Cross (4), p. 80.

5. For horns see chapters 5, 6, 9, and 12.

6. The symbolism of the earth was explained in chapter 4.

7. Yukteswar, p. 29.

8. The term *buddhi* has been given somewhat different meanings depending on context. I follow here Sri Yukteswar. He explains that *manas* will lead man ever deeper into the delusion and *buddhi* will lead him into liberation According to my interpretation, the idea behind Revelation is that there are two opposite forces at work in man: the universal Self and the delusion. Thus, man's abilities and characteristics form a continuum according to how well they penetrate the power of delusion. In the Indian philosophy, man's characteristics are described also with words *sattva, rajas,* and *tamas, sattva* meaning the most pure and *tamas* the most delusory; along with the words *buddhi* and *manas*, the expressions *sattwa* and *anandatwa* are used in India to denote the opposite ends of the scale. (Yukteswar, pp. 7, 9).

9. E.g. Vivekananda (3), pp. 201, 299–301; Ramana Maharshi, p. 24 (I used this quote in chapter 5).

10. For Christian beliefs, e.g., Gilson, pp. 44–45, and for Oriental understanding, e.g., Daya Mata, pp. 39, 198.

11. Ramana Maharsi, p. 121.

12. I explained Jung's concept of ego briefly in chapter 5. Freud presented his views e.g., in Freud (1), pp. 76–82, esp. p. 81. According to Freud ego was man's common sense principle that considered the outer world, and part of its 'realm' could remain subconscious.

13. For example, Freud (2), pp. 146–157. For more general religious philosophical views see, e.g., Hegel, pp. 328–394, and Voltaire, p. 58.

14. Ramana Maharsi, pp. 21, 121.

15. For Jungian psychological views see chapter 5. Freud's theory, e.g. Freud (1), pp. 66–74, 79–81.

16. I interpret the expression "in the sight of the beast" appearing in this verse (Rev. 13:14) only here in the note. Greek language uses the preposition *enōpion*, and therefore the translation "in the sight" is not the only possible one. Actually, the same expression appeared already in the verse Rev. 13:12, where the New King James version translates it with words "in his [the first beast] presence". Should we follow this translation, the context is logical. In terms of modern psychology, the conscious and subconscious levels are both present, and the conscious level draws strength from the subconscious level. We could also say that the more narrow form of the delusion receives strength from the broader and more basic form of the delusion.

In the verse Rev. 13:12 it is also said that the beast rising from the earth causes men to worship the beast rising from the sea. St. John emphasizes here the power of the delusion. Man's specific abilities, symbolized in Revelation by men, are submitted to the power of delusion, they start, as if, to worship the beast.

17. Charles, pp. 355–357. Charles differentiates between three versions, but the second and the third differ only by one word.

18. Gal. 6:7.

19. Matt. 26:52.

20. Jer. 15:2. See also Jer. 43:11–12.

21. Grace and man's own action: e.g. Catherine of Genoa, p. 33; The Art of Prayer, pp. 132–134; Ramana Maharshi, pp. 104–105.

22. Dan. 7:1, 3–7.

23. Materiality, which the bear symbolizes along with the subconscious, does not explain the whole nature of delusion. Delusion means essentially a wrong order of values, or thinking of that which is unessential as essential. Man can be free from attachment to materiality, although he, at the same time, acts in the material world. (For more on this thought see the concluding chapters.)

24. Lion's jaw as the threatening mouth of the beast appeared in chapter 9. For the meaning of the lion as a symbol for the basic energy and the level of high spiritual reality, see chapters 4, 5, and 6.

25. Yogananda (1), p. 145. The Greek word in question is *plēgē* meaning a blow, scar, and plague. Generally, it has been translated as plague in Revelation. (For its interpretation see also Court, pp. 132–133.) In interpreting the place, I rely on the idea that the beast symbolizes man's own ego-consciousness. The bliss experience, like a blow, 'stuns' the delusory consciousness. Therefore, from the beast's point of view, bliss experience is like a plague.

26. Eckhart (1), p. 56.

27. Bowman (2), pp. 381–382; Charles, pp. 366–367. See Irenaeus' views also in Court, pp. 5–6.

28. Tolstoy, pp. 337–339. Tolstoy allows Pierre Bezuhov's finding of the connection between the numbers of his and the beast's names awaken in Bezuhov expectation for heroism and happiness. Essential, however, is that man is brought to ponder what the number of the beast's name means in his own case.

29. The beast's number in some of the manuscripts of Revelation is 616 (Bowman (2) pp. 381–382). This, too, is easily interpreted symbolically. Man is tied to constant changes derived from conflicts, and this is symbolized

by the number six. He can live also oneness received from value experiences symbolized by the number one, but tied to the desires and the delusion he must soon return to the conflicts and changes caused by them. Paraphrasing Plato, we might say that man is like a homeless wanderer, Eros, who quickly looses the things he acquires, or the momentary satisfaction, and must again begin his travels as a poor wanderer (Plato (5), 203c–e, pp. 180–181). Because the number one appears along the six in this version of the beast's number, this relates to the light half of the Buddhist wheel of life.

30. Gilson, pp. 44–45, 58; St. Bernard of Clairvaux (3), p. 985.

31. Illustrations of the wheel of life can be found, for example, in Dagyab, figure 6; Lauf, figure 59 (see also text op. cit., pp. 140–143); Jung (3), figure 3 (see also text op. cit., § 644, p. 360).

14th chapter

1. E.g. Isa. 1:27; Jer. 14:19; Amos 6:1; Hebr. 12:22.

2. Avalon, p. 147.

3. St. John of the Cross (3), pp. 602–603; see also Bonaventure (1), pp. 89, 113.

4. E.g. Daya Mata, p. 172.

5. Eckhart (1), p. 71; Eckhart (2), pp. 139, 142. I explained the symbolism of the union on the level of the ego in chapter 9 clarifying it with a quote from St. Teresa; see note 25, chapter 9.

6. St. Teresa of Avila (2), e.g. pp. 283, 338, 421, 441. See also Eckhart (1), p. 5.

7. Eckhart does not speak of this explicitly, but it becomes clear in Eckhart (1), p. 191, and Eckhart (2), p. 184.

8. For the symbolism of exile and the strange lands see chapters 7 and 9.

9. The Art of Prayer, p. 73.

10. For fornication symbolism see chapter 9.

11. The chapter quotes in order of appearance: St. John of the Cross (2), p. 320; St. John of the Cross (3), p. 606; St. John of the Cross (2), pp. 323, 318, 311.

12. Bible references: John 5:27; Luke 17:30, 33.

13. For example, Dan. 7:13; Mark 13:26; 14:62.

14. For an explanation on the meaning of the word *stephanos* see note 42, chapter 4.

15. Wine in the meaning of man's core-essence was introduced in chapter 6.

16. St. John of the Cross (2), pp. 321–322.

17. Op. cit., pp. 311–318.

18. Op. cit., pp. 322, 313–324.

19. Op. cit,. p. 337.

20. Op. cit., p. 337; for God's wrath see also chapter 6.

21. Op. cit., p. 336.

22. Op. cit., p. 337.

23. Blood symbolism was discussed in chapters 6, 7, 8, and 11.

24. St. Teresa of Avila (2), pp. 323–324.

25. Teresa of Avila (4), p. 107. The horse can be probably interpreted here also as man's energy, although, for the sake of simplicity, I have used in the text only the word 'consciousness'.

15th chapter

1. St. John of the Cross (2), p. 326.

2. The quote from Wittgenstein appeared in chapter 8, see note 7 of that chapter; Bhagavadgita (1), II:69, pp. 154–155. In the Oriental literature, the sea of *samsara* is often used in an imprecise meaning. If the sea of samsara refers to the *entire* realm of delusion, the parallel between the sea of glass in Revelation and the sea of samsara is not, in this chapter, complete. St. John merely speaks of those victorious over the beast, and they have not yet accomplished the victory over the dragon, which illustrates the broader meaning of the delusion. For the literal meaning of samsara, see e.g. Yogananda (1), p. 471.

3. Bhagavadgita (1), III:39, p. 206.

4. St. John of the Cross (2), pp. 318–319.

5. Op. cit., p. 335.

6. The bowl symbolism was explained in chapter 5. St. John tells also that the angels leaving the temple are clothed in pure bright linen and have their chests girded with golden bands (Rev. 15:6). The pure, bright clothing of the angels reflect the purity of St. John's consciousness and particularly that of his intuition. (For the symbolism of white clothing see, for example, chapters 6 and 7, and later chapter 19.) The golden bands on the angels' chests probably emphasize that the love burning in St. John's chest is 'refined' to gold. (A golden band appears already in the verse Rev. 1:13.) I doubt that the bands here would have a meaning of being bound, although that, too, could be possible, because St. John's spiritual intuition is not yet completely liberated.

7. St. John of the Cross (2), p. 336.

8. Op. cit., p. 335.

9. Op. cit., p. 336.

16th chapter

1. The plagues associated with the trumpet blows were presented in chapters 8, 9, and 11. These, as well as the bowl plagues, parallel also the Egyptian plagues described in the Old Testament and other apocalyptic excerpts of the New Testament (see Court, pp. 50–54, 75–77).

2. St. John of the Cross (2), e.g. pp. 295, 334.

3. St. John of the Cross (3), p. 586.

4. The connection between love and agony was explained already in chapter 8 in discussing the hail mixed with blood.

5. St. John of the Cross (2), pp. 354–355; quote p. 354.

6. River and spring symbolism was explained in chapter 8.

7. St. John of the Cross (2), pp. 352–353.

8. I use as my source Patanjali's yoga sutras, which are included in complete works by Vivekananda in Sanskrit and English translations including Vivekananda's interpretations. This is the work Vivekananda (3) in the bibliography. Nevertheless, I mention in parenthesis also Patajali's most important yoga sutra numbers after the page numbers from Vivekananda's work. Although we don't know with certainty when Patajali lived, he is often placed to the second century B.C. (for example, Yogananda (1), pp. 224–225, 224n).

For matters mentioned in the text see Vivekananda (3), pp. 189–190; Sivananda, pp. 72–74. I presented an interpretation on rivers and springs based on yoga theory in chapter 8.

9. The verses Rev. 16:5–7, "And I heard the angel of the waters saying: 'You are righteous, O Lord, the one who is and was and who is to be, because you have judged these things. For they have shed the blood of saints and prophets, and you have given them blood to drink. For it is their just due.' And I heard another from the altar saying, 'Even so, Lord God Almighty, true and righteous are your judgments.'" These words appear after men have received wounds, and the sea, the rivers and the springs have become blood. I feel that the words repeat these early events of the chapter. When "they," that is, apparently men, have shed the blood of the holy, St. John has wounded himself with his self-knowledge, so that his deeper and inner level, the Self or the blood, has flown forth. The change means, at the same time, St. John's deepening so that also the more superficial levels symbolized by men are changed. They must drink blood and then they, too, are to learn to love. In the verses, St. John calls his experience a judgment. And a judgment is a fitting word because the death of the ego brought about by the change has been painful. But that experience has also been good, and therefore it is *God's* judgment.

10. St. John of the Cross (2), p. 339.

11. Op. cit., p. 333.

12. The river Euphrates was interpreted in chapter 9.

13. St. John of the Cross (2), pp. 333, 321.

14. Op. cit., p. 325.

15. Op. cit., p. 333.

16. Op. cit., pp. 333–334.

17. Vivekananda (3), pp. 137, 171, 174.

18. Athanasius, pp. 27–29.

19. St. John of the Cross (2), pp. 384–385, 328.

20. Tibet's Great Yogi Milarepa, pp. 235, 238. For meeting with the demon see also, for example, Allione, pp. 144, 146–148.

21. For example, C.G. Jung tells in his memoirs of an experience where he felt clearly the presence of several spirits and understood their 'speech.' Jung's experience, however, was not a tormenting one like the one in Revelation. (Jung (2), p. 215–216.)

22. St. Teresa of Avila (2), pp. 363–364.
23. St. John of the Cross (2), p. 328.
24. Matt. 4:8–9.
25. 2 Kgs. 23:29; 9:27; see also Judg. 5:19; 2 Chr. 35:22; Zech. 12:11.
26. St. John of the Cross (3), pp. 587–588; St. John of the Cross (2), p. 336.
27. Bhagavadgita (1), I:11, p. 40; the Indian interpretation: Shyamananda, p. 40.
28. For the symbolical meaning of clothing see chapter 6.
29. 1 Th. 5:2; see also Luke 12:36–43.
30. For the poverty of the spirit see, for example, St. John of the Cross (2), p. 334. I will return to this concept more in chapter 18.
31. St. Teresa of Avila (2), p. 364.
32. For hail see chapters 8 and 11. The hail appeared in verses Rev. 8:7; 11:19.
33. St. John of the Cross (2), p. 330. The parable presented by St. John of the Cross is based on the psalms.

17th chapter

1. Vivekananda (6), p. 17.
2. St. John of the Cross (3), pp. 638–639.
3. Yogananda (1), p. 266.
4. For example Vivekananda (6), pp. 16–17; Yogananda (5), pp. 162, 169–170. The expression "a direct and immediate experience of the supreme Truth" comes from Ramana Maharshi (Ramana Maharshi, p. 120).
5. I explained this attitude toward life a saint feels in chapter 5, where the verse Gal. 2:20 came through more clearly.
6. Irion, p. 348. Irion continues Cayce's interpretation and presents it more broadly, but that interpretation is different from my understanding. According to Irion, Babylon is a general sense of self, which develops in a child as early as at six years of age.
7. Edinger (2), p. 120

8. St. John of the Cross (4), p. 88; see also op. cit., p. 248.

9. St. Bernard of Clairvaux (2), p. 476; see also op. cit., pp. 391, 115, 164.

10. St. Gregory the Great (2), p. 235.

11. The night of the senses and the night of the spirit were mentioned in chapter 16.

12. St. Teresa of Avila (2), pp. 341–342, 421, 434–435.

13. For the individuation theory of the Jungian psychology see note 22, chapter 5; for the rest see Jung (6), §§ 377–381, pp. 226–227, §§ 389–399, pp. 231–236.

14. Ezek. 16:8, 26, 28–30, 62–63. The events I am quoting do not cover Ezekiel's entire vision of the prostitute.

15. For example, Gilson, pp. 119–123. See also Ramana Maharshi, pp. 44–53; Yogananda (1), p. 412.

16. This parable will be completed later in connection with the holy city (in chapter 21). A saint who is fully liberated from his desires can, as if, freely walk between immanence and transcendence without the door, or the self tied to the desires, closing the doorway. The doorway is then the gate opening to the holy city, and St. John does say fittingly that the gates of the holy city will never be closed.

17. St. Teresa of Avila (2), pp. 284, 287.

18. Ramana Maharsi, p. 149.

19. Op. cit., pp. 119–120.

20. I presented the wilderness as a symbol for spiritual preparation in chapter 12.

21. St. John of the Cross (2), pp. 329–331.

22. Op. cit., p. 333.

23. Isa. 1:18. Redness already appeared in chapters 6 and 12.

24. St. John of the Cross (2), pp. 332–333.

25. Op. cit., p. 333.

26. Op. cit., p. 330.

27. Op. cit., p. 332.

28. Op. cit., p. 330.

29. For example Vivekananda (2), pp. 254–255.

30. For example, The Art of Prayer, p. 129.

31. The mountain symbolism was explained in chapters 6, 8, and 14.

32. St. John of the Cross (2), p. 332.

33. The Bible reference Isa. 14:13. Interpreting the king of Babylon as Satan is also fitting; any one interpretation does not annul others. Satan interpretation is supported, among others, by the fact that the morning star Venus is kind of a harbinger of light or Lucifer. Additionally, Satan falling from the heaven can be associated with Rev. 12:9 and Luke 10:18. In the latter, Jesus says having seen Satan fall from heaven like a lightning. I will return to the king of Babylon of the Book of Isaiah in the last note of chapter 22.

34. St. John of the Cross (2), p. 332.

35. Ramana Maharshi, pp. 21, 36, 120.

36. Bhagavadgita (1), II:71, p. 157, XII:13, pp. 610–611, XVIII:53, pp. 820–821.

37. St. John of the Cross (2), p. 333.

38. Ramana Maharshi, pp. 120–121.

39. St. John of the Cross (2), pp. 333, 334, 321.

40. Op. cit., p. 337.

41. The angel prophesies to St. John also events which will follow the destruction of the prostitute. Because these angels' words only anticipate what will happen later, I interpret them here in the notes. The angel says to St. John: "[They]... give their kingdom to the beast, until the words of God are fulfilled" (Rev. 17:17). It is not clear who "they" are. "They" can mean the beast's horns or the peoples, multitudes, and nations or all of these. The general meaning of the words is, however, easily understood. Once the prostitute has been destroyed, the beast who eats the prostitute will still be left. St. John will not be immediately liberated from the entire delusory consciousness, even if he were able to let go of his sense of self. He still needs to fight the victory over the beast; the complete liberation from the beast, or the delusion, means the fulfillment of God's words.

Revelation has foretold the events leading to the liberation already a few verses earlier when the angel says of the approaching battle, "These [the different mythical images associated with the beast] will make war with the Lamb, and the Lamb will overcome them" (Rev. 17:14). The battle has again two opposite sides: on the one hand, there are the different delusory attachments, and on the other, the Self. This kind of settling of a conflict, or a battle, is described in chapters 19 and 20 (Rev. 19:17–21; 20:8–9) after St. John has been freed from the prostitute of Babylon during his following vision.

I will interpret a few more much written about verses of the angel's declaration. During the centuries different authors have, for example, read in these verses Caesar Nero's rebirth (e.g. Bowman (1), p. 61). In the following, I will suggest a psychological interpretation.

The angel relates to St. John, "The beast that you saw was, and is not, and will ascend out of the bottomless pit and go to perdition" (Rev. 17:8). The angel says that the beast was, because St. John has personally experienced delusory states of consciousness. This happened in the previous vision, particularly while St. John was tormented (Rev. 16:13). When the angel says that the beast is not, it means that presently (in this chapter 17) St. John lives a tranquil and intuitively keen state of consciousness. During such a state of consciousness the delusion, or the beast, has withdrawn into St. John's subconscious or to the depths. But soon St. John must again live delusory states, and then the beast will rise from the depths. This kind of an experience will be described particularly in the verse Rev. 19:19. The beast will, however, be overcome and it is thrown into a fiery lake in the verse 19:20. Then the beast goes to perdition.

The same matters are repeated yet a little differently in the verse 17:11 when the angel explains to St. John: "And the beast that was, and is not, is himself also the eight, and is of the seven, and is going to perdition." To understand the verse, I will quote a part from the previous verse 17:10 which brings the kings to the stage: "There are also seven kings." The kings represent in my interpretation the lower centers of the consciousness; human beings are kings when they, for instance, act or think or will consciously. Kings represent the level of the conscious mind. The beast, on the other hand, belongs to the level of the subconscious when it "is not." At that time, it is, as if, in the depths of St. John's subconscious. The angel calls the beast the eighth when it is not; that is, the beast is an outsider compared to the kings representing the level of the conscious mind. But when the beast rises from the depths, St. John must clearly and personally live the delusion it represents, and then the beast as well belongs to the level of the conscious mind. Then it is "of the seven." But the angel repeats that the beast goes to perdition.

I think Revelation emphasizes in these verses, which at first appear strange, that to be fully liberated we must confront the delusions in our consciousness openly and overcome them. They may not remain repressed or hidden on the bottom of our consciousness.

18th chapter

1. The thoughts of St. John of the Cross, which I refer to in this chapter, have already come up earlier. As I have explained (in chapters 16 and 17), he divides the purification in two main stages, the night of the senses or the purification of the senses and the night of the spirit or the purification of the spirit. The thought that the purification of the senses is not complete until the spirit has been purified, was discussed in the previous chapter when I interpreted the prostitute as the mother of the abominations.

2. Because a city has many buildings and inhabitants, the city probably illustrates the states of consciousness associated with man's self, whereas the prostitute as an individual mythical image symbolizes well the actual self. Even when St. John speaks of Babylon as a city he, nevertheless, seems to personify it. For the city as a symbol for the state of consciousness see chapters 11 and 16.

3. Eckhart (1), p. 55; Matt. 21:12.

4. St. John of the Cross (2), p. 330.

5. For fornication see chapters 9 and 17.

6. For incense see chapters 5 and 8.

7. St. John of the Cross (2), p. 358. A translation more true to the original language would be 'captive' rather than a slave, but the meaning is essentially the same.

8. St. John of the Cross (3), pp. 627–628.

9. St. John of the Cross (2), p. 309.

10. Bhagavadgita (1), II:47, p. 132, II:49, p. 134, II:51, p. 136. The last quote is my own translation. Instead of the word 'bliss' the original text uses the word *anamayam*, which means literally 'without suffering.' The state without suffering is *samadhi*. Perhaps for this reason the line has been also translated, "The highest seats of bliss" (Bhagavadgita (2), p. 20).

11. St. Teresa of Avila (2), pp. 301, 349, 417–418. The thought is, of course, quite common in Christian literature, see for example Gilson, p. 135.

12. St. John of the Cross (2), p. 331.

13. Vivekananda (3), pp. 191, 208, 270 (=Patanjali III:1) and p. 310.

14. The quote includes the words, "Repay her double according to her works; in the cup which she has mixed, mix for her double" (Rev. 18:6). That the prostitute must receive double for her works illustrates perhaps the terrifying

nature of the night of the spirit, but a double revenge may also have an interesting theoretical origin, one that fits well the progress of St. John's visions. One's sense of self is, as if, doubly delusory. First, it is merely a phantom created by the conscious mind, and secondly, it is based on a delusory ego-consciousness, the beast, that is broader than the conscious mind. In this way the final destruction of the prostitute requires a double destruction, or revenge, like I explained in the last note of the previous chapter: the first one is directed toward the prostitute, and the second, toward the beast.

15. St. John of the Cross (2), pp. 311–312.

16. For the words of St. John of the Cross see note 8, this chapter. For virgins see chapter 14.

17. Isa. 13:19–20; see also Jer. 51.

18. St. John of the Cross (3), p. 586. Fire as a mythical image was discussed earlier, particularly in chapter 8.

19. Yogananda (6), p. 98; for the burning of the old karma in the fire of wisdom see chapter 8.

20. St. John of the Cross (2), pp. 346, 350, 355. Darkening was explained in chapter 16.

21. St. John of the Cross (2), p. 346.

22. Op. cit., p. 342.

23. Op. cit., p. 347.

24. Op. cit., p. 333.

25. Op. cit., pp. 339, 348–349.

26. Op. cit., p. 351.

27. Op. cit., p. 351.

28. Singing and playing appeared in the meaning of spiritual value experience already in chapters 5 and 14.

29. For the undesirous saintly action see chapters 5 and 16, and later chapter 21. The destruction of Babylon is described in the end of this chapter also in the following words, which repeat what was said previously, "And in her was found the blood of prophets and saints, and all who were slain on the earth" (Rev. 18:24). I explained in chapter 17 that man's sense of self, as if, draws to itself a value experience in a limited way so that this experience cannot expand to a state of genuine bliss. Therefore, the blood of the saints

and others are found in the prostitute, and when the prostitute is destroyed, the blood can manifest freely as bliss.

30. The verse Rev. 19:3 does no longer speak of the smoke from a fire but only of smoke, and this may be significant emphasizing the darkening and delusory nature of the ego. The expression "the smokescreen of delusion" appears, for example, in Yogananda (4), p. 418. The smoke rising up for ever and ever could, of course, express also the emotional power of the revenge St. John decrees to the prostitute; it is as if St. John would wish the prostitute to scorch for ever and ever. However, I see the theoretical interpretation to be more important.

31. Jer. 51:63–64.

32. Mark 9:42.

33. St. Teresa of Avila (2), p. 322. St. Teresa may include also the "disturbing noises," which she hears in her head (op. cit. pp. 320–322), to the movements of the mill. Because those sounds are, according to my understanding, Om-vibration, I do not include them in my own interpretation to the troubles caused by the millstone of Babylon. The mill parable appears also in St. Teresa of Avila (3), p. 142, where St. Teresa compares specifically man's understanding to a grinding mill.

34. The Buddhist wheel of life was discussed in chapter 13. The millstone, in the sense that I am interpreting it here, and the wheel of life do not parallel each other as pictures otherwise than both being round figures. In the wheel of life, the center is presented as the most delusory, but I am interpreting the millstone so that the center means liberation.

19th chapter

1. St. John of the Cross (2), pp. 356–358.

2. St. Teresa of Avila (2), pp. 359–378.

3. New Larousse Encyclopedia, pp. 60, 57 (Babylonian myths); Homer (2), book 14, verses 346–352, pp. 92–93.

4. S. of S. 6:3.

5. St. John of the Cross (3), p. 609.

6. Op. cit., p. 578.

7. Vivekananda (1), pp. 96–100.

8. Avalon, pp. 282, 287–288, 295–296.

9. St. Bernard of Clairvaux (4), pp. 290, 297. However, St. Bernard speaks also of the church as the bride of the Christ (for example, St. Bernard of Clairvaux (5), p. 271). Already Origen presented a twofold interpretation on the bride symbolism—bride as a human soul and as the church—in his treatise on the Song of Songs (Origen, p. 21). Later Bonaventure, among others, interpreted Christian bride symbolism, and according to my understanding also the bride symbolism in Revelation, so that the bride means both the human soul and the church (Bonaventure (1), p. 91; see also op. cit., pp. 89, 93).

10. The early Dominicans, p. 421. The nun mentioned in the text was sister Agnes von Ochsenstein from Unterlinden convent; for more specific information on the source see op. cit., p. 480. Schlink, p. 267. Schlink uses the bride of the Lamb also in the meaning of the congregation. op. cit., p. 638.

11. Jung (16), §§ 223–225, pp. 180–182, and Jung (1), § 743, pp. 457–458. Jung explained that in the days of Revelation the immediate and urgent problem was not the union of opposites in attaining personal wholeness. Instead, it was important to strengthen the light and the good "against the advent of the Antichrist." Therefore, the marriage in Revelation takes place "in heaven, where nothing unclean enters, high above the devastated world." Only in future would the reconciliation of the opposites be possible. The child which was born in the 12th chapter would be a reconciliation between the opposites, yet, the child was snatched into the heaven, because in Jung's words "he belongs to another, future world." Jung explained that "only in the last days will the vision of the sun-woman be fulfilled." (See also Jung (1), § 712, p. 439). Irion, interprets the Lamb's wedding clearly as healing on the individual level (Irion, p. 370).

12. This theory was explained in chapter 6.

13. See also Yogananda (1), pp. 145, 239.

14. The Bible reference Matt. 22:2–4; see also Matt. 25:1–13, and Luke 12:35–38. St. John of the Cross (1), p. 474.

15. The sacred meal of Mithraism was mentioned in chapter 10. Drinking *amrita* nectar appears in Yogananda (1), p. 143; the quote including *amrita* nectar can be found in the end of the chapter 11.

16. I explained in the note 39 of chapter 5 that interpreting more objectively, the angels refer to spirits. According to this kind of interpretation St. John would emphasize with his words the difference between the original divinity

and those spiritual levels of the reality to which the angels belong. This interpretation, too, fits well to Revelation because St. John gives God ever more clearly a transcendent meaning as his visions progress.

17. These words of the angel can also be interpreted more objectively. With his words the angel would again emphasize the difference between, on the one hand, transcendent God, and on the other, the lower levels of the spiritual reality. The angels belong to the latter level and are thus comparable to men in their relationship to the transcendent God (see previous note).

18. Ramana Maharshi, pp. 186–187; Tao Tê Ching, e.g. §§ 47–48, pp. 73–74, and § 63, p. 90.

19. See chapter 4 and for example Yogananda (3), p. 300.

20. Vivekananda (3), p. 192 and p. 270 (=Patanjali III:1–3); Yogananda (1), p. 237; Yogananda (4), pp. 340, 351, 365–367.

21. Ramana Maharshi, p. 148.

22. Yukteswar, pp. 3, 19–20, 22–23, 56, 60, 62, 65; Rev. 3:14.

23. Yogananda (3), p. 300; the similarity of merging into the Om-vibration and the infusion of the Holy Spirit has been presented clearly in the work of Sri Gyanamata, a Canadian disciple of Yogananda (Gyanamata, pp. 140–141). St. John of the Cross (1), pp. 166–467.

24. Acts 2:1–4.

25. For Indian thought Yogananda (4), pp. 340–341. St. John of the Cross (1), p. 467.

26. Eph. 6:17.

27. St. Teresa of Avila (2), pp. 370–371. "Communications" are mentioned e.g. in St. John of the Cross (2), p. 330.

28. St. Teresa of Avila (2), p. 367.

29. St. Teresa of Avila (3), p. 252; see also St. Teresa of Avila (1), p. 430.

30. St. John of the Cross (3), p. 598.

31. Yukteswar, pp. 20–21.

32. An experience like this is described, for example, in Yogananda (1), p. 139, where Yogananda tells of having seen a spiritual light as lightning.

33. St. Teresa of Avila (2), pp. 359–360 (quote). I have used the experiences mentioned by St. Teresa as my examples when describing the meeting with the tormentors and the battle of Armageddon in chapter 16.

34. The expression is from Daya Mata, p. 236. The fire of delusion is mentioned also, among others, in Yogananda (3), p. 45.

35. Brimstone appears in chapter 9.

36. It is said, for example, in the Gospel of Mark, "And if your hand makes you sin, cut it off. It is better for you to enter into life maimed, than having two hands, to go to hell, into the fire that shall never be quenched" (Mark 9:43). Here, the hell could be a state of mind where the ego-desires torment man and keep him from entering true life. The hand that makes one sin would refer to any action preventing liberation, and the fire of the desires would be unquenched because it burns as long as man is not rescued from it through being liberated from his desires. Interpreting in a more metaphysical way, fire never to be quenched could mean that the fire burns as long as there are men attached to their desires. In this case, also, an individual human being can free himself from the fire by freeing himself of his ego-desires. Once free, he will be able to enter life.

37. Yukteswar, p. 22.

38. Jung (1), §§ 725–733, pp. 446–451. According to Jung, a false prophet could be also "the dark counterpart of Christ" (op. cit., § 725, p. 447). As far as I understand Jung's interpretation of Revelation, its central idea was that Revelation revealed the duality included in divinity: evil along with the good. But, this duality does not synthesize, or its synthesis will not happen before the end of time. It is only at the end of the world that the vision of the celestial woman giving birth to a child—who will bring the opposites together—will come true (see op. cit., § 733, pp. 450–451, § 743, pp. 457–458 and the note 11 of this chapter).

39. The angel, whom St. John sees in the verse 19:17, stands in the sun. The sun, in this connection, probably means, in the first place, the light of the spiritual eye. That is, St. John is evidently in deep meditation while he sees the vision. But the sun parable may occur also because St. John is about to reach the final settlement with his ego-attachments, and in general, with the different forms of delusion. Only this kind of resolve can permanently free him of his old God-concept symbolized in Revelation by the sun.

40. Ramana Maharshi, pp. 107–108; see also Bhagavadgita (1), II:22, pp. 101–102. Flesh as a mythical image can also have a broader meaning than that of physical being because the Greek word *sarx*, flesh, is used in the New Testament in a broad sense. The broad meaning of flesh is well apparent in the verses Gal. 5:13–26.

41. Early Dominicans, p. 410. A more detailed source: Letter of St. Peter Martyr to the Prioress of St. Peter's in Campo Santo, Milan (op. cit., pp. 410–

411); the letter has been written close to the middle of the 13th century (op. cit., p. 429). See also Bonaventure (2), p. 281.

42. St. Teresa of Avila (2), pp. 386, 388. St. Teresa, however, places these experiences in the next stage of spiritual evolution. Because the inner path cannot be forged to a certain form, we can perhaps think that St. John experiences something similar to them already in this vision.

43. Teresa of Avila (3), pp. 173, 181.

44. Clarke, p. 254; New Larousse Encyclopedia, p. 45; Yogananda (1), p. 252, 252n.

45. For eagle symbolism see chapter 6. The eagle as a symbol for intuition is also appropriate here, see chapter 8.

20th chapter

1. St. Teresa of Avila (2), the quotes of the first paragraph pp. 379–380; the quote of the second p. 384.

2. Vivekananda (3), p. 180, p. 260 (=Patanjali II:24), p. 270 (=Patanjali III:3).

3. Yogananda (1), p. 238 (quote) and p. 238n.

4. For example, St. Teresa of Avila (2), pp. 386–387.

5. Yogananda (4), pp. 69–70.

6. Daya Mata, p. 187.

7. Yogananda (4), p. 227.

8. Yogananda (7), see the back cover of the source.

9. Yogananda (4), p. 70.

10. Vivekananda (3), p. 231; Yogananda (4), pp. 49–50.

11. Ezek. 38:2–3, 16; 39:11–13.

12. Vivekananda (3), p. 272.

13. Vivekananda (3), pp. 234, 272; Yogananda (4), p. 49.

14. St. John of the Cross (2), pp. 355, 360.

15. St. Teresa of Avila (2), pp. 421–422; I have added St. Teresa's words in parenthesis from a place little later in the text, p. 423, so that the nature of the torment would become clear for the reader.

16. Op. cit., pp. 424-426.

17. Ezek. 39:11-15.

18. These Oriental views of the cycle of birth and death can be found, for example, in Yogananda (1), pp. 400–414; see also Vivekananda (5), pp. 316–317. (For the sake of simplicity, I speak in the text only of the astral levels, although the Oriental literature recognizes also higher, so called idea levels.) Plato, as well, presented a similar view of man's fate in his Phaedo (Plato (4), 112e–114d, pp. 384–391).

19. Matt. 8:22; St. John of the Cross (3), pp. 25, 62.

21st chapter

1. Yogananda (1), pp. 238, 400, 400n; Ramana Maharshi, pp. 183–184.

2. Waltari, pp. 183–184.

3. Tara Mata, pp. 9–13.

4. Ramana Maharshi, p. 191.

5. Op. cit., pp. 190–191 (the first paragraph of the quote); op. cit., p. 185 (the second paragraph of the quote).

6. St. Teresa of Avila (2), p. 444. The information I mention is based on the book The Interior Castle, but St. Teresa lived many years of active life after this book, founding several convents. She wrote about this activity yet another book where she, however, does no longer speak of the inner matters of the spiritual marriage, so I do not know whether the information I mention pertains to all of the last part of her life.

7. St. Teresa of Avila (2), pp. 432–433.

8. St. Teresa of Avila (1), p. 402.

9. The quotes are from St. Teresa (2), but I have rearranged their order. The quotes are, in the order of appearance, separated by the ellipses, from pages 438, 438, 442, 434, 430.

10. See chapters 5, 6, and 16, and for example St. John of the Cross (2), p. 333.

11. St. Teresa of Avila (2), pp. 440, 439.

12. St. John of the Cross (3), p. 609 (St. John of the Cross writes here in Latin); Ramana Maharshi, p. 185.

13. Ramana Maharshi, p. 189.

14. St. Teresa of Avila (2), p. 440.

15. St. Teresa of Avila (4), pp. 117, 163; St. Teresa of Avila (2), p. 442; see also St. John of the Cross (3), p. 579. After the verse I discuss, Revelation reads, "But the cowardly, unbelieving, abominable, murderers, sexually immoral, sorcerers, idolaters, and all liars shall have their part in the lake which burns with fire and brimstone, which is the second death" (Rev. 21:8). The meaning of the verse is probably clear already based on the interpretations I have presented so far. As long as man is tied to different ego-desires, he must wander in the sea of delusion or the cycle of death and birth represented by the fiery lake in my interpretation of Revelation. For the symbols in the verse see, among others, chapters 9 and 20.

16. Eckhart (1), pp. 201–202; St. John of the Cross (3), p. 592; St. Teresa of Avila (2), pp. 283, 288; I referred to this St. Teresa's view that God lives in the innermost room of the castle in chapter 14 while interpreting the virgin parable. The diamond castle appears also in the work by St. Teresa, The Way of Perfection (St. Teresa of Avila (4), p. 143).

17. Julian of Norwich, chapter 67, p. 183; see also op. cit., chapter 51, pp. 145, 151.

18. Bhagavadgita (1), V:13, p. 285 (the city with nine gates); for the spiritual body and the astral body see chapter 6; Liu Hua Yang, p. 116 (diamond body).

19. Tai I Ging Hua Dsung Dshi, p. 77.

20. Lauf, p. 118, Lauf says that the mandala palace is "an archetypal picture of a divine city."

21. St. John of the Cross (3), p. 584.

22. Teresa of Calcutta (2), p. 77.

23. Vivekananda (3), p. 228 (=Patanjali I:41); Yogananda (2), p. 4, see also op. cit., p. 93.

24. Tai I Ging Hua Dsung Dshi, p. 102; for the concentration of the life energy see chapters 16 and 18.

25. St. John of the Cross (2), p. 333; see chapter 17.

26. These kinds of experiences have been described, for example, in Zander, pp. 90–91, 110, 112, 126. The halo can be compared to the golden wreath received by the victorious in Revelation, and applying the chakra teaching, to the enlightened state when the life energy has moved into sahasrara.

27. For the interpretation on the alchemists see e.g. Jung (4), § 40, p. 34.

28. Tai I Ging Hua Dsung Dshi, pp. 77, 100–102.

29. See 2 Chron. 3:8. According to some Bible translations, the holy of holies in Salomon's temple is even cubic in its form, since also its hight can be seen to be twenty cubits, see e.g. New American Bible (Revised Edition) 2 Chron. 3:4. These kinds of Tibetan mandalas have been presented, for example, in Lauf, figures 49, 51, 55.

30. Pictures like this can be found, for example, in Maclagan, pp. 34, 91.

31. Jung (4), § 165, p. 124; see also Jung (3), § 715, p. 388.

32. Lauf, pp. 118–119.

33. One furlong equals 1/8 mile.

34. Luke 6:47–48; Matt. 16:18.

35. E.g. The Teachings of the Compassionate Buddha, pp. 28–29.

36. Tai I Ging Hua Dsung Dshi, pp. 102–103.

37. Amitayur-Dhyana-Sutra, p. 170.

38. E.g. Avalon, pp. 253, 295.

39. E.g. op. cit., p. 253 (the six-fold path), and op. cit., p. 355 (petals and pericarps); Yogananda (1), p. 238 (the number 12). Additionally, different sources relate different number of chakras, among others 13 and 144, because there are more and less important energy centers (Sivananda, p. 38). When 13 chakras are counted and when the highest chakra is sahasrara, the number of the chakras lower than sahasrara is again 12.

40. Ramana Maharshi, pp. 127–129; Yogananda (1), p. 143; Yogananda (4), p. 4; Chandogya Upanishad (1), pp. 120–121; Chandogya Upanishad (2), p. 107. The more detailed interpretation of the understanding I apply in the text varies in the Oriental literature. According to Paramahansa Yogananda the center in question is the heart center. Ramana Maharshi, on his behalf, teaches that the center in question is not the heart center but the so called spiritual heart. Probably the meditation exercise of the Amitayur-Dhyana-Sutra mentioned in the text is also founded on the spiritual heart concept, because there the base is supported by seven precious stones.

41. Zander (Seraphim of Sarov), p. 16; Bonaventure (1), p. 90.

42. Dorotheus, § 17, pp. 344–347.

43. More precisely, the tribes of the children of Israel are classes of characteristics; for this symbolism see chapters 5 and 7.

44. St. Teresa of Avila (2), pp. 431–432.

45. Op. cit., p. 384.

46. Ramana Maharshi, p. 26.

47. St. Teresa of Avila (2), p. 438.

48. E.g. Lauf, p. 120, and p. 132 (the caption for the figure 51).

49. Teresa of Calcutta (1), p. 68.

50. Op. cit., p. 49.

51. St. Teresa of Avila (2), p. 439.

52. Bhagavadgita (1), V:11, p. 283, III:30, pp. 195–196.

53. Bhagavadgita (1), XV:5–6, pp. 699–700.

22nd chapter

1. Homer (3), book 4, verses 564–569, pp. 148–149.

2. Ovid, book 1, verses 89–112, pp. 3–4; Hesiod, verses 334–335, p. 46; New Larousse Encyclopedia, pp. 144, 172.

3. St. John of the Cross (3), pp. 579, 613; St. John of the Cross (2), p. 326.

4. St. Teresa of Avila (2), pp. 288–289 (the first quote), p. 288 (the last quote).

5. St. Bernard of Clairvaux (6), p. 315.

6. Amitayur-Dhyana-Sutra, pp. 166–181. Buddha Amitabha's Western land is a popular subject in Buddhism. For more information on this see, for example, The Teachings of the Compassionate Buddha, pp. 204–222. The connection between that land and the holy city of Revelation is so obvious that, for example, the editor of that work, E.A. Burtt, mentions it (op. cit., p. 206). For yoga theory see Avalon, p. 253.

7. Waltari, pp. 184–145.

8. St. Teresa of Avila (2), p. 441. St. Teresa's parable of the living water as a perfect contemplation was used in the previous chapter, see note 15, chapter 21. The Bible reference: John 7:38.

9. Gen. 3:22.

10. The Bible reference Gen. 3:7.

11. Gen. 3:17.

12. According to Today's English Version, "The river... flows down the middle of the city's street. On each side of the river was a tree of life" (Rev. 22:1–2).

13. For example, New Larousse Encyclopedia, p. 144.

14. St. John of the Cross (3), p. 649. St. John of the Cross uses the word *gloria* which in this context has, so I think, the meaning of brightness. Another possible translation would be, of course, glory.

15. Avalon, p. 428 (Sat Chakra Nirupana text); The Tibetan Book of the Dead, p. 96; Yogananda (5), pp. 158, 170.

16. For *vajra* symbolism see Snodgrass, pp. 174–175, and Jung (3), figure 1, and § 636, p. 358.

17. 1 Cor. 15:24–28.

18. Rev. 3:12 was interpreted in chapter 6. Paramahansa Yogananda uses the end of the world in this kind of meaning, explaining that the end of the world can mean not only the end of the entire world but also the end of the world in a person's life when he reaches complete perfection (Yogananda (4), pp. 67–68). According to the Oriental theory, man can incarnate even after he has reached perfection, but then he will not incarnate because he must, but he comes as a so called Avatar to liberate human beings.

19. I will yet interpret the more central ideas from the concluding verses of Revelation.

The prophesy

"Blessed is he who keeps the words of the prophecy of this book" (Rev. 22:7). "Do not seal the words of the prophesy of this book" (Rev. 22:10). According to my interpretation, Revelation describes in mythical language man's spiritual path all the way to perfection and bliss. But we, for whom the message of the book is directed, have not reached perfection, and therefore, the book is so far only a prophesy for us about what is possible. Additionally, should we apply the Oriental teaching of reincarnation, the Book of Revelation can be a prophesy in a more demanding sense as well. According to this teaching, everyone is to incarnate as many times as it takes him to reach the perfection, and along with that, permanent bliss.

"I am coming quickly"

"And the Lord God... sent his angel to show his servants the things which must shortly take place" (Rev. 22:6). "The time is at hand" (Rev. 22:10). "Behold, I am coming quickly!" (Rev. 22:7). The words "I am coming quickly" are repeated also in the verses 22:12 and 22:20; in the latter verse the speaker is clearly Jesus.

The Bible researchers maintain that during the New Testament times the end was thought to be near and God's kingdom was expected to manifest soon (e.g. Räisänen, pp. 45, 72–73). The second coming of Jesus is indeed clearly prophesied in the New Testament. For example, in the Gospel of John Jesus says, "And if I go... I will come again and receive you to myself" (John 14:3). In the Acts of the Apostles the angels say, "This same Jesus... will so come in like manner as you saw him go into heaven" (Acts 1:11).

I assume, however, that by the end of Revelation St. John has realized the inner meaning of such beliefs: the new coming of Jesus is the manifestation of a deeply spiritual state of consciousness in man. In fact, this interpretation is also used in religious literature. Paramahansa Yogananda emphasizes that Christ has two sides, Christ as man and Christ as the universal Spirit, and when one has progressed on the inner path living the universal Spirit in himself, he experiences Christ's second coming (Yogananda (4), p. 254). Interpreting in this way, the words "I am coming quickly" are like an encouragement: one who takes heed of the words in Revelation, will reach the goal quickly and find bliss.

Entering the holy city

"He who is unjust, let him be unjust still; he who is filthy, let him be filthy still; he who is righteous, let him be righteous still; he who is holy, let him be holy still" (Rev. 22:11). The words sound odd within religious tradition, but based on St. John's previous analysis, it is possible to suggest appropriate interpretations for them.

Over the Book of Revelation, St. John has disconnected from his old religion, according to which God would be a punishing and rewarding power outside man. According to his new understanding, human life is, instead, governed by an inner law: how we each think, choose, act, and feel, determines what we become. Should we act wrong, we become morally unworthy and indifferent and must suffer inwardly in many ways even when outwardly successful. An indifferent person also tends to make wrong choices whereas an understanding person tends to choose well, not unlike to the famous biblical words, "For whoever has, to him more will be given... but whoever does not have, even what he has will be taken away from him" (Matt. 13:12). The verse in Revelation may derive from St. John's realization: he need not preach to others repentance nor threaten them with judgment. Everyone will reward and punish himself; and we can learn from the inner misery that we sometimes bring ourselves into, and change ourselves. Everyone will progress at his own pace.

The reward

"And behold, I am coming quickly, and my reward is with me, to give to everyone according to his work" (Rev. 22:12). The speaker of the words is probably Jesus although the angels transmit his words to St. John. When man is freed to experience the spirituality represented by Christ, that experience is the reward in itself. One who experiences it does not need an outer reward for his striving. The words "to give to everyone according to his work" express again the law of karma that the previous verse was based on. Everyone can experience the spiritual value to the decree that he has prepared himself for it.

"Blessed are those who do his commandments, that they may have the right to the tree of life, and may enter through the gates into the city" (Rev. 22:14). Another version, as well, can be found in the manuscripts for this verse, also used in Bible translations. According to this version the beginning of the verse would be, "Blessed are those who wash their robes." Both versions emphasize that man must change himself to be able to experience more genuine spirituality. We must purify our consciousness, or our clothes, from attachments, and then we are able to receive spiritual nourishment and experience high spiritual values.

The Morning Star

"I, Jesus... I am the Root and the Offspring of David, the Bright and Morning Star" (Rev. 22:16). Also here the expression "the Root of David" actually means the scion or the branch from the root of David (see chapter 5, note 23).

The morning star is mentioned already in the second chapter of Revelation, where it is said, "And I will give him [who overcomes] the morning star" (Rev. 2:26–28). Astronomically the morning star is Venus, but its symbolism in the Bible crystallizes some of the essential message of Revelation, and therefore St. John probably feels that it is appropriate as the guiding star of human life.

In the Old Testament, the morning star appears in Isaiah in a place which I have already partially used as a comparison for the prostitute of Babylon (chapter 17, where it speaks of the prostitute on the mountains). In the King James translation, the morning star in Isaiah is called Lucifer, but the "morning star," more true to the original language, appears, for example, in the New English translation. The following quotes are otherwise from the New King

James translation, but I have substituted the word Lucifer with the words "morning star." According to Isaiah, the king of Babylon will once receive the mockery, "How you are fallen from heaven, O morning star, son of the morning... You have said in your heart: 'I will ascend into heaven... I will be like the Most High'... But you are... like an abominable branch... like a corpse trodden underfoot" (Isa. 14:4, 12–14, 19).

Therefore, the morning star in the Bible is, on the one hand, a symbol for Jesus and spiritual victory, and on the other, a name for the king of Babylon. One way to understand this strange symbolism of the morning star is to interpret the morning star as man's pure, 'original' soul; for example, in Egypt the stars were seen, among others, as human souls (Clark, p. 265). When a pure soul falls from heaven, like man in the beginning of the Bible falls away from the original paradise, it takes on an ego-covering. Then man identifies with his physical body and narrow consciousness, and he is like the king of Babylon or ego. As an ego he then goes about bragging and thinking of himself to be the most magnificent of all. But in the end man is brought to realize the true nature of the ego. The ego is nothing but a weed that must be pulled out and beaten to death. When the ego finally dies and the human soul returns to its original pure state, man has overcome and Christ experiences the second coming in him. Then he, too, will become a valuable offspring of David, a branch from the root of David, instead of an abominable branch. The morning star is born in his heart, and Peter's words, "Until the day dawns and the morning star rises in your hearts," will be fulfilled (2 Pet. 1:19).

Additions and removals

"For I testify to everyone who hears the words of the prophecy of this book: If anyone adds to these things, God will add to him the plagues that are written in this book; and if anyone takes away from the words of the book of this prophecy, God shall take away his part from the book of life, from the holy city, and from the things which are written in this book" (Rev. 22:18–19). The verses strive to guarantee that the text in the Book of Revelation would remain unchanged. Because the events in Revelation often seem confusing and even insane from the viewpoint of conceptual thinking, it is no misjudgment from the author's part to try to prevent any possible changes. In addition to this obvious purpose, I suggest the verses a deeper interpretation.

Although man's spiritual evolution cannot be forged into one and the same mold, St. John perhaps feels he has presented something essential of that inner journey. When he says that one may not take anything away from Revelation, he is perhaps warning the reader of many easily taken shortcuts. Should our inner change remain too superficial, we will not reach the highest levels of the spiritual life, and the holy city will not emerge from us.

The beginning of the warning "if anyone adds to these things, God will add to him the plagues that are written in this book", I would like to interpret in the following way. Everyone who begins to ponder Revelation and to read it with abandon, will add to it his own thoughts, visions, and experiences. The attentive pondering of mythical images and becoming personally involved in them, function suggestively to initiate an inner change. Thus, the interpreter must wrestle with the problems which he reads into the visions, and he will receive the same plagues as St. John did, because he begins to *live* the images and the events of Revelation.

BIBLIOGRAPHY

Allione, Tsultrim: Women of Wisdom, Arkana, London 1986.

The Amitayur-Dhyana-Sutra (The Sutra of the Meditation on Amitayus), in Sacred Books of the East, vol. 49, Buddhist Mahayana Sutras, pp. 159–201 (ed. F. Max Müller), Motilal Banarsidass, New Delhi 1985.

Anandamayi Ma: Sad Vani; A Collection of the Teaching of Sri Anandamayi Ma as reported by Bhaiji (J. C. Roy), Shree Shree Anandamayee Charitable Society, Calcutta 1992.

Arndt, William F. and Gingrich, F. Wilbur: A Greek-English Lexicon of the New Testament and Other Early Christian Literature; A translation and adaption of the fourth revised and augmented edition of Walter Bauer's Griechisch-Deutsches Wörterbuch zu den Schriften des Neuen Testaments und der übrigen urchristlichen Literatur; Second edition, revised and augmented by F. Wilbur Gingrich and Frederick W. Danker from Walter Bauer's fifth edition, 1958, The University of Chicago Press, Chicago 1979.

The Art of Prayer; An Orthodox Anthology (compiled by Igumen Chariton of Valamo), Faber and Faber, London 1997.

Artemidorus: The Interpretation of Dreams; The Oneirocritica of Artemidorus (transl. Robert White), Noyes Press, Park Ridge, New Jersey 1975.

Athanasius, St.: The Life of Saint Antony (transl. Robert T. Meyer), The Newman Press, Westminster, Maryland 1950.

Augustine:
(1) Confessions, Introduction and Text (James J. O'Donnel), Clarendon Press, Oxford 1992.

(2) City of God (ed. David Knowles), Penguin Books, Harmondsworth 1980.

Avalon: Arthur (Sir John Woodroffe): The Serpent Power, Ganesh & Co., Madras 1958.

St. Bernard of Clairvaux:
(1) S. Bernardi, abbatis primi Clarae-Vallensis: Tractatus de gradibus humilitatis et superbiae, in Migne: Patrologia latina, vol. 182, ss. 942–971, Paris 1879.

(2) The Letters of Saint Bernard of Clairvaux (ed. Bruno Scott James), Burns Oates, London 1953.

(3) S. Bernardi, abbatis primi Clarae-Vallensis: Liber de diligendo Deo, in Migne: Patrologia latina, vol. 182, pp. 974–999, Paris 1879.

(4) Des Menschen Wert und Unwert, in Die Schriften des honigfliessenden Lehrers Bernhard von Clairvaux, vol. 3, pp. 289–298, Georg Fischer Verlag, Wittlich 1935.

(5) Die Zähne der Braut Christi, der Kirche, in Die Schriften des honigfliessenden Lehrers Bernhard von Clairvaux, vol. 4, pp. 271–273, Georg Fischer Verlag, Wittlich 1936.

(6) Paradiesesquellen, in Die Schriften des honigfliessenden Lehrers Bernhard von Clairvaux, vol. 4, ss. 315–317, Georg Fischer Verlag, Wittlich 1936.

Bhagavadgita:
(1) Bhagavad-gita, As It Is, Complete Edition with original Sanskrit text (A.C. Bhaktivedanta Swami Prabhupada), Macmillan Publishing Co., New York 1972.

(2) The Song Celestial, Bhagavad-Gita (transl. Sir Edwin Arnold), Self-Realization Fellowship, Los Angeles 1981.

Blyth, R. H.: Zen and Zen Classics, vol. 1, The Hokuseido Press, Tokyo 1977.

Bodhipuun juurella (Under the Bodhi-tree, in Finnish), (ed. René Gothóni and Mikael Tenzin Dönden), Otava, Helsinki 1984.

Bonaventure:
(1) The Soul's Journey into God, in Bonaventure: The Soul's Journey into God, The Tree of Life, The Life of St. Francis, pp. 53–116, Paulist Press, New York 1978.

(2) The Life of St. Francis, in Bonaventure: The Soul's Journey into God, The Tree of Life, The Life of St. Francis, pp. 179–327, Paulist Press, New York 1978.

Bowman, J. W.:
(1) Revelation, (Book of Revelation), in The Interpreter's Dictionary of the Bible, vol. 4, pp. 58–71, Abingdon Press, New York 1962.

(2) Six Hundred and Sixty-six, in The Interpreter's Dictionary of the Bible, vol. 4. pp. 381–382, Abingdon Press, New York 1962.

Brontë, Charlotte: Jane Eyre, Clarendon Press, Oxford 1969.

Brother Lawrence of the Resurrection: The Practise of the Presence of God, Double Day, New York 1977.

Brunton, Paul: A Search in Secret India, Samuel Weiser, York Beach 1989.

Campbell, Joseph: The Hero with a Thousand Faces, Meridian Books, New York 1956.

Catherine of Genoa: Purgation and Purgatory, The Spiritual Dialogue (introduction: Benedict J. Groeschel), SPCK, London, 1979.

Catherine of Siena: The Dialogue (transl. Suzanne Noffke), SPCK, London, 1980.

Chandogya Upanishad:
(1) From the Chandogya, in The Upanishads, pp. 113–126 (transl. Juan Mascaró), Penguin Books, Harmondsworth 1978.

(2) The Doctrine of the Chhandogyas, in The Ten Principal Upanishads, pp. 85–117 (transl. Swami Shree Purohit and W. B. Yeats), Faber and Faber, London 1975.

Charles, R. H.: The Revelation of St. John; A Critical and Exegetical Commentary, vol. 1, Charles Scribner's Sons, New York 1920.

Cirlot, J. E.: A Dictionary of Symbols, Routledge, London 1971.

Clark, R. T. Rundle: Myth and Symbol in Ancient Egypt, Thames and Hudson, London 1959.

Cook, Roger: The Tree of Life, Thames and Hudson, London 1988.

Corney, R. W.: Colors, in The Interpreter's Dictionary of the Bible, vol 1, pp. 657–658, Abingdon Press, New York 1962.

Court, John, M.: Myth and History in the Book of Revelation, SPCK, London 1979.

Cowen, Painton: Rose Windows, Thames and Hudson, London 1979.

Cumont, Franz: The Mysteries of Mithra, Dover Publications, New York 1956.

Dagyab, Loden Sherap: Tibetan Religious Art, vol. 2, Otto Harrassowitz, Wiesbaden 1977.

Dante: The Divine Comedy (ed. Edmund Gardner), J. M. Dent & Sons, London 1961.

Davidson, Gustav: A Dictionary of Angels; Including the Fallen Angels, The Free Press, New York 1967.

Daya Mata: "Only Love", Self-Realization Fellowship, Los Angeles 1976.

Dorotheus: Dorothée de Gaza: Æuvres spirituelles; Introduction, Texte Grek, Traduction et Notes (transl. L. Regnault and J. de Préville), Les Éditions du Cerf, Paris 1963.

Dostoevski, F. M.: The Idiot (transl. Alan Myers), Oxdord University Press, Oxford 1992.

Early Dominicans, Selected Writings (ed. Simon Tugwell), SPCK, London 1982.

Eckhart:
(1) Eckhart, Meister: Sermons & Treatises, vol. 1 (ed. M. O'C. Walshe), Element, Shaftesbury 1991.

(2) Eckhart, Meister: Sermons & Treatises, vol. 2 (ed. M. O'C. Walshe), Element, Shaftesbury 1989.

Edinger, Edward F.:
(1) Ego and Archtype, Penguin Books, Harmondsworth 1980.

(2) The Bible and the Psyche, Inner City Books, Toronto 1986.

Encyclopedia Britannica, vol. 2, William Benton, Chicago, 1973.

Engelmann, Paul: Letters from Ludwig Wittgenstein with a Memoir, Basil Blackwell, Oxford 1967.

Engels, Friedrich:
(1) Zur Geschichte des Urchristentums, in Karl Marx, Friedrich Engels: Werke, vol. 22, pp. 447–473, Dietz Verlag, Berlin 1972.

(2) Das Buch der Offenbarung, in Karl Marx, Friedrich Engels: Werke, vol. 21, pp. 9–15, Dietz Verlag, Berlin 1972.

Freud, Sigmund:
(1) Die Zerlegung der psychischen Persönlichkeit, in Sigmund Freud: Gesammelte Werke, vol. 15, pp. 62–86, Imago Publishing, London 1946.

(2) Totem and Tabu, Ark Paperbacks, London 1983.

Gaster, T. H.: Michael, in The Interpreter's Dictionary of the Bible, vol. 3, pp. 372–373, Abingdon Press, New York 1962.

Gilson, Étienne: The Mystical Theology of Saint Bernard, Sheed and Ward, London 1955.

Gossner, Simone D.: Zodiac, in The Encyclopedia Americana, vol. 29, pp. 787–788, American Corporation, Danbury 1978.

St. Gregory the Great:
(1) Sancti Gregorii Magni: Homiliarum in Ezechielem prophetam, in Migne: Patrologia latina, vol. 76, pp. 786–1072, Paris 1878.

(2) St. Gregory the Great: Pastoral Care (Regula Pastoralis), The Newman Press, London 1950.

Grof, Stanislav and Christina: Beyond Death, Thames and Hudson, London 1990.

Gyanamata, Sri: God Alone, Self-Realization Fellowship, Los Angeles 1984.

Haavio, Martti: Suomalainen mytologia (Finnish Mythology, in Finnish), WSOY, Porvoo, 1967.

Hammer, P. L.: Devil, in The Interpreter's Dictionary of the Bible, vol. 1, p. 838, Abingdom Press, New York 1962.

Harper's Bible Dictionary, Harper & Row, San Francisco 1985.

Harzer, Edeltraud: Samkhya, in The Encyclopedia of Religion (chief editor Mircea Eliade), vol. 13, pp. 47–51, Macmillan Publishing Company, New York 1987.

Hegel, G. W. F.: Hegel's Phenomenology of Spirit (transl. A.V. Miller, foreword, J. N. Findlay), Oxford University Press, Oxford 1979.

Hesiod: The Poems of Hesiod (transl. R. M. Frazer), University of Oklahoma Press, Norman 1985.

Hesse, Herman: Siddhartha, Suhrkamp Verlag, Eschwege 1971.

Hindu Myths, A Sourcebook Translated from the Sanskrit, Penguin Book, Harmondsworth 1980.

Homer:
(1) The Iliad, vol. 1 (books I–XII), The Clarendon Press, Oxford 1963.

(2) The Iliad, vol. 2 (books XIII–XXIV), Harvard University Press, Cambridge 1957.

(3) The Odyssey, vol. 1, Harvard University Press, Cambridge 1960.

Humphreys, Christmas: The Buddhist Way of Life, Unwin Books, London 1969.

Huxley, Francis: The Dragon, Thames and Hudson, London 1979.

I Ching, The Book of Change (transl. John Blofeld), Mandala Books Unwin Paperbacs, London 1976.

Irion, J. Everett: Interpreting the Revelation with Edgar Cayce, A.R.E. Press, Virginia Beach 1982.

St. John of the Cross:
(1) The Spiritual Canticle, in The Collected Works of St. John of the Cross, pp. 393–565 (transl. Kieran Kavanaugh ja Otilio Rodriguez), ICS Publications (Institute of Carmelite Studies), Washington, D.C. 1979.

(2) The Dark Night, in The Collected Works of St. John of the Cross, pp. 293–389, ICS Publications, Washington, D.C. 1979.

(3) The Living Flame of Love, in The Collected Works of St. John of the Cross, pp. 567–649, ICS Publications, Washington D.C. 1979.

(4) The Ascent of Mount Carmel, in The Collected Works of St. John of the Cross, pp. 43–292, ICS Publications, Washington, D.C. 1979.

Julian of Norwich: Revelations of Divine Love (transl. Clifton Wolters), Penguin Books, Harmondsworth 1978.

Jung, C. G.:
(1) Answer to Job, in The Collected Works of C. G. Jung, vol. 11, pp. 355–470, Routledge & Kegan Paul, London 1981.

(2) Memories, Dreams, Reflections, Collins Fount Paperbacks, Glasgow 1980.

(3) Concerning Mandala Symbolism (with Appendix), in The Collected Works of C. G. Jung, vol. 9i, pp. 355–390, Routledge & Kegan Paul, London 1980.

(4) Psychology and Alchemy, The Collected Works of C. G. Jung, vol. 12, Routledge & Kegan Paul, London 1981.

(5) Psychological Types, The Collected Works of C. G. Jung, vol. 6, Routledge & Kegan Paul, London 1981.

(6) The Relations between the Ego and the Unconscious, in The Collected Works of C. G. Jung, vol. 7, pp. 121–292, Routledge & Kegan Paul, London 1977.

(7) Symbols of Transformation, The Collected Works of C. G. Jung, vol. 5, Routledge & Kegan Paul, London 1981.

(8) Preface to de Laszlo: 'Psyche and Symbol', in The Collected Works of C. G. Jung, vol. 18, pp. 537–542, Routledge & Kegan Paul, London 1977.

(9) Foreword to Allenby: 'A Psychological Study of the Origins of Monotheism', in The Collected Works of C. G. Jung, vol. 18, pp. 656–659, Routledge & Kegan Paul, London 1977.

(10) Concerning Rebirth, in The Collected Works of C. G. Jung, vol. 9i, pp. 113–147, Routledge & Kegan Paul, London 1980.

(11) Jung and Religious Belief, in The Collected Works of C. G. Jung, vol. 18, pp. 702–744, Routledge & Kegan Paul, London 1977.

(12) Aion, The Collected Works of C. G. Jung, vol. 9ii, Routledge & Kegan Paul, London 1978.

(13) On the Psychogenesis of Schizophrenia, in The Collected Works of C. G. Jung, vol. 3, pp. 233–249, Routledge & Kegan Paul, London 1977.

(14) Psychology and Religion, in The Collected Works of C. G. Jung, vol. 11, pp. 3–105, Routledge and Kegan Paul, London 1981.

(15) A Psychological Approach to the Dogma of the Trinity, in The Collected Works of C. G. Jung, vol. 11, pp. 107–200, Routledge & Kegan Paul, London 1981.

(16) Paracelsus as a Spiritual Phenomenon, in The Collected Works of C. G. Jung, vol. 13, pp. 109–189, Routledge and Kegan Paul, London 1978.

Kant, Immanuel: Grundlegung zur Metaphysik der Sitten, in Immanuel Kant: Werke in sechs Bänden, vol. 4, pp. 9–102 (ed. W. Weishedel), Buchgesellschaft, Darmstadt 1966.

Kenny, Anthony: Wittgenstein, Allen Lane The Penguin Press, London 1973.

Lange, K. and Hirmer, M.: Egypt; Architecture, Sculpture, Painting, Phaidon Press, London 1961.

Lauf, Detlef Ingo: Tibetan Sacred Art, Shambala, Berkeley 1976.

Lawrence, D. H.: Apocalypse, Benguin Books, Harmondsworth 1980.

Liu Hua Yang: Hui Ming Ging, das Buch von Bewusstsein und Leben, in Das Geheimnis der Goldenen Blüte, Ein chinesisches Lebensbuch (transl. Richard Wilhelm), pp. 116–124, Walter Verlag, Olten 1984).

Loyola, Ignatius: Der Bericht des Pilgers, Verlag Herder, Freiburg im Breisgau 1956.

Maclagan, David: Creation Myths, Thames and Hudson, London 1977.

Mann, Thomas: Doktor Faustus, Bermann-Fischer Verlag, Stockholm 1947.

Matarasso, P. M.: Introduction, in The Quest of the Holy Grail, pp. 9–29, Penguin Books, Harmondsworth 1981.

Moody, Raymond A.:
(1) Reflections on Life after Life, Bantam Books, New York 1978.

(2) Life after Life, Bantam Books, New York 1976.

Murray, Alexander: Who's Who in Mythology; Classic Guide to the Ancient World, Studio Editions, London 1992.

Neumann, Erich: The Great Mother, Princeton University Press, Princeton 1974.

New Larousse Encyclopedia of Mythology (introduction: Robert Graves), Hamlyn, London 1979.

Origen: The Song of Songs; Commentary and Homilies, The Newman Press, Westminster 1957.

Ovid: Metamorphoses (transl. A. D. Melville), Oxford University Press, Oxford 1986.

Pagels, Elaine: The Gnostic Gospels, Vintage Books, New York 1981.

Plato:
(1) Timaeus, in Plato in Twelve Volumes, vol. 9, pp. 2–253, Harvard University Press, Cambridge 1966.

(2) Timaeus and Critias (translation and introduction: Desmond Lee), Penguin Books, Harmondsworth, 1979.

(3) The Republic, vol. 2, in Plato in Twelve Volumes, vol. 6, Harvard University Press, Cambridge 1987.

(4) Phaedo, in Plato in Twelve Volumes, vol. 1, pp. 193–403, Harvard University Press, Cambridge 1971.

(5) Symposium, in Plato in Twelve Volumes, vol. 3, pp. 73–245, Harvard University Press, Cambridge 1967.

Plutarch: Isis and Osiris, in Plutarch's Moralia with an English Translation by Frank Cole Babbit, in fifteen volumes, part 5, pp. 6–191, William Heinemann, London 1957.

Purge, Jill: The Mystic Spiral, Thames and Hudson, London 1987.

Ramana Maharshi: The Teachings of Ramana Maharshi (ed. Arthur Osborn), Rider, London 1987.

Rist, Martin: Revelation (The Book of Revelation), in The Encyclopedia Americana, vol. 23, pp. 440–442, American Corporation, Danbury 1978.

Räisänen, Heikki: Tuhat ja yksi tulkintaa (Thousand and One Interpretations, in Finnish), Yliopistopaino (Helsinki University Press), Helsinki 1989.

Sayce, Archibald Henry: Astronomy and Astrology of the Babylonians, with Translations of the Tablets Relating to These Subjects, Wizards Bookshelf, San Diego 1981 (the original work in Transactions of the Society of Biblical Archeology, vol. 3, no. 1, 1874).

Schlink, M. Basilea: Wie ich Gott erlebte: Sein Weg mit mir durch sieben Jahrzente, Evangelische Marienschwesternschaft, Darmstadt-Eberstadt 1975.

Science Says, in Self-Realization, vol. 51, 1980, no. 3, pp. 21–26 and pp. 54–57 (Publisher: Self-Realization Fellowship, Los Angeles).

Shyamananda, Swami: Kriya Yoga and the Spiritual Meaning of the Bhagavad Gita, in Self-Realization, vol. 60, 1989, no. 4, pp. 37–45, 64 (Self-Realization Fellowship, Los Angeles).

Sivananda, Swami: Kundalini Yoga, A Divine Life Society Publication, Durban 1994.

Smend, Rudolf: Die Entstehung des Alten Testaments, Verlag W. Kohlhammer, Stuttgart, 1978

Snodgrass, Adrian: The Symbolism of the Stupa, Cornell University, Ithaca 1985.

Spinoza: The Ethics, in The Chief Works of Benedict de Spinoza, vol. 2, pp. 42–271 (transl. R. H. M. Elwes), Dover Publications, New York 1955.

Steiner, Rudolf: Wie erlangt man Erkenntnisse der höherer Welten, Philosophisch-Anthroposophischer Verlag, Berlin 1920.

Suomen kansan vanhat runot (Finnish Folk Poems, in Finnish):
(1) Vol. 1: Vienan läänin runot 1, Suomalaisen Kirjallisuuden Seura, Helsinki 1908.

(2) Vol. 7: Raja- ja Pohjois-Karjalan runot 4, Suomalaisen Kirjallisuuden Seura, Helsinki 1933.

(3) Vol. 7: Raja- ja Pohjois-Karjalan runot 1, Suomalaisen Kirjallisuuden Seura, Helsinki 1929.

Swedenborg, Emanuel:
(1) The Apocalypse Explained according to the Spiritual Sense, vol. 1, The Swedenborg Society, London 1854.

(2) The Apocalypse Revealed, vol. 1, The Swedenborg Society, London 1851.

(3) The Apocalypse Revealed, vol. 2, The Swedenborg Society, London 1851.

Tai I Ging Hua Dsung Dshi, in Das Geheimnis der Goldenen Blüte, Ein chinesisches Lebensbuch (transl. Richard Wilhelm), pp. 76–115, Walter Verlag, Olten 1984).

Tansley, David V.: Subtle Body, Thames and Hudson, London 1988.

Tao Tê Ching (transl. Ch'u Ta-Kao), Mandala Books Unwin Paperbacks, London 1982.

Tara Mata: A Forerunner of the New Race, Self-Realization Fellowship, Los Angeles 1981.

The Teachings of the Compassionate Buddha, ed. E. A. Burtt, New American Library, New York 1955.

St. Teresa of Avila:
(1) Spiritual Testimonies, in The Collected Works of Saint Teresa of Avila, vol. 1, pp. 369–438 (transl. Kieran Kavanaugh and Otilio Rodriguez), ICS Publications (Institute of Carmelite Studies), Washington, D.C. 1987.

(2) The Interior Castle, in The Collected Works of Saint Teresa of Avila, vol. 2, pp. 261–452, ICS Publications, Washington D.C. 1980.

(3) The Book of Her Life, in The Collected Works of Saint Teresa of Avila, vol. 1, pp. 5–365, ICS Publications, Washington, D.C. 1987.

(4) The Way of Perfection, in The Collected Works of Saint Teresa of Avila, Vol. 2, pp. 13–204, ICS Publications, Washington D.C. 1980.

Teresa of Calcutta:
(1) A Gift for God: Prayers and Meditations, Harper Collins Publishers, San Francisco 1996.

(2) The Love of Christ: Spiritual Councels (ed. Georges Gorrée and Jean Barbier), Harper & Row Publishers, San Francisco 1982.

St. Thérèse of Lisieux: Collected Letters of Saint Thérèse of Lisieux (ed. Abbé Combes), Sheed & Ward, London 1949.

The Tibetan Book of the Dead (ed. W. Y. Evans-Wentz), Oxford University Press, Oxford 1980.

Tibetan Yoga and Secret Doctrines (ed. W. Y. Evans-Wentz), Oxford University Press, London 1958.

Tibet's Great Yogi Milarepa (ed. W. Y. Evans-Wentz), Oxford University Press. London 1974.

Tillich, Paul: Love, Power, and Justice, Oxford University Press, London 1969.

Tolstoy, Leo: War and Peace, vol. 2, Wordsworth Classics, Hertfordshire 1993.

Vivekananda, Swami:
(1) Bhakti-Yoga or the Yoga of Love and Devotion (includes: Para-Bhakti or Supreme Devotion), in The Complete Works of Swami Vivekananda, vol. 3, pp. 29–100, Advaita Ashrama, Calcutta 1979.

(2) Conversations and Dialogues, in The Complete Works of Swami Vivekananda, vol. 7, pp. 105–294, Advaita Ashrama, Calcutta 1979.

(3) Raja-yoga, in The Complete Works of Swami Vivekananda, vol. 1, pp. 119–313, Advaita Ashrama, Calcutta 1984.

(4) Six Lessons on Raja-yoga, in The Complete Works of Swami Vivekananda, vol. 8, pp. 36–52, Advaita Ashrama, Calkutta 1985.

(5) The Practical Vedanta and Other Lectures, in The Complete Works of Swami Vivekananda, vol. 2, pp. 291–474, Advaita Ashrama, Calcutta 1983.

(6) Addresses at the Parliament of Religions, in The Complete Works of Swami Vivekananda, vol. 1, pp. 1–24, Advaita Ashrama, Calcutta 1984.

Voltaire: Philosophical Dictionary, ed. Theodore Besterman, Penguin Books, Harmondsworth 1971.

Walker, Benjamin: Gnosticism, The Aquarian Press, Wellingborough 1983.

Waltari, Mika: Ihmisen ääni (A Voice of Man, in Finnish), (ed. Ritva Haavikko), WSOY, Porvoo 1978.

Wheelwright, Philip: Heraclitus, Princeton University Press, Princeton 1968.

William of Saint-Thierry (Guillelmi, abbatis Sancti Theoderici): Tractatus de contemplando Deo, in Migne: Patrologia latina, vol. 184, pp. 366–379, Paris 1879.

Wittgenstein, Ludwig: Tractatus Logico-Philosophicus, Routledge & Kegan Paul, New York 1963.

Yogananda, Paramahansa:
(1) Autobiography of a Yogi, Self-Realization Fellowship, Los Angeles 1981.

(2) Whispers from Eternity, Self-Realization Fellowship, Los Angeles 1975.

(3) Man's Eternal Quest, Self-Realization Fellowship, Los Angeles 1982.

(4) The Divine Romance, Self-Realization Fellowship, Los Angeles 1986.

(5) Where There is Light, Self-Realization Fellowship, Los Angeles 1989.

(6) Metaphysical Meditations, Self-Realization Fellowship, Los Angeles 1982.

(7) Easter Prayer, in Self-Realization, vol. 48, 1977, no. 2, back cover (Publisher: Self-Realization Fellowship, Los Angeles).

Yukteswar, Swami Sri: The Holy Science, Self-Realization Fellowship, Los Angeles 1977.

Zander, Valentine: St. Seraphim of Sarov, St. Vladimir's Seminary Press, Crestwood 1975.